Allen E. Goldenthal

Blood of Trinity

Allen E. Goldenthal

BLOOD OF TRINITY

(Ninth Book of the Kahana Chronicles)

A family historical novel by

Allen E. Goldenthal

Val d'Or

Allen E. Goldenthal

Val d'Or Publishing
ISBN: 978-0-9942559-8-3
Printed in the United States of America

LETTER FROM THE AUTHOR

Since first publishing **Shadows of Trinity** ten years ago, one of the most common questions that I'm asked by the readers is, "Are these events in the book fiction or truth?" A fair question, since the storyline appears too fantastic to have been a record of actual events. But I assure you, all the people mentioned did live and events did occur essentially as described. Perhaps not exactly as detailed in the book, since it is an author's prerogative to embellish the events and enhance the characters within the story but nonetheless, the series of murders, the culprits, the villains, the heroes and the outcome are essentially true.

My readers had their favourite characters and they were quick to notify me when some of those individuals died along the journey towards the conclusion that they weren't happy. But sadly, when a writer incorporates the actual lives of real people that left behind historical footprints into a storyline, then the reality that we must accept is that these people did die, and often as in the case of Giordano Bruno, it was in a horrific manner. What matters most is how they lived, and as a writer it is my greatest wish that I was able to capture their spark and their essence, which made them stand out from among other men or women of significance. That is the achievement that every writer desires.

Fortunately, every epoch, every century has its heroes. Even though Yakov Kahana and Giordano Bruno never survived into the seventeenth century, their spirit did, and that is where this latest tale of the family history will begin. As Caesar de Nostradame soon learned, his life was inextricably drawn into the whirlwind that hovered dangerously over the heads of the Kahana for almost two millennia. As history has proven, the theatre of events often revolves around certain families that for inexplicable reasons cannot escape destiny's clutch and have no other choice but to surrender to the whims of fate. One merely has to look at the Kennedy family in the last century to recognize this inescapable truth. Generations of that family had to resign to the simple truth that they must endure what appeared to the rest of us to be a series of never ending tragedies.

Whether it be a curse or a blessing, acceptance that free will is merely an illusion that is dangled before us like the proverbial carrot before the horse, that is the reality that we must all face at some point in our lives. Caesar came to that realization as soon as he recognized that his father's prophecies never actually provided him with any options other than to fulfil them. He never had any personal choice in the matter, his father, Nostradamus imprinting his quatrains into his son's memories to a degree that every response was already hardwired into Caesar's reactions.

Nostradamus knew that his son would be living during troubled times. A strange new world where the manifestation of evil would spread like a vicious plague throughout Europe, affecting every one and everything that it came in contact with. A Europe where monsters were the norm, preying on the innocent and the unsuspecting. How and why this came to be, historians can't really say, since the dark ages were already defeated by the enlightenment of the Renaissance and the Reformation. Perhaps it was a last attempt by the forces of darkness to regain control of society through the spreading of ignorance and black magic; a desperate last gasp by the days of sorcery and medieval fantasies. But whatever the reason, those in the east of the Habsburg Empire were victimized by what can only be described as a Satanic tsunami that swept away everything in its path. The Golem was merely the crest of the towering wave seen far off in the distance, a barely perceptible hint of what was yet to come.

So you will ask, "Is what I'm about to read in *Blood of Trinity* real or imagined?" And once again I will answer, the people, the events, the horrors as described were very real. The outcomes for those involved, as described in the book, are precisely as we know and believe them to be from the biographical details of these individuals. As we connect the dots from the beginning of the events to the final chapter, you, the reader, will realize that history is never a straight line from A to Z, and sometimes the most improbable of tales is ultimately the truth.

Dr. Allen E. Goldenthal

The words of the Rabbis are like the songs of birds; beautiful to listen to, but when you think about what they say, you realize their song is absolutely meaningless...

\- 8th century Karaite Sage

Anan ben David

PROLOGUE

Nadia Fogarasy had already berated herself over a hundred times this evening for having been so incredibly stupid. Why she just didn't wait along with all the other girls to return home the next morning was now a moot point. She couldn't wholly justify her decision at this moment in time. Certainly, she wanted to be home with her family for Christmas, but tomorrow was only Christmas eve and in retrospect, her going home a day early was simply her way of telling the other girls that she was special. After all, how could she possibly refuse when the head mistress unexpectedly announced that she had arranged for a carriage to be available for any girl that had an urgent desire or need to return home the day before school actually ended. As a Fogarasy, it seemed only natural that she would seize the opportunity. Clearly, the offer was intended for her.

Among the ranks of Hungarian nobility, the Fogarasy family were as close to old royalty in the Eastern regions of the Empire as anyone could be without actually wearing a crown. To them, being offered special privileges was as natural as breathing. But where was the estate's carriage her brother was sending to pick her up from the western depot in Trencin. The head mistress had assured her that morning that everything had been arranged and that she had received a reply days earlier from Count Fogarasy to inform his sister that all the arrangements had been made and not to worry. 'Well, if that was true, then where was Estafan with the carriage,' she fumed, stamping her feet in a show of temper.

Her family estate was five miles from the transfer station, a distance too far and too dangerous to walk this late at night. She couldn't decide if she was more furious or frightened by her current predicament. At first, she thought about asking the private carriage driver that picked her up from the school to take her directly home, offering to pay him whatever additional charge he requested. In retrospect, it should have been arranged that way in the beginning but then she was reminded of how angry her brother was with her the last time she failed to wait for their carriage to arrive on a previous journey to Bratislava and she thought better of it, choosing instead to dismiss the driver as she stepped down from his carriage. Estafan probably just misjudged the time it would take to travel the distance from the school to Trencin and he'd be arriving at any time soon. At least that is what she convinced herself to believe almost an hour ago. Now she wasn't quite sure if he'd be arriving at all.

To make matters worse, the night fog began to roll in from the Van River, swirling between the buildings that lined the streets to the north of the station. She knew it was only a matter of time before it would blanket the area with its heavy mist. She watched in dread as the fog floated eerily along the cobblestone laid streets, moving steadily closer as if it was reaching for her, trying to grasp her in its gray mist-laden tendrils. The more she tried to dismiss it from her mind, the more the terror grew within her until she felt herself suffocating from the tightness pressing upon her chest. "Where was Estafan?" her mind panicked with the thought that he might not be coming. She tried to think of a thousand reasons why he might be late but every single one was dismissed by her knowledge that Estafan was never late. Something had gone terribly wrong. She could feel it within every bone of her young body.

As the thick fog moved closer, she found herself pacing in the other direction, attempting to stay several yards ahead of its clutches. She couldn't recall a night when the mist was so heavy, concealing everything laying beyond ten yards. It was only a short matter of time before she would be totally enveloped within its obscurity, unable to recognize any familiar places and certainly unable to know in which direction she should be moving. She had reached the point where she just wanted to sit and cry, unable to will her legs to take another step forward.

Just when she thought her situation was hopeless, she thought she heard someone calling out her name. Then she heard it again, 'Nadia', it was quite clear this time. "Over here," she cried out, a sense of relief flooding through her veins but the euphoria was short lived. Estafan would never call her by her Christian name. "Mistress Fogarasy" was as familiar as he would ever allow himself to become. Perhaps her brother, she thought momentarily, but dismissed that thought as well since she had always been 'Natty' to him for as long as she could remember. Whomever it was, they knew she was there, but she had no idea who else might have been aware of her arrival back in Trencin that night. She heard her name called out again, obviously her rescuer was as lost in the thick fog as she was. At that moment it didn't matter who it might be as long as they could help her get home. "Over here," she called to him, directing his approach through the sound of her voice. For the briefest of moments, she thought she could make out the shadow of someone moving through the mist but then the image disappeared completely. "Over here," she shouted in desperation, fearing that she would not be found. Suddenly she felt a moist cloth being held tightly over her nose and mouth. She could barely breathe and the few breaths she did takes smelled sweet like distilled wine. Her eyelids felt exceedingly heavy as she listened to the final words whispered in her ear.

"Don't worry Nadia. We found you now," the disembodied voice cooed softly.

Chapter One

Zhuhai, China; Present

"I told you John that there was going to be a sequel."

Having just pitched the second edition of *Shadows of Trinity* to him, Pearce looked like he was ready to fall asleep in his chair.

Suddenly he was fully awake and sitting on the edge of the couch.

"How can there be a sequel Doc? You planning on resurrecting the dead?" Pearce sounded more confused now than sleepy.

"Haven't you ever wondered John how my third-great grandfather Jacob could mysteriously become a director at the University of Vienna and the Empress's private tutor for her children, and yet he never had a formal education?"

"Doc, when it comes to your family, nothing ever surprises me," he retorted, followed by a snickering laugh. "With all your family's hocus pocus, anything is possible."

"John, we're talking no formal college education at all. I have a letter in my possession from a professor at the university who is commenting, or he could be criticizing, hard to say exactly, on how amazed he was that my ancestor never even attended a gymnasia."

"So he wasn't into physical fitness, what's the big deal?" Pearce questioned.

"No John, gymnasia wasn't a gym as we know it; it was the common vernacular for high school at that time. Imagine! He didn't even graduate high school! And yet he becomes a full professor at one of the most prestigious universities of its day and then the Dean of the College of Languages and Literature. Imagine the unimaginable!"

Pearce scratched the unruly mop of hair on the top of his head. "So what's your point Doc?"

"The point is that there was this ongoing and long-lasting relationship between my family and the Habsburg monarchy. It wasn't a one-off event as one might assume reading *Shadows of Trinity.* By the time that my third great grandfather was born, the debt owed to my family was huge. That is how this relatively uneducated Jewish boy attained one of the most prestigious positions in the Empire and had his dalliance with the most beautiful Empress that ever lived."

"Aha," Pearce shouted, taking me by surprise. "I knew it! All those years you've been waving the prospect of writing the book about that episode in your family's history but never getting around to it. It's because of that, isn't it. This romance between your whatever number grandfather and the Empress Sissi was a big deal, wasn't it? That's why you've been holding off. Because of the repercussions."

I nodded my head in a partial acknowledgement. "Yes, it's a big deal, but no, that's not the reason I haven't got around to telling the story."

"Then what is it?" Pearce pressed me for an answer.

"If I simply wrote the story without the background you have from *Shadows of Trinity* and what you will find out in *Blood of Trinity*, then the reader is only going to pass the story off as so much fiction. Yes, there will always be the proof that my ancestor became a professor at the University of Vienna. And furthermore there will be the royal archives to show that he became Sissi's personal tutor and afterwards the tutor for the royal children. But what they won't have is the explanation of how he could so easily ingratiate himself into the Emperor's household. Or how he could simply write his own ticket to become whomever and whatever he wanted to be. Karaite Jew or not, as far as the palace was concerned, he was simply a Jew, so to suddenly exert the influence he did, he needed to have something he could hold over their heads. Once my readers see what he held in his possession, then everything else will make sense. Capishe, John?"

"Yeah, I got it Doc."

"Good. Now I'll get on with the task of explaining how *Blood of Trinity* finally gave my family the leverage over the Habsburg royal family, and afterwards you can get back to your task of sleeping.

"Sounds like a plan Doc."

"But I will admit that finding the underlying facts to this story was much harder than I could ever imagine. For *Shadows of Trinity* all the details were clearly laid out for anyone to discover. But this story I only had the vaguest of memories to steer me in the right direction. It wasn't until I was actually in the Czech Republic that the memories of my ancestors became much clearer to me. It was then that I realized that all the monsters that we had come to cherish in our current love affair with Hollywood stemmed from this one particular event and to be honest with you, Bela Legosi didn't even come close to the real story.

"Bela who?" Pearce showed off his lack of appreciation for the classics.

"Legosi," I reiterated. "Sheesh John, you'd think you would at least be familiar with the RKO horror movies. Boris Karloff as the mummy and Frankenstein, Bela Legosi as Dracula, Claude Rains Junior as the wolfman?"

The blank stare on his face told me that he didn't have a clue about what I was saying. "How could you have lived your life and never seen any of these classic movies?"

"Just not my cup of tea, Doc. Me and the missus are more in to the romantic comedy type movies."

Now there's something I didn't expect. John Pearce and romantic comedies mentioned in the same breath. That's like sugar on top of cheese. If there's any two things that don't belong together, those are it. "Well, just to edify you, those are the original stories that put Transylvania on the map. Bram Stoker, Mary Shelley, they knew that there was something very real behind the stories that they wrote about, but they could never have known that the truth would make their telling of the events nothing more than a child's bedtime tale. The real story was far more horrific and far more terrorizing for everyone that lived during those dark terrifying times."

"So you're trying to convince me that those stories are actually true? Let's face it Doc, you were able to provide a convincing alternative reality behind the Golem, and I'll concede all your facts checked out but now you're trying to tell me these monsters are real...Dracula? Let's not take me for a fool, Doc. One monster, maybe, but all the rest, no way! I'm not buying that one! Not at all!"

"I was a skeptic too, John. But if you could see what I can see, I'm certain you would change your mind, much in the way that I did. I never asked to envision these things but obviously I didn't have much choice in the matter. But now that my ancestor's path has been laid out for me, it has become clear how my family was able to move through the aristocratic society of Vienna with ease. It's as if every event, every improbable and unbelievable tale and legend of eastern Europe had only one purpose. Designed solely to explain how my third great grandfather was to become intimately involved with the Habsburg royal family."

"It's about time!" Pearce exclaimed. "I didn't ever think I was ever going to hear you admit that your grandfather number whatever and the Empress Elizabeth had something going."

"I never denied it John. Like I said, I just wanted you and the readers to understand how such a thing could happen. This is the story that will explain to everyone how it was possible."

"If that's true Doc, then let's have it."

"Okay. I need you to sit back in your chair and be prepared to be shocked, because everything I'm about to tell you in regards to the horrific events of the beginning of the seventeenth century is absolutely true. Trust me when I tell you John, there were monsters that haunted those mountains bordering Slovakia and Romania. Monsters that violated the laws of man, but more importantly betrayed the rules of nature.

"Fire away Doc!"

Brody; November, 1609 A.D.

In a city under the protection of the Polish king, an entourage sent from the Habsburg Empire was an unusual event. For those that had been around two decades earlier, they may have remembered the last time they saw such a display, but in general, this was a unique event for most of the populace living there.

"Make way for the Emissary of his Highness, Emperor Matthias," the heralds shouted as the white ornate carriage trimmed in gold leaf rolled through the streets behind its escort of twenty grenadiers.

The Emperor's name meant nothing to the townspeople, for in reality they had no particular allegiance, since Brody was a merchant town, established on the main corridor of goods passing between east and west, and long ago it had been agreed by all the kingdoms that it would remain a commercial centre without taxation or loyalty to any particular monarchy. Instead, a tribute was paid to the Polish throne to ensure their army would protect them if ever attacked, but that was the full extent of any presence of sovereignty. It had been that way for five hundred years and not even the appearance of an entourage from the Holy Roman Emperor could influence their independent mindset. The complete lack of interest or enthusiasm only served to make the grenadiers more wary.

The carriage rolled on towards its destination in the southern quarter of the city, crossing over a small stone bridge and passing along the narrow streets until the entourage was surrounded by a square of small shops and stores with signs written in Hebrew characters, clearly denoting that they were now in the Jewish sector of town. With a sense of purpose, the Austrian contingent rolled directly towards the courtyard of the great synagogue that dominated that quarter's skyline. Passing by the massive stone wall that encircled the synagogue, the carriage arrived at the adjoining home, equally as impressive with its formidable turrets and high portico through which the horsemen and the carriage easily passed. The captain of the grenadiers swung the heavy brass ring on the oak door, its thundering clap making their presence known to anyone and everyone residing inside.

Creaking as it swung inward, the ornately carved wooden door rolled back upon its iron hinges and a scraggly bearded man in his mid forties emerged into the light of the portico to greet the travelers. Around his shoulders hung a prayer shawl, and on his head, a wool skull cap that failed to cover the bald patch of his scalp.

"Can I help you?" he asked in thickly accented German.

"Our Lord wishes to speak to the chief Rabbi of Brody," the captain responded in the more pleasant sounding high German of Austria.

"I am him," the man responded.

Suddenly the door of the carriage swung open, and without waiting for any assistance, the passenger stepped down to the ground and approached. "No, no," he rebutted the Rabbi's answer. "You are not him. Where is the other one?"

"I assure you," the Rabbi responded, "I am most certainly the Chief Rabbi. There is no other."

His voice rising in pitch, the Emissary in his fancy white and gold jacket with its fringed epaulets was beginning to sound a twinge hysterical, "The old Rabbi! Where is Isaac ben Shakna? I need to speak to him urgently."

"You cannot," the Rabbi was firm in his answer.

"He's the one I want. Where can I find him?"

"In the cemetery," the Rabbi answered calmly. "He's been dead for several years now."

"Then let me speak to his daughter, Raisa," the stranger insisted as he wiped the nervous sweat from his forehead, just below the band of his wide brimmed hat surmounted with ostrich feathers.

"You cannot," the Rabbi responded once more.

"Why," the traveler pleaded, "are you going to tell me that she's dead too?"

"Yes," the response was short and curt.

The Emissary shook his head in dismay. "Oh, I didn't know. Surely everyone cannot be dead. Where are her children? I need to find them."

The Rabbi scratched his beard while he thought on the matter. "I believe both children still reside in the city. If I am not mistaken, they live by the cemetery on Lwowska Street."

"By a cemetery?" the Emissary sounded positively flabbergasted. "They can't live by a cemetery! That would place them practically outside the city...in what would be the poorest part of town. They're children of one of your high priests. They are forbidden to be by the cemetery. Clearly you must be wrong!"

"I can only tell you what I recall," the Rabbi remained calm.

"The last I heard, that is where they were residing. Now please go. I do not mean to sound offensive but the longer I am seen talking with you, the more suspicious it will appear to the townspeople that I am in some way involved in some manner of subterfuge with a foreign government."

"Tell me how I find this Lwowska Street," the Emissary requested directions.

"Follow this road which is Boznicza. Soon afterwards you will make a turn on to Lazionna, which continues as Zyblikiewicza on the other side of town. That will take you to Lwowska. When you come to Kwolska, turn left. The cemetery is at the end of the road. If you reach the cemetery then you have gone too far. I have told you everything I know. Now please go."

Turning to his driver the Emissary inquired if the man had memorized the directions. The nod of his head signified that he had done so.

"I'm sorry to have troubled you Rabbi but I do appreciate your assistance no matter how reluctantly you may have been in providing it. If it is any consolation to you, let me just say that your help in this matter may have possibly saved the world."

Shaking his head mildly as if to disagree, the Rabbi commented, "Our world is always safe. We have God to protect us. The only time we our in danger is when your world believes yourselves to be in danger. Then you always seek a scapegoat. So please, leave us in peace and do not be offended if I pray that we do not see one another again."

Bowing the Emissary turned and returned to the carriage where he climbed the metal step and sat down inside. Leaning out the window he made one last parting comment to the Rabbi. "Long ago one of your greatest Jewish leaders reminded me that it is not our religious beliefs that set us apart but the level of courage that we hold within our hearts. Men of courage will never fear the shadows of what may be, because they shine a light on the darkest corners of our world. You cannot remain separate forever Rabbi." Tapping the side of the carriage, the driver was given the signal to roll on and the entourage turned and departed from beneath the portico into the street beyond the synagogue.

The route towards the cemetery provided multiple views of the city in stark contrast to one another. From pictures of wealth seen as villas with lavish gardens to three walled leaning structures with nothing more than a canvas sheet to serve in place of a missing roof. Essentially, the further east the entourage traveled, the older and more disheveled the buildings and structures became, to such a degree that the Emissary feared what form the accommodation that the children of

Yakov Kahana might be living in. The southeast sector of the city had been neglected for almost a century. It was as if Kolejowa Road acted as a dividing line between two worlds. East of the line dwelt the poor, the desolate, and the abandoned. Those that had lost hope in a city that promoted prosperity to all those that had a desire to achieve in a mercantile world. That encouraged those with specific sets of skills, or those that possessed a knowledge of the sciences to flock to the city. And wherever the elite gathered, it also served to attract artisans and thespians, those capable of providing this elite populace with the best that society could offer. But for every ten success stories there would be someone that had either migrated with nothing to offer, or those born in the city, but not gifted with any skills to compete in a world that thrived on competition. A city capable of crushing as many dreams as it supported.

Brody

Nowy Cmentarz Żydowski
7

Cmentarz Katolicki

Castle

WAŁY SZPITALINE

PLAN MIASTA BRODY

Ghetto
1 Old Synagogue
2 New Synagogue
3 Jew. Municipality House
4 Jew. School
5 Jew. Hall
6 Orphanage
7 New Cemetery
8 Old Cemetery
9 Catholic Church

TARGOWICA (Park Miejski)

SUCHOWÓLKA

STARE BRODY

Stary Cmentarz Żydowski 8

Do Lwowa Przez Krasne

SZWABY

Do Radziwiłłowa

As far as the eye could see, here in the Eastern Sector lay the remains of shattered dreams and eternally lost souls. The forgotten lives that struggled with their own failure to succeed; an elephant graveyard of deprivation and misery.

Holding his head between his shaking hands, the Emissary could not believe what lay in his path. This was not what he expected to see upon his return. This was not how he had envisioned his reunion with the children of Yakov Kahana would take place. Perhaps he should have made a point to visit the family during the past twenty years. If not a visit then at least to have made an effort to reach out to Raisa to see how she was doing. He castigated himself for not having even made the barest effort. In his role as mayor of his little town in Provence, he had permitted himself to become preoccupied with less significant matters. Too busy in fact with absolutely nothing. 'Forgive me Yakov,' he muttered beneath his breath.

Looking to his right he saw a young boy in rags searching through a refuse-pile, but unable to identify at first what he was hunting for. Suddenly the boy's right hand snaked into the heart of the pile and with an exuberant smile on his face he pulled a fat rat by the tail from the garbage heap. With a quick flick of his wrist he swung the rat by the tail so that its head smashed against a broken concrete brick, crushing its skull in the process. Hanging it by the tail, he let the blood drain from its nose until if flowed no longer and then he dropped it into the small sac on the ground that already bulged from whatever else he had caught that day.

"Boy," the Emissary yelled out, "What are you doing there?" He realized how ignorant the question was as soon as he asked it. He knew exactly what the young lad was doing.

"Finding dinner," the boy shouted back, proudly displaying his prowess as a hunter as he held up the bag for all to see.

"Come here boy. I have a gold ducat for you if you can provide me with information." The Emissary held up the coin so that the lad knew he was serious about his offer.

"A gold ducat!" the boy screamed excitedly, as he climbed down from the scrap-pile and almost forgot to pick us his sac in the excitement of returning to his family with what would be more money than they had probably seen in months. He ran to the carriage until he stood panting directly beneath the open window. "What do I have to do Mister," he barely could get the words out.

"I need to find someone," the man explained. "Actually two people. A man and his sister. They'd both be in the twenties. They probably don't interact much with anyone else. Their mannerisms and habits will be different from the people that you might know. In fact they probably look different from anyone else you know. Do you know where I might find these two people?"

The boy ran his dirty fingers through his grease streaked hair while he thought about what the man had just said. He then looked up and there was a twinkle in his eyes. "Do Jews count?"

"Yes boy, Jews especially count. Do you know of these two?"

"Everyone knows them here," the boy responded. "He's our teacher. He teaches all the children here in the Miodova ghetto."

"He teaches you?" the Emissary was quite surprised by the response. "Here, in this slum, he is your teacher?"

"Yes," the boy nodded his head.

"And don't be offended by this next question but why and what exactly does he teach you?" The man still could not believe that the son of Yakov Kahana would have fallen so low that he'd be teaching anyone anything of value in this poor man's ghetto.

"No one else will come to Miodova to teach us and since he was here already, it seemed like the proper thing to do. He knew so many things, so many languages, and I don't think there was anything else he knows how to do. He has no hunting skills like the rest of us and he doesn't know how to build anything. So he teaches."

"How does he survive from day to day if he is busy teaching the children?"

"The older boys pay him from their daily take," the boy was quick to explain. "Sometimes it's just the vegetables they find, sometimes it is coins or even jewellery if they have a good day."

"And they just happen to find these things," the man smiled at the boy's effort to conceal the truth. "I guess I would be very surprised to know just how many items fall off the back of wagons everyday in this city," he laughed.

"You would," the boy snickered in return.

"Well, here's one coin that didn't fall off the back of a wagon," the Emissary joked as he flicked the ducat into the air and watched as the young boy deftly snatched it out of the air as it flew. "You keep that one. No need to give it to this teacher. So where do I find him; is his home close by?"

"Follow me," the boy commanded the leader of the entourage as he ran out in front of the grenadiers and waved for them to follow.

Staying close on the boy's heels, they could see the cemetery getting closer in the distance. Nearing the tall, iron lettered gates to the Cemetarz Zydowski, the boy darted sharply to the left and led them down Cicha Lane. The Emissary ordered the entourage to stop and dismounted from the carriage. "I will proceed the rest of the way on foot," he said to someone else that had been riding with him in the carriage. Then turning to the entourage leader said, "See that everyone remains here Captain. I don't want to make any of the denizens of this neighbourhood any more nervous than they probably already are if they've witnessed our approach."

The boy pulled the Emissary along by the cuff of his long sleeve. "Teacher Joe, teacher Joe, there is someone here to see you," the boy shouted excitedly.

Before the Emissary got within twenty-five yards of the hovel where Teacher Joe resided, he realized the boy was directing him towards a huge beast that had emerged from the shadows to block their way. The Emissary froze solid in his tracks. "What the hell is that?" was all that he could manage to say.

"Oh, don't mind him," the boy tried to pull the Emissary towards the home but the man strongly resisted. "How can you not mind him? It's a monster!"

"Naw, that's just the dog. He's harmless," the boy insisted.

Standing over two feet at the shoulder, and easily weighing over sixty pounds, the beast did not resemble any dog that the Emissary was familiar with. With fangs bared, and a vicious snarl on its lips, the animal refused to move out of the way. "Then why doesn't he look harmless?" the terrified man questioned the lad.

"He won't do anything," the lad insisted. Picking up a stick, the boy tossed it as far as he could throw. "Go fetch boy!"

Darting down the lane, the dog disappeared from sight as it searched for that one, particular stick among a pile of fallen branches.

Teacher Joe was already standing at the opening of the dilapidated shed that served as his home, arms crossed over his chest as he awaited the approaching stranger. "Thank you Micha. You can run home now. Your job here is finished."

"But can't I stay," the boy pleaded. "Can't I play with your dog?"

"I think the rest of your family is waiting for dinner," the teacher commented as he noticed the bag hanging from the boy's left hand. "You wouldn't want to keep them waiting too long. Some of your older brothers are probably very hungry by now."

"Aw, but I wanted to stay," the boy kicked the dirt with the heal of his right foot.

"Not today Micha. Go now," the teacher commanded

Reluctantly the boy turned and trudged off in the direction of his home.

"If you've come to lay charges for any of the property that may have been misplaced by their owners, then first I must say that none of the children had anything to do with the disappearances. You can search my home all you want. You will find nothing of value within. It is always easiest for persons of wealth to blame the waifs of the city for their lost property than assume responsibility for their own losses."

"What is that thing?" the Emissary asked, apparently not hearing a single word that the teacher had spoken but looking behind at the dog.

"What do you mean," the teacher didn't fully understand the question. "That's my dog."

"It's not a dog," the Emissary insisted. "That's a wolf," he answered his own question.

Shaking his head, Teacher Joe attempted to correct the stranger. "I assure you it's not a wolf. That's my dog. I've had him since he was a pup. He just never knew when to stop growing."

"Because he's a wolf," the Emissary insisted.

"Most definitely a dog," the teacher repeated.

"If you say so," the man conceded, "But it certainly looks like a wolf to me."

"As I was saying," Teacher Joe continued, "Whatever you are looking for, it is not here. All we wish is to be left alone."

While the teacher attempted to explain their innocence, the Emissary remained motionless, staring silently into the dark eyes of the young Kahana, breaking his silence only when the teacher finished his explanation. "You don't recognize me, do you?"

Teacher Joe furrowed his brow and scanned the visitor from head to toe and then back to his face, looking for any recognizable feature that would stir a distant memory. It was the frilled lace collar that provided a clue to the man's identity "You're that Frenchman; the one that came to our home to tell us of my father's death so many years ago."

The Emissary nodded his head. "And had I known what fate was going to befall you and your sister, I never would have remained away for so long. I am so sorry Yusef."

"Joseph."

"What?"

"Joseph. I go by Joseph now. Yusef ended when the community threw us out on to the street. I prefer to be called by the common tongue of the Galician people."

"And you may call me Caesar. Caesar de Nostradame. So much has changed since we last met. I do not understand what has happened here. How did you end up like this? What has happened to the money I left your mother? This does not make any sense." Caesar looked around at Joseph's surroundings and he could not believe what he was seeing.

"Tanit! Come on out sister and see whom we have visiting our humble abode." At the same time Joseph called for his sister, the dog returned, dropping the stick by his master's feet and wagging its long bushy tail, waiting patiently for another toss.

Caesar could sense the anger mixed with sarcastic tone in Joseph's voice. It was obvious that the young man had every reason to be angry. Life had been cruel to Joseph and his sister since they last met and he knew there was nothing that he could say now that would erase all their years of pain and frustration.

Appearing in the doorway, the young woman hardly looked young at all. Her dress was worn thin and tattered in numerous places. Her face had become sallow, dark shadows beneath her sunken eyes, eyes that testified to how hard her life had been thus far. Caesar quickly calculated from memory that she would only be twenty-five years old but by the way she looked and the way she moved she easily could have been mistaken for a woman in her late forties.

"Who is he Joseph?" she asked.

"Don't you remember sister. This is the man that came to us almost twenty years ago to tell us that our father had died in Prague. The man that told us that everything was going to be fine. That our lives would be taken care of. That we'd be rewarded for our terrible loss."

Caesar could feel her dagger like eyes penetrating straight through his trembling heart. The bitterness that shrouded her face was clearly evident. He had failed them both and most of all he had failed their father. He had promised Yakov they would be taken care of in the event of his death and it was his responsibility alone to see that it was done. While he had been living a life of affluence and respect back in Provence for the past two decades, Yakov's children had been fighting for survival. Not in his wildest imagination could he ever dream their lives would have come to this. He was lost for any words of consolation. "I don't understand. How did this happen?" he repeated while he shook his head.

"What did you think would happen?" Joseph retaliated.

"What happened to the money the Emperor gave you? Why didn't you use his letter of entitlement? This never should have happened." Caesar waved his hands frantically in a gesture of confusion.

"What was our mother without our father. She was weak, she was frail and you knew exactly what kind of man our grandfather was!" Joseph shouted at Caesar, which prompted the Captain of the guard to come running down the road.

"Stay back," Caesar ordered the Captain. "Everything is fine. I have this under control. So tell me, Joseph, because I am surprised by all this. Your grandfather was not a nice man, that was obvious, but I know he loved you both. He would not have done anything to intentionally harm you. He loved your mother. He never would have hurt her. Just help me understand."

The tears welled in Joseph's eyes. "Did you think that standing in front of the people and telling them a story about how brave and heroic our father had been in saving Prague was going to even be remembered the following day? Did you think that in some way the enemies of my father were going to leave him rest in peace? How long did you think that Rabbi Loew would remain silent before he started telling everyone that it was all a lie? How long before the other Rabbis would turn the entire event upside down because of the antipathy they bore for my father's Karaite heritage?"

Caesar had been oblivious to everything that had befallen the family. "But the letter from Emperor Rudolf explained everything. It was a promise that every door would be open to you. Every request you made would be supported and backed by the throne. It gave you unlimited authority to practically do as you pleased."

"This is Brody," Joseph exclaimed. "A letter from the Holy Roman Emperor is meaningless here. The Habsburgs have no authority here. The only response I had from that letter was a collector of artifacts that was enthralled by the signature and the wax seal. He offered a handful of silver thalers for it."

"I surely hope you didn't sell it to him."

"Of course not," Joseph reassured Caesar. "It is the only memory I have of my father. I would never have sold it. But it just proves to you how my father died for nothing. After the Rabbanite all agreed that Judah Loew was the true hero of Prague, there was no convincing the community otherwise. Then our grandfather saw an opportunity to expand his influence by throwing his lot in with the detractors of our father. Not that he ever respected my father to begin with. The Rabbinic Council promised he would secure his own place in history if he lent his voice in condemning Yakov Kahana. He used their promise to blackmail our mother into handing over the bag of money you gave her into his possession. He said that he would use the money to build a Talmudic school dedicated to her husband's memory. Otherwise he promised he would lend his voice to the Rabbinic Council, swearing that all the stories about Yakov were a lie. What could my mother do? Had my father still been alive, he would have surely died if he knew his name was linked to a Talmudic school. What greater dishonour could you do to a Karaite. But my mother could not bear the shame and acquiesced to her father's pressure."

Caesar shook his head in disbelief. "I knew your father well. That certainly would have been a death blow to your father. And let me guess, your grandfather squandered the money instead of building the school as promised."

"Oh he started the school," Joseph explained, "but what became obvious was that my grandfather was no scholar. The stories had been true. Practically all of his published papers and dissertations were from his father and he had just plagiarized them. As soon as the students realized he was not an authority on the subject matter that he was attempting to teach them, they deserted him until no one was left in his classroom. I guess the embarrassment and ridicule by his colleagues was too much for him and one day his heart just gave out."

"So all the money was gone?"

"Everything," Joseph sighed. "But it was not before the entire Jewish Community in Brody had been turned against us. Our father had been stripped of his heroism. Our grandfather had been proven to be a fraud and did not deserve the respect he had been given as a Chief Rabbi in Brody. We had no money to support ourselves and no friends that would dare place themselves in conflict with the Rabbinic Council by taking us in or coming to our defence. They removed us from the home attached to the synagogue and forced us into the streets with what little of our belongings we could carry. They labeled us 'traif', lepers, untouchables, and what could a widowed mother of two young children do but become a wash-woman in the dye workers yards. For years she struggled in the yards, knowing that the chemicals would eventually kill her but she had to take care of us and that kept her going as long as possible. But even that inner strength had its limitations and after a decade of toiling in the most terrible labour imaginable, she finally succumbed and passed away.

We were now two teenagers left to fend for ourselves on the streets but fortunately for us, there were others living on the streets and they helped us to survive. Now I teach them to survive and provide them with a level of education that should some of them ever be lucky enough to escape this life then at least they have a chance to blend back in to society." Having finished his story, Joseph let out a deep sigh. His sister rubbed the back of his neck tenderly, knowing how difficult it was for her brother to recount all the hardships of their lives.

Caesar de Nostradame stood in silent reflection of all he had heard and for what felt like minutes, was speechless. Finally he recovered his voice. "I can't imagine what your life has been like," he pointed with his hands to their surroundings to emphasize his comment. "I won't even try because what ever I think it might have been like would only be a fraction of how terrible it probably was. Even an apology would seem hollow. But I assure you, had I known, I would have been here much sooner to correct matters."

"And just why are you here," Joseph interrupted Caesar before he could continue with his comments.

"I would like to say that I have come simply to check on your well-being but that would be a lie too. I am here on a mission for the Emperor," Caesar confessed.

"And exactly which Emperor would that be?" Joseph's voice carried a distinct tone of anger. "The one locked away in his castle in Prague, or his brother that now calls himself Emperor in Vienna?"

"I see that you have managed to keep up to date with events in the Habsburg Empire, even though some of what you just mentioned has taken place only recently."

"There is nothing that is not known in Brody," Joseph explained. "But you still have not answered my question."

"Matthias. I am here on behalf of the Emperor Matthias."

"So what is it that this usurper wants from me? Hasn't he already stripped me of all dignity when he let that murderer return to Prague?"

Caesar knew exactly whom he was talking about. "Hardly a usurper," Caesar corrected him. "Officially named as Emperor by the governors of all the separate states within the Empire and even Rudolf conceded as much."

"Usurper," Joseph repeated. "Rudolf has not abdicated, so he is still the Emperor. Not that it matters here in Brody what occurs within the Empire, but just so that it is clear, as far as my father was concerned, Rudolph was and is the Emperor. At least he saw to it that the murderer was exiled and disgraced. So why would this false Emperor have you seek my sister and myself out after so many years of forgetting of our existence. Is he suddenly concerned about our welfare?"

The acid dripping from Joseph's last comment was hard to miss. "The Empire has encountered another crisis that needs the services of the son of Yakov. Another encounter with dark forces that are beyond their capabilities to deal with it themselves."

"So why come to me," Joseph dismissed the Emperor's needs with a shrug of his shoulders and a wave of his hand.

"Because Matthias acknowledges what your father achieved under his brother's rule was extraordinary and therefore extraordinary circumstances calls for extraordinary people."

"A shame then that you are the only one of those extraordinary people still alive then. It looks like you will have to resolve this crisis on your own, Joseph was flippant with his answer dismissing Caesar at the same time.

"On the advice of Cardinal Klesl, chief magistrate of the Empire, Matthias has been told that the prophecy buried in the old church documents applies equally to the events occurring now as it did twenty years ago in Prague. They are somehow connected. Which means that they can only be stopped by a heretic priest, a failed prophet and a king without a kingdom. Now you can understand why I have come to you. Your situation is no different than your father's."

"Except it is," Joseph corrected him. "Firstly, I make no claim to the throne of my heritage. In fact my grandfather saw to it that I had as little exposure to my Karaite roots as possible. And secondly, my father was forced to tag along on your mission because the Church threatened to destroy our community in Brody if he did not comply. I will let you in on my little secret, I hope that someone does destroy this God-forsaken community and everyone that lives in it" Joseph grinned wickedly as he passed on his secret wish to Caesar.

"You don't understand," Caesar tried to explain. "If what is happening in the Carpathians is not stopped now, then it will result in the deaths of thousands, perhaps hundreds of thousands. And the Jews will be slaughtered most of all. We need you on this mission. Your people need you," Caesar pleaded.

"Do you know," Joseph diverted the conversation from the main discussion, "I don't even know where my father is buried. With all their wants, and needs, neither of your two emperors, your cardinals, or all your political appointees could even bother to give me the one thing I desired most; the opportunity to say goodbye to my father. Now they ask me to save the world when they couldn't even provide me with that one little bit of consolation. You probably know where he is buried but did you ever pass on that information to my mother? No! You didn't. So give me one good reason why I should even listen to your request for me to travel to some far off land in order to save a world that has spat on myself and my sister and reduced us to living like animals in these conditions you see."

"It was wrong," Caesar admitted. "Keeping your father's burial place a secret was wrong and never should have been permitted. I should have never let Rudolf do so because I see now how cruel such an action truly was. He feared that it would become a site of pilgrimage, that it would fuel the anxieties between all the communities because the grave of the hero of Prague would be contested by Christian, Jew and Karaite alike, leading to exactly what Yakov gave his life to stop, more bloodshed. The Emperor knew that as a high priest, you could not visit the grave-site because of your religious convictions. He made a decision he thought was best for everyone."

"He made the wrong decision!" Joseph suddenly screamed. "He took my father away from me twice! So now if my refusal to go along on this insane mission of yours means that they know what it feels like to feel excruciating loss and suffering, then so be it!"

"Your father would not have hesitated when it came to saving even a single life," Caesar chastised the son."

Moving forward, Joseph stood a mere couple of feet in front of Caesar, glaring in to the older man's eyes with cold hatred. "Take a good look and recognize me, I am not my father!"

"Of that I am certain," Caesar concurred, "But every man has his price. It is clear you want revenge, so take it! If that's what you want then name your price!"

"There is not enough gifts and gold in this world that you could offer that would quench my thirst for revenge," Joseph growled, his fists clenched in anger.

"Try me," Caesar responded coolly. "Name your price."

"What?" the response by Caesar took Joseph off guard. "What do you mean? You can't be serious?"

"Exactly what I said, name your price."

Taking a step backwards, Joseph unclenched his fists and looked left and right as if magically there would appear some mystical writing on the wall that would tell him what he actually wanted. He then turned his head to look at his sister, only to see that she bore an expression of shock and surprise on her face as well.

"Well, you want revenge on all those that have wronged you, so here's your opportunity," Caesar challenged the young Kahana. "Tell me what it is that you want."

"I...I...I need a moment to think about this," Joseph hesitated.

"Captain," Caesar shouted to the captain of the guard still standing frozen in the lane way. "Return to the carriage and ask your Lord to step this way please."

The Captain immediately turned on his heels to fulfill the request. Within minutes the a tall stately looking gentleman was standing beside Caesar in front of the still speechless Joseph Kahana.

"So this is the young man I have traveled these hundreds of miles to see," the man smiled, extending his right hand in friendship towards Joseph. No sooner had he reached towards Joseph, when a ferocious and guttural snarl surfaced from deep in the dog's throat.

"Settle down boy!" Joseph commanded and immediately the dog quieted and resumed gnawing on the stick. "My apologies. He's very defensive if anyone tries to touch me."

"I guess he doesn't know who I am," the man replied jovially.

"I don't even know who you are," Joseph commented.

"This is the man that can make all your wishes come true," Caesar replied calmly. "This is the Archduke Maximilian, brother to the Emperor."

"Right," Joseph refused to believe Caesar. "As if the second highest ranking member of the Austrian monarchy would be sneaking around Brody unheralded? I doubt that very much," Joseph scoffed.

"I don't know," the Archduke rebutted. "Seemed like a clever idea at the time. It's not exactly as if Galicia is part of the Empire…yet. Not to mention I have my grenadiers, which are an unmatched elite fighting force. I had actually hoped that I could come and go completely undetected and never have to set foot out of my carriage but it would appear that Caesar has met a stumbling block, namely you, young Master Kahana."

"You are really the Archduke?" Joseph's jaw dropped. "Standing here in the ghetto like a real person."

Looking around at his surrounding, Maximilian nodded his head, "Yes, it certainly would appear that I am standing in a ghetto. Not that I visit them that often," he quipped.

"But…but…you're the Archduke of Austria…" Joseph gasped in surprise.

"Yes, the Archduke, the prince of the realm, third in line to the throne, Grand Master of the Army, Master of the Horse, and all that."

"You really are the Archduke," Joseph questioned and answered simultaneously as he ran his eyes up and down the dashing gentlemen dressed in his finest dress military uniform. At the same time, Tanit moved to her brother's side and attempted a somewhat clumsy curtsy in front of the very distinguished aristocrat.

"It is an honour to meet you sir," she finally spoke.

"The honour is all mine," Maximilian replied. "I have traveled a long way to meet the children of Yakov Kahana. I presume that Caesar de Nostradame has explained to you why we are here."

"That I have done, Excellency," Caesar confirmed. "But young Master Kahana is somewhat reluctant to aid us in this quest. Which is why I have asked you to step from our carriage. It would appear that he requires some convincing to aid us in our mission."

Maximilian smacked his lips, "Perfectly understandable, considering the circumstances of his living and how he must feel that we have abandoned him during these intervening years." From a quick survey of the surroundings, Maximilian was able to summarize the events thus far in a simple statement. He then inhaled deeply while shaking his head, a motion clearly acknowledging his regret. "Had my brother Rudolf known about this he would have taken you to live in his palace. Such was the esteem with which he held your father. It serves no purpose to say that now, I know, but I want you to know it is true. We had no idea of your present circumstances, which is no excuse for our failing you, but I am here to confirm that we will not do so again."

"I have just informed Master Joseph that we will indulge all of his requests. Whatever he asks, we will attempt to fulfil, as long as he aids us on this mission."

Bowing his head slightly, Joseph finally found his voice. "Excellency, I doubt that even you will be able to fulfil all the requests that I would make. They are beyond any man's capacity, even that of a prince."

"If you don't ask, you will never know," the Archduke replied temptingly. "So ask me what I can do for you."

"Our lives have been destroyed. There are some things that can never be repaired." Joseph wrapped his arm around his sister's shoulders. "Tanit should have been married long ago into a respectable family but after being driven from the community and having our family honour destroyed, she is now considered '*shunda*'; no Jewish man will touch her. If our father was a king, then she's a princess and she deserved a better life than what she has been tethered to. I doubt very much you can restore her reputation or give her a life of happiness with a family of her own. Not even God has seemed fit to make that happen. So you want to know my first impossible wish; restore to her all those missing years; replace the life she should have had; make her a princess again." Folding his arms across his chest, Joseph awaited the inevitable apologies and excuses of why his first request could not be met.

Caesar looked towards the Archduke to see how he would respond to what certainly appeared to be an impossible request.

Holding his hands out pontifically towards Joseph, Maximilian winked as he responded. "Consider it done."

"What do you mean?" both Joseph and Caesar responded simultaneously, while Tanit swooned and fell towards her brother, only to be caught up in Joseph's arms.

"This is hardly the time to jest, Excellency," Caesar commented, fearing that they were only going to antagonize Joseph further.

"I am most serious, Caesar. I have her future husband in mind already."

"Seriously?" Caesar still could not believe the answer. "You can do this?"

"I wouldn't have said yes if it wasn't possible," Maximilian admonished him for his doubt. "She won't be a princess, but I'm certain she will be content with being named a countess. Her betrothed, Otto von Wallerstein, is fair to look at but I'm afraid not the most intelligent of my relatives. Some might even say dim-witted but that only serves to make him very compliant when she advises him of her wishes. That would even include raising their children in the Jewish faith if she should be blessed with a family. Your sister will want for nothing. He will cherish her, he will love her, and it will not matter if she cannot love him back equally, although with time, I'm certain she will develop a fondness for him. Is that serious enough for you, Master Joseph?"

Tanit began to stir in her brother's arms just as the Archduke finished describing her future. "Brother, did I hear the Lord correctly, did he say I will be wed?"

"Not only that sister, but you will be a countess."

Her hand immediately shot to cover her mouth as she gasped with unbridled jubilation. It was far too much to believe and she felt as if she would faint again but Joseph's supported her on to her feet and held her until she was steadied.

"But one further condition," Joseph insisted. "The wedding takes place before I go on this mission."

"Consider it done," Maximilian confirmed. "We will have the wedding take place in the palace in Vienna. I will take care of all the arrangements myself. Is there anything else you desire in order to convince you to accept this mission?"

Thinking for a moment, Joseph was still not persuaded that all the wounds he had suffered over the years could be so easily repaired. He was happy that his sister's life would be seemingly repaired but he feared nothing could ever compensate for his own losses.

"If I may intercede into your thoughts for a moment, Master Joseph, Caesar interrupted. "Your father never had the opportunity to tell you about me but if he had survived, I'm certain he would have told you that I had a gift of insight, a special intuition that helps me solve certain riddles that might alter people's lives. The anger that drives you now will not fade. I can see that. Not until you feel that you have taken your revenge on those that have inflicted these hardships upon your family, will you ever be satisfied. So, I suggest you look for one or two supreme events that would be sufficient to quell that rage inside you and ease the pain and anger that fills your heart. There are those that will tell you revenge solves nothing; I will disagree and tell you otherwise. Revenge solves everything, as my father proved long ago."

"So you're instructing me to ask for something that will humble my family's enemies, rob them of their happiness, make them the subject of ridicule, just as they have done to myself and my sister," Joseph wished to clarify the message he was hearing from Caesar.

"Exactly," Caesar de Nostradame responded.

The response sent a jolt through Joseph's subconsciousness. "I think I recall my father saying that word a lot. For the moment, I even thought I heard him speaking."

"Perhaps he was. So what act of revenge would be sufficient to quell the pain you have suffered," the Archduke inquired. "Don't be afraid to ask for the impossible. The impossible is something we Habsburgs make happen all the time."

"Rabbi Judah Loew and his disciples were the ones responsible for causing my family's demise. They were the ones that caused my father's death. They were the ones, over the years following my father's passing, that stripped away any of the honors that had been bestowed on my father. They took his honor, they destroyed his memory, they robbed him of his place in history. Loew and his underlings need to be punished."

"I don't disagree with you," Caesar sympathized, "But in order to restore calm into the Jewish community, the Emperor Matthias thought it necessary to pardon Rabbi Loew of the crimes of which he had been accused. He was permitted to return to Prague and all the edicts against him raised by Rudolf were rescinded. I assure you, there was strong objection, but peace between the various communities was the priority. You must understand that."

"You want my assistance," Joseph objected, "then you need to make them pay for what they did. Not only for the murders they committed, but for what they did to my family afterwards. You want me, then that's the price."

"So what do you have in mind, Master Joseph," Maximilian sounded surprisingly calm, though Caesar thought this demand to be too preposterous.

"Loew has to pay dearly for his crimes," Joseph demanded.

"That will be a little difficult to do," the Archduke advised. "I suppose you don't receive much news in this part of the city, especially news from the Jews in Prague, but Rabbi Loew died two months ago. I'm afraid you've missed the opportunity to exact vengeance on him."

"But not on his closest allies and family. What about his son-in-law, Singer. Or perhaps one of his chief students. The price must still be paid."

"And how shall they pay it?" Maximilian questioned further. "In blood? Is that what you would seek from these others that might have had nothing to do with their master's nefarious crimes? Tell me true, what is it you really want?"

"I want my family name restored. I want the name Kahana to be recognized along with all the great scholars of our religion. I want to be part of the great Jewish families that everyone adulates. I want what should have been my father's by birth-right. You asked and now you have my answer. Give me that and I know for a fact that my walking among them with my head held high will be like driving a knife through their black hearts."

"How interesting," Maximilian muttered audibly. "Fate certainly has a twisted sense of humor. Let me make a suggestion," the Archduke interrupted Joseph's rambling thoughts. "I would propose that you should be married to the most beautiful daughter, of one of the most prominent Jewish scholar families in the Empire. Not only into such a prominent family, but her father should be the recognized heir to Rabbi Judah Loew. His heir apparent; his most famous student. Would that be acceptable?"

"Seriously?" Caesar interjected. "Excellency, do you truly believe you could make that happen? Let's not get the young Master Joseph's hopes up only for us to fail to deliver."

"How long have we ridden in that carriage together Caesar?" the Archduke asked.

"A long time Excellency."

"And in all that time that we took to become acquainted, was there any of my stories that I told you that cast doubt regarding my abilities to achieve my goals once I set my mind to it."

"No Excellency, but this is quite different," Caesar defended his position. "You are talking about manipulating the Jewish community to do your bidding and if it is one thing I know, they are a stubborn lot that resent interference by the government. Trying to force them to do anything against their will has always been a disaster."

"What say you, Master Joseph. How would you like to be the husband of one of the daughters of the one they call Yom Tov Lipmann of Heller?"

Joseph couldn't believe what he was hearing. "Excellency, you know Rabbi Loew's most prominent student personally?"

"You might say we are very close," the Archduke replied with a Cheshire grin spread across his face.

"How is that even possible," Joseph questioned.

"Yes, how is that possible?" Caesar inquired as well.

"You might say that he currently is a guest in my palace. Like his mentor and teacher, he has a propensity for causing trouble. Rather than confine himself to religious matters, he likes to stick his nose into governmental affairs. Recently, he has gone too far, publishing pamphlets calling for the overthrow of the government. He proclaims that only God has the right to rule and therefore the royal family must be overthrown. He calls it religion but I disagree. I call it treason. As such, his life is mine to do with as I please. I will make him an offer that I doubt he will refuse. Even the most religious stalwarts all seem to crumble in their faith when their lives are at stake."

"And his daughter is beautiful?" Tanit suddenly joined the conversation upon hearing that her brother now had the opportunity to be wed as well.

"My dear, he has six daughters. I'm certain that at least one of them will appeal to your brother. As a betting man, I would say the odds are in his favor."

"You can do this?" Joseph needed a moment to process all that the Archduke was claiming within his authority.

"And much more, Master Joseph. Is there anything else you'd like to be done to ensure your participation in our mission?"

"My head is spinning. This is so much to comprehend. I never dreamed this would ever be possible. I couldn't even imagine our lives would have the opportunity to be restored. Even my dreams of the Jewish community in Brody being punished for their ostracizing and exiling us into this life of misery now seems possible."

"You need not worry about that wish," Caesar interjected before Joseph had a chance to continue or the Archduke had a chance to announce some other miracle by which he would punish an entire city. "It has already been prophesied though it will not be your doing but instead by the hand of one of your descendants."

"I don't understand," Joseph shook his head, not aware of Caesar's talent to interpret his father's visions of the future.

"It was how I already knew you'd be joining our quest. My father's prophecies are never wrong. He wrote them, but I am the key to understanding them. Bear with me, but in this particular scenario he wrote the following according to Century I, Quatrain 96:

> *'A man will be charged with the destruction of Temples*
> *And Sects, altered by fantasy.*
> *He will harm the rocks rather than the living,*
> *Ears filled with ornate speeches.'*

"I don't understand that at all."

"Don't worry. It took your father a while, but eventually he could interpret them as well. He never doubted my ability to solve the riddles, even when I had no faith in myself to do so."

"But how can you be so certain that it refers to one of my descendants and that he exacts vengeance on the community of Brody? It doesn't mention any of that"

"But it does, once you learn how to unlock the riddle," Caesar explained. "You consider the Rabbanites to be nothing more than a sect of Judaism, correct?"

"Yes," Joseph replied, "the same way that Karaism is a sect."

"And the best way to destroy the temple or synagogue is to steal its treasury. If they have no money, they can't operate and if they can't operate, then it will ultimately lead their failure. Correct?"

"Agreed, but how do you know it relates to Brody and to my family?"

"Because of the nature of this man. He is one of them at the time he destroys them. That is evident by his ability to make speeches and convince them to provide him with the treasury funds. You, as you are well aware, are not part of the community, so it has to be one of your descendants after your family reputation is restored."

"And you know for a fact that he does this for revenge because of what they did to my family."

"Notice how it explains he does this to the rocks and not against the living. He is not punishing those of things they do in his own time but rather those that had died long ago and are buried in a garden of rocks or tombstones."

"And you calculated the timing…"

"Well into the future. I would think at least two hundred years because he lives in an age of fantasy. An age where there are inventions and machines that we couldn't even dare to imagine. What would be pure fantasy to us is common place for him. And this fantasy leads him to believe he can follow whatever path of his choosing. "

"I still don't know if I believe all that you say, but it is a comforting thought to think that sometime in the future, one of my own bloodline will exact the vengeance I crave," Joseph sighed.

"Trust him," the Archduke advised. "In time you will come to understand that Caesar's abilities are beyond questioning. You will need to rely on his ability to interpret his father's prophecies if you are going to succeed in this mission."

"All these things that we discussed," Joseph refocused on their agreement, "you promise that you will arrange for all of them to happen."

"If these are what comprises your list of demands, then I can promise they all will be granted," Maximilian guaranteed.

Looking at his sister, Joseph grabbed her hands in his two hands and looked into her eyes to see if she was happy. From the presence of the smile that he had not seen on her face for such a long time he didn't need her to say a word, he knew immediately what she was thinking. "We are agreed then," he confirmed.

"Good. I told you we could find a way to satisfy even the impossible," the Archduke gloated. Reaching into his vest, he withdrew a small leather sac filled with coins and tossed it towards Joseph who caught it in his left hand. "There's your initial payment. Get yourself and your sister some decent clothes and be in Vienna by the beginning of the new year."

"Thank you Excellency, thank you. I promise, we will be there in plenty of time. I don't know how to repay you."

"That will be the easy part, "Maximilian advised. "Find and slay the monster that inhabits the mountains, restore the peace in the land and there will be plenty more bags of silver from where that one came."

"Monster?" The word rolled off Joseph's tongue with some trepidation.

"Isn't that what you family is famous for? If it was an ordinary killer plaguing the kingdom, we wouldn't need to recruit the three legendary monster hunters, now would we?"

"I guess not," Joseph replied. "But no one ever mentioned that this mission involved some creature from the netherworld."

"Let me tell you what your father told me once, long ago," Caesar attempted to calm Joseph's nerves. "There are no such things as monsters, only people that behave as such. He did not believe in any of this superstitious nonsense and neither should you."

"It just caught me by surprise momentarily," Joseph reassured the others. "I will not fail you. I swear it upon my father's memory." Having said those words, Joseph looked around at the wooden shed he called home and examined his immediate surroundings as if to say goodbye forever. Looking far down the lane, he caught a glimpse of Micha, attempting to hide behind an outcrop of trees but failing terribly to do so. The sight of his young pupil made him realize that there was still some unfinished business.

"I have one more demand, two actually," he stated firmly, not willing to back down, even though he had already given his word to the Archduke.

"Why does that not surprise me," Maximilian nodded, willing to hear his remaining requests.

"I am all the children of this ghetto have in the way of an instructor. For years I have helped to keep them safe. Some of them have families that reside here, but the majority are orphans. When I'm gone, they will need somewhere safe they can go in times of trouble. They will need a place they can receive a meal when there is no food to be found in the streets. A place to sleep when the storms come and destroy what little shelter they have at present. I ask this of you, not as a request for myself, but on behalf of them. Please, are you able to build an orphanage in Brody to take care of these children?"

Caesar could not hide the smile that spread across his lips. "Now you do sound like your father."

The Archduke didn't need to think about his response for long. "We already own several buildings in this city. I can't see why we couldn't convert one of them into an orphanage. Actually, I think my brother would be delighted to have his name engraved on the lintel of a building in Brody. The Matthias Home for Wayward Children and Orphans. He would make certain that his benevolence was known to everyone. It wouldn't surprise me if he didn't visit it once or twice in his lifetime for the sake of the publicity. Consider it done. Now for this second of your final demands, let me hear it."

"I want to take my dog with me."

"Most certainly," the Archduke agreed immediately. "I would never dream of separating a man from his dog," Maximilian agreed. "What is his name?"

"We call him Wolf."

"It is a good, strong name," Maximilian nodded.

Turning as he prepared to walk back to the carriage, Caesar muttered under his breath. "I knew it was a goddam wolf."

Galicia in the Seventeenth Century

Chapter Two

Venice: November, 1609 A.D.

As the gondola slowly paddled its way along the Grand Canal from the Piazza San Marco, where Senor Paolo Sarpi had his office towards the Rio di San Marino, where he had his home, the city magistrate deliberated in his mind the case that he would be presenting before the court the next morning. At fifty-seven years of age, he also was seriously thinking that perhaps the time to retire was quickly approaching. The hair was thinning, the lines permanently engraved into his brow, and the eyesight not as sharp as it once was, all suggesting that perhaps it was time to relocate to his country villa where he could pursue his passion for writing his memoirs. Having assumed the role of state counsel since the now famous court case against the Vatican in 1607 when he successfully argued for the separation of State and Church, he had not enjoyed a single day's rest and he sorrowfully reminisced about the days he would just sit idly by the river with his fishing pole without a care in the world. Now he feared he would never see those days again. He then laughed at the thought of retirement and dismissed it completely from his mind. It would never happen. As long as the city of Venice needed a defender of the liberties of the Republic, he would be there. He knew there was no one else with the strength of his convictions. No one else that would protect the Freedom of the Press, preventing both governmental and ecclesiastical censorship.

While deep in his thoughts, the gondolier eased the boat into the slip outside Sarpi's home and wrapped the tie-line over the tethering post. "Senor Sarpi, we are here," the gondolier interrupted Sarpi's meditations.

"Oh, already?" Sarpi snapped out of his daydream and reached in his pocket to find a quarter florin to flick to the boatman. Stepping onto the pier he made his way to the front door of his three storey home. Waiting for him on the veranda was his house keeper, who helped remove his black woolen overcoat the moment he stepped on to the first porch step.

"Good evening Senor Sarpi," she greeted her employer, "You have a guest waiting in the salon for you."

"Madame Ricci," he responded in tones signaling his displeasure, "How many times have I told you that you must be firm with these people. If they wish to see me they must make an appointment at my office. When I come home, it is my time to do as I please and it does not please me to have these interlopers steal from me what precious little time I have." He gave her a stern look of disapproval as he reprimanded her but after so many years serving in his employ, she paid little attention to the scolding. The scowls and sternness of his visage were well known to all, and there wasn't a single painting in the city that ever portrayed Chief Magistrate Sarpi with a smile on his face.

"I know Sir," she replied, "But this gentleman was quite insistent. I believe when you see who it is you will understand."

"Oh, well then. Bring me a glass of cognac and I will go see to my uninvited guest. Bring him one too if you haven't already served him."

"Immediately Sir," she bent her knee and left to retrieve the glass of cognac as requested.

Sarpi entered his salon and immediately upon seeing his guest, he revolved on his heels, searching every corner of the room for any hidden threats."

"You could at least say hello, old friend," the man seated on the green and white striped settee suggested.

"Cardinal Klesl, I would be lying if I said it was an honour to have you here."

Chuckling, the cardinal removed his red cap and placed it in his lap. "Why so formal, Brother? Surely you can still refer to me as Melchior, old friend."

Sarpi continued to look into the shadows and corners of his salon. "Forgive me Cardinal if somehow I don't feel the bonds of friendship right now."

"Oh, stop looking for assassins already Brother Paolo. I come in peace. If I wanted you dead you never would have had the opportunity to set a foot outside your office. Now sit down already, so we can talk." The cardinal patted the empty seat beside him on the settee.

"I think I prefer to sit a distance from you Klesl." Sarpi sat down in stylishly curved chair with its padded armrests across the table from the Cardinal. "And stop calling me brother. Those days in the Church are long gone and you certainly are no brother of mine!"

"I can see you are still harboring ill feelings towards us Paolo. That pains me to no end."

"No, what you consider pain Melchior, is nothing at all. Pain is the scars left behind from seventeen stab wounds. That's real pain."

"Seventeen? Don't you mean fifteen?"

"Shall I show you all of the scars Cardinal? Seventeen!"

"I was certain it was only fifteen," the Cardinal insisted.

"Definitely seventeen," Sarpi corrected him once more.

"Oh my," the Cardinal feigned astonishment. "We only had reports of fifteen wounds. There must still be someone out there that we haven't accounted for."

"You mean someone you haven't paid yet," Sarpi corrected him.

"We cannot be held accountable for everyone that tries to kill you," the Cardinal explained. "Sometimes there are those that act on their own volition."

Sarpi just shook his head in disbelief. "I would think that when you place a bounty of eight thousand crowns on someone's head you are inviting a lot of freelancers to try their hand at assassination. That makes you responsible!"

"I want you to know that it was not with my approval. Pope Paul insisted you had to be silenced and he wasn't going to let anyone disagree with him."

"So am I to be grateful for your lack of cooperation in His Holiness's efforts to have me killed."

"A little gratitude might be in order," Klesl suggested. "After all, I wouldn't be here today unless I managed to negotiate a clemency for you."

"Somehow your argument in a court of law that you managed to momentarily quell the homicidal urges of your fanatical Papal leader will not award you absolution from all the other times you failed to stop him. Your Pope is a crazed lunatic that murders everyone that stands in his way. How can you seriously sit here and tell me that you are all men of God in good standing?"

"Even his holiness is human," Klesl tried to excuse the Pope's actions. "We all tend to sin but the Lord grants us his forgiveness."

"And you wonder why I left the clergy. If only you could hear the hypocrisy you spew, through my ears. Thank God, the Lord has seen fit to protect me. Even after all your attempts, and the seventeen stiletto wounds that now adorn my torso, God was not prepared to let me die. Your plots failed! God made it clear that he disapproves of Paul's election to the Papal throne. So keep your bullshit regarding Paul being forgiven to a minimum. Jesus Christ has not forgiven any of you. Not then, not now, not ever!"

Klesl sat motionless as Sarpi railed against the Vatican, bowing his head once or twice as if to acknowledge the truth of Sarpi's comments. "Your right, God did not want you dead. No man could survive fifteen stabbings if it were not for the Almighty's protection."

"Seventeen," Sarpi corrected him once again.

"Yes, seventeen," the Cardinal corrected himself. "Even Pope Paul had to admit that you had divine protection. But still, he wanted you dead but I was able to convince him otherwise as long as you accept our offer."

"Always a catch with you Cardinal," Sarpi sounded disgusted upon hearing that the price of not being assassinated had to be negotiated. "If you think that I'm going to retract our laws separating Church and State in some manner, then you might as well stab me right now and get it over with. It's not going to happen."

Klesl patted the air with his right hand, the gesture suggesting that Sarpi had to wait and settle down. "Nothing to do with the Venetian Edicts of two years ago. Rest assured they will remain in place. What I need to discuss with you has far more serous repercussions."

"More serious than the rights of the Church in the city-state of Venice?" Sarpi found that hard to believed.

"Are you willing to listen to me now Paolo?" the Cardinal suggested it would be in his best interest.

Leaning back in chair, Sarpi waved for Madame Ricci to enter the room with the two glasses of cognac. The housekeeper placed the glasses on the table between the two men and exited the room as quickly as possible having overheard a bit of their emotional discussion as she passed through the hallway and wanted no part of it.

"Ah, cognac," Klesl sighed. Taking a quick sip, he licked his lips and smiled. "There are still some good things in this world to enjoy, even in bad times. I can safely assume my glass has not been poisoned?"

"Assume nothing Klesl. Drink at your own risk. I'm presuming this cryptic message regarding bad times has something to do with the reason you are here," Sarpi interpreted the Cardinal's last comment.

"I'm afraid we are facing dark times again, Paolo. Do you recall how two decades ago we were facing Armageddon and if not for our timely intervention, Satan would be dominating this world right now?"

"If you're referring to the events in Prague at that time, then I think you forget that it was my good friend Giordano Bruno and two others that saved your world, and as far as he explained it to me, the Church had actually very little to do with resolving the murders other than interfering in their investigation."

"Perhaps that is how Brother Bruno viewed the situation, but I can assure you the Church was actively involved in bringing an end to the monster that was rampaging through the city." Cardinal Klesl was not backing down from his statement.

"Still, in my view," Sarpi summarized, "the murder of just over a dozen people and the theft of millions of crowns does not constitute a world ending doomsday."

"Well, that is how some of the clergy are viewing that event in light of what is happening now. They think we may have misjudged the timing of the doomsday prophecy. What happened in Prague may have been a prelude but the actual end of the world scenario may be happening now!"

"Then it's a real shame that you managed to kill two of your three saviors in your rush to judgment. Guess you really should have thought twice before you decided to burn Giordano at the stake."

"Yes, that was a serious misjudgment on the Church's part but we believe we have a solution offered to us by Nostradamus."

"You mean by his son, don't you. Nostradamus has been dead for quite some time now."

"Caesar may have interpreted it for us but the solution came from his father," Klesl explained. It was buried into what Nostradamus labeled as Century III Quatrain 36. It read as follows:

> *'Buried apoplectic not dead,*
> *He will be found to have his hands eaten:*
> *When the city will condemn the heretic,*
> *He who it seemed to them had changed their laws.'*

You see, it is obvious," the Cardinal drew his conclusion.

"Perhaps to you," Sarpi shrugged his shoulders, "But I don't see anything but a bunch of words that are nothing more than childish gibberish."

"It is describing you, Paolo. Can't you see it?" Klesl challenged the magistrate to see the connection. How many times you should have been buried but each time you wake up from your semi-comatose condition and spit on death right into his face. As we have come to realize, you just won't die like any other normal man. You, a former lay priest in the Church are now branded by all as a heretic, or at least we have branded you as one. You chose to prosecute the Vatican and succeeded in establishing laws that separated Church and State."

"Exactly the reasons that you attempted to assassinate me repeatedly. So now you want me to believe that you view what I have done in a completely different light? I find it very hard to accept that you are able to put our mutual past behind you and we can move on from it. You certainly didn't move on from your past resentments for Bruno after all he did for you. You executed him. You burnt him at the stake. So why should I believe you will behave any differently in my case?"

Klesl was already prepared to provide the answer, knowing that the question was certain to arise in their conversation. Reaching into the interior pocket of his red robes he pulled out a sealed letter."

"And what is that supposed to be?" Sarpi was suspicious of anything the Cardinal had to offer.

"It is your letter of clemency. A guarantee from the Pontiff that no further attacks will take place upon your life. Pope Paul will rescind his original papal bull and pronounce an edict you are under the protection of the Vatican.

"I believe Bruno had one of those letters too, if I'm not mistaken," Sarpi sniped at Klesl sarcastically. "Didn't prove to be worth the paper it was written on."

"He had a letter of pardon from Pope Sixtus. It was Pope Clement that ordered him to be executed."

"So, you're saying I'm only safe as long as Pope Paul remains alive. That's not very reassuring. What am I supposed to do in order to make certain the agreement is upheld?" Sarpi knew that he could never trust the Papacy but his desire to finally end the attempts on his life was sorely tempting.

"I suggest first that you pray for Pope Paul to have a long life. That is all I can suggest other than the fact that the Emperor will do everything in his power to protect you."

"Oh my, you have just infused me with confidence," Sarpi commented with his usual sarcastic wit. "And what's this nonsense of having my hands eaten. Is the Pope now demanding that I am to have my limbs amputated rather than have my life forfeited."

"Don't be ridiculous Paolo! Of course the Pope would not demand such a thing. According to the explanation from the son of Nostradamus, it refers to hands in the context of aides or assistants. We would know which heretic priest to recruit not only because we couldn't kill him but also because he was forced to work alone since no young solicitor would enter into his services for fear of losing their own life." Holding out his hands placably, Klesl expected a response. "Isn't it true Paolo, no one dares work for you because of the taint of death that surrounds you."

"Because you have made it so. And I'd appreciate if you didn't refer to me as a heretic priest. Those days are long behind me and I am no priest."

Smiling at Sarpi's refusal to have any connection to the Vatican, Klesl could not resist to taunt him further. "As I said earlier Brother

Paolo, you never leave the services of the Catholic Church, no matter what you choose to call yourself. There is no divorce from the Church."

"Not divorced, merely annulled," Sarpi voiced his perspective. "And since it is obvious that you are desperate to have me join your band of adventurers, then I think it is time you provide a little more detail regarding this mission." Paolo took a long sip of his cognac as he waited for Klesl to tell the story.

"We have been sitting on a powder keg for over a decade with the hope that it would go away but the situation has only grown worse, I'm afraid," the Cardinal replied. "For years now, young women in the eastern part of the Empire have been disappearing but we paid little attention to the matter. It didn't really concern us."

"Because…" Sarpi pushed for a clarification.

"Because the early victims were all peasants, gypsies and Jews. They were of little concern to us. The less of them, the better."

"But now…" Sarpi knew that something had changed.

"Now what or whomever is killing them has begun to slaughter women of the aristocracy. Powerful people are now demanding a solution and the Emperor and I have none to offer thus far."

Sarpi scratched top of his head, the hair thinning in his middle age and now approaching a point where the baldness was beginning to definitively show. "How many disappearances are we talking about?"

"Four thus far. The first was the sister of Count Fogarasy of Hungary a couple of Christmases ago."

"Four hardly seems to be significant enough to catch the attention of the Church. Other than the aristocratic girls, how many are we talking about?" Sarpi knew there had to be much more to the story than the disappearance of four wealthy privileged girls.

Klesl was hesitant to respond. His speech became barely audible as he replied, "Perhaps a few hundred. Maybe more."

"What!" Sarpi practically shouted. "You let the disappearance of hundreds of innocent girls go uninvestigated and now because of a handful of rich and spoiled offspring you are actually going to do something. Perhaps you should all rot in hell."

"Paolo," the Cardinal pleaded with the magistrate to listen, "It is not because of them but a matter far greater than the sum of the girls. The religious affiliation of the four was equally spread among the Christian sects. Most of the peasant girls tended to be Calvinists and the gypsies and Jews are nothing more than heathens. But now the embers of religious dissent have been stirred in the East and the flames are growing higher. The first thing the Calvinists did was blame the Lutherans. So the Vatican stayed far away from internal struggles between Protestants. But then the Turks decided to meddle into these affairs and they prodded the people to rise up against the Lutherans. Much as the Lutherans always do when they find themselves hard pressed, they attack the local Catholic clergy. Several of our priests have been beaten badly."

"Forgive me if I do not shed a tear for your priests," Sarpi scarcely lamented. "Still, this hardly appears to be prelude to world ending events."

"It is when you consider the further ramifications," the Cardinal attempted to educate the Venetian. "The natural response, we all know will be for the Vatican to bring the blood libel against the Jews. In that way we cast the suspicion on them so that the others are left alone. But the Protestants will accuse the Gypsies of performing witchcraft and before you know it, they will all be killing each other."

"Isn't that your usual way of dealing with your opponents? Let them kill one another before they can strike against you? I thought that was Church doctrine," Sarpi jested as he took another sip of his cognac.

"Except this time it is different," Klesl sounded worried. "What the Vatican didn't appreciate at first was that we aren't talking about a few small villages of Jews in the Carpathians. We are talking about millions. And the gypsies probably number in the tens of thousands. I have no idea where they all came from but when we last tried to perform a census, we were forced to abandon the project because we couldn't number them all and then the Jews especially began to resist being counted. They actually began to fight back physically and our wardens were no match for them. If they should come to realize just how powerful a force they are, they will wipe us from the globe."

"But that still doesn't tell me why you think that eventuality will occur. What made you draw the conclusion that the end of the world was inevitable?" Sarpi pressed the Cardinal for answer.

"While the Emperor and I were informing the Vatican of the danger of pursuing any form of retribution that would antagonize the Jews, we received a letter from Caesar de Nostradame. He had experienced another episode where his father had communicated to him from beyond the grave and one quatrain in particular became fixed in his mind. Century VIII Quatrain 80:

'The blood of innocents, widow and virgin,
So many evils committed by means of the Great Red One,
Holy images placed over burning candles,
Terrified by fear, none will be seen to move.'

That is why we are so alarmed. He knew exactly what we were facing and his father was warning us of what would happen unless we found a way to stop it."

"Pardon my ignorance but I'm afraid that I'm still not very good at resolving these prophetic riddles. What exactly does it say?" Sarpi scratched his head again, confused by the words of the long dead Nostradamus.

"Even those of us not accustomed to these prophecies, knew the meaning, immediately. All these disappearances of young women were going to ultimately be blamed on the Catholic Church. We are the Great Red One, as is obvious by the frocks of our senior clergy. All the factions will rise against us for presumed evils they believe we have done."

"As is true," Sarpi interrupted. "Maybe it is time for the Church to fade away."

"True or not, it will be the Jews that destroy us completely. That is the image of our holy Icons being burned by the flames of their Sabbath candles. If it's anything the Jews are renown for, its their constant burning of candles at every occasion and festival. So great will be their reprisals that none of us will be able to stop their path of destruction. Is that what you want? A world where Jews become the dominant power! Not Catholic, not Protestant, I doubt even the Turks would want that. It will be the end of days according to the book of Zechariah, an end where they rebuild their Jerusalem and dominate the world. An end we cannot let happen."

"So the world trades one brutal and prejudicial force for another. Hardly my concern," Sarpi rejected the Cardinal's plea for help.

"But we offered you freedom from fear of being assassinated in the future. Is that not enough to convince you how dire is our need." Klesl couldn't understand how Paolo Sarpi could refuse his offer.

"You offer me nothing," Sarpi rebutted. "As you are certainly aware after all your attempts to kill me, you will not succeed. Not then, not now, not ever. Not only that, but the mere fact that you have tried to kill me all these years attests to the fact that your Church is hardly fit to dominate the world."

"So you would let another religion take our place and dominate the world in our stead," Klesl argued.

"No religion should ever be in a position of dominance. Only the State should provide order to the people. Religion must be kept out of the affairs of State at all cost." Having said those words, Sarpi took a moment to reflect upon exactly what they meant. In doing so he knew precisely what he wanted in payment for his services. Shaking a finger in the Cardinal's face, the magistrate made his point, "I will take your letter of clemency but there is one other condition you will agree to if you want my services on this quest of yours."

"Tell me," Klesl was eager to hear the demand, knowing that Sarpi had finally shown a willingness to cooperate.

"You will have Matthias and the Church sign the Rudophine Letter of Majesty," Sarpi demanded.

"You're joking," the response blurted out from Klesl spontaneously.

"I am very serious. Sign it or no deal"

"The letter is an abomination," Klesl grew angry and his face turned red.

Sarpi simply shook his head. "Having helped write it, I hardly consider it an abomination. Merely a treatise well ahead of its time. You will agree that no man can be forced against his will into Catholicism or any other faith. All men are to be guaranteed freedom of religion no matter what their status. A council of faiths will be established so all religions can express their needs equally before government. Sign it and we have an agreement.

The original letter drafted by Emperor Rudolf had been dismissed in its entirety when presented in July of this year to his brother, the usurper who now referred to himself as Emperor Matthias.

"Sign it and have Matthias announce it formally at council and you will have my assistance, otherwise you can leave my house now Cardinal."

"You are being unreasonable Paolo," Klesl complained bitterly. "You will have us willingly do what this prophetic threat will do should it come to pass. There is no difference."

"Cardinal, there is a world of difference. If the prophecy comes true, your Catholic Church will no longer exist. You will be celebrating your Sabbath starting on Friday night and you will forfeit your foreskin, which I understand at your age will be quite painful. What I ask is that you learn to share the world with those beliefs that are in no way inferior to your own. It is the subjugation of other religions which has rendered you the target of this prophecy. Sign the agreement and you have removed that which thy despise you most for. They will have no reason to rise up against you."

"If that is the case, and you have quelled the fire that will consume our world and bring down the Empire with a simple treatise promising equality, then why join the mission at all?"

"Because in all your efforts to save your own world you have completely ignored the overwhelming fact that hundreds of young women, all equal, all deserving of life, have disappeared and must be presumed dead. Their souls cry out for justice! I'm willing to join this mission to save the lives of the future innocents mentioned in that quatrain. If you were truly a man of God, you would have been concerned for their well-being as well."

Pushing the letter of clemency towards Sarpi, the Cardinal rose from the settee and proceeded towards the salon door. Turning back he begrudgingly flung his final words in Sarpi's general direction. "The Rudolphine letter will be signed and announced. See to it that you're in Vienna by the end of next month!" With that, he donned his red tri-cornered cap and stomped from the home.

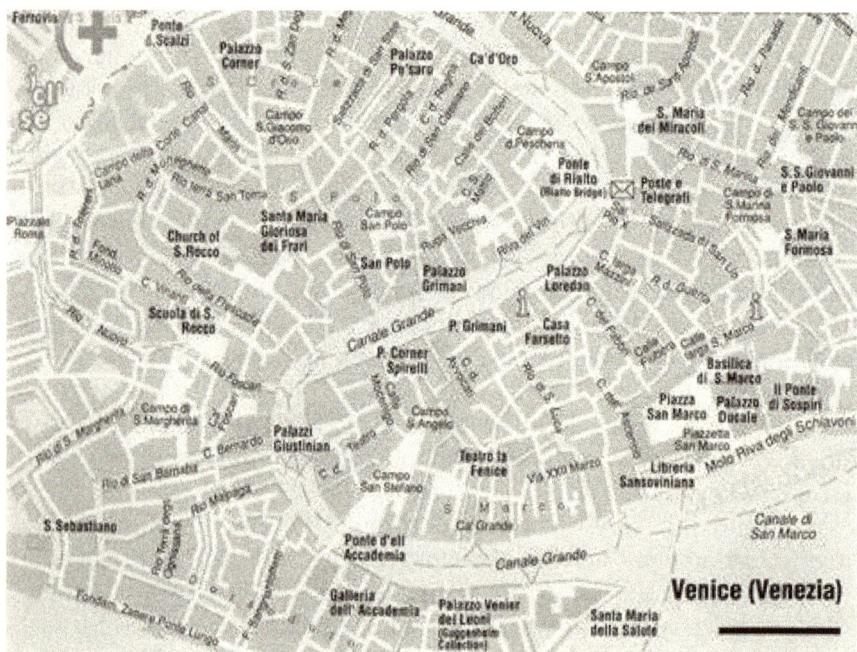

Map of Venice

Chapter Three

The Hofburg; December 1609

True to his promise, the Archduke Maximilian had taken care of all the wedding arrangements for Joseph's sister, Tanit. As the third week of December approached, the city of Vienna was flooded with countless visitors that specifically came to the capital to attend this very special royal event.

Tanit had met her betrothed on several occasions, and in spite of the fact that he had suffered irreparable brain damage through a fall from his horse in his teenage years, Count Otto von Wallerstein, was still one of the most handsome men of the aristocracy, with his long wavy blonde hair and dazzling blue eyes. Though childlike in both speech and mannerisms, neither debility appeared to bother Tanit in the least, as she immediately felt a maternal instinct for her soon-to-be husband.

As the only surviving son of the Oettingen-Wallerstein family, Otto was in possession of incredible wealth but his finances had been managed the past ten years by Archduke Maximilian on account of his debilitation. The Archduke had been very protective of his distant cousin, taking him in as his ward and carefully managing all his affairs, some saying that he did so in order to hide the fact that he had been freely dipping into the wealth of the Von Wallerstein estate. There had been other women from among the aristocracy that had requested the opportunity to liaison with the young count for the purpose of marriage but each one had been refused and turned away by the Archduke. So it was a surprise to everyone that he had agreed to this particular marriage, to a woman considered low-born and possessing no apparent wealth or estate of her own.

But that certainly did not stop anyone from attending. A wedding at the palace was always a lavish affair and a necessity to attend and be seen if aristocratic families were going to reinforce their loyalty to the crown. In an age when so many wanted to call themselves Emperor, it was important to be seen with the one having the best prospects of achieving that station. The guest-list included anyone of significance in the Austrian Empire, as well as numerous foreign dignitaries that had come as representatives of their own monarchs, but like everyone else, they would also take this golden opportunity to petition the Holy Roman Emperor on matters to their own personal benefit. From princes and dukes to the top scholars and financiers of the Empire and from those far beyond the borders, they came to celebrate the union of the houses of Oettingen-Wallerstein and the Kahana; some out of curiosity, others to merely court favor.

Carriages had lined the Ringstrasse since noon, as most guests decided to arrive well in advance of the ceremony, knowing that parts of the road had been closed off due to the ongoing construction the palace had been undergoing for months already. Matthias had begun a massive reconstruction process, intending to return the Imperial Court to the Hofburg Palace, now that the matter of who actually ruled the empire had been resolved with his brother Rudolf who previously laid claim to rule from his palace in Prague. Now, a virtual prisoner in his palace, Rudolf had not received an invitation to the wedding, his brothers purposely ignoring the fact that the previous Emperor and Tanit's father had been extremely close, almost to the point of being considered friends. They considered that a dangerous combination.

Guests had to pass through the impressive gates designed in the Renaissance style of the prior century, The moat and drawbridge were reminders of an earlier time when the Habsburgs first began their rule in Vienna, the family having originated deep in the Swiss Alps. The four towers were a reminder that the Empire had been engaged in a never ending war of expansion. As a composite of almost four centuries of architectural styles, the Hofburg was a living museum of the ages, a testimony to the greatness of the Austrian Empire. The four wings that connected into a square, created the lavish central garden, a huge park-like setting where the ceremony would take place. Among the trees and flowers, the numerous statues strove to provide a connection from ancient Greek and Roman civilizations to the ascension of Austria as the new Rome. The glass canopies that stretched towards the sky from each of the four wings shielded the garden from the Austrian winter, ensuring that for a full twelve months the gardens bloomed with colour. Few places could provide such a spectacular backdrop for a wedding. But to many of the guests, the most exciting part of the palace and a royal wedding was the three storey wine cellar in the basement of the Hofburg Palace, which guaranteed practically everyone would have a fabulous time.

The entire affair was carefully orchestrated as a civil ceremony, thereby avoiding the controversial issue of providing a religious service, which would have normally taken place in St. Michael's Church. Fearing that holding to tradition would have been contentious to all parties involved, Maximilian arranged for the ceremony to take place within the palace walls under the auspices of the city's chief magistrate, Herr Lukas Lausser. A palace wedding also meant that there was no need to begin the service early in the morning, which was normally necessary in order to make it possible for all the guests to eventually make their way from the church to the ballroom of the palace in time to participate and partake of the meal and celebrations that would follow. A late start also meant that Maximilian would have sufficient time to prepare the groom properly. An over anxious groom in this case could and probably would easily turn into a disaster, as there was no way of knowing how Otto was going to react to being the center of attention of the hundreds of people gathered to witness the wedding. Throughout the morning, Maximilian repeatedly reminded his cousin that he was only to say what he would tell him to say at the appropriate time and at all times he was to do as he was instructed. Otto nodded his head, appearing to understand the instructions, though admittedly it was difficult for Maximilian to be certain.

"I get to kiss Tanit," was Otto's immediate response.

"Yes, you get to kiss her when I tell you to kiss her. Understand? Only when I tell you that it is the time to kiss her," Maximilian explained.

Blushing, Otto donned a big grin, acting like any school boy about to receive his first kiss. "I want to kiss Tanit," he informed the Archduke.

"I know you want to kiss her Otto. And you will do so, but only when I tell you it is the right time. Do you understand me?" The Archduke feared his cousin didn't understand at all.

"I get to kiss Tanit. I get to kiss Tanit," the young count repeated over and over again.

"When I say so," Maximilian desperately tried to get a confirmation from Otto that he understood. "Do we have a deal?"

Holding out his hand, he waited for his cousin to shake it. "Deal", Otto said as he shook the hand vigorously.

"Yes, a deal," repeated the Archduke, finally content that he was able to convince his cousin to follow his instructions.

At the same time, preparations for the bride were also under way as the stylists coiffed her raven tresses and the make up artist applied just the right amount of rouge to her cheeks and lips. Her eyelashes were lined with mascara, while her eyelids were powdered a silvery-blue. The outline of her aquiline nose was shadowed to accent its perfection and the same shadowing was applied to elevate even further the height of her cheekbones.

Since her father had passed away, the honor of walking the bride down the aisle fell to her brother. The once disheveled, haggard, aged well beyond her youthful years undesirable, deemed too old to be married within her own community had been miraculously transformed into a beautiful swan for her wedding day and the tears welled in Joseph's eyes as he gazed upon his sister as if seeing her for the very first time. Gowned in the magnificent bone white, silver lace trimmed wedding dress that the Empress Anne, wife of Matthias, had personally selected for this special occasion, she was the very picture of perfection. Her smile visibly radiated as she gazed upon herself in the looking glass. It had been years since he had seen his sister so happy, thinking back to the few occasions he had ever seen her smile since their parents died. 'Even if he failed to return from this mission,' he thought to himself, seeing his sister this happy would be worth the price of failure. It was almost time for the ceremony to begin. Her two bridesmaids, the royal princesses, Constance and Magdalen, the daughters of the Duchess of Bavaria began to gather the long train of her gown. Joseph closed his eyes and for the first time in a long time he thanked God for making this day possible.

The groom was escorted into the garden by his caregiver, the Archduke Maximilian. Wearing a blue and gold military uniform, characteristic of Otto's position as a Bavarian Count, the gold brocade ropes hung from his epaulets, neatly looping across his chest and attaching to the lapels of his jacket. Gold buttons in double breasted rows ran the length of the overcoat, which hung slightly below his waist. The white gloves appeared to bother Otto, but each time he attempted to remove them, the Archduke would swat his hands away and warn him from doing it again with a stern crisp, 'No'. Once satisfied that the young Count was ready, Maximilian signaled the leader of the small chamber ensemble to begin the wedding march.

Urging his cousin to march in step on his left, Maximilian began the slow walk along the red carpeted path that led to the podium at the center of the garden. Seeing relatives and friends seated among the guests, Otto began to wave excitedly to catch their attention. Some of the people began to laugh, which only encouraged the young Count to wave even more vigorously. "Stop that," Maximilian could be overheard muttering in a low but still audible tone. "Stop that immediately, do you hear me!" It was evident Otto must have heard because he hung his head down, chin upon his chest, while shrugging his soldiers as he marched in step beside the Archduke. Mounting the podium, the Archduke locked his elbow under Otto's right arm, ensuring that his cousin would not be able to go any where unexpectedly.

The music became more brisk as Princess Magdalen entered onto the garden path carrying a basket of white rose petals that she sprinkled across the ground, covering the red carpet behind her. That was the moment that Tanit entered the arboretum, her brother proudly walking on her left as he held her hand firmly, and the Princess Constance, trailing behind to ensure that the train of the gown remained spread like the feathers of a peacock. A collective sigh of awe emanated from the assembled guests, as the bride radiated such beauty and charm that it was dazzling to behold. Taking their place on the podium, Joseph released his grip, permitting Herr Lausser to take his sister's right hand and place it over top of Otto's extended left hand. Gazing upon his bride, a transformation appeared to overcome the young Count. He stood more erect, more confident in his own sense of being, puffing out his chest as he gave Tanit a slight nod of reassurance. Otto made no mistake in repeating the words that were being whispered to him by his cousin. In fact, the ceremony was performed so perfectly without incident that many came to question whether the Count still suffered from an impairment at all.

———————

Following the elaborate meal and the early entertainment provided by the musicians, acrobats and jugglers, it was time for the newly married couple to consummate their vows, while the rest of the guests would continue to eat and drink their fill into the long hours of the morning. Carried to the bridal suite on the shoulders of family and new found friends, the newlyweds were thrust together into the room. Maximilian posted two guards to stand outside the room to ensure that they would not be disturbed. Some of the celebrators were overheard joking as to whether Otto would know what to do as they returned to the hall, raising a burst of laughter from the others. "I can assure you all," Maximilian spoke up, "Otto will not disappoint. Every young boy already knows what his tool can do from a very young age. He may not know about the consequences of his actions but he certainly knows what feels good." This invited another round of laughter from those surrounding him.

Reaching the doors to the hall, the Archduke searched among the revelers for the whereabouts of Joseph, Caesar and Paolo. It wasn't until he let his eyes roll up the white winding staircase that he saw them gathered together on the first landing. They appeared to be engaged in an animated conversation and he thought it would be wise to let them discuss the matters at hand before he intruded on them. But that did not stop him from ascending half way to their location so that he could overhear what they were discussing.

"So let me see if I understand this clearly," Sarpi was saying. "In order for you to join this mission, you demanded two weddings, an orphanage and a pile of money."

"I will admit," Joseph responded, "it may not seem altruistic but I have absolutely no reason to give up my life for matters that have nothing to do with me."

"That certainly was not the thinking of your father," Caesar reminisced.

"And look what happened to my father and the rest of us," Joseph reminded him. "My father is dead and nothing you say is going to resurrect his spirit within me. So don't even bother to try."

"I don't expect you to understand your father's motivation," Caesar admitted, "he was different from any other man I have ever known. But no matter how much you wish to deny it, I know that part of you made the decision to join this mission because you know it is the right thing to do."

"Of course it was the right thing to do," Joseph confirmed. "Did you see the look on my sister's face. Seeing that look of happiness on her face, after thinking I would never see it ever again, tells me it was the right thing to do. The same way when I will look at the sheer misery evident on the face of Yom Tov Lipmann Heller, it will be well worth the price of my commitment to this quest. How is my motivation any different from Senor Sarpi's? All he wants is for the Pope to stop trying to have him assassinated."

"Not to mention a proclamation of the equivalency and freedom of all religions in the Empire."

"A very noble expectation," Caesar agreed, "but just because the Emperor Matthias signs an edict and proclaims it to the public does not mean it will be fulfilled."

"No, but it is a start," Sarpi shook his finger in the air to emphasize his point. "And what about you Caesar? Why bother to do these things at all? What is your motivation?"

"Because...as my father made me appreciate, it is my inescapable destiny."

"All men have free will," Sarpi challenged Caesar.

"If you believe so," Caesar replied nonchalantly, dismissing Sarpi's comment as if it was the naive belief of a young child. "My father made it obvious to me that all our destinies are predetermined. Do you think it was mere coincidence that the three of us are gathered here and even discussing what has united us? Do you think it was luck that permitted you to survive being stabbed a dozen times, only to have your ability to survive be used to induce you to join this mission?"

"Seventeen times," Sarpi corrected him.

"Seventeen times then," Caesar corrected himself. "Or do you think it was mere coincidence that your unmarried sister would have the opportunity to marry into one of the oldest aristocratic families in the Empire, only because at the time to persuade you to join our cause there just happened to be a brain addled only son of such a family ripe to be married?" he directed the line of questioning towards Joseph. "Or that the most recognized and acclaimed disciple of the man responsible for killing your father and shaming your family,just happens to have six daughters and coincidentally also happens to be rotting in a jail cell as we speak? That is not coincidence, gentlemen. That is predetermination!"

"I'm afraid I'm a scientist," Sarpi tried to deny Caesar's conclusions. "Serendipity certainly happens and therefore we cannot claim that chance is always the result of predetermined destinies."

"But you were also a lay priest at one point in your life and as much as you may wish to deny it, God does work in mysterious ways," Caesar reminded the Venetian magistrate. "No matter what your feelings, Joseph, you as the Kahana know that is true."

"I must admit," Joseph turned towards Sarpi, "he does make a compelling argument. It does seem quite odd that all these events took place exactly at the right time."

"My father even made a better one," Caesar Nostradame continued. "In Century VI Quatrain 11 he wrote this:

'The seven branches will be reduced to three,
The elder ones will be surprised by death,
The two will be seduced to fratricide,
The conspirators will be dead while sleeping."

It was this quatrain that became my prime motivations for reaching out to the Emperor in the first place. Do you see it?"

Both Joseph and Paolo shook their heads, failing to understand.

"Then let me explain," Caesar sighed disappointingly, unable to fathom why everyone was having such difficulty resolving his father's riddles. "Often my father would hide the date of the events in the numbers he assigned to the quatrain. In this particular case he was saying we have just about one year to resolve these mysterious deaths or we will fail. The sixth century of this millennium is this one. The eleventh year is one year from now. Our deadline is 1611 gentlemen. Furthermore, what has seven branches, Joseph?"

"A menorah," Joseph answered without hesitation.

"Yes, the symbol of the Holy House of Israel; You! You are the key piece of solving these murders. Once you agreed to join the mission, then we would have the three required to fulfil the prophecy. The two elder ones, being myself and Senor Sarpi, though both of us have been exposed to death so many times in the past, we are still able to be shocked by the deaths of these girls because what we find is not natural and if I dare say so, 'not human'. But there was another issue I had to warn both Matthias and Maximilian about. They must not lay a hand on their brother Rudolf, lest they risk their own lives."

Upon hearing Caesar recite and explain that particular quatrain, Maximilian decided it was time to intercede and he began climbing the final steps to the landing. "No point in giving away all the family secrets," he instructed Caesar. "But now you know why we have confined my elder brother to his palace in Prague and not fully stripped him of his title as Emperor. But more importantly, I see that all three of you have become acquainted," the Archduke commented as he climbed the last step on to the shared landing. "I was hoping that you would all manage to meet of your own accord."

"I wish to thank you Excellency," Joseph bowed to the Archduke in gratitude. "You have made this the happiest day of my sister's existence. For that, I am eternally grateful."

"And I am grateful to you," Maximilian replied. "The care of my cousin now falls to someone else. I cannot tell you what a relief that is. But at the same time there is sadness. As you may have noticed neither I nor my brothers have any children of our own. In Rudolph's case, it is most likely by choice, but for Matthias and myself, it is not due to lack of trying. Otto provided me with the experience of having a son. It is a feeling I will always cherish. But he is the perpetual child, and in my role as Grand Master of the Teutonic Order, I need to spend more time on the battlefield as the army's commander, and that leaves me no time to take care of his needs any longer. It will not be easy for your sister, but she has embraced the challenge gladly."

"I believe someone like Otto was exactly what she needed," Joseph reasoned. "All the emotion she has pent up for twenty years she can pour out and lavish on him."

The Archduke agreed. "Other men would probably run from the sensation of being suffocated by her attention but Otto will not only absorb what she provides but will probably ask for more. He has a high demand for attention."

"He will be well taken care of by my sister," Joseph reassured the Archduke.

"I am well aware of that," Maximilian replied. "If I did not believe it so, I would never have agreed to this marriage. There will be those that will accuse me of having manipulated the situation for gain, but what mattered most to me is Otto's happiness.

"He did not appear to happy with the meal he was served tonight," Paolo Sarpi reflected on the nights events. It had not gone unnoticed that Joseph, Tanit and Otto had been served especially prepared meals.

"Well, he better get used to it," Maximilian quipped. "I doubt very much he's ever going to have the chance to eat suckling pig ever again." It was then that Paolo Sarpi fully understood the extent of Joseph's arrangements in order to join the mission. "But let us toast to what lies ahead gentlemen." Maximilian waved for one of the servants to bring the tray of full wine glasses over to them immediately. But his shouting and arm waving caught the attention of someone else looking on from the crowd as well.

As they all gazed upward towards the servant that was now approaching, their attention was immediately diverted to the slim elegant figure of a woman standing on her own at the top landing of the marble staircase. Her pale white skin contrasted sharply with her long auburn tresses that were braided and weaved into a high cone that surmounted her head. A gold tiara kept her locks tidily in place. Her neck was long, longer than most, a simple gold necklace complimenting the perfection of her skin, drawing one's eyes from the nape of her elongated neck into the well demarcated cleavage of her breasts. Dark eyes penetrated deep into their flesh as they came to rest one by one on the three visitors. The mysterious woman showed no hesitation or shyness as she descended the winding stairway towards the platform upon which they were standing. She immediately moved to the Archduke's side, grabbing his upper left arm in her delicately shaped hands, in an obvious display of familiarity that made him uncomfortable. "Maxie, you have been hiding your guests away from the celebration. How terrible of you. That is not how the host is to behave, especially when we have new visitors to our usually very dreary family get-togethers. You must introduce me."

Taking a deep breath, the Archduke's reaction clearly suggested that whomever this beautiful lady was, she was definitely not one of his favourite people. "Elizabeth, please stop referring to me as Maxie, especially when in front of guests."

"But dear cousin, how else am I to refer to you? Maximilian is far too formal and Max lacks any evidence of the fondness I bear you. But if you insist, I will simply call you Cousin." It was evident that the woman took great delight in grating on the Archduke's nerves.

"Cousin will be fine," he confirmed. "Gentlemen, permit me to introduce the Countess Nadasdy, a cousin on my mother's side, or is it my grandmother's. I can never keep it straight with so many marriages of convenience taking place among the gentry these past few generations." All three quickly noted the subtle but snide remark by Maximilian, suggesting that many of the inter family commitments were loveless arrangements and that the Countess Nadasdy was a likely representative of one such marriage.

"I wouldn't know Cousin," the Countess responded without hesitation, "Because unlike my uncles and aunts, I preferred to marry within my own circle of Hungarian nobility. But I must compliment you on this wedding; it has been a beautiful affair. You certainly outdid yourself. How you ever managed to keep the poor boy under control is beyond imagination. I never expected cousin Otto to ever make it this far in life. Truly incredible! I commend you cousin. And the lavishness of this wedding, you must have spent a fortune. At least this time I can see that the money you have borrowed from my family has finally been put to good use." She had quickly turned the tables, implying that any marriages of convenience were entirely contrived by the Habsburgs in order to supplement their constantly dwindling reserves of cash in the treasury.

Feigning to laugh, the Archduke recognized that his cousin was far better at playing this game of veiled insults than he could ever be. "I had no idea that you would be attending Cousin. You never bothered to reply. I thought you preferred to live the life of a spinster in that dreary remote castle of yours up in the mountains." She may have been better at the insults but the Archduke was no amateur when it came to making his own stabbing remarks. "So tell me Elizabeth, have you enjoyed the festivities of the day at least?"

"Of course Cousin. You should have known that I would be coming. I could not resist attending an event where there is new blood being brought into the family. Pray tell, what are her family lines. She is too beautiful and exotic looking to be from your side of the family Cousin. Is she Spanish? I definitely see a trace of the Mediterranean in her." It was obvious to all that the Countess had not yet decided to let Maximilian escape so easily with his blistering remarks. The Habsburg grip on its Spanish territories was frightfully weak and she knew that the Emperor would do anything to shore up that relationship.

"If you must know Cousin, since it is your habit to try to know everything, she comes from a very rare and ancient blood line. A matter-of-fact, dear Elizabeth, far older than either yours or mine, if I am to be precise. But I'm afraid you are wrong, she is far more Eastern than Western. Correct me if I'm wrong Joseph, but as far as I understand, you are descended from the House of King David. At least that is how my brother Rudolf described your lineage."

"A maternal connection," Joseph clarified. "More precisely from the House of Aaron paternally but the considerable number of marriages between our two Houses made us practically indistinguishable."

"There, you see Cousin," Maximilian highlighted his explanation, "an ancient and immortal blood line. One that we have to be respectful of."

"You mean immortal like the one rumored to have been extinguished in Prague several years back," the Countess challenged the explanation, expressing some doubts.

"Hardly extinguished, Elizabeth. That was a false rumor put out by enemies of the family. This is that man's son. Allow me to introduce Joseph Kahana. Last male heir to the Kingdom of Israel. Or as they liked to say about his father, a king without a kingdom." Maximilian laughed as he made that last statement. To those born to rule, being a king without property seemed ludicrous. It also reinforced anyone's thinking, that should they ever believe that having now married into the Austrian aristocracy, they would somehow be on an equal footing with their peers, that was never going to be possible.

Nonetheless, the countess appeared impressed. Holding out her hand delicately, she waited for Joseph to take it into his own hand and gently press his lips against the top of her fingers. As he did so, Joseph was captivated by the softness of her skin and the fragrance of her flesh as his nose came in contact. The countess did not withdraw her hand quickly, letting it linger there longer than usual as if she sensed Joseph's enchantment. Joseph savored the aroma that he found inexplicably intoxicating.

Not willing to let her sink her hidden talons any further into Joseph, the Archduke quickly moved on to the next introduction. "And this gentlemen is Caesar de Nostradame, son of the famous seer and prophet Nostradamus." The Archduke turned her attention to the gentleman standing directly to the left of Joseph.

Slowly withdrawing her hand so that Joseph felt it slide smoothly across the flesh of his own fingertips, she then held it out for Caesar to acknowledge their acquaintance. "This is a surprise Monsieur Nostradamus. Once again, you are one of the men they speak of when they talk about the monster of Prague. One of the three that defeated the evil, if the stories are to be believed. How strange that the both of you should be here."

Having kissed her hand, Caesar quickly released it as if he had been stung by an insect. "Sometimes stories become exaggerated,

Countess. People choose to believe what they wish to believe. Even now they change the story, giving it different heroes that they find more acceptable. But as Yakov Kahana was a cherished friend, of course I would be attending his daughter's wedding."

"I have heard that the events have been altered, but I am old enough to remember the actual circumstances when they occurred," she informed him.

"You must have been a very young girl to recall the events of twenty years ago," Caesar commented. "I am surprised."

"Yes, very young," she smiled as if concealing a secret.

"And finally, this gentlemen is Senor Paolo Sarpi, chief advocate and magistrate of Venice. You may have heard of him. He is the man who outfoxed the Vatican and my brother, getting them to sign the Treaty of Venice."

"Oh, you mean the treaty where the Catholic Church lost almost all of its entitlements in Venice," she smugly replied to Maximilian, as if to say I know far more than you think. "A pleasure to meet the man that can take the Church down a rung or two," she offered her hand out once again. "I congratulate you Sir."

Snapping his feet together, Sarpi kissed her hand in proper Italian fashion, showing the others how it should be done.

"This wedding truly is a delight, Cousin," she complimented the Archduke once more. "To have the opportunity to meet so many distinguished gentlemen in one place, I cannot believe how fortunate I have been. The three of you together, it is almost as if you are on some sort of mission," she said the last sentence with a girlish laugh. She was merely guessing but Caesar noticed the way she watched their eyes in response to her comment as if she could read their innermost thoughts.

"Don't be ridiculous Elizabeth," the Archduke rebuked her. "What could these three men have in common that they'd actually be working together."

"Certainly not what they have in common but the sum of their combined differences. I'm surprised you didn't notice it yourself Cousin," she deftly planted her sublime insult squarely on Maximilian. "Well I must be going gentlemen," she excused herself. "It certainly has been a pleasure to meet your acquaintances. Should you find yourself in Slovakia, you must come and visit my home in Cachtice."

The three men watched in silence as the Countess descended to the landing immediately below and engaged in conversation with the next set of guests she encountered.

Maximilian was the first to break their entranced silence. "Don't pay her any attention gentlemen," he warned. "Elizabeth, it is said has a habit of making good men act stupidly."

"Where is her husband?" Caesar asked, not knowing why he was suddenly interested in her marital status and even asking a question in that regard.

"Dead, five years ago," the Archduke informed him. "If you ask me, I think he used it as an excuse to escape from her. But don't be upset for her, she has never played the part of the sorrowful widow. Her husband was always away fighting one war or another. I doubt she had time to miss him when he wasn't around. Take my words to heart, stay away from that one, she is nothing but trouble."

"So young and beautiful to be a widow," Joseph sighed, still smelling the fragrance of her perfume in his nostrils.

"Ha!" was Maximilian's immediate reaction. "How old do you think she is?"

"Thirty?" Joseph guessed.

"Perhaps a little older," Caesar contemplated the question "Thirty-three perhaps?"

"Gentlemen, take it from an Venetian when it comes to women. The tautness of her skin, the lack of a single crease on her neck or by the corners of her eyes, the flush of her cheekbones, trust me, she is in her late twenties at best."

Maximilian clapped his hands together in applause. "Well done Gentleman. You are all so wrong that it is extremely amusing. My cousin is fifty years old. She uses her youthful beauty to trap young, ignorant men in her web. Mark my words, that woman is a spider and you'd better be careful not to be caught in her web. Anyway, we have another bride in mind for you Joseph, so put her far from any thoughts."

Snapping out of his trance, Joseph shook his head in denial. "What are you even suggesting. Of course I have no interest in the Countess," he denied, feeling somewhat embarrassed. "I was very clear about my conditions of marriage for being part of this mission. I have no intention to change my mind."

"Good," Maximilian felt reassured. "Just heed my warning. Stay far away from her. She possesses an incredible ability to bend men to her will. I wouldn't want to see you become one of the many puppets that I suspect pass through her bed chamber each night."

Joseph was reluctant to admit that in some way he was attracted to the Countess, but even as he tried to deny it, the faint remnant of her perfume still lingered and played upon his thoughts.

"There is something more to that woman," Caesar voiced his opinion. "I felt it when I touched her hand. It was as if I had been bitten by a viper, the pain shot the length of my arm.".

"Static electricity," Sarpi tried to explain away the sensation that

Caesar had experienced. "It is a natural phenomenon. Probably from the fabric of her dress. Nothing to worry about"

Caesar was not accepting the explanation "No it was more than that. If it was static electricity then it would not have triggered one of my father's quatrains to rattle around my brain. Century IV Quatrain 41 appeared as soon as she touched my hand. It gave me a passing headache, it came on so strong:

> *'Female sex captive as a hostage,*
> *Will come by night to deceive the guards,*
> *The chief of the army deceived by her language,*
> *Will abandon her to the people, it will be pitiful to see.'*

Everything I witnessed today would appear to fit that description."

"What do you mean?" the Archduke questioned, knowing by now that the flashes of insight from Caesar's father's quatrains were not to be taken lightly.

"Let us just take it apart sentence by sentence," Caesar suggested. "You already told us she can use her sexuality as a trap for any man she wants. So there is the reference to her taking control sexually and holding her lovers hostage."

"I definitely see that," Joseph agreed, then suddenly felt embarrassed to admitting she had an effect on him.

"And here we are at night, the three guardians against Armageddon gathered together with the Commander-in-Chief of the army and she played us with words, and I will be honest if the rest of you won't be; at the moment, I would have done anything she asked of me. She certainly has a gift to manipulate men and I'm not one easily manipulated by the fairer sex."

Sarpi dismissed the suggestion that she could have manipulated him like a puppet.

"As for how much power she has over her people, I guess only you can answer that question Excellency," Caesar deferred to the Archduke. "You know her best."

"There are about fifteen villages she personally holds dominion over in Hungary and Transylvania. Not including her castle in Moravia when she mentioned Cachtice," Maximilian did a quick calculation in his head. "But what about her making a man do as she wishes? Wealth and power are what men pursue."

"So she's a rich, powerful and sexually attractive woman that can even turn the head of one like myself not normally predisposed to women," Caesar remarked. "History is filled with such women. Helen of Troy and Cleopatra, just to name two. They can turn any man into a puppet!"

"Exactly why you must stay clear of her; I fear she could jeopardize our mission if we are not careful." Maximilian warned them. "Let's hope she leaves the city quickly and does not seek any of you out afterwards."

"Surely you can hold your emotions in check, dear Caesar," Sarpi joked.

"It's not me I'm worried about. But you two on the other hand, especially young Kahana over here, that is a worry?"

"Then not another word about my cousin, gentlemen. Are we in agreement?

Having finally been served their glasses of wine, the four of them toasted to not giving another thought about the beautiful Countess Nadasdy.

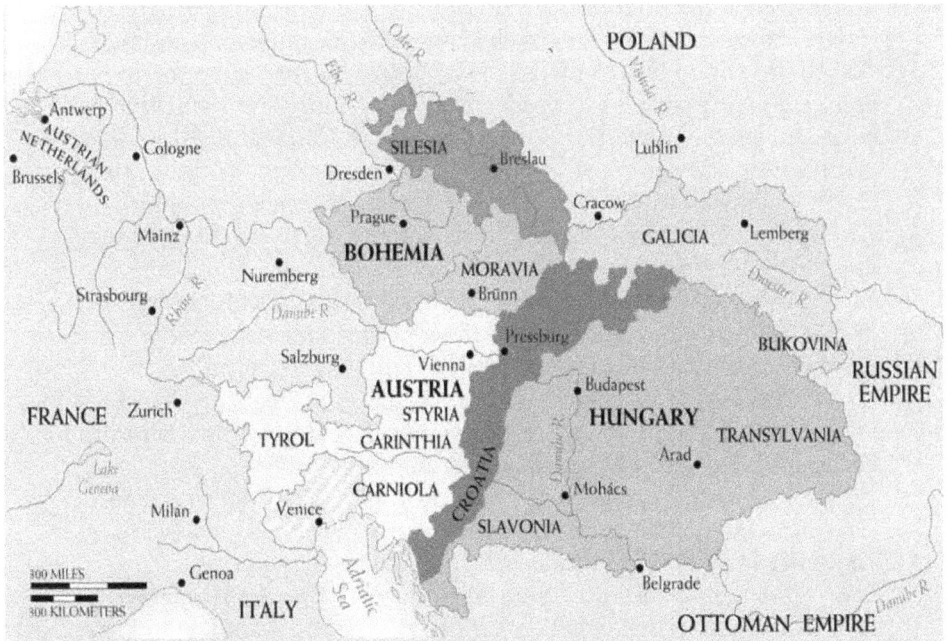

The Austro-Hungarian Empire 16th to 18th Century

Chapter Four

Hofburg Castle: December 1609

"So here they are brother," Maximilian announced as he led the guests into the throne room. "The guardians of the Empire."

Seated on his silver and gold embossed throne, dressed in the robes of the reigning Emperor, even though Rudolf still officially held that title, Matthias' head appeared to be disproportionately small as a result of the huge white frilled ruff he wore about his neck. "Are you certain these are the saviors of the Empire," the Emperor questioned. "What do you think Cardinal?" Matthias appeared doubtful as he peered down from his red padded chaise upon the three men standing beside his brother, deferring for comment from Cardinal Klesl in order to settle the matter.

"Your Majesty, they are as the prophesy said they should be," the Cardinal responded, not realizing that Matthias knew exactly who they were and was remarking only on their appearance.

"There is no mistake brother," Maximilian quickly intervened, offering a broad smile and a wink before Klesl would realize that he had now become part of the joke. "These are definitely the three."

"Fra Sarpi," the Emperor directed his gaze upon the Venetian. "We've met before, but you certainly appear different from that time. Far more frail and much paler than I recall."

"That is to be expected, Excellency," the magistrate responded. "Having been so close to death so many times in the recent past, I guess I have begun to look like death itself."

"Yes, I have heard of your misfortunes. Yet, the Almighty has favored you and fortunately you are still with us. I want you to know that neither the Cardinal nor myself had any part in those attacks upon your person. So you are safe and under my protection if you should have any concerns while staying in the palace as my guest."

"If I was concerned Excellency, I would not be here." The response was curt and cold.

"Yes, I know that to be true. You have always been a man that says exactly what is on his mind. A trait which has repeatedly landed you in trouble with the Pope. Nevertheless, I encourage you to speak openly and frankly in my presence. There will be no punishment for doing so. I give you my word." It was evident to all that the Emperor was well aware of the risk he had undertaken in convincing the Pope to cease his vendetta against Fra Sarpi.

"Thank you Excellency," Sarpi bowed his head.

"I must admit, I knew not what to expect regarding you Monsieur de Nostradame." Matthias turned his attention towards Caesar. "Rudolf told me much about you long ago, and described you far differently from what I see today."

"Your Majesty," Caesar replied. "That was twenty years ago. I would have been shocked had you said I looked exactly as I was described. That would mean that Rudolf must have thought I was old and fat looking, even two decades ago."

"And then there is this one," the Emperor now directed his attention towards Joseph. "It saddens me that I never had the opportunity to meet your father. They say he was a great man. There are those that recall his time in Prague and say he had the look of a king no matter how he was dressed. But sadly, if I am to be honest, you don't appear to have inherited that same regal stature. I had a much different picture of you in my mind."

"I can barely remember my father," Joseph confessed. "So I can neither confirm nor refute what you say, but if you were looking for a duplicate of my father then that truly is not me. I have been molded by my environment and that has left me with a rancid and bitter taste in my mouth."

"As you have adequately expressed to Maximilian in order to persuade him to negotiate far more than I would have given, had I been there. But surely the bitterness has been sweetened, even if only a little bit by what you have thus far obtained." The comment left Joseph thinking which part of the negotiations did the Emperor think was far too much.

"My apologies for not attending your sister's wedding," the Emperor continued. "I hear that it was a beautiful affair. I hope you can appreciate that as Holy Roman Emperor, it would have been entirely inappropriate for myself or Cardinal Klesl to attend a secular event of that nature. I may have agreed to Fra Sarpi's requirement that I sign my brother's policy on the freedom and equality of religion within the Empire, but that doesn't mean that I personally have to show my approval of the proclamation. I am the defender of the faith, after all!"

"Your Majesty, if I may be permitted to speak," Joseph responded, "I appreciate your situation and I think everyone knew that although you were not in a position to attend, nonetheless, the wedding was still permitted to transpire, which as far as I am concerned, meant it had your blessing. On behalf of my sister and myself, I am eternally grateful."

"Well, you may not have the stature and appearance of a king, but you certainly know how to talk like one when the need arises," Matthias admitted. "I think you managed to give slight insult and heap praise on me, all in the same breath."

"It was a magnificent affair brother," Maximilian interjected. "It was a true shame you could not attend."

"I hear that Count von Wallerstein has apparently gained a lot more self confidence and has become far more coherent in his speech of late," the Emperor addressed his brother. "I presume this is all the result of his taking a wife."

"The transformation of his character has been in some ways quite remarkable," Maximilian confirmed. "A miracle one might say. There are times when he is so lucid that you swear he talks and behaves like any other man. Had I known that marriage would have made such a change in him, I would have sought out Master Joseph's sister long ago."

The Emperor banged his right fist against the mahogany rim of his throne, a rare moment of showing a tinge of anger. "And for that you have my sincere apologies Master Kahana, that you were left to exist in desolation for so long." Matthias looked down his long nose, his eyes burrowing into Cardinal Klesl at his side. "It was unforgivable of Rudolf and his ministers to have abandoned you after all your father had done in the service to the Crown and the Church. I want you to know that I took no pleasure in permitting Rabbi Loew to return to Prague this year. I did so only because I thought it was prudent in order to keep the peace with the Jewish community. I am certain you can understand that I was caught in a difficult situation. If the truth of Rabbi Loew and his Golem was ever to come out, the Christians would have burned the Jewish Quarter to the ground for his role in unleashing the terror upon the city that killed so many. But by keeping him in exile and denying him the privilege to die in Prague, it would have eventually become obvious that the Rabbi was being punished for being in some way responsible for the tragedies those families suffered twenty years ago. I even had to give part of Maisel's fortune back to his nephews, just to hide the fact that the man almost bankrupted the Empire.

As Maximilian has already informed me that you bore some hostility towards my actions, I wanted you to be aware that I had no other choice. And frankly, I knew Rabbi Loew had only a short time to live. So letting him return also appeared to be an act of mercy on my part. There are three requirements to be a king. One, he must be strong and resolute in his actions. Two, he must be wise just like Solomon of old. But most of all a king must appear merciful, otherwise he will not be king for long. Surely you can appreciate that?"

"I thank you for your frankness, your Majesty," Joseph bowed his head in a sign of respect. "But to be more precise as to the cause of my resentment, the part that Prince Maximilian may have overlooked, is the fact that I was never told where my father was buried and that grieved me most certainly. A son must pay his final respects to his father and I was denied that personal privilege and right."

"Again, a decision that I had no part in." Almost unnoticed was that the Emperor flashed another glaring stare at his Cardinal. "Rudolf with his counselors thought it best not to have the burial site become a commemorative for a martyr, which again they believed would have raised tensions in the city. Anonymity of the individual interred within the grave was deemed crucial. If you knew where it was, they did not feel they could preserve that anonymity. But I strongly disagreed. Personally, I believed your father represented a unifying force between all the populations of the city and should not have been buried in secret. Instead a tomb should have been erected in the city square so people of all faiths could make pilgrimage to the hero of the city. But it is your right to know! You should know! Your father is buried in the corner of the Old Jewish Cemetery of Prague, beside the caretakers shed but there is only a grass path to reach his grave. From what I understand, you are forbidden to walk on the grass in a cemetery. Once again my brother buckled to the advice of his counselors rather than do what was right for the family of Yakov Kahana. I deeply regret our failure to properly honour your father."

"And I appreciate and am grateful to your Majesty's openness regarding this matter." Joseph bowed his head. "The truth is all I ever wanted."

"This is my promise to you Master Kahana, when you return from this mission, I will see to it that you are escorted to the cemetery by military guard for everyone to see, and my engineers will erect some manner of temporary bridge over the grass so that you can visit your father's grave and say your final farewell to him. This I promise you!"

Bowing again but this time at the waist, Joseph Kahana thanked the Emperor profusely.

"As for you, Monsieur de Nostradame, you are still an enigma to me," Matthias confessed. "I can understand what has been the motivation for young Master Kahana and Fra Sarpi, but why are you so eager to place your life at risk? You have asked nothing of the Crown.

You have a comfortable life, even if it is choosing one without wife or children, so it is not fame or fortune you seek. So tell me, why are you here?" Matthias ran his fingers down his goatee as he pondered what could be the reason why Caesar had been so eager to join this mission.

"The answer is quite obvious, your Majesty," Caesar replied. "Because I am the son of Nostradamus."

"We are all the son of somebody," Matthias laughed as he discarded Caesar's comment, "but that doesn't mean we have to put our life in danger for the sake of our fathers. That would make no sense at all."

"It does when your father is Michel de Nostradame, your Majesty. From the day I was born my father groomed me for one purpose only; to see that his prophecies were fulfilled. He managed to burn all of them into my memory, knowing that when the time was right, those which were applicable would surface from my memory and guide me in the right direction."

"Seems a little harsh to use your only son as a conduit for one's own glorification," Cardinal Kesl interjected his opinion.

"At one time I believed so too," Caesar agreed. "It was only when I was in Prague twenty years ago that I realized what he did was for my own survival. He knew I was different from most and as such I was going to need his protection."

"Different as in being an aberration to the godliness of a man and a woman," the Cardinal pressed the matter.

"If you are asking Sir if I am like your former Emperor Rudolf, whom you served for years and then so eagerly turned upon, in preferring the flesh of a young boy to that of a shapely woman, then the answer is no, Sir! Mine is a far more serious burden. I have no feeling for either sex. That is my curse to bear. Neither man nor woman stirs my heart or makes my loins ache. If that makes me an aberration, then so be it but isn't that exactly what you ask of your clergy; to be asexual. I make no effort to conceal my nature. Perhaps it would be better for the Church if your priests did a better job concealing their own."

"I am well aware of your detestation for the Mother Church," Klesl admonished Caesar, "But don't think you can hide behind the threat to release your father's writings against the Church forever as a shield for your own protection."

"I would think Cardinal, you have your hands full with the Lutherans and the Calvinists, that you don't need Nostradamus adding to your woes," Caesar smiled sardonically as he said his words.

"I believe he has you there, Cardinal," the Emperor interjected. "We have enough enemies without adding a prophet and seer to the list."

The Cardinal was still not prepared to back down. "Your Majesty, he claims to have nothing to hide but if that is so," Klesl continued, "then why do the Church stories speak of his hiding behind the skirt of Mademoiselle Claire, pretending that she is more than his housemaid?"

"For the very reason Sir that the Church feels the need to spy on my everyday life as you have so readily admitted," Caesar defended himself. "If you are watching me, as is apparently the case, then I must provide a showing that puts your hounds off the scent. Mademoiselle Claire is far more than simply my housemaid as you have described her. She is my confidante, my associate, my friend. One of many that would come to my defense should the Church ever decide to attempt to punish my choice of lifestyle."

"I meant no threat," the Cardinal attempted to apologize, having glanced to his right and seeing that the Emperor had grown irritated by his repeated attempts to bait Caesar.

"But I do," Caesar snapped back. "I know the Church's sentiments against me quite well and as you have already stated, you know that any attempt to raise a hand against me will result in my burying your Church in the prophecies left to me by my father. Prophecies that have never appeared in his books. Prophecies that make what he has revealed in his quatrains about the Church thus far look like harmless bedtime stories. Have I made myself perfectly clear Cardinal?"

Caesar's outburst took everyone by surprise. His usual calm and soft spoken demeanor now revealed an inner fury that he kept carefully buried behind the diplomatic facade he presented outwardly.

"Everyone," Matthias shouted, banging his fist against the armrest once again. "Cease this bantering immediately. Cardinal, are you clear regarding Monsieur Nostradame's stance?"

"Perfectly clear, your Highness," Klesl replied but even so still addressed Caesar on the subject matter, "We know your father has left you with a number of prophecies with which to bury the Church. Apparently, from what I understand, he could look into the past as well, not just the future. We're not ready to have our past deeds exposed. But a day will come when none of that will matter and your strangle hold on the Church will no longer be effective."

"Fortunately I will no longer be alive when that day comes, Cardinal," Caesar snapped back in response. "And I won't have any children that you can threaten afterwards, so as you can see, you cannot coerce or threaten me."

"Once again Monsieur, you have misinterpreted my intent, that was not a threat," Klesl countered. "Merely a statement of fact. There will come a time when the sins of the Church are no longer considered sins. I don't need to be a prophet to see that such a day will come."

"But that day is not now," Caesar dismissed the Cardinal's foretelling of the future, "And the truth is that 'now' you still need me."

"Very true," Klesl replied. "We need you now but now is not forever."

"Enough!" the Emperor demanded silence. "Sometimes you are a fool Klesl. The man says he is here to help, so let him help. Nothing more needs to be said by you."

"Your Majesty, you asked why am I doing this, placing myself in danger? Let us agree that it is your present need which has brought me here. It is my need to prove to my dead father that I was worthy of his name and that is why I am here. But this time the ending will be different from Prague. This time there will be acknowledgement of our success when this mission is over. That is when I will let you know what will be the compensation for my time and effort."

"Very well," the Matthias conceded. "After all, it is the mission that must take precedent. And with that in mind," Matthias continued, "I think it is time we actually discuss the nature of the mission gentlemen."

"I have already given Fra Sarpi a summary of the circumstances," Klesl mentioned.

"But not to the full extent, I would suspect," the Emperor surmised. "As they say, the Devil is in the details. Once they appreciate that this time the demon is stalking young noblewomen, then they will appreciate why they have been summoned. Would you not say so Cardinal," the Emperor explained while he waited for the clergyman to agree. "Our sins in this matter must be fully exposed," Matthias proclaimed."

"Sins?" Paolo Sarpi inquired, "You failed to mention your involvement Melchior, when we last talked."

"Sins of omission," the Cardinal clarified. "In this case decades of turning a blind eye. I did touch upon this matter with you."

"Now we are talking decades," Sarpi interjected. "Before it was only talk from a few to ten years."

Holding up his hand to speak, Matthias assumed control of the conversation once again. "A few years concerns the young women from the nobility. Prior to that it was simply a civil matter that did not require our involvement."

"Even a civil matter requires attention, your Majesty," Sarpi commented. "From what Melchior explained, the matter never received any attention."

"It was always dealt with at a local level," Matthias corrected the magistrate's criticism. "Over the years my Palatine dealt with the matter and he had taken many statements and made many arrests but obviously they had not been arrests of those actually responsible."

"Clearly they were incorrect," Sarpi remained sarcastic. "How many hundreds had to die for the Cardinal to come to that realization?"

"This matter is not between you and the Cardinal," Matthias grew angry. "The matter is far bigger than the two of you! It is far bigger than all of us!"

The young Kahana could no longer hold himself back from entering the bickering conversation. "Obviously you all have an idea of what is being discussed," Joseph interjected, "But I have not heard any of this before. What has been transpiring for decades? I think it is time you tell it to myself as well."

"Murder, young Kahana," Sarpi answered. "Hundreds and hundreds of murders perpetrated on young girls."

Joseph shook his head in disbelief. "And suddenly today we are assembled here in Vienna, deciding to take action." He could not even contemplate the numbers that Sarpi was referring to. "So, even while my father was chasing a monster across the rooftops of Prague, the Crown was concealing the real evil that threatened the Empire. One must ask themself, who were the real monsters?"

Mathias disliked having the Crown's motives being questioned in this manner. "We concealed nothing. I already told you it was being dealt with by the local authorities. The problem has only been recently heightened," he explained.

"Hundreds over decades and only now you can seriously state the problem has been heightened, your Majesty?" Sarpi questioned how Matthias could make such a statement.

"Do not try my patience," the Emperor warned them all.

"This all should have been revealed when you first sought me out," Joseph complained. "You have requested my services upon this mission, your Highness. It was your brother that came to me along with Caesar de Nostradame and spoke of a monster killing in the woods. Now you speak of hundreds over decades. Anyone can see this may be the work of a much greater magnitude, which may even suggests a nest of monsters. I did not seek you out. I deserved to have known these facts in the beginning."

Gripping the armrests of his throne tightly, the lines across the Emperor's forehead furrowed deeply. "Am I to interpret your misgivings as an unwillingness to join in this mission," Matthias demanded to know. "Everything you have been given thus far, I can remove with a snap of my fingers."

Maximilian stepped from the shadows of the room and moved towards his brother's throne, ready to intercede before the atmosphere became too intense and all the parties regretted what they were about to say.

"Yes you can, your Highness. You can take it all away," Joseph admitted. "And I can go back to living in the streets of Brody. Which according to the little I have been told thus far, will be a very safe place from which to watch your Empire crumble and the Church burned down to ashes. That's assuming all the prophecies are correct, which they must be or else you would not have made all those promises to me in the first place. If I seem impudent, your Highness, then forgive me, but as I said, I am not my father. If you expect this mission to succeed, then everything needs to be revealed. All the information must be set on the table before us. We all must be honest with one another. Otherwise, I fear this mission will be doomed to failure. Had all been revealed to me at first meeting, you would find that I would still be here, standing in this room, ready to face whatever monsters or madmen, or even armies that dwell in your dark, foreboding forests. I am not a man to cower in fear. But neither am I a child to be shielded from the truth. I gave you my word to destroy this evil and on my honour I will either do so or perish in the attempt."

The Emperor rose from his throne and descended the few steps of the dais,then walked sternly towards Joseph. Approaching within a foot of Master Kahana, Matthias raised his arm and then brought it down, firmly grasping Joseph on his left shoulder. "I like this lad," he shouted. "He's got courage. He fears nothing. Not even angering an Emperor. There is the strength of Kings in him. And I have no doubt we will find he possesses wisdom and mercy too. Tell him everything Cardinal, I insist." Having congratulated Joseph Kahana on his display of courage, Matthias turned and strode back to his throne to take his seat.

The Cardinal began relaying everything that they knew. "In truth, we have been sitting on the knowledge of this powder keg for well over a decade with the hope that it would go away but the situation has only grown worse. Only once we began to investigate did we realize the killings had been going on for much longer," the Cardinal explained. "For years now, young women in the eastern part of the Empire have been disappearing but we paid little attention to the matter, leaving it to the local authorities in Transylvania. It didn't really concern us."

"Because..." Sarpi pushed for the clarification that he already knew.

"Because the early victims were all peasants, gypsies and Jews. They were dispensable. You want the truth, then the truth is, the less of them, the better in the eyes of the Church."

"But now…" Sarpi was disgusted by the cavalier attitude of the Church towards murder.

"Now what or whomever is killing them has begun to slaughter women of the aristocracy. Powerful people are now demanding a solution and the Emperor and I have none to offer them thus far."

Sarpi scratched top of his head, the hair thinning in his middle age and now the baldness was beginning to definitively show. "How many disappearances are we talking about?" Again, it was a figure that Sarpi already knew but he wanted his colleagues fully aware as well.

"Four thus far. The first was the sister of Count Fogarasy of Hungary a couple of Christmases ago."

"Four hardly seems to be significant enough to catch the attention of the Church. Other than these aristocratic girls, how many are we talking about that weren't gypsies or Jews?" Sarpi knew there had to be much more to the story than the disappearance of four wealthy girls. Facts that still hadn't been revealed even to him.

Klesl was hesitant to respond. His speech became barely audible as he replied, "Perhaps a few hundred. Maybe more."

"What!" Sarpi practically shouted. "You let the disappearance of hundreds of innocent Christian village girls go uninvestigated and now because of a handful of rich and spoiled offspring, you actually have a desire to do something."

"It is more than the wealthy girls precipitating this urgency. The villagers have gone to their burgermeisters. There is talk of open revolt. A challenge to the monarchy. They even talk of joining with the Ottomans to overthrown the Crown."

"Perhaps they are right. Perhaps you should all rot in hell," Sarpi commented. "Tell them everything that you told me, Klesl!"

"Gentlemen," the Cardinal pleaded with the others to listen, "It is not only because of the threat of revolt but a matter far greater than the sum of the girls. The religious affiliation of the four was equally spread among the Christian sects. Two were Catholics, the other two Protestants. But now the embers of religious dissent have been stirred and the flames are growing higher. The first thing the Calvinists did was blame the Lutherans. So the Vatican had little concern for the animosity between Protestants. But then the Turks decided to meddle into these affairs and they prodded the people to rise up against the Lutherans. Much as the Lutherans always do when they find themselves hard pressed, they attack the local Catholic clergy. Several of our priests have been beaten badly. The Jews are talking of allying themselves with their Muslim cousins. The resulting conflagration will be a disaster for everyone. There will be no Empire left for anyone to rule."

"The Empire has survived similar uprising in the past," Sarpi commented. "Why are you so certain that this time it is the end of the world? There is obviously more that you haven't told me."

"Because of the ancient texts in the Habsburg library and what Caesar has told us of his father's prophecies," Klesl responded very concerned.

"You are referring to the same ancient text that you used to convince my father to come to Prague. Correct?" Joseph sounded slightly confused.

"Yes, the very same one," the Cardinal agreed. "But we had overlooked a paragraph that followed the others concerning the poor man's Trinity."

"Excuse me," Joseph interrupted, "Poor man's Trinity?"

"That is how the text referred to Yakov Kahana, Brother Giordano Bruno and Caesar de Nostradame," the Cardinal clarified. "There would be three of them; a heretic priest, a false prophet, and a king without a kingdom."

"But if they were the three that fulfilled the prophecy, then why are we three here. That matter was done with twenty years ago," Joseph was confused.

"Or so we believed," the Emperor interceded and continued the story line. "It would appear that the Ecclesiastical Librarians are not as thorough as they'd like us to believe."

The three listened intently as Matthias continued to tell the story.

"After the monster in Prague had been killed by young Master Joseph's father, one of the librarians thought it would behoove them to ensure the matter had been settled by confirming that the original text had been satisfied. To this day he swears that the paragraph following the description of the Trinity did not exist when they first opened the Tome. I prefer to believe that in their rush to deal with the threat of Armageddon, that they had overlooked reading further into the text and in that haste did not recognize that it was a tale of two halves."

"And in this second half......"

"An indication that the monster in Prague was merely the prelude of an even greater disaster. An Empire that would be washed away by the rivers of blood that would flow down from the mountains. Rivers that would never be able to quench the thirst of Lilith 'the devourer'. Whereas the first paragraph spoke of a limited number of deaths, now during this second wave of destruction the death toll would eventually be in the hundreds if not thousands if left unchecked."

"And you think these deaths of several hundred young girls is related in some way to this writing in your ancient text," the Venetian

Magistrate questioned."

"We don't think Fra Sarpi, we know," the Emperor was adamant in his opinion. "What may have been a doubt initially was rendered into fact when Caesar came to us with the same dire warning."

"This is true, Caesar?" The magistrate turned to Caesar, seeking his help to understand.

"I'm afraid so," Caesar confirmed the tale thus far. "It mattered not when they discovered the second paragraph concerning the End of Days. What mattered were the quatrains my father had written to confirm that it was the second coming they needed to fear most."

"Surely you are about to tell us what your father said..." Sarpi held out his hands supplicatingly.

"The first was from Century I, Quatrain 82," Caesar explained:

'When the great wooden columns tremble,
In the southerly wind covered with blood.
Such a great assembly then pours forth,
That Vienna and the land of Austria will tremble.

It matched almost identically with what was written in the ancient text. From the forested mountains of the Northeast, from where they southerlies blow, they will flood the Empire with blood. Do you see?"

Sarpi and Joseph first looked at one another and then slowly nodded their heads.

"I guess one could see it that way," Sarpi admitted halfheartedly.

"I have no idea which way the winds blow into Vienna," Joseph apologized but if your father says that is the way they blow then I can see how this quatrain can relate."

Caesar could see that they were still not convinced, "Then listen to this next quatrain and you will understand completely how I knew this was the time being spoken of and why I warned the Emperor of what would take place. Remember, I had no idea that they had already been alerted by something similar from their own books in their library. This is from Century VIII, Quatrain 15:

'Great exertions towards the North by a man-woman to vex
Europe and almost all the Universe.
The two eclipses will be put into such a rout that they will
reinforce life or death for the Hungarians.

Do you see the connection now?"

"I'm afraid Caesar that I never quite understood your father's gift. I don't know if the others can understand it immediately but I'm afraid I don't have that ability," Paolo Sarpi apologized.

"Wait," Joseph interjected. "I think I might actually see the connection. The text in the library referred to Lilith. Lilith the demon-angel; possessing traits of both men and women. Who's name means the Night-Wind. And the eclipses must refer to two forces, each considering themselves to be the light but Lilith manages to block out their light, hence destroy both of them."

"Aha!" Caesar exclaimed. "You do see it now."

"Catholicism and Protestantism, both thinking they are the light, each trying to eclipse the other but now with the advent of the demon-angel they both are annihilated. But the Hungarians, why refer to them?" Joseph asked.

"Because as in the first quatrain and the ancient text, it is telling us where the threat stems from. We three are all that stand in the path of the evil coming from the Northeast. Hungary and everything that lies beyond it will either live or die depending on our success. It is crystal clear," Caesar snapped his fingers to make his point."

"But why us," Joseph was still not entirely convinced. "You already had your 'poor man's Trinity' so why come to us?"

"Because this newly translated paragraph said it will only be stopped by the Trinity's wayward sons. You three are those sons. Each of you have strayed from your belief in God because of what you have suffered. Only through the suffering and loss of the original Trinity could you three have been created. The loss of a father, of a friend, of hope is what made you wander from the path."

"Well gentlemen," the Emperor intervened, "If it is now crystal clear as Cardinal Klesl has explained and indicated, then let us get busy, for as this hidden passage has revealed, you have a world to save."

Chapter Five

Der Kerker: Christmas 1609

"Is that him?" Joseph asked as he peered through the grate in the floor at the prisoner seated in the dark and dank room below.

Except for a small desk, holding a book and a jug of water, a chair, a straw mattress and a chamber pot in one far corner, the room was nothing more than four solid stone walls and a heavy iron door, locked from the outside. The only light into the room was from the grating that both men were standing over, casting the room into shadow.

"Yes, that's him," replied Maximilian. "Yom Tov Lipmann Heller, born around 1570 and depending on how he responds today, dead by 1610."

"Who's up there?" the croaking voice asked in thick accented German. "I know you're up there. Who are you?"

"Don't worry Herr Lipmann, we are on our way down," the Archduke replied.

"I know that voice," the Rabbi shouted in reply.

"You should," Maximilian joked, "I'm the one that put you in this hell-hole. The one you wrote about as being a blood-thirsty war monger that took delight in sending his men into the Jewish ghettos and villages to rape and pillage. And that was one of the kinder stories you disseminated about myself and the Royal family."

"If you don't think my articles rang with truth then come down and join me and we can discuss it face to face like real men," the Rabbi challenged the Archduke.

"Oh, have no fear, we will be joining you shortly. Do tidy up though. You want to look your best for your visitors."

The Rabbi continued talking but by this time they all had moved away from the grate and the words were falling upon deaf ears. The party accompanying Archduke Maximilian made their way down the narrow winding steps towards the cell blocks. As they braced themselves against the walls to stop from falling, the cold sweat off the granite stones dripped from their fingers. The putrid smell of death blew up from below, stinging their nostrils as they descended further and further down into the crypt like atmosphere. The Archduke signaled his guards to stay back with the rest of the visitors, while he, his personal attache', and Joseph continued forward towards the cell holding Rabbi Lipmann. He would send his attache' back to retrieve the others when the time was right.

As they approached the cell, one of the prison guards suddenly appeared in the corridor, key ring in hand. Searching through the large number of keys that were strung on the ring, the guard finally identified the correct one, opening the iron gate to the cell, and then immediately closing and locking it the moment that the Archduke and Joseph had entered. The Rabbi remained seated at the little wooden desk, the only actual piece of furniture that had been provided, practically ignoring the two men that had entered his cell.

"Rabbi Lipmann, you really have to learn some etiquette if you ever intend to leave this cell alive."

Refusing to show any deference to a member of the Royal family, the defiant Rabbi Yom Tov Lipmann Heller pretended that it mattered not if he lived or died, refusing to let any trace of emotion cross his face. "I had grown accustomed to this place. It is quite comfortable," he responded, knowing that his answer would irk the Archduke to no end.

"I am glad then," Maximilian responded in kind. "I had become worried that you weren't enjoying my hospitality. But if you insist on becoming a permanent guest, then I'm certain some better accommodations can be arranged."

"Very well then Prince Maximilian, we can play this game forever, but you know it always ends the same way. Someone from my community or one of the other religious centers arrives with my bail, and like a wave of a magic wand, I'm suddenly a free man."

"Yes, that has been our usual history Rabbi," Maximilian agreed. "But this time I promise you, it will be different. You crossed the line this time with your political diatribes. The charges this time are no longer of a minor civil nature."

Joseph leaned forward to whisper into the Archduke's ear, "You mean he's done this before?"

The question made Maximilian laugh. "The Rabbi is a regular visitor to our prisons. He has a tendency to write virulent polemics against the Church and the government, rather than adhere to his primary role as a community religious leader. This time he was caught red-handed agitating against the Royal family and that is tantamount to treason."

"I provide the people with the truth," the Rabbi argued in his own defence. In the eyes of God, telling the truth can never be a crime."

"Well then, we can let God judge you after the Viennese court is through with you," the Archduke warned his captive.

"I did not realize that he was such a rebel," Joseph commented.

"Who is this annoyance?" Lipmann demanded to know. "His accent sounds like a Galiciano. Why is he here?"

"Rabbi, you are in no position to question me about anything, You may have been born in the German provinces where they preach to you that all men are created equal, but let me remind you, this is Austria and here we definitely have a monarchy and one way or another you will learn to respect that."

The Rabbi refused to be threatened. "When your family of despots learns to respect the people, that will be the day that I will give you the respect you demand. Now, I ask again, who is this stranger you brought to see me?"

Maximilian simply shook his head in disbelief of the level of arrogance and defiance that had still not been stripped from the rabbi. On one hand he admired the spirit of the man, on the other hand he'd remind the guards to be a little more forceful next time they were disciplining Herr Lipmann.

"How rude of me Rabbi Lipmann," the Archduke feigned a mock bow towards his captive. "How could I have overlooked introducing you to your new son-in-law."

"What...," Lipmann screamed as he suddenly launched himself from the chair, only to fall backwards once he reached the limit of the chain firmly locked around his left ankle.

Wagging a finger in front of the Rabbi's face, the prince made a tsk-tsk sound with his tongue. "Now is that any way for you to behave in front of your future family member."

Joseph had not noticed the metal chain until that moment. It was now apparent that Maximilian knew exactly where they should stand and why he had not felt it necessary for the prison guard to enter the cell along with them.

"Let me repeat myself," the Archduke goaded his prisoner. "This gentleman is your new, or should I say, soon to be son-in-law. Just a matter of his deciding which of your daughters he prefers, but I think he may have already decided. I noticed a twinkle in his eye when he spoke to one of them."

"You cannot do this," the Rabbi screamed at the Prince. "You cannot force any of my daughters to marry against their will!"

"Sure I can," Maximilian taunted. "As I explained to you, Herr Lipmann, you are no longer in North Swabia. This is my brother's empire, you now find yourself residing in, and I can do whatever I please. When are you ever going to understand that? But have no fear, I'm certain your daughter, whichever it may be, will gladly accept the offer of marriage."

"Who are you?" Lipmann demanded to know, directing his question at the stranger.

The Archduke motioned with his hand for Joseph to answer directly.

"I'm probably the one person you'd wish your daughters would never marry," Joseph initially replied.

"What could be worse than a Galiciano?" the Rabbi expressed his disdain for the province renown for its secular Judaism.

"Perhaps the Karaite Prince. The son of the one man that knew exactly what your mentor had done and how you are nothing more than a conspirator and a murderer. A liar and a fraud within your own community."

The revulsion was evident as Lipmann spoke, "You are the Kahana. A curse upon your house and all your descendants." The Rabbi spat a wad a phlegm narrowly missing Joseph's feet.

"I believe you have just cursed your own descendants Rabbi because as it has been explained, I will be marrying one of your daughters and she will bear my children. So I'd think very carefully about what you say in the future."

"I will not permit it," Lipmann screamed. "I will see you dead before you lay a hand on one of my daughters."

"Allow me to respond," the Archduke inserted himself into the fray. "Understand this Herr Lipmann. You are a dead man. You will see to nothing because you won't be around to deal with any of your daughters' betrothals in the future. I will do as I please with you family, even throw your daughters to my soldiers if I so desire and you will not be alive to stop any of it. Your daughters are well aware of that possible future. They are also aware that if one of them marries young Master Kahana here, then none of that future needs to transpire. You will live, the rest of them can marry as they please, and the one that is chosen will live a life befitting a princess. And though it may surprise you, they most willingly embraced the opportunity I presented to them."

"My daughters would never agree to sell themselves like whores to the likes of him," Lipmann denied the Archduke's words, cursing under his breath as he looked up at Joseph and felt disgusted by what he saw.

"Apparently you do not know your daughters as well as you think, Herr Lipmann. Perhaps if you spent more time with them rather than leading your crusades and railing against the government you'd actually come to know what it is that they wish and hope for. Certainly, they want their father to live, but even more than that, every girl dreams of being a princess and being carried away by the handsome young prince on his snow white stallion. That is what a young woman wants, not to be a pawn in their father's foolish games."

"You know nothing about my daughters," the Rabbi refused to listen to Maximilian's lies.

"Actually I know everything there is about your daughters," Joseph interjected himself back into the discussion. "I have had the pleasure of having a long conversation with each of the one's that are not betrothed. Even a Galiciano like myself will respect the sanctity of a marriage contract, so I did not press myself upon those that are taken. So, of the four that remained uncommitted, I had the opportunity to tell them all about who I was and who my father was. I even told them the truth about your teacher and how he was one of the most vile creatures that ever stalked this earth and what was most surprising, they didn't appear to be shocked by this information. I'm guessing you provided them the opportunity to meet him before he died. Women have an incredible innate ability to peer into a man's soul and judge what kind of man he is even if just a single acquaintance. I know this from studying my sister. Being so, I believe your daughters would have seen for themselves exactly what kind of monster the Maharal was. You should be grateful that they didn't resent you for your association with him. But I digress. So permit me to return to the topic at hand and to summarize my long conversations with each of them. They all expressed their willingness to be my wife."

Practically in tears, Lipmann sounded defeated as he responded, "Only because they feared for my life. They would agree to anything in order to save me. Never would any of them agree to marry one of the Kahana of their own accord."

"I thought of that too, so I told them that if any time during the courtship they decided they did not wish to go ahead with the marriage then I would release them from their promise and I swore that there would be no retribution against their father."

"What does that prove?" the Rabbi scoffed at what he considered his opponent's naivety. "They still know that they had to initially agree in order to save my life. That does not mean they actually wanted to marry you. You are a fool no less than your father," he stated contemptuously.

"No, you are right, it doesn't prove a thing," Joseph explained. "What it means simply is that they can be free from the arrangement if they desire it so. It means that while I'm away that you will have ample opportunity to convince them to leave me and return to you. I accept that is all true, but there is another truth that I hold on to and it goes like this; after all your cajoling, all your pleading, all your berating, and even after all your threatening, if the daughter I have chosen to be my wife still makes the decision to wed with me, then God has guided my decision and that daughter truly does love me and perhaps it might even suggest that she despises you."

"You are a fool to think that one of my daughters would be so easily taken in by a charlatan. You are a fool if you see this in some manner as a challenge. Thinking that one of my daughters is some play thing that you move like a chess piece on the board under your control?"

"I will let the Lord decide which one of us is the fool Lipmann. Your master took someone very dear and important from me. A man of far greater worth than you could ever be. So now the Almighty has placed me in a position where I have the opportunity to do the same to you," Joseph enlightened his adversary. "You must admit that God has a wonderful sense of irony. Perhaps you should write about that some day. But I am not like you and I certainly am not a cold-hearted killer like your esteemed master. What I take from you will be done in the name of love, and as my wife, your daughter will be cherished and cared for with the fullness of my heart.

What your kind did was through the evil blackness of hate. You never gave my father the opportunity to return to his wife and children. The same way those killed in Prague by your monster could never return to their loved ones. And for what; power, money? You parade around thinking yourself to be blessed by God. Take a good look at this cell and recognize you are here because God despises you and the only reason you will be released is because the Kahana can find mercy for your dark soul."

Sitting himself back in his chair, the Rabbi was visibly shaken but restored himself after a few deep breaths to a level where he could speak calmly. "You are ignorant no different from you father if you think what the Maharal did was the result of a lust for money or power. Those material things were never of interest to him. What he did was in the name of love. A love for his people, a love for the Children of Israel. He suffered for the hundreds, no more like the thousands of our own that died at the hands of the petty rulers of this kingdom. They permit their citizens to beat us and burn us out from our homes, time and time again. The pogroms are performed with Royal blessing and we are left to bury our dead and wail over their graves. He suffered for all those innocents that lost their lives because no one would stand up for us. Where were any of the Kahana to defend us? Nowhere to be found. So he took it upon himself to find a way to make them stop their slaughter of our people. By creating a defender of the weak and helpless that filled the hearts of our enemies with such fear that they dared not raise a hand against us. The Golem restored a balance where the goyim would no longer risk attacking us out of fear for their own lives. Only to have your father destroy all that we had achieved and now once again we find ourselves oppressed by the tyranny of our enemies."

"You had achieved nothing, you stopped nothing," Joseph challenged the Rabbi's interpretation of events. "You may think that you brought a degree of peace to Prague, but those in other cities within the Empire were about to pay the price for your defiance by having their Jewish communities wiped from existence. Even my community in Brody, which isn't even under Habsburg domination was threatened because of your delusions of having achieved a status quo. While you were saving your thousands, tens of thousands would have been slaughtered elsewhere. The only one that stood between our genocide as a result of your madness was Yakov Kahana and that is why both of us are here today, still alive and still free to disagree on how we interpret our fates."

"The only reality that your father, Yakov Kahana, prevented was the realization by our brothers that if they were all to rise up and challenge our enemies as a united force, as we did in Prague, then we would deliver ourselves from evil everywhere in the world."

"And how many would die in this insanity of yours?" Joseph scorned the Rabbi's concept of a universal revolt. "Do you think if every Jew, in every city of the world was to take up a sword simultaneously that we would be victorious? Can the lake tell the river to reverse its flow and no longer fill up the oceans? Can the moon refuse to give way to the sun at dawn and remain as the sole light in the heavens? For every one of us there are a hundred of them. Not even if each of us were a gifted warrior like the Maccabees could we ever prevail. As I said, this illusion of yours of a universal uprising by our people is nothing more than madness."

"No more a madness than you believing that any of my daughters would choose marriage to you over returning to my home," Lipmann laughed.

"Then you have nothing to fear when I tell your daughter Reisel that I want her to be my wife."

"You will leave my youngest daughter alone," Rabbi Lipmann screamed, losing completely the calm that had been restored. "She is still a mere child. What kind of man selects a child…only a foul, godless creature would do so." This time genuine tears did stream from his eyes as he protested Joseph's choice of his youngest daughter.

"Perhaps if you spent more time with your daughters as the Archduke suggested," Joseph replied, "You would have realized that Reisel has already passed her thirteenth birthday. Isn't it the custom among you rabbis to marry your daughters off to each other at the age of twelve. I will at least practice the more tasteful custom of the Empire and not wed her until after her fourteenth birthday."

"She is just a child..." the Rabbi pleaded once more.

"There you are wrong," Joseph corrected him. "She is very much a woman. I have sat and talked with her and she is far more aware of her womanhood than you are obviously aware. Of all your daughters she is the most beautiful both externally and within. She will be my princess and I will give her the love and kindness she has never received from you. If you believe that she will only consent to be my wife in order to save your life, then I will accept the outcome if she chooses to return to your house after the courtship period. I am a man of my word."

"I will never accept you as my son-in-law," Lipmann threatened.

"Then we are equal because I will never acknowledge you as my father-in-law. Nothing would want to make me vomit more."

"Shall I bring your family in now, Herr Lipmann," the Archduke suggested. "It is time we inform them of our decisions."

"No, wait! I don't want them to see me like this." The Rabbi hesitated to have his daughters see him in his current disheveled condition.

"They have been waiting all this time to see their father," Maximilian reminded him. "They need to know that you are fine, if not for your sake, then at least theirs."

"If you release me as promised, then I will see them all soon enough," Lipmann rationalized. "There is no reason for all of them to see me like this. Let Reisel come in alone and she can tell the others afterwards. I need to speak to her."

Neither Maximilian nor Joseph were comfortable with the request. Being alone meant that the Rabbi was already planning to influence his youngest daughter's decision.

Noticing their reluctance to agree to his request, Lipmann explained himself further. "You obviously don't trust me, much in the same way that I distrust you. If the being alone is too much to ask for, then both of you may stay while I speak with her. After all, if you intend to take my youngest daughter from me then you need to know there are going to be some rules that I intend to impose as a father. You said God guided your choice and you believe you will be able to convince her to stay with you, then you should have no fear of what I have to say now. I referred to this as a game of chess, did I not? If God truly plays in your corner, then let the opening moves be made."

"Agreed," Joseph accepted the challenge.

"Are you certain about this," Maximilian questioned the young Kahana.

"I am certain," came the reply.

"Bring in the daughter called Reisel," the Archduke instructed the guard standing by the cell gate.

The iron gate creaked noisily as it swung back on its rusted hinges. The young girl was unceremoniously ushered into the room, looking somewhat frightened at first but then immediately relieved as soon as she saw her father sitting in the corner of the room. Her chestnut red hair hung in long tresses that flowed enchantingly as she ran to her father. Tall for her age, and amply developed, she easily could pass for a girl sixteen years of age. Her face was already losing its childish features, replaced by high cheekbones and a long straight nose with emerald green eyes that shone brightly in the dim light of the cell. Jumping into her father's lap she hung her arms around his neck and planted several kisses on the side of his heavily bearded face.

It was then that another side to the irascible rabbi surfaced, as he embraced his youngest daughter tenderly, holding her tightly in his arms as tears rolled down his face. He kissed his daughter on the top of her head, referring to her as his little bird as he did so. Neither Maximilian nor Joseph interfered as father and daughter reunited, willingly standing aside as long as necessary. Eventually, Lipmann lowered his daughter from his lap and had her stand by his side. If it was not evident previously, it now became obvious just how tall she truly was, her waist in line with her father's head while he sat in his chair.

Slender, tall and beautiful, the Archduke thought to himself; young Master Kahana had chosen well. "Do you know why I asked you to come in, girl?" Maximilian asked her, paying no attention to her father who kept wiping a relentless stream of tears away from his eyes.

"I think so, my Lord," she replied.

Clever girl, the Archduke thought, at least she knows how to address her superiors unlike her father. "They tell me your name is Reisel. Is that so?"

The young girl nodded.

"And you also know who this gentleman is, correct?" he pointed towards Joseph.

"Yes, my Lord. That is Mar Kahana," she replied, flashing a brief smile towards Joseph as she looked upon him.

"Yes, that is right. That is Joseph Kahana. Do you know who the

Kahana are, Reisel?"

"My father said that they are a family of wicked priests that once ruled over and enslaved our people. But that was a long time ago and the Rabbis stripped all their power away, so now they have no kingdom either on earth or in heaven any longer to rule."

Maximilian looked amused. "Why would your father ever tell you such a thing?" he asked.

"He didn't," she was quick to point out. "I overheard him talking one night with the old Rabbi in Prague. I think the old Rabbi was asking for forgiveness for what he had done against the Kahana. My father was telling him not to worry, that God would not hold it against him because of that family's past misdeeds."

"And what do you think dear Reisel about the Kahana now that you have met Mar Kahana."

"He explained to me what the old Rabbi had done and how he lost his father because of it. I know in his heart he believes that anyone associated with the old Rabbi was in some way also responsible for his father's death. Because of that I know that he bears no admiration or kindness for my father. It is a heavy burden to carry if you believe that everyone else is to blame for the life we choose to live. No man can force another to make the choices we make. But I understand his pain. There comes a time though, when we must be responsible for our own decisions and accept the consequences."

"She is a smart girl, Joseph," the Archduke stated to his companion. "Obviously she knows exactly what is going on here. Perhaps her father is right and this a chess match you are not going to win."

Solemnly hanging his head, Joseph Kahana realized for the first time that his demand to force a daughter from a leading rabbinical family into a marriage they did not want made him no better, perhaps even worse, than the people he blamed for the death of his father. Turning sideways to shield his face from Reisel, he exposed his feelings of guilt. "Yes, she is a very clever girl," he admitted openly, " A characteristic that I found extremely attractive. A girl that deserves far better than be bound to a self-serving husband that uses people like pawns, just as the others do, in order to seek revenge."

Too ashamed to directly face the girl, Joseph turned his back towards the others, staring blankly at the dungeon wall. No one was more surprised than himself when he felt the pair of small, soft, delicate hands wrap around his tightly clenched right fist. As he turned in disbelief, all he could see was Reisel's smiling face looking at him with an expression of deep warmth.

"You still don't understand," she shook her head. "You cannot force someone to act against their will but that does not discount the fact that as a woman, I can certainly decide for myself how to conduct my own life and with whom I wish to share it."

"Reisel!" her father shouted. "What are you saying? Get away from him immediately. I forbid you to be with him! Get away from him now!"

"No Papa," she refused to let go of Joseph's hand. "I have seen the gentleness within his heart. I have known this man from the moment he said he would not bind me to the betrothal if I chose to leave of my own accord. I knew then that he was the one that the Lord has chosen for me. I will never be able to explain to you in a million years why the two of us belong together but we do. I am taking responsibility for my own life, Papa. I can ask you for your blessing, father, but I know you will not give it. That saddens me but I will not change my mind."

"I forbid you to marry that man, Reisel. You are only a child. You know nothing about love or marriage. I will not let you do this!" Her father was sounding hysterical at that moment as he pounded his fist against the table.

"Was I merely a child when I overheard you promise the Rabbi of Prague that you would marry me to some old Rabbi in Lodz. A widower that already had children from his deceased wife. Suddenly I was not too young to raise and tend to a family that wasn't even my own. Where was your concern for my lack of knowledge in love or marriage then, Papa? Did you even give a thought for my own happiness then, Papa?

"You will not speak to me this way! I am your father and I forbid it! Now go back to your mother and I will deal with you when I return home." Her father was adamant that his daughter would not marry Joseph Kahana.

"Home?" the Archduke interrupted. "You clearly don't understand the reality of your situation, do you Herr Lipmann? You are going no where if you don't agree to your daughter's wishes. I must admit, I like your daughter's spirit. For her sake, I won't have you executed but that doesn't mean I won't have you spend the rest of your life rotting in this cell."

"I will never agree to permit her to marry this…this…Karaite!" he sputtered and spat again upon the stone floor.

"It is my choice Papa," Reisel insisted. "Mar Kahana has asked me to consider his proposal and I have given my word willingly to accept if he selected me from among my sisters." Clasping Joseph's hand against her breasts she stared into the depths of his dark eyes.

"Will you have me as your wife, Sir?"

"If you will have me," Joseph gladly accepted, "it would be my most cherished blessing from heaven to have you as my wife. Sadly, I must go away now but upon my return, I promise to court you properly and if you still want me, then I pledge my heart and soul to you."

"No, no," Maximilian interrupted at that moment. "I'm afraid that will not do," the Archduke objected vehemently. "You cannot expect that someone like Rabbi Lipmann would simply sit about with his family residing in Vienna, eagerly waiting for your return. I am almost certain that he would be on the first coach back to Germany with his daughters in tow before you were even gone a full day from the city. Once in Germany, I'm afraid that would place him beyond our reach."

"Well, we can't keep him a prisoner until I return either," Joseph dismissed that idea in case the Archduke was considering it. "I gave my word that he would be set free once there was a betrothal with one of his daughters. I cannot go back on my word. How are we going to deal with this dilemma?"

"Yes, I agree. That was my promise to him as well that he would be released as soon as one of his daughters agreed to a marriage with you. I too am a man of my word. Though it would be tempting to keep him locked away where he can no longer do us any harm," the Archduke contemplated continuing the incarceration.

"But we both swore a promise," Joseph reminded the Prince.

"Yes, we did," Maximilian admitted reluctantly. "Actually, young Master Kahana," Maximilian stroked his moustache, "I believe the answer may be quite simple. Since we can't trust her father, then we need to ensure that Reisel is well beyond his reach. She will remain a guest in the castle and I will place her under royal protection until you return."

"I will not be kept like a prisoner in a castle, while my betrothed is off in some distant land fighting some monster on your behalf, with no guarantee of returning alive," she responded furiously to the thought of being restrained in the palace.

Maximilian was shocked. Not by the girl's defiant refusal of his offer but by the fact she knew of Joseph's mission. "You told her?" he asked quite alarmed.

"Excellency," Joseph tried to explain, "I couldn't exactly say to them, I intend to marry one of you but by the way, it won't be until much later after some unknown length of time, and furthermore, you won't be seeing me during that extended wait. I had to say something a little more substantial. Don't you think so?"

"But a monster? Why did you think it was necessary to mention that you are going on a mission to hunt down a monster? You know we are trying to keep the events surrounding these hundreds of murders as quiet as possible."

"Yes, and that is why I didn't say anything about the murders. You just mentioned that part," he notified the Archduke.

"I guess I did," Maximilian rubbed his chin. "Oh well, now I definitely have to detain them until this matter is completely dealt with. We can't have any information regarding the murders entering into the public arena."

"No!" Reisel shouted, then felt sheepish realizing that she had just yelled at a member of royalty.

"No?" the Archduke was taken back by her outburst. "I admire your strength of character girl but even so, you do not have the authority to ever say 'no' to me."

"I did not mean it that way Excellency," she apologized. "Forgive me. I meant to say, no, I have a better idea."

"This girl may even be too clever for you," the Archduke chided Joseph. "If you don't marry her, I may do so myself," he joked. "Well, let's hear it girl. Speak up," the Prince commanded.

"I need to get to know my betrothed. He needs to get to know me. We can't do that if we're apart for an unspecified length of time. I propose that I go along on the mission."

"Preposterous," her father exclaimed. "I will not let my daughter place herself in danger on some fantastic goose-chase after your so-called monster. Reisel, I forbid you to go!"

"Absolutely not!" Joseph strangely found himself in agreement with Rabbi Lipmann. "What kind of husband would I be if I placed the life of my betrothed at risk?"

Still rubbing his chin, the Archduke thought heavily on the matter. "Actually, not that preposterous an idea at all. I mean, there's already will be train of guards and officials accompanying you. She'd find herself more protected with you than if she was walking the streets of Vienna. That being the case, what difference would it make if we add another wagon for the young lady and a couple of handmaidens to watch over her and tend to her needs."

"No, I must agree with her father," Joseph refused the Archduke's suggestion. "It would be too dangerous for her to come with us. I could never forgive myself if she was harmed in any way."

"I am not some child hanging on to my mother's skirt," Reisel countered angrily. "As you have already indicated by selecting me as you future bride, I am a grown woman. Either you truly believe that or you have lied to me. And as a woman, I have the right to choose to go where my husband goes, otherwise there will be no marriage and that is my final word on the matter." She stamped her foot in defiance.

"Mein Gott, are you certain she is only thirteen," Maximilian looked askance at Joseph Kahana. "Definitely sounds like a grown woman to me."

"Is there any way I can change your mind?" Joseph looked pleadingly at his young bride to be.

"Absolutely not," she was resolute.

"Then I guess I have no other choice but to agree."

"Then I'm coming along too," Rabbi Lipmann voiced his condition.

"Don't you have some liturgical paper to write, or some book to editorialize," the Archduke tried to dissuade the Rabbi.

"If there's a gap in my writings, then so be it. It will teach my students patience until my return. In the meantime they can speculate on my previous papers and discuss the Talmudic impact of my editorials."

"It's your decision," the Archduke placed the matter in Joseph's lap. "Personally I suggest you leave him behind. He will be nothing but a thorn in your side."

"True, but he is my wife's-to-be father and he does have her best interests at heart even if he is a liability." Taking a moment to see what Reisel's opinion might be, he noticed that she was nodding her head in agreement. "Alright then, it is decided. We all go. Let us make the necessary preparations and be on our way as soon as possible."

Chapter Six

Pressburg:Christmas 1609

"So why am I here?" Caesar sounded perplexed as he and Fra Paolo Sarpi entered the mortuary in the city of Pressburg accompanied by Count Gyorgy Thurzo, the Palatine, or also known as the chief security administrator of Hungary. Now assigned by the Emperor Matthias to accommodate every need of his select trio of new investigators, and from the expression on his face, it was obvious to the two of them that he resented every second of this duty.

"Because this is where we will find the latest victim of this killer," Thurzo responded while rolling his eyes and clearly displaying his disdain for what he considered a foolish question.

"Yes, I understand that, but why am I here?" he asked once more.

"Because I need you," Sarpi filled in the missing information.

"You need me?" Caesar scoffed at the response. "I thought you didn't believe in fortune tellers. Some how it went against your scientific ethics."

"I still don't," Sarpi confirmed, "but I cannot deny your father had some form of special gift and you are his interpreter. Right now an interpreter is exactly what we need. So Count Thurzo, what do we know about this latest victim?"

The Count held the door open to the mortuary as the party moved inside. "A young girl of noble birth," Thurzo began his description of the homicide. "Maria Zapolya was on her way home to Pressburg to join her family for the holidays. A very similar story to a young girl that was killed a couple of years ago. But where that victim was accidentally left off in the nearby village to her estate in the middle of the night because her family failed to receive notice in time of her early return, this girl was a different matter in that she had been expected early but failed to arrive on the day that had been originally planned."

"Planned, not planned, what are you referring to Count?" Sarpi immediately adopted his chief legislative role and attempted to narrow down the answers.

The dates of their return from school of course," Thurzo snapped, surprised that the famed Venetian legal expert could not have ascertained that fact for himself. "The girls from aristocratic families all attend the best private schools in the land. At these schools they learn how to be proper young ladies. That is not something they would teach them in the government school curriculum. Fortunately we are blessed with some of the best private schools in all of Europe. Unfortunately, it means the girls have to board away from their families for very long periods of time."

"So you're saying that both these girls attended private schools," Sarpi surmised.

"No, I'm saying that they both attended the same private school," Thurzo corrected him.

"Aha! So there's our common denominator," Paolo Sarpi was elated in making his first deduction.

"Yes, for these two girls," Thurzo stated a matter-of-factly. But certainly not for any of the others. And when you consider the total number of deaths, then these two sharing the same school are probably nothing more than a mere coincidence. And anyway, it is my cousin that operates this particular finishing school and I can assure you that she offers the best care possible for the girls while they remain at her estate. These two deaths have occurred well after the girls have left her property and many miles away. One can hardly hold the school responsible for matters well beyond their control!"

"True," Sarpi agreed, "But we must look at every possibility, no matter how remote it might seem. As much as we'd like to find a common denominator, each separate strand may lead to an eventual conclusion. We need to talk to the families and find out if there was an issue that was common to both."

"No we don't," Thurzo was adamant in his response. "I have already talked to the families. They don't need the likes of you disturbing them any further. They are distraught enough without you picking at their wound further."

Paolo Sarpi was not used to someone refusing his wishes. "But I need to know why they were expecting her early. Why she came late. Why for the other they didn't come at all."

"Are you suggesting that I don't know how to do my job?" the Palatine was practically right in Sarpi's face when he asked the question.

Slightly intimidated, Paolo Sarpi backed away. "No! Of course not," he responded. "I merely was asking for the details."

"Good," Thurzo commented. "Because I certainly wouldn't want someone like me coming to Venice and telling you how to conduct an investigation. Of course if you wish to know the details, then you can certainly ask me."

"Count Thurzo, I really would like to know the details if you don't mind," Sarpi tried to make it sound like he wasn't begging but that was impossible after the Count's invitation to be asked.

"I appears that Maria Zapolya was having a difficult time at school. Not surprising considering who her family was. For a brief time, her great-grandfather was King of Hungary around 1540. Not that he had the blood for it. No, he was one of the 'new men' of this era. The ones that are as rich as kings but still have the dirt under their fingernails from working their way up the ladder. That tends to anger those that do have blue blood coursing through their veins, especially when they're denied a throne that they believe to be rightfully theirs."

"But that was over half a century ago," Sarpi found it hard to believe.

"Could be a millennium ago and they still won't forget," the Count advised. "So the other girls were giving Maria a rough time, insisting that she did belong in the school. I doubt very much the headmistress did anything to stop the girls either. You see, if anyone had a claim to the throne of Hungary, it would be my cousin."

"This is all nonsense," Paolo Sarpi criticized the actions of the girls from the aristocratic families. "There are no kings in Hungary any longer. The Habsburgs now sit on the throne of the Empire and there will never be a separate kingdom of Hungary again."

"Those of you not born of aristocratic families will never understand. As long as there is a Hungary, there will be those holding titles that will dream of the day when once more they might sit on a restored throne. If you believe that to be true, then any threat to that dream, even the great granddaughter of a usurper, must be removed."

"Are you suggesting there was a political motive to this murder," Frau Sarpi jumped on the possible accusation.

"Don't be ridiculous," Thurzo dismissed the question. "I'm explaining why the girl was wanting to leave school early and come back home. But her parents insisted she stay until the term officially ended. Maria threatened she would just leave and show up on the doorstep of her home. Her parents had no idea if she would carry out her threat or not. Turns out she did wait until the end of the term but her parents didn't know that and had no idea where and when she would be arriving here in Pressburg."

"And the first girl?"

"Nadia Fogarasy," Count Thurzo rolled the name across his tongue. "The family is about as blue blood as you can get. So there goes any thoughts of these murders being a crime of political passion. Peasant, 'new man', aristocrat, doesn't matter at all to the killer. All that matters is having the opportunity."

"But you said she arrived a day early?"

"As it often happens, there was a private carriage leaving the school the day before the regular transport would take the girls back to the respective homes for the holidays. The headmistress mentioned that anyone wishing to leave a day early could ride in this private carriage. The Fogarasy girl accepted the offer. Unfortunately the letter she wrote advising her family of the choice she made didn't arrive until after the day she had been killed. Tragic case of being in the wrong place, at the wrong time. The killer obviously was out stalking victims that night and she happened to be there. And now you know everything that I know Fra Sarpi; no reason to go and bother the families any further."

"That being the case," Sarpi conceded, "Then let's hope this dead girl can tell us a thing or two."

The morgue where the bodies were held prior to preparation was damp and cold. Caesar de Nostradame felt a shiver run up and down his spine the moment he set foot in the room. The mortician stood solemnly alongside the steel table where the young girl's body was fully displayed.

"I thought we had agreed there would be no preparation of the body prior to our examination," Sarpi complained to the mortician.

"I have not done anything, my Lord," the mortician responded nervously, somewhat afraid of the prominence of the individuals standing in his morgue. "This is exactly how she was brought to me."

"Then why is she so pale," Sarpi didn't believe the man. "She looks as if you've applied talc to her already."

"Check for yourself, my Lord. I have not applied anything," the mortician defended himself. "This is the colour of her flesh. I swear to it."

Sarpi raised the girl's arm, turning it over and then replacing it by her side, only to pick it up again and examine the palms more closely, pinching each finger just below he finger nails.

"What are you looking for?" Caesar questioned Paolo Sarpi.

"The obvious," Fra Sarpi responded as he closely examined the rest of the body lying on the table. "Surely you must be able to recognize what I'm seeing."

"It was my father that practiced medicine, not me," Caesar replied.

"This is all very fascinating," the Venetian commented as he used a magnifying lens, raising her hands for a third time but this time to more closely examine the fingernails.

Every where he looked, Fra Paolo Sarpi made these barely audible sounds that the others could only interpret as oohs and aahs.

"I am so glad that you are enjoying yourself," Caesar remarked somewhat sarcastically, "but I don't know about anyone else, but all I see is that we have one more dead young girl and no real answers to what is actually happening."

Standing erect, Sarpi confronted his companions. "No, that is where you are very wrong Monsieur de Nostradame. This girl has a significant story to tell and we are definitely getting closer to the killer. We are extremely fortunate to have been given the opportunity to view one of the victims so freshly murdered."

"I doubt very much that the girl shares the same sentiments," Count Thurzo was sympathetic to the family's loss of their only daughter.

"Do not worry gentlemen, Maria Zapolya will be rewarded by revealing her killer to us and she will have her retribution. I swear it!"

Caesar scratched his head. "How can you be so certain. The dead cannot speak. Or should I say, at least not to us. They apparently do speak to members of Joseph's family but he's not here."

"Ah, yes, the legendary necromancers of the Bible. And for that reason he cannot be with us because the same religious paradigm that makes them capable of crossing over into the nether regions, also forbids them from coming in contact with the dead. Somewhat of a paradox. Otherwise I'm certain the young Kahana would have been here."

"Actually, he still wouldn't be here," Caesar corrected his colleague, "because he's busy selecting a wife, in case you've forgotten."

"That too," Sarpi agreed, "but the ability to communicate with the dead would actually be of great service to us. I know what you are thinking," Sarpi immediately responded to what he knew Caesar would say next. "If he becomes possessed by the spirits of the dead then he can become lost forever. I believe his father already told you that. And even the slightest contact with a corpse requires his seclusion and ritual baths for thirty days. Neither of those outcomes would be of much use to us. But I still say that the ability to communicate with the dead would be a most welcome asset at this time."

"I thought you said the Zapolya girl is telling you everything you need to know," he reminded Fra Sarpi.

"A lot but not everything," Paolo sighed. "Here, take a look at these nails." Sarpi held out the girls hand for Caesar to examine.

Caesar shook his head. "I see a hand, nothing special. Perhaps a little pale," he added.

"Exactly," Sarpi congratulated him. "Not only her hand but her fingernails are pale as well. They should be almost black from the blood congealing in the nail-beds. And look at her lips, practically white. Not purplish as expected." Paolo Sarpi indicated to the mortician to roll the girl on to her right side. "Now let us see what else she can tell us."

"What are you thinking," Caesar questioned.

"As I expected," Sarpi pointed to her elevated left buttocks. "The blood will normally settle to the lowest points of the body when lying prone. The flesh should be darker there. But her backside is the same colour as the rest of her skin. The whiteness of her skin is unnatural. Were the other girls like this?" Paolo Sarpi directed his last question to the count.

"They may have been," Thurzo responded without directly answering the question.

"You don't know?" Sarpi pressed harder for an answer.

"The Fogarasy girl, yes, may have been. I'm not certain, but I believe so. As for the peasant girls, I don't believe my men paid that much attention."

"I'm betting they were," Sarpi challenged his colleagues.

"Meaning…," Caesar encouraged him to continue.

"Meaning my friend…" Sarpi brushed the hair away exposing her neck, revealing two welts, perhaps four fingers in distance apart. Using the magnifying glass he examined the centers of each welt, noticing that each bore evidence of puncture marks. "…that I believe the body has been drained of blood," he continued. Looking up at the mortician, he flashed an angry stare at the man. "I thought you said you had done nothing to the girl. Then how do you explain the marks from the embalming needles!"

Hearing the accusation, the mortician moved closer to the table to examine the girl's neck for himself.

"Here, see for yourself," Sarpi could not withhold his anger. "Did you do this?"

No sooner had the Venetian magistrate pointed out the two marks on the neck to the man, the mortician became practically hysterical, running from the room shouting, "Upiri" over and over again.

"Come back here you fool," Thurzo shouted but it was too late. The mortician was long gone and there was no way to stop him.

"What was that all about?" Caesar inquired of the Count.

"An old wife's tale that persists in this land," the Count shook his head as he explained. "You would think the Slovak people would get over this nonsense but it seems they never do. The man was yelling in

Slovak, 'vampires.' An old fable of the undead to frighten children and make them obey their parents. Pay him no mind."

"Well that's going to be hard to do," Sarpi complained. "Since the fool is going to spread this nonsense around town and before we know it this place is going to get very crowded with onlookers and the like. It will become impossible to do anything more with the body."

"It is nonsense, isn't it?" Caesar was not too certain.

"Of course it's nonsense," Count Thurzo affirmed. "But don't tell that to a Slovakian."

"But you did say that you could see two puncture wounds on the neck…right?" Caesar was beginning to have his own doubts. "And it's clear from the morticians actions that he certainly didn't do it."

"Two holes of a very small diameter that appear to have been very accurately placed. One over the jugular vein and the other over the carotid artery," Sarpi explained

"Which sounds very much like a vampire," Caesar suggested. "Unless the mortician comes back and says he forgot that he had started to embalm the body, I certainly can't think of another explanation."

"Exactly what the murderer wants you to think," Paolo punctuated his statement by stabbing his finger into the air. "People that are afraid won't investigate. The murderer will protect himself by paralyzing investigators in a shroud of fear."

"So you already think it is a man," Caesar concluded from Paolo's statement.

"Certainly," Sarpi confirmed. "Only a man would be preying upon these young girls. These are crimes of lust, of passion, of a desire to exert power over his victims. But at the same time, I must confess they are the trademark of what must be of a highly skilled professional with access to sophisticated equipment. The killer knows his anatomy well and is quite skillful with the use of tiny bores. That could suggest that the killer might be a medical man, perhaps even a doctor and thus I know it must be a man."

"Because all doctors tend to be men," Caesar extrapolated Sarpi's meaning. "But perhaps it could be a nurse. She would have medical training and know how to pass a blood bore as well."

"But a woman would not have the physical strength to overpower all these girls and then force them to submit to the bloodletting."

"Even so, how would a man manage to subdue them and at the same time insert the needles? From the look of her neck," Caesar pointed at Maria Zapolya's, "it does not appear that he needed more than the one attempt to precisely hit both targets and she shows no signs of having resisted. That would suggest he must be highly trained."

"Or…" Sarpi rolled the girl once more on to her back and then opened her mouth with his fingers. He leaned over and placed his nose just above her lips. "As I thought, " he answered his own open question. "She was drugged. There is still a sweet fruity smell in her lungs. Check for yourself," he suggested.

Caesar shook his head. "I will take your word for it. And you know this smell because…"

"As I told you and Joseph, I had met with Brother Giordano Bruno on numerous occasions. He was always one to demonstrate his latest inventions and once exposed to the smell of his little anaesthetic ampules, one does not forget that smell. Ever!"

"But I thought that was one of Bruno's inventions," Caesar tried to recall precisely what his old friend had told him. "How could someone else have them?"

"Of course not!" Sarpi objected. "Like so many of Giordano's inventions, he merely burrowed what the Turks had developed centuries before and modified it by putting it into little glass balls. Anyone that can read Turkish papers can find out these things for themself."

Caesar sensed a modicum of bitter rivalry that must have existed between these two heretical byproducts of the Church. Best not to dwell too much on Bruno's accomplishments, that being the case. "So you think we are dealing with a medical person," Caesar summarized what they had learned thus far. "He drains the body of its blood but that would create quite a mess, wouldn't it? Did the constables at the scene of the crime describe the surroundings as being covered in blood?"

"No, they didn't," Thurzo replied thoughtfully. "In fact when they first found the girl they though she was merely sleeping in the alleyway."

"Then where is all the blood?" Caesar repeated his question.

"A good question, my friend," Sarpi commented as he became deep in thought. "Where is all the blood?" he asked, talking to no one but himself. "A girl her size would likely have just over two quarts of blood. If he found a way to actually contain it, perhaps he took it with him but to do so would take hours to fully drain through such small bores and I doubt anyone would stay at the scene of the crime that long. Which meant…"

"This is beginning to sound very much like a vampire to me," Caesar commented.

"Don't be foolish; there's no such thing," Sarpi scolded him, agreeing with the Count that it was nothing more than a foolish tale of the uneducated and superstitious masses.

"Then where's the blood?" Caesar demanded to know.

"Perhaps where she was found was not the site of her death,"

Sarpi postulated. "The blood could have been spilled at one location and then she was moved to another where she would be found."

"Except we found no other sites covered in blood, in or around the surrounding area," Thurzo was quick to interject.

"Then perhaps they were moved over a much larger distance," Caesar surmised.

"Possible," Sarpi nodded in agreement. "If the blood trail was close to my home then moving the body far away would make sense. As the killer I wouldn't want my lair discovered."

"That doesn't explain how some of these bodies have been discovered hundreds of miles apart," Count Thurzo challenged the line of thought, having dealt with this case for over a decade. "You might drop the bodies a moderate distance from where you are performing this act of draining their blood but that certainly can't account for literally hundreds of miles over the years."

Thinking long and hard, Sarpi searched for possible explanations. "If the killer did not always reside in the same place, then as he changes his location, so too will the sites where the bodies are found. Over the years he could have easily migrated hundreds of miles."

"True, but during my investigations, at some time, some place, someone would have reported to me a large amount of blood being splattered about. Especially if a new party moved in to a building or area recently vacated by the killer. No one could always be that meticulous that they can drain the body of blood in one place and then transport it to another without ever leaving some evidence behind. And trust me, in these little towns and villages, if someone new suddenly appears and there's a wave of murders occurring about the same time, the townspeople are going to put the two together long before I arrive on the scene."

"But only if that stranger actually lives in the town and is seen by the people. You're assuming he would live like a regular person in a building or domicile." Caesar still wrestled with the notion that it wasn't a vampire.

"I know what you're thinking Monsieur de Nostradame, but once more I assure you that this is the work of a man and not of some mythological creature of the night."

"I know that you refuse to believe in monsters Fra Sarpi but I can assure you after the experience that Giordano, Yakov and I shared together back in Prague, there are still those things which defy explanation. The Golem may have been a man, but he was unlike any other man you may have known. So why not believe that there is someone, man or creature that is harvesting blood for some nefarious reason that we don't understand. There is no blood trail because by some means they consume it and thereby leave us with no evidence to follow."

"It is still far easier to believe that they are bled out in one location and then moved to another," Sarpi contested.

"But Fra Sarpi," Count Thurzo interjected, "As I mentioned, in all those towns and villages, somewhere there is going to be an actual crime scene horrifically painted in the girl's blood, but to date we have not found a single one."

"Are you suggesting that Caesar is correct in suspecting the supernatural?"

"Of course not," the Count snapped at Sarpi's insinuation. "Don't be ridiculous."

"Perhaps then we are looking at this incorrectly," Sarpi rubbed his forehead as he pondered the riddle. "Perhaps we should look at places where blood drenched walls are the norm and not the exception."

"I am not sure I understand," Thurzo furled his brow.

"We can't find something if its sitting right in front of us," Paolo had a wry smile smeared across his face. "Imagine a place where blood is always spattered across the floors and walls and no one even bothers to give it a second thought. For example, a doctor could work in a hospital and if he killed his victims in a surgery wing, no one would even recognize that it was being done under their noses. Or perhaps a medical university. We already know medical students in training practically get away with murder in those colleges."

"But surgeons don't move around that freely," the Count was quick to douse that possible explanation. "They have to be aligned to a hospital in order to perform work there and that takes years to establish a relationship."

"But college professors and their associates do. They are constantly moving about from university to university."

Thurzo shook his head in disagreement. "Universities and hospitals only exist in the large cities. Some of the body locations were in remote places that even the nearest university or hospital was hundreds of miles away."

Sarpi agreed that Thurzo had just made a very valid point. Universities were limited by their locations to big cities. As for doctors, they would not have been allowed to freely walk in to a hospital and make use of its surgical rooms if they were not already employed at such institutions. And to perform these acts anywhere else certainly would have raised suspicions and left evidence, no matter how much the murderer may have tried to conceal it.

"Let us not be too hasty to rule out medical personnel as a

possibility," Sarpi was conceding it may have to be placed much lower on his list of possible suspects. "But there are other vocations, which require consideration. Let us examine what we already know. If it is another craft other than medicine, then the killer has to be strong, carrying these bodies to and from a discrete location without being noticed. And it is obvious he has some knowledge of the anatomy and function of blood vessels and the circulatory system. Furthermore, it must be a man with a trade that permits him to move easily from one location to the next without any suspicion or notice. It would need to be a vocation that people are used to seeing a different face in town without raising any eyebrows."

"Speak up already," Caesar blurted. "It is obvious you have already thought of such a vocation and have a suspected profession in mind."

"Yes, I do," Sarpi responded. "I believe we could possibly be looking for a livestock slaughter-man. Such a man would easily possess all the skills and knowledge required to be responsible for the death of all these girls. He would have the necessary tools to commit such acts. He could easily walk through the streets with blood drenched clothes and no one would even give him a second look. As journeymen, they could take their trade throughout the countryside and they would be welcomed every where they go."

"But there will be thousands of butchers that have worked in the towns and villages where these girls have been murdered," Thurzo protested the insurmountable task of actually identifying such a person. "You are presenting us with a task of screening through the impossible!"

"Difficult, yes, but not impossible. How many will be journeymen, having a history of moving from town to town over several decades. Admittedly, we are no longer a society of small villages lacking the services of shopkeepers and merchants as we once were, in the past. The days of the travelling merchants and vendors are nearly over. Journeymen butchers are coming to an end and that means there will only be a handful that still pursue that lifestyle any longer."

"We are still searching for the proverbial needle in a haystack," Count Thurzo gave his opinion of finding such a person.

"Don't forget Count that I am the renown Chief Magistrate of Venice. Finding needles in haystacks is what I do every day. We must start making a plan on how we will identify all the suspects and then we must take them all into custody where we can question them." Looking upon his colleague's face, Sarpi could see that he still had not convinced Caesar. "What is the matter now?" he inquired.

"It just doesn't seem right," Caesar expressed his doubts. "As I learned in Prague, twenty years ago, nothing is ever that simple.

"That is because you weren't working with the expertise of Paolo Sarpi," the Venetian laughed. "Scientist extraordinaire and master criminologist as the courts of Venice have come to know. Not every mystery has to prove itself unsolvable."

Thurzo was not convinced either. "The trochars that these butchers use to bleed out the animals are huge as compared to those tiny bores you refer to in this case. How would such a man come to learn how to use them properly?"

"Whether a thousand pound beast or a hundred pound girl, the blood vessels in the neck are identical, just smaller. If you know where to place the instruments, what matters the size of them, it is all proportional."

"Still, I think you give this butcher theory too much credit," the Count continued his argument. "You said you detect a chemical odour with which the victim was rendered unconscious. How would some meat processor find such a chemical or even know how to use it properly?"

"For that answer, we must ask the suspect himself, once we identify one," Sarpi dismissed the question as an unnecessary detail at this time. "How does anyone find anything they require. They simply find a vendor that deals in such items. Being on the road, I'm certain our killer would come across many merchants selling a variety of chemicals."

"But that still doesn't explain if our killer is a slaughter house worker, why leave a body at all. He could make the entire corpse disappear. Grind the bones, mince the muscles, throw whatever else he couldn't use down their lime pits. He'd be a fool to continually deposit the bodies in places where we can find them." Count Thurzo had been imposing the law for too long throughout Hungary to accept that this killer that he had been pursuing and eluding him for so long would be so reckless and sloppy in his methods.

"Not a fool," Sarpi corrected the Count, "A genius! He sees you as an unworthy adversary."

Fra Sarpi's suggestion stung the Count sharply but he resisted taking offense.

"He obviously considers himself to be intellectually superior and every body he leaves behind is a personal challenge to you. 'Catch me if you can,' he's saying but he doubts you ever will. Which suggests to me that in some way his killing spree may be the result of something personal against you. Perhaps someone you offended or took into custody a long time ago and this is his retribution against you. I believe this killer knows you."

Thurzo shook his head in disgust. "This is sheer nonsense. This killer is no genius, just someone who has been very lucky thus far. But that luck is about to run out. And this has nothing to do with me. If I had encountered a man capable of doing this at some time in the past, I can guarantee you Magistrate Sarpi, that man would be buried six feet under after having swung from one of my ropes by now."

"Well, perhaps after so many years of denial, it's time to admit that this particular murderer has outsmarted you at every step." Paolo Sarpi made no attempt to hide his contempt for Thurzo's refusal to admit that luck had nothing to do with the killer's ability to evade being caught.

"Exactly what are you inferring sir!" The Count's hand was automatically moving towards the hilt of his rapier. He was not a man to take an insult lightly.

"Enough!" Caesar screamed as he held the sides of his head as if he was in agony. His outburst and apparent anguish did serve to stop both men in their tracks before they made a serious mistake. "Century IV, Quatrain 71, the answer is apparently there," Caesar stated, his words interspersed by grunts and groans as if in pain.

'In place of the bride the daughters slaughtered,
Murder with great error no survivor to be:
Within the well vestals inundated,
The bride extinguished by a drink of Aconite!'

"What the hell was that?" Count Thurzo was baffled by Caesar's sudden rendering of what appeared to be a unintelligible riddle.

"That is what we have been waiting for," Sarpi informed the Count. "I had hoped that by exposing Caesar to the victim, she might be able to tell us something through his dead father!"

"Necromancy!" Thurzo sounded alarmed that they would be participating in an unlawful and forbidden practice.

"Not at all," Paolo Sarpi clarified, "More like prophesy. You are now listening to the voice of the seer Nostradamus.

Forgetting completely about the previous affront to his honour, Thurzo was desirous to find out the meaning. Even in Hungary he had heard stories about the famed astrologer and seer. "So what is he telling us?"

"We have to give Caesar some time to recover. These quatrains generally make no sense at all to me. But in some way his son is gifted with an ability to interpret them. From what I've seen, he can do it fairly accurately. Are you able to tell us anything, Caesar?"

Still rubbing both temples, Caesar de Nostradame took a deep breath before replying. "It's not a slaughterer. This is not someone killing for the mere thrill of the kill. It's a ritual. Some form of ceremony is involved, like a wedding but this is not for the sake of becoming a bride to the killer but instead they are all his children. When they reach the age of puberty, just as the vestal virgin must never take a man, these girls all need to be sacrificed so that they never marry. They are pristine. There can be no survivors. That would be his undoing. They have to be young. If any were to survive they would destroy whatever this ceremony is designed to achieve."

"I know of no such ceremony," Sarpi tapped his skull as if he could rattle through the recesses of his mind to find obscure facts.

"What's this about an inundated well," Thurzo demanded an answer.

"We are mistaken to think that there is only one girl involved at a time," Caesar interpreted the quatrain further. "More like a bottomless well, where the killer has a collection of girls already in his possession to choose from."

"So he keeps them underground?" Thurzo questioned.

Caesar shrugged his shoulders. "It may be literal or it could simply be a metaphor. I don't know."

"But that can't be," Thurzo countered. "Maria Zapolya was on her way home from the school. The Same with the Fogarasy girl. They were never in his possession like you said. Maybe the others, the peasant girls were held captive for some time, but definitely not these two. And their bodies were recovered alone without any other victims at the same time."

"Perhaps the words are merely an indication that the killer in some way has access to all these girls at any time of his choosing. That they already know him before their abduction and he knows exactly how and where to find them whenever he desires to perform this mystic ritual."

"How can a slaughterhouse worker know the daughters of aristocratic families?" Thurzo directed the question towards Sarpi, still unable to place his faith in such things a prophecies but definitely doubting Sarpi's choice of a suspect.

"Only a few aristocratic daughters," Sarpi rationalized, "The rest have all been girls from among the common folk. Perhaps this is someone that has now gained some recognition for his produce among the gentry and elite of Hungary. Maybe even does his own deliveries to the estates where he could possibly encounter the girls and befriend them. Just because Caesar says this is some form of ritual doesn't mean it can't be an abattoir worker. We all know the Jews practice ritual slaughter. Perhaps this is similar. Let's see if any of these noble families can tell us if there's been some new supplier of provisions to their households."

"You now want to accuse a Jew of doing these heinous murders," Caesar jumped on Sarpi's choice of words. "You say something like that to Joseph and I seriously doubt you will survive your next stabbing."

"No,no, you're twisting my words I merely brought up the reference to show you that such things as ritual slaughter do exist. The two aren't mutually exclusive. I would never infer that this is a crime committed by the Jews."

"But it is still a possibility," Count Thurzo was not so willing to dismiss the suggestion. "Jews often journey throughout the Empire and their butchers are few and in high demand. So they still practice a journeyman trade. And many an aristocratic household will only seek medical aid from a Jewish doctor and meat from a Jewish butcher. They consider both professions to be more hygienic and trustworthy." If there had been prior contact between the victim and the killer then someone working in the castles might have seen or heard something. A visit by a Jew around the same time would definitely be remembered."

"You are right," Sarpi agreed with the Count. "Jews do move about without anyone paying notice and as a people, they would definitely have reasons to hate the aristocracy. Would not be the first Jewish doctor to exact revenge on a Christian employer."

"Wait!" Caesar sounded alarmed. "Stop it, both of you! Clearly neither of you knows anything about the Jews. They abhor murder. They just want to be left alone."

"How can you possibly say that?" Sarpi pressed him for an answer. "Twenty years ago you exposed a Jewish cabal that had no remorse in committing multiple murders of Christians. One of them was a doctor, wasn't he."

"That was different," Caesar insisted. "The victims were purposely selected as acts of revenge for crimes they committed."

"Wasn't there a little girl killed as well?" Thurzo recollected the case in Prague. "What was her crime?"

"I'm telling you both that you are wrong," Caesar insisted. "If Jews were involved, my father would have no hesitation in saying so. You're both overlooking the aconite!"

"Not at all," Sarpi denied having done so. "Aconite is well known for a variety of medicinal effects. Particularly for reducing pain. If there is a ritual slaughter being performed as your father suggests, then perhaps these girls are not fully somnolent when the killer is committing these acts. It also will cause paralysis, and that could explain any lack of signs of resistance or struggle by the victims."

"But you already said you could smell the same substance that Giordano used in his little glass balls. Now you are saying it's aconite?"

"I never said that the killer could not be using more than one drug.

"You don't understand my father," Caesar shook his head. "He wants you to focus on the less obvious, knowing full well that most people will merely look superficially at the obvious."

"I know you believe your father is a master of illusion," Sarpi commented, "But perhaps sometimes he is just providing us with a clear and precise message that doesn't need further interpretation. After all, he was a master of herbs and floral medicines himself. Wasn't he the man that stopped the spread of the plague with his concoction of rose petals? He knows what these plants can do and as I explained, aconite would be the perfect drug for someone perpetrating a sadistic ritual where the victim has to be immobilized. No reason that couldn't be a Jewish doctor. Why can't you accept that your father might actually be stating what is obvious?"

"Because I know my father," Caesar countered. "You don't! He doesn't want us being misled and searching for the obvious He is directing us to think beyond the veil of our normal world. Last time he directed us to find a monster and this time is no different. I can assure you, we are on the trail of a monster this time as well."

"Certainly," Thurzo agreed. "Whomever is committing these murders is a monster by any description. We are all in agreement on that point. But he is still only a man."

"No, you're both missing the point. Instead of the bride being killed, the ritual requires the sacrifice of the daughters. So the bride is never given the aconite, so that person is never extinguished. Don't you see? He does all this for the bride!"

"Aconite besides numbing the pain, causing paralysis, will also kill if taken internally in too great a quantity," Fra Paolo Sarpi reiterated his medical knowledge, not seeing Caesar's point at all.

"Can you for once think like a monk," Caesar threw up his arms in exasperation. "After all, you were trained as one before you became this other thing you profess now to be."

"What is that supposed to mean," Sarpi sounded offended.

"Exactly what I meant it to mean. Now think like a monk and tell me what the plant is used for."

"That's nothing but superstitious nonsense."

"Good, for once think like the rest of us and deal with the fears that the rest of us simple people share every day. Do that, and then you will understand my father. And by the way, Giordano Bruno was a great scientist!" Caesar had been dying to get that last line off his chest, ever since Sarpi had denigrated his friend.

"So you want me to believe that your father says aconite when he really means wolfsbane."

"Also known as monkshood because my father is trying directly to make a point to you, since he knows no matter how much you see with your own eyes, or how much you hear, you'll still remain blind and deaf on this mission. And if you remain that way then you'll be useless to help any of us. Why do you think you are here? It's not because of your superior knowledge that you enjoy flaunting in front of us repeatedly, it's because of your ability to not die."

"That's ridiculous," Sarpi grew defiant.

"Is it?" Caesar placed his faces but inches from Sarpi's own face. "When I was brought to the court several months back to select this group, that was exactly the reason I provided why you should be part of this team. I needed someone that had a history similar to Bruno and what made you stand out most was that God apparently was not ready to let you depart this world until you had done His will, whether you realize it or not. That was sign enough to me that you were someone special. You were the one."

"I thought it was because the Vatican had some foolish prophecy about a heretic priest," Sarpi reminded Caesar of the documents that had been uncovered over twenty years ago.

"Heretic Priest," Caesar laughed. "I can find a hundred of those now with all the Calvinist and Lutheran insurgencies taking place across Europe. What made you different is God won't let you die."

"You can't die?" Thurzo's mind was still lingering on Caesar's first comment, oblivious to everything else that had been said.

"Three attempts on his life. Fifteen stab wounds," Caesar recounted the list of Sarpi's near death encounters.

"Seventeen...seventeen stab wounds to be exact," Paolo Sarpi prided himself on accuracy.

Thurzo was impressed. "Yes, that does sound to me like a man that can't be killed. But seriously, you want us to believe your father was referring to wolfsbane as the solution to these murders?"

"If you knew Michel de Nostradame, then you wouldn't be asking that question."

"But you're inferring that country superstition has some basis in reality," Sarpi still refused to accept Caesar's interpretation. "That is ridiculous!"

"I'm saying that Nostradamus wants us to look into the superstition and then we will find the truth of what is really happening."

"Seriously?" Thurzo was still struggling with the nature of the conversation. "Wolfsbane, as in dealing with werewolves and vampires? You cannot be serious."

"Wolfsbane as in a lethal instrument that kills werewolves and wards off the undead," Caesar offered further explanation. "We may not be dealing with actual vampires or werewolves but what if there's someone that believes they are one of these creatures and these killings are all part of their effort to live out some horrific fantasy."

At that moment Sarpi and Thurzo looked at each other puzzling over the possibility, and then having analyzed it internally, both turned to Caesar simultaneously and responded. "Nah, don't think so."

"I'll start looking into a journeyman slaughterer immediately," Thurzo advised Sarpi. "Especially if there's been any Jewish butchers new to those areas where the bodies were found. But I still doubt you're right."

"And perhaps we should still check to see if there have been any new doctors moving through the territories," Sarpi added.

"Let us get away from this building before any crowds start showing up looking for evidence of a vampire," the Count suggested. "The mortician must be already spreading the rumour. Right now, I think its best we stick to the facts."

Chapter Seven

Vienna: January 1610

"It is clear that we're going to be at odds over the direction this investigation is going to take," Maximilian observed.

Wringing his hands, Thurzo appeared obviously frustrated. "Excellency, I have been investigating this series of murders for over ten years now and I must protest the interjection of these lay people into that investigation. One has me chasing after some journeyman slaughterhouse worker that no one can identify or has ever seen and the other wants me to hunt down legendary monsters that haunt the forests under full moons."

"And have you been successful in finding any of their suspects yet," Maximilian inquired in all seriousness.

"Excellency, you cannot be serious," Thurzo shook his head.

"When it comes to this matter, my brother, your Emperor, and myself can be deadly serious." Maximilian was not willing to brook any further dissension. "We need to put an end to this killing spree immediately. It has gone on for far too long. It was bad enough when the people just considered our law enforcement agencies incompetent, but now word is spreading of supernatural creatures since your debacle in Pressburg. If things go wrong will hold you accountable, Gyorgy."

"We did nothing wrong, Excellency."

"Of course you did," Matthias who had been listening to the banter between his brother and the Count replied. "In front of this mortician you spoke of an individual draining the blood from perhaps hundreds of victims. You know that can only mean one thing to these provincials. Vampires, the undead. Do you want to know what they are saying in Hungary? Felall a sotetseg! The darkness has risen! And it is beginning to spread like wildfire. How long before you think we have an open revolt on our hands?"

"It's nonsense, your Majesty. There are no hobgoblins, dark magic forces, or vampires causing these murders. We live in a modern age where we can understand and appreciate such things do not exist. We are stalking a killer that is very much flesh and blood but who has a very uncanny means of evading detection. But sooner or later he will make a mistake and we will catch him."

"You have been telling me that same thing for years Gyorgy. If you weren't my cousin, how long do you think you would have lasted in this posting?" Maximilian asked.

"As long as your family still owes my family millions of thalers, I guess," the Count was quick to respond and remind the Archduke of the debt owed by the throne. "We both know that the only thing keeping Matthias as Emperor is my family's bank rolling his rule. So let's not pretend that my position as head of law enforcement as the Palatine is anything more than one of the many benefits that is doled out for our support of you and your brother. Yes, I'm your cousin but this position has been bought and paid for."

"I'm not denying any of that," Maximilian conceded. "All I'm trying to say is that whether you believe it or not, our world is facing annihilation at the hands of the Antichrist! The Vatican was the first to find this interpretation within their ancient documents but one doesn't need a crystal ball to see where this chain of events is going to lead us if we don't find the killer quickly. Whether you are willing to accept it, this is a matter of religious, political and civil significance. For that reason, I need you working with this group we have assembled to deal with this emergency and stop resisting them! Perhaps we should re-examine everyone's roles in this affair," the Archduke suggested.

"Am I in charge or aren't I," Thurzo's tone became sharp and resonated with an anger seething just below the surface.

"I am not saying that you are not in charge of the three of them. I only think that it would be wise for you to give them the opportunity to demonstrate to you their individual strengths. One thing I do recall is that those ancient documents suggested, in order for us to succeed, then those three must become as one. They are the weapon. It matters not who wields the weapon as long as we use it properly."

"You truly believe all this nonsense," Thurzo questioned the Archduke.

"I was there when it happened to the three that were chosen to save Prague and I'm certain it can happen again. But this will only be achieved if you are able to forge a commonality between themselves and make them into this divine weapon that was foretold. Let that be your undertaking, to see that they do unite in this endeavor and once that occurs, then I'm certain they will be ready to report to you and accept your instructions."

"Since when have I become the royal baby sitter?" Thurzo

objected.

"Since I have told you to be so," came the reply from Emperor Matthias that was tiring quickly of the squabbling.

"I have one that thinks he is so intellectually superior to the rest of us that we are nothing more than ants walking in his shadow. Another that spouts unintelligible rhymes from time to time that don't even make for good poetry and insists they are coming from his long dead father. And as for the third, he's so busy parading around the castle with his fiance' that he doesn't appear to have a care at all what the rest of us are doing. I still don't know what he does."

"Don't be fooled," Maximilian wagged a finger at his cousin. "Joseph Kahana may appear to be uninvolved in this matter, but trust me when I say that he is the cog that will bring this entire wheel together."

"Well that will be a surprise to me," Thurzo sneered. "Because the only useful thing I see about the man is his big dog. I guarantee that monster can take down any vampires or werewolves should we encounter one. It's a beast!"

"You will see, cousin," the Archduke reassured him, "When the right time comes, Joseph Kahana will be our saviour. It is written."

"Written in the stars in the heavens," Thurzo mocked Maximilian. "I will indulge you both this request for now but my patience won't last forever. I need to get back to Hungary, do some serious investigative work and find this killer. Being here in Vienna does not help us in the least."

"You will indulge our request as long as I say you will," Matthias interrupted their discussion.

"Wait brother, the Count is right," the Archduke agreed with Thurzo. "Remaining in Vienna serves us no purpose at all. That's why they all will be leaving tomorrow. I need you to assemble a guard for your companions on this journey."

"Journey?"

"Yes. You will be heading east. As I said, when necessary, Joseph Kahana will be vital to your success and apparently he has come to the conclusion you must go towards the Black Sea to find the answers. I see no reason why we don't begin this tomorrow."

"The killer is in Hungary, not in Romania. Why are we wasting our time," Gyorgy Thurzo grew even more perplexed.

Ignoring his protest, Maximilian continued his train of thought. "Don't assemble too many of your men. Nothing too large to draw attention. Remember, you'll require both speed and stealth but still have enough men to protect everyone. Ten to fifteen at the most I would think. Trusted men that have served you well in the past. Soldiers that don't ask too many questions. But also I need soldiers that don't share the common superstitions one usually finds in army barracks."

"Such as?"

"Such as women accompanying your mission will only bring you bad luck," Maximilian explained.

"Women? Now I am babysitting women as well! Excellency, tell me that this isn't true and you are merely jesting."

"Two or three at most," Archduke Maximilian attempted to make it sound as if it was a minor detail. "The Kahana's fiance' and a couple of her attendants. Hardly a burden. Oh yes, and her father as well."

The count couldn't believe what he had just been told. "I'm taking a wedding part along on a dangerous mission to find a pathological killer, who might possibly even be a monster according to some, because the Church says the world is coming to an end. Is that what you are actually saying?"

"Exactly," the Archduke confirmed.

"Am I the only sane person in this castle?" Thurzo could not believe what he was being told. Yes, he understood that in he had failed to bring the killer to justice in over a decade but if he was going to be punished for his failure, then arrest him and throw away the key. That would warrant far less suffering as compared to the burden that was currently being placed upon his shoulders.

"How can you even be asking me to do this," the Count turned to the Emperor, dropping all formalities of addressing his superior.

"Because my brother has told you to do it," Matthias responded.

"I know it sounds complicated," the Archduke felt some sympathy for the concerns of the Palatine.

"Complicated my ass! It's insane!"

Matthias rose quickly from his chair, his face drawn and contorted into a fierce mask that Thurzo found extremely threatening. "Remember who you are addressing Gyorgy! We may owe a debt to your family but there are far more in your family than just you and they may not miss your absence if you overstep too far. You are talking to me as well, not just my brother!"

"My apologies your Majesty." As much as it infuriated the Count he knew that Matthias was right. There were more than enough siblings and cousins that would jump at the opportunity to take his place without shedding a single tear in mourning.

"Do we have an understanding," Matthias demanded an answer from his cousin.

"Yes your Majesty, we have an understanding," Thurzo conceded.

"Good!" Maximilian jumped back into the conversation. "Just one more thing I need to mention. The girl's father absolutely loathes Joseph. See to it that they don't end up killing each other during the journey."

"Explain this to me one more time," the Count insisted.

"It is clearly evident that we must begin our search in the region of the Carpathians," Joseph reiterated.

"And how may I ask did you come to that conclusion?" Although Gyorgy Thurzo promised that he would work along side these three paragons supposedly predicted from some ancient text that no one even knew existed until twenty years ago, he never promised that he would not remain skeptical of their every suggestion.

"The evidence is clear that you all have been approaching this matter from the wrong direction," Joseph addressed his response to the three others in the cabin. "You," he pointed his finger at the Count, "have been searching for this killer for years unsuccessfully because you are unable to think like him. Once you appreciate what the killer is trying to achieve through these murders, understand his goals and his needs, then you will find him easily. As for you," he next pointed his finger at Sarpi, "You can only think in one dimension. The killer must be this, or that but you fail to appreciate that he could be many things all at once. A butcher, a doctor, a lover, even someone that already has power and authority, rather than some pathetic man trying to simply exert power over weak and defenseless girls. And as for you," he turned towards Caesar, "When are you ever going to accept that no matter how absurd your father's instruction might be, they are correct?"

It was obvious that Joseph had been told everything they had discussed that day in the mortuary by Caesar.

"And you suddenly know all this because…?" Thurzo felt he had heard enough and he need more than Joseph's instincts to make this journey eastward. "And whatever you do, don't tell me you now because you just know!"

"I know because I actually pay attention to everything that you all have said. Rather than think of it in terms of either this or that, I believe it makes far more sense to think of it in terms of this, and this, and also that."

"That makes no sense at all," Sarpi twisted uncomfortably in his seat, gazing through the carriage window to see the road sign pointing towards Raab.

"Actually, it might make more sense than we think," Caesar

offered his opinion. "Several nights ago I received more messages from my father. I couldn't make any sense of them by myself so I discussed them with Joseph."

"And you failed to mention this, why?" Thurzo questioned if Caesar had any reason not to share this information previously.

"No point in sharing what you consider nonsensical rhymes until I can actually make some sense from them that you will find acceptable," Caesar defended his decision.

Turning his head back towards his colleagues in the black carriage sedan, Sarpi asked the question that was already on Thurzo's lips. "So what did he say?"

"The first was Century I, Quatrain 45. It read as follows…"

'A founder of sects, much trouble for the accuser:
A beast in the theater prepares the scene and plot.
The author ennobled by acts of older times;
The world is confused by schismatic sects.'

"I couldn't make any sense of it at all," Caesar confessed, "Until Joseph walked me through it. And it is exactly as he says. The killer isn't someone that fits into a single pigeon hole. They are as he says, 'multidimensional.' That is why we couldn't find this journeyman butcher, or a doctor as you had suggested, Fra Sarpi."

"Now explain it to me," Thurzo demanded.

"Best if I let Joseph do that," Caesar hesitated. "I don't want to make a mistake and after all, he was the one to see the true meaning."

"Well, then…" Thurzo turned his stare on Joseph sitting directly across from him.

"I approached it from the last sentence first," Joseph explained. "The world being confused by schismatic sects provides us with a motive and a purpose on behalf of the killer. They have been directly impacted by the schism that has erupted in Christianity. Perhaps part of their family is Catholic, the other half Lutheran, and now those two halves may be at each others throats. The divisiveness has caused them some immeasurable pain and they long for the old ways. But Nostradamus chooses to use the word author as if to suggest that the killer is trying to write a new story based on old histories. This ritual that Caesar spoke of in Pressburg must have come from that older time referred to. The killer is ennobled by it. They are certain they are doing the right thing by reviving this ages old ritual. They want to restore a religion and practice that predates Christianity."

"All very well and good," Thurzo commended, "But how could they even think they could achieve this restoration? It would be impossible and by now they must realize that."

"See, that is where you have been led astray all these years," Joseph pointed out. "They are already achieving it. The first line tells us so. The killer has already founded this sect. Which means there are followers. This is no longer the acts committed by one individual. The murders are being committed by a group of them that follow this leader."

"As in a coven?" Sarpi questioned.

"I guess if we consider them in the possession of dark forces, then you could refer to them as a coven," Joseph agreed.

"That could explain the movements around the countryside where the bodies were found," the Count agreed. "If it wasn't always the same killer but several practicing the same ritual, then it starts to make sense."

"Of course it does," Joseph responded. "The beast stands center stage in the theater from where he sets the scenes and directs the plot. That is why no one could ever identify a single individual common to all the crime scenes. Because it has not been one person responsible for these crimes for a very long time."

"A good story," Sarpi was willing to admit, "But its hard to establish a criminal prosecution based on the dreams of a seer. I'm still not convinced we are not witnessing the actions of an individual."

"Granted it may be one or many," Caesar agreed, "That is why we have to catch this 'beast' in the perpetration of the crime. But to do that we must understand the killer's motives which is why we are going to search in the East where this all began."

"Exactly where in the East?" Thurzo preferred not to stumble around blindly.

"We're working on that," Caesar replied.

"That's your answer?" the Count stammered. "We just head east."

"Well, we know the first victims were found in the eastern Carpathians, so that's a good a place as any to start. Plus we had some sense of where we should look from the other quatrain that recently appeared in my head but Joseph and I haven't yet deciphered it completely."

"Let me hear it," Sarpi requested, now suddenly sounding like a believer.

"Its from Century III, Quatrain 44:

'When the animal domesticated by man,
After great pains and leaps will come to speak:
The lightning to the virgin will be very harmful,
Taken from earth and suspended in the air.'

"We think it gives us the location but we are still working on it,"

Caesar explained.

"How far have you gotten," Thurzo asked.

"Once again the wolf appears to be central to this mystery," Joseph took over the explanation. Between this quatrain and the last, it is explaining that the old ways have something to do with both man and wolf being one. Part of their religion had to do with human sacrifice. Sacrificing virgins, just as they're doing now. As a young boy I recall my father telling me the history of this part of the world because my family had lived in these regions for some time. He spoke of people that worshiped the wolf a long time ago. But they are all gone now. Wherever they lived, that's where we must look We must find the place they conducted their sacrifices."

"That could be anywhere in Romania," the Count sighed. "The wolf was a god to those people a thousand years ago and for a thousand years before that. Another needle in the haystack."

"Of which I told you Count, I'm a master at finding. I know exactly where we must look."

"Of course you do," Thurzo replied sarcastically.

"A matter-of-fact, I do. I think I can interpret and resolve this quatrain quite easily. One does not become a Chief Magistrate without knowing the socio-political history of all these lands. After all, we are all the continuation of that once great Roman civilization. They really should make the teaching of Roman history compulsory in the schools."

"Yes, yes… a fine idea," Thurzo agreed less than sincerely, "But where are we going already?"

"The answer is Brasov, my friends. You should have come to me with this quatrain when you first received it Caesar."

"And how did you come to that conclusion," Thurzo challenged Sarpi as if it was the inquisition.

"And how is it that you do not know this, if you are an aristocrat of a Hungarian family?" Sarpi fired right back at the Count. "I can excuse these other two as they aren't from around here, but you most certainly have known about the Dacians."

"Of course I know about the Dacians," Gyorgy Thurzo countered. "But that still doesn't tell me how you decided it was Brasov."

"Did you know the Romans referred to the Dacians as the wolf warriors?" Sarpi looked at the faces of the others to see if any were aware of that fact. No one responded. "You see, all cultures had some connection to the wolf; even the Romans considered the wolf sacred, as the mother of their civilization by nursing Romulus and Remus but they considered her to be a benevolent creature. On the other hand, the Dacians saw the wolf as their chief god. A god of power and a malevolent force of nature. They worshiped the wolf, they hunted like the wolf, they fought in formations like a pack of wolves, and some say that their noblemen could even become wolves on certain nights of the year."

"Yes, yes, all very good," Thurzo agreed, "But why Brasov?"

"Because the area around Brasov was their holy ground. You might say it was their Vatican. Their sanctum santorum. The very heart of their religion."

"And how do you know this is where we must go for a certainty?" Thurzo was still doubtful.

"Because Nostradamus says so," Sarpi winked and nodded towards Caesar. "Listen, I know you find these prophecy matters hard to digest. The truth is, so do I. But I have to admit that when a coincidence keeps repeating itself, then it probably is not a coincidence. The fact that time and time again we seem to be directed towards taking a certain action by the sayings from a man dead for over fifty years suggests to me that perhaps I should stop questioning and just start listening. And for someone like me, that is not easy to admit." Having said that, Sarpi winked and nodded to Caesar once more.

Count Thurzo clasped his hands together and after clearing his throat repeatedly, spoke, "Well, if Magistrate Sarpi can admit that he doesn't know everything and even he has to listen to others, then I guess that's the day that I have to sit up and pay attention too. So tell me about these Dacians before I change my mind!"

"That reference to lightning is what convinced me that Joseph was taking us in the right direction. There are few people in the world that would know the Dacian god was Zamolxis and besides being a wolf, he was also considered the god of the lightning. The Dacians made sacrifice to this god of theirs, human sacrifice. They would use these sacrifices to send a messenger to Zamolxis. Or as the quatrain says, taken from earth and suspended in air, because the messenger had to meet their god up in the clouds in order to deliver the message. They performed this ritual every four years and their priest known as the Deceneus, whom it was said could transform between wolf and man, performed the ceremony. Sometimes howling, sometimes speaking, but the transformations were said to be accompanied only with great pain."

"And these sacrifices you spoke of," Thurzo prodded Sarpi for more information and less narration.

"It had to do with a quest for immortality. The messenger they would send would be one of their own warriors as only he was considered suitable to speak to their god. He would bargain with Zamolxis to grant them immortality so that they would not die in battle. But to sweeten the bargain he would take along with him the souls of a number of young virgins. Usually girls from conquered villages, but if they didn't have any prisoners at the time, then they would sacrifice their own young girls. Apparently it was an honour to be selected. The Greeks called their race the Daai and that became Dahae in Persian, the word for wolf. Their enemies believed the Dacians were descended from wolves. I think they believed it themselves."

"But they are all gone, right?" Thurzo questioned.

"Supposed to be," Sarpi answered but sounding less than convinced of that fact. "They are said to have died out over a thousand years ago."

"But what if they didn't," Joseph postulated. "What if there was still a remnant of them that have been secretly living within our civilization, just waiting for the opportunity to resurface and revive their old way of life."

"All the more reason I guess we need to go to Brasov," Sarpi rubbed his chin as he replied. "Like you said Joseph, we need to know how this all began in order to put an end to what we are dealing with now."

"It is going to be a long uncomfortable journey, gentlemen. I will tell you this now, so that when you all start complaining you will remember that it was your decision," the Count warned them.

"How long," was Caesar's first complaint.

"Four hundred and fifty miles long," Thurzo replied. "We should be there in about fifteen days if we don't make any long delays." He specifically directed that comment towards Joseph because they were already hours behind their anticipated departure from Vienna. Not that it was Joseph's fault, but his future father-in-law had to ensure that everything intended for his use and that of his daughter was *kashruth*, from the food they would eat to the linens they would use to prepare their beds. Only once he was personally satisfied, having ignored the assurance provided by Abel Weissman, the city's unofficial mayor of the Jewish community, did he agree to get into the carriage with his daughter. Of course that was after forcing her two attending handmaidens to ride in a separate carriage that trailed behind, insisting that he had to be the one to ride along with Reisel in order to protect her innocence.

"Is that including or excluding today," Caesar requested further clarification regarding the journey's duration.

"Does it really matter," Sarpi laughed at the question, "By the time we've spent two weeks riding in this carriage along these bumpy roads, we will already be so sore that the only answer you need to know is that whichever it is, it is too long."

"I guess I better go tell the others," Joseph mentioned as he signaled to the driver to stop so that he could dismount from the carriage.

"I'm sure she's going to appreciate it when you inform her how long she needs to be sitting in that carriage with her father," Caesar said mockingly.

"Not as much I am guessing that her father will be when I tell him," Joseph laughed thinking about Rabbi Lipmann bouncing around in his carriage for two weeks. "I might even start feeling sorry for the man."

The others responded in unison, "Nah, we seriously doubt that."

Chapter Eight

The Road to Heve: January 1610

It was the dog, Wolf, that first noticed that their little caravan was apparently not alone on the road. Normally running along side or behind the carriage in which Joseph rode, the dog suddenly darted to the front of the caravan, forcing the train of horses to stop dead in their tracks. Snarling and growling, the hair rose along his spine as it hunched its back, green eyes shining like mirrors as it stared into the woods that lined the road. The sudden halt to their progress and the horrific noise coming from his dog, certainly made Joseph and the others aware that there was something seriously amiss.

"What is it?" Sarpi asked.

"Don't know yet, but the only time I've seen and heard him act like this is when there were wild animals in the forests surrounding our neighbourhood in Galicia. Could be that we're being stalked by some beast hidden in the forest."

"Well tell him to get out of the way and stop blocking the carriage," Sarpi instructed. "He's beginning to scare the horses."

Joseph whistled for Wolf to move aside and get back behind their carriage where he had been keeping in stride with the horses' pace, but this time the dog refused to listen to his master's command. "That's not like him to ignore me. I better take a closer look," Joseph advised the others. "I trust Wolf with my life. If he thinks there is something there, then we all should believe him." Instructing the driver to calm down and just keep the horses still, Joseph dismounted from the carriage and approached his dog. "It's alright boy. Nothing to be frightened of. Relax," he instructed Wolf as he approached, kneeling down beside the animal and stroking his head softly between its ears. The others could only stare, noticing that from their position they could see little difference in size between master and pet. It was a point that everyone else was well aware of, but no matter how many times they made the comment, in Joseph's mind Wolf was still just a little puppy he found abandoned in the woods. The dog appeared to relax under Joseph's tender touch, until there was the sound of twigs snapping somewhere among the trees, and Wolf's growls were now followed by repeated gnashing of his exposed razor-like teeth as he curled up his lips. Joseph heard it too and was now equally aware that they were definitely not alone.

"Whoever is there, come out now and show yourselves," Joseph shouted, masking any fears he might have with a false bravado.

Hearing Joseph's shout, Count Thurzo dismounted and ran to Joseph's side with his rapier already drawn in hand. Waving his left arm, he instructed the men of the guard to ride forward from their position behind the train of carriages and join with him at the forefront.

They didn't have to wait long to find that the creatures stalking them were human. "Tell your men to relax," came the request as a squadron of eight men armed with both short musket and cutlass hanging from their belts emerged from the sheltering treeline. "We had to ensure that you weren't going to cause us any trouble," the leader of this unknown force explained as they entered into the clearing.

"And you honestly believed a caravan of carriages and wagons represents a threat," Count Thurzo inquired, finding it hard to accept the explanation. "You have a very strange definition of threats my friend."

"One can never be to certain of anyone these days," the squadron leader answered. "In the past week several of the local farms had been pillaged by roving bands of thieves. Soon you learn not to trust even your own eyes."

"Then you should have reported it to the proper authorities," Thurzo advised. "As far as I know, the Palatine is still responsible for policing these territories."

"These lands are under the ownership, authority and protection of Castle Ecsed," immediately came the spoke-person's reply. "If anything happens within these parts then we hold full jurisdiction in application of the law to act upon our own lands. Not even the famed Palatine, can enforce every law across the countryside. Is that not so?"

"What is going on here?" Joseph asked Count Thurzo in a hushed voice so as not to be overheard. "Whoever they are, Wolf doesn't like them at all." The dog became even more excited now that it could see and smell the strangers. "He usually never reacts this way."

"Merely a difference of opinion," the Palatine answered, now knowing full well who's men these were. His comment was meant to answer both Joseph and the armed men.

"Am I to understand your mistress is now in residence," Thurzo asked their leader.

"She is Count Gyorgy Thurzo and she invites you and your fellow travelers to be her guests to stay the night."

"I suspected you always knew who we were," the Count did not appreciate playing games. "So why then the pretence of following us from out of sight as if you didn't know our identity?"

"Forgive me," their leader apologized. "I am Captain Valerie Rodescu. You are well known throughout all of Hungary. Your tracking skills are legendary. I was curious to see if you were also as good at knowing when you were being tracked."

"That is an odd matter to be curious about Captain, unless you intended to use that information some time in the future."

"Certainly not, Count Thurzo, merely as you say, a curiosity."

"And what is your conclusion?" Thurzo was interested in knowing.

"Your animal is actually very good. It picked up our scent almost immediately. I could use a beast like that when I hunt. Is he for sale?" Captain Rodescu began to approach Wolf, only to retreat when the dog bared his teeth ferociously and tried to break free of Joseph's hold attempting to leap at the stranger.

Now that the squadron of men had all stepped into the open, Joseph could see that every one of them was draped in what appeared to be a red cape adorned with wolf-skin across the shoulders and clasped across their chests. He wondered if that was what could be the cause of triggering such a vicious response in his dog.

"Not mine," Thurzo responded. "It's his and I doubt very much he's willing to part with him. But you can always try to approach again and see if you can discuss your offer."

Rodescu shook his head. "I think I will pass on this one. I doubt he'd get along with my own animal. Their character would be too much alike."

"So what now Captain?" Thurzo inquired.

"If you would care to follow us," the Captain pointed to a side road heading slightly north, "then we should be back to the castle in time for dinner."

"I think I can speak for my companions in saying they would enjoy the comfort of your castle at least for one night. What do you think Joseph?"

"I know for a certainty that Reisel would enjoy spending the night in a warm bed under a roof that keeps the winds out. Not to mention having an end to the never-ending stream of complaints I hear from her father. With a little luck we can convince him to stay behind and wait for us in this castle until we make our return journey."

"And my men will certainly enjoy having a warm meal in their bellies rather than eat another day of hardtack. So, lead on Captain, it will be good to see my dear cousin once again."

Castle Ecsed stood perched imposingly on the crest of the hill overlooking the forest of Nyirbator. Its massive stones were ancient, having withstood the onslaught of storms and wars for over four centuries. Never having been taken in battle, it had remained a defiant symbol of Hungarian independence, so much so, that even the Habsburgs never insisted that the family stop calling themselves Princes of Hungary and Transylvania.

It had been a long time since Count Thurzo last visited Castle Ecsed. One thing he never forgot was how impregnable the eastern wall appeared. It was against this wall that the structure of the castle actually stood, But the wall itself was built into a massive rock-face that was short of the walls summit by twenty feet. The rock was a fatal lure over the centuries for all the armies that attacked and tried to breach those heavy stone walls. The forty-five degree slope of the rock reduced the enemy to crawling on all four limbs to reach the top, while the castle defenders rained down upon them with missiles and arrows. By the time the few survivors did manage to reach the rock's peak, there weren't enough of them to raise the ladders the final twenty feet to scale the walls.

Extending outward from both the north and south of the castle was another wall which curved into a circle, meeting in the west where it completed wrapping the crest of the hill within its protective embrace. It was inside this outer wall that a few selected villagers would live and set up their merchant stalls for the benefit of their patron. There were two roads leading up to the massive iron gates of the outer wall; one to the north and one to the south, but once inside the village area, there was only a single gate into the inner courtyard of the castle, heavily guarded by at least twenty more of Captain Rodescu's men.

As the travelers approached the castle they noticed that they were being closely watched by the men manning the castle parapets. It was obvious from their actions that the castle did not receive a lot of visitors. When they reached the base of the hill, Rodescu signaled for the caravan to stop advancing, pointing to the high portico with its iron grill built into the hillside.

"Count Thurzo, if you would be so kind to instruct your men to take their horses through that gate where they will find quarters to lodge in the livery and stables. I am certain they will find the barracks most comfortable and the interaction with my men far more entertaining than sitting in the village square while we dine."

Without hesitation Count Thurzo instructed his men to follow Captain Rodescu's squadron members through the livery gates. Leading their horses, the men disappeared into the yawning darkness below the castle.

Within the first carriage, Sarpi questioned his companions as to the wisdom of such a move. "Why would he have his men separate from us?" he sounded worried. "He knows they are the only protection we have. We don't know anything about this castle and its occupants." The alarm in Sarpi's voice was obvious.

"Thurzo may be a lot of things but he's no fool," Caesar countered in an effort to calm his companion. "If he thinks we are safe without our guards present then I have to assume he knows far more about the inhabitants of this castle than we do and he doesn't consider them a threat. So why should we?"

"I still don't like it," Paolo Sarpi objected. "How did that captain even know who we were? Our mission I thought was secret. Yet he was well aware of our travels along the road and who was in charge of our welfare. It doesn't seem right."

At that moment, Joseph interjected himself into the conversation. "Gentlemen, we all know that if there was anything serious or insidious, then in some way Nostradamus would make us aware of it As you can see, Paolo, Caesar is fine, he doesn't have anything to say, and that means at least for the time being, we are probably safe. That is of course if you finally believe that Caesar does have this innate ability to tap his father's prophecies to our benefit."

"And you're saying you have no doubts at all about Caesar's abilities?"

"I'm saying that my father had no doubts and he was a far wiser man than I could ever be. So if he believed it to be true, then who am I to say otherwise."

"I just hope you are right," Fra Sarpi groaned as suddenly there was a knock on their carriage door. Sarpi immediately opened the shutter to see who was knocking.

Captain Rodescu smiled at the three men sitting inside the carriage. Addressing Joseph, he asked, "Sir, if you could kindly have your animal follow the men into the livery. The kennels are down there and he should stay with the other animals."

Sticking his head out the window, Joseph looked behind the carriage to see Wolf sitting haunched and growling in a low rumble as he stared coldly with his ice green eyes at the Captain. "I don't believe he wants to go down there, Captain. I think it is best for all your men's sake that he stays with me."

"Sir," the Captain began to object, "My mistress would probably not be pleased with the presence of your beast in her hall."

"Captain, if Wolf does not attend me in the hall, then I will not go there either and you can explain my absence to your mistress. The choice is yours."

"So be it," the Captain acquiesced. "Take your carriages up the road," he shouted to the drivers who were waiting patiently as he was discussing matters with Joseph Kahana.

The road was steep, but with the proper urging, the horses pulled against their harnesses with an increased exertion and the carriages appeared to surmount the obstacle, rolling forward.

"So trust in Caesar's abilities," Sarpi mentioned somewhat sarcastically to Joseph as their carriage rolled towards the outer gates.

"I also learned long ago to trust in my dog as well," Joseph replied.

"Probably the better choice," Sarpi nodded his head.

Once past the outer gates, it was a short distance through the heart of the small village that inhabited the lower plateau of the hill to the tall iron gates that were set into the wall that surrounded the castle courtyard. All the travelers descended from their respective carriages and joined Count Thurzo and Captain Rodescu in front of the open gate to the inner courtyard.

"Everyone," Rodescu announced, "If you will kindly follow me, it is time that you meet your host." He then pointed to the series of stalls set into the wall where the drivers could hitch up their horses and tend to them with hay and water. From the gates to the entrance of the castle was approximately a hundred paces and already a feeling of dread hovered above their heads as an ominous gloom emanating from the exterior of the castle enshrouded them in a cold shadow. Above the archway of the entrance hung the family crest, a creature so hideous that even a man like Paolo Sarpi, who had abandoned his faith, felt the urge to cross his chest for protection. At first one could assume it was a dragon, but upon closer inspection the beaked mouth and ears that were shaped like horns clearly suggested a creature of demonic origin. The neck was ringed, with rows of spikes that resembled flames lining its spine. The coiled arrow-headed tail was matched by a tongue that was identical. The creature hung tenaciously to the shield in its grasp, which bore as its only emblem, three sharp and threatening claws.

The large iron bar that served as the knocker was coiled exactly like the tail of the creature on the crest. Rodescu raised the bar and let it fall, resounding against the black walnut set of doors like cannon-fire. He let it strike against the block three times, waiting for a response. From the other side of the door, footsteps could be heard approaching, then the ornate wooden doors rolled back on their hinges and the visitors were greeted with a simple, 'hello.'

As they all stared past the steward into the lobby of the castle, they were surprised to see that the interior was in sharp contrast to the exterior of the building. Candles were seen illuminating every corner of castle, casting each room with bright and lively gaiety that was totally unexpected. Colourful tapestries adorned the walls and beautiful artwork from around the Empire, many easily identified as being from the most famous painters of their time, were interspersed between the marble statues and ornate flower-filled vases that stood stolidly as if guarding every alcove.

"Please come in," the steward welcomed them, holding the door open invitingly, at least until she saw Wolf walking along side Joseph. The expression on her pleasantly rounded face changed dramatically into an disproving scowl. "Oh, we usually don't let anyone bring their animals in with them," she commented. Joseph was about to make a reply, when she suddenly held up a finger to silence him and just as suddenly as it had disappeared, the smile returned. "But, I have been instructed specifically to see that your every wish is tended to, so that obviously means that you can bring your animal in as well."

"I am most appreciative," Joseph thanked the steward. "Did you mean me specifically, or our group in general?"

"You will understand soon enough," she responded as if concealing some big secret, "But don't thank me, thank my mistress. She has an obvious soft heart for strangers."

Joseph flashed Reisel a quizzical look as if to say he had no idea who their hostess might be after noticing that she did not appreciate the inference that somehow he had been a familiar to the owner of the estate. As far as her father was concerned, it would give him one more argument why she should have nothing to do with the son of a Kahana.

"Everyone, please follow me," she directed as she led them into the dining hall. "Please take your seats according to my instructions. Count Thurzo, if you don't mind sitting to the right of the head of the table. Master Kahana to the left. Lady Reisel to the left of your betrothed and I will sit to the right of the Count. Signor Sarpi, if you don't mind sitting to my right…"

"It would be a pleasure to sit beside you," Paolo Sarpi felt it necessary to compliment her as a typical Venetian.

"Thank you," the steward responded. "Mine as well. Rabbi, please sit to the left of your daughter and then one of her handmaidens will sit beside you."

"I'm afraid my daughter and I will not be able to eat anything and therefore it is unnecessary that we dine at your table. My apologies to our hostess but we have a strict dietary code. I hope you understand. We will simply retire to our room if you could point them out to us. I hope your mistress will not be offended."

"Actually, we understand fully Rabbi Lipmann," the steward responded. "And you need not have any concerns. Everything we eat at Castle Ecsed is strictly kosher. I can assure you that there is nothing that will be served that you cannot eat. So if you don't mind, please take your seats as instructed."

"Well then, I must object to my daughter's handmaiden sitting next to me. It would be discomforting for me to be so close to another woman that is not my wife."

The refusal of the Rabbi to sit next to the handmaiden did not phase the steward at all "Monsieur Nostradame, *veuillez-vous asseoir a cote de* Rabbi Lipmann."

"*Certainment*," Caesar agreed in French. "Well Rabbi, it looks like you and I will be dinner companions tonight instead. I'm certain we will have such pleasant conversation over dinner." The jest was well received by the others and even Reisel had to laugh as her father grunted his obvious displeasure.

The food being kosher was a point that did not go unnoticed by Joseph, who was left wondering why there would be food prepared to Jewish religious law available in a remote Hungarian castle. But even more disconcerting was the fact that the steward was familiar with everyone's name. The castle had obviously been prepared well in advance to expect their arrival. This was all very highly suspicious.

"As for the rest of the chairs, Captain Rodescu, if you could make yourself comfortable. Our hostess's other attendants will sit at that end of the table when they arrive."

The weary travelers were overjoyed at the opportunity to sit around a formal dining room table and enjoy a banquet especially prepared for them.

"And one more thing," the steward continued. "Master Kahana, if you don't mind having your dog rest and eat in the adjoining room. A bowl of water and food will be brought out for it."

Although not happy to have Wolf out of eyesight, Joseph agreed and led the dog into the next room where he commanded him to stay. Obediently, Wolf lay down on carpeted floor and rested his head between his forelegs.

"I don't believe we met the last time I was here," Thurzo appeared to find the steward's knowledge of the members of his mission also unsettling and felt it was time to ask some questions of his own. "You must be new here. What happened to my cousin's other assistant? The one that served as her personal physician as well."

"I am not that new, Count Thurzo. More likely that you have not been here in such a long time that makes it seem that way. I have been at Castle Ecsed a few years now. I am Erzsi Majorova, and I took over the position of steward and personal assistant when Anna passed away last year."

"Oh, I am sorry to hear that. I presume Anna was the doctor I was referring to."

"Yes, Anna Darvula. Most unfortunate. They say something happened to her brain. At first she was paralyzed on one half of her body and after a month or so, she finally succumbed to the illness."

"Sounds like a stroke from your account," Paolo Sarpi interceded. "You say she was a physician; how intriguing. I thought I knew most of the female physicians within the Empire," he continued. "But I don't recall anyone by that name."

"You keep track of female physicians?" Caesar sounded both shocked and surprised. "That sounds somewhat perverse," he joked.

"Only because as the Chief Magistrate of Venice I am always looking for the brightest and best in all the professions to come to my city to work. For a woman to be accepted into the medical colleges is extremely rare and it means she must be far superior in intellect and skill than her male counterparts. That is why I am aware of most of them but this one obviously had escaped my attention."

"So you know our host extremely well, Count," Joseph's mind was still puzzling over how the castle staff had knowledge of their travels and knew who they were. He was just about to inquire from Count Thurzo who their mysterious hostess might be, when that question was suddenly answered by her spectacular entry into the dining hall accompanied by her attendants.

"I am so sorry to have kept you waiting," she apologized in her soft lilting voice. "Vanity is such a terrible vice, but I could not dare let you see me unless I was looking my best." Resplendent in a high fan collared gown, beaded with small pearls that complimented the heavy pearl necklace she wore abut her neck, their hostess was the epitome of statuesque beauty.

Rising from their chairs, the party of travelers stood dumbfounded, with mouths hanging open as if attempting to utter a word or a phrase but remaining speechless until Count Thurzo decided it was time to fill in the silence. "As always Cousin, you are and always will be the most beautiful women in any room you enter. You look ravishing."

"Thank you Gyorgy. As usual, you always have the right words to say to me. It is why you will always be my favourite cousin."

"Gentlemen, and Lady Reisel, may I introduce to you the Countess Erzsibet Bathory," Erzsi Majorova introduced her employer.

"I believe we have already had the pleasure of meeting before," her eyes twinkled as she spoke with a slight girlish laugh. "Don't look so surprised gentlemen, I did say we would obviously meet again and I am always a woman of my word. I hope you don't mind if my ladies in waiting join us for dinner?" Addressing the young woman on her right, "Allow me to introduce Lady Dorottya Szentes, who you may call Dorka." The handmaiden bore obvious traits of her Spanish heritage, having raven black hair and eyes that were equally as dark but dazzled in the candlelight. Though not as beautiful as the Countess, Dorottya certainly would attract most men's attention. "And this young lady is Ilona Jo, who you may call Inna. I don't know what I'd do without either of them. They attend to my every need."

They still found it difficult to speak, staring at the same elegant and slim figure that had descended the steps between landings at the Hofburg Palace several weeks back during the wedding. This time she wore her auburn hair down, flowing across her back until it reached just above her waist, intertwined with silver and gold ribbons that kept it neatly in place.

"So how is your darling sister, Joseph. I do hope she is managing to keep Otto in line. The dear boy can be such a handful at times."

The informality of addressing Joseph by his first name made Rabbi Lipmann nudge his daughter with his elbow, as if to suggest that there was some clandestine relationship between the two.

Clearing his throat, Joseph inhaled deeply as he managed to restore his voice. "She is fine Countess. I know she would send her regards and appreciation for the lavish gift she received from you at her wedding."

"I won't hear a word of it," the Countess held up her hand in order to stop the praise. "She is family now, and exchanging gifts is what we do all the time. And you are family now too, so please, Elizabeth is fine, we don't need to use titles among family members."

"Of course Countess...I mean Elizabeth," Joseph quickly corrected himself. "I must admit and I think I speak for all of us, we are quite surprised, perhaps even shocked to see you so soon after our last meeting."

"And I'm surprised that Maxi didn't tell you that you always had the option to stay in my castles while travelling through these lands. It was foolish that he made you sleep in your carriages when I can make you so much more comfortable on your travels. It is a good thing that I became aware of your whereabouts so I could send my Captain to rescue you from one more horrible night under the stars. "

Caesar's eyes were drawn to the perfection of her ivory skin, on obvious display by way of the low cut of her silver shimmering gown, highlighting her bountiful breasts and accentuating her neck that was longer than that gifted to most other women but suited her admirably. Once again he experienced that unusual sensation that attracted him before to the countess even though he admittedly had little sexual attraction for either sex. A strange sensation that he could neither explain or identify.

"Are you not happy to see me Caesar," she caught the son of Nostradamus staring unblinkingly and decided to interrupt his daydreaming by teasing him.

"Er...of course I am Countess. I am just surprised, that is all. And a little confused. I could swear that I recall you being introduced to us as the Countess Nadasdy the last time we met but your steward just used the surname Bathory for your introduction."

"My husband has been dead for six years now," she bowed her head and half closed her eyes as if in remorse, "My friends tell me it is time that I shed my grief and the best way to begin was to resume my maiden name. I still have a life of my own to live dear Caesar. Would you not agree?" She was very suggestive in the flirtatious manner in which she questioned him.

"Ah...certainly," Caesar was at a loss for words, having difficulty in understanding why the Countess had such an unsettling effect upon him.

"Bathory as in King Stefan Bathory of Poland?" Paolo Sarpi finally recovered his voice, rescuing Caesar from an embarrassing and awkward situation.

"My uncle," she replied. "A dear sweet man if I might say so. The stories about him can be so cruel but I assure you they are not true."

"I was not implying anything in that manner of your relationship Countess," Sarpi was quick to defend himself. "I have only heard good things about King Stefan, I assure you."

"And no offense taken good Sir," the Countess responded, "Spoken like a true politician. But we all know my uncle has been a stern ruler and that is a matter of fact that you need not deny. But if a ruler is not stern, they only invite disaffection, which eventually leads to revolt. It would be a good lesson if it were to be followed in this Empire but I'm afraid it is lost on my cousin Matthias."

"Erzsibet, it is best not to discuss such things in the company of your guests," Count Thurzo cautioned her. As a loyal agent of the Empire, he was uncomfortable with his cousin's criticism of the Emperor.

"Why Gyorgy? Are you going to arrest me. Have the Habsburgs become the masters of your thoughts now as well that you cannot hear a truth lest it should displease them?"

"You know I'm not saying that at all cousin. Only that there is a right time and place to discuss politics and this is not that time."

"You're right. Of course you are right Gyorgy. How terrible of me to forget my manners. We haven't even finished introductions and here I am discussing politics. I hope you all can forgive me."

The guests around the table all indicated that there was nothing to forgive, from their various mutterings, while nodding their approvals.

"So please tell me Joseph, who is this beautiful young girl sitting with us," the Countess begged him to provide the details.

"Well Elizabeth," Joseph struggled to say her name, still preferring to use the word Countess as if it provided protection from being too close and personal, "I believe you are already aware of her identity, but this is my beautiful fiance', Reisel Lipmann and of course sitting beside her is her father, Rabbi Yom Tov Lipmann."

The Countess watched intently the expression on Rabbi Lipmann's face as Joseph introduced the young girl as his fiance'. It was obvious from his bared grimace that not everyone was particularly happy with this arrangement of the Kahana taking Reisel for a wife. This deserved further investigation, she thought to herself. Always one to play with people's emotions, just as Maximilian had forewarned them, she was desirous to see if her suspicions were correct. Over the course of the meal, she decided to intersperse a few more comments into their discussion to uncover the Rabbi's true sentiments.

Clapping her hands, the maids entered the dining hall carrying the five course meal upon silver platters. From salads and soup, to pheasant and goose, accompanied by tarot and potatoes, carrots and legumes, the meal had been fabulously prepared. As a finale, an assortment of sweet-cakes and fruits were provided, to be washed down by wine also supplied by the local Jewish community.

"So Rabbi Lipmann, I hope you enjoyed the food tonight?" the Countess questioned her guest.

"I am absolutely delighted Countess," he replied. "It was delicious Countess," he bowed his head in gratitude. "I was quite surprised to hear that you actually had kosher food available for me."

"Not just for you, Rabbi, but for everyone that dines with me," she laughed at his implication that the meal had been especially prepared just for him.

"I don't understand," the Rabbi scratched the top of his graying head.

"There is no great mystery," Countess Bathory explained. "My lands are at the crossroads of the Holy Roman Empire and the Ottoman

Empire. Many times both sides will be negotiating within one of my estates and I have to play hostess to them. Like yourself, the Muslims that eat at my table have dietary restrictions that I need to meet. I may not have many Muslims that can prepare their Halal meals within my towns' borders but I certainly have enough Jews that can prepare the food to their dietary laws."

"Still, it is different," the Rabbi insisted.

"In your mind perhaps," the Countess laughed, that same girlish giggle that won over many a man's heart. "But in reality, you are merely two sides of the same coin. There is little difference between your people. And as you may already know, its says in the Qur'an that a Muslim, and therefore any representative from the Ottoman Empire, can eat at the Jew's table but not at that of a Christian. So it was expedient to me to simply have all my kitchens in all my castles operate to a strictly kosher standard. In that way we can all eat well without any pangs of guilt that we may have enjoyed something that was forbidden."

The whimsical smile with which she made her last comment did not go unnoticed by Joseph. Just how much enjoyment has the Countess obtained from forbidden pleasures, he wondered.

"It was quite unexpected," the Rabbi explained. "But why continue to serve only kosher meals if you don't always have Turkish guests to entertain. You would only need to serve it at the times that require it."

"That is a personal restriction that I imposed upon myself. You see, I will not let my lips ever touch the blood of an animal. It is a foreign impurity that must never enter my body. As only the Jews ensure that the blood is completely drained from the carcass by their method of kill and the soaking of the meat in saline, it was obvious to me that I should have Jewish chefs prepare all my meals. Which reminds me, that since I have numerous castles throughout these lands, I can provide you the assurance that you never have to worry about your meals along your journey as long as you partake in my hospitality."

"At this time Erzsibet," Count Thurzo interrupted, "We are not certain which direction we might be taking in our travels and therefore we cannot say for certain we will be in the vicinity of one of your castles."

"Merely a suggestion Cousin," she replied. "But unless you tell me exactly where you intend to go, then how can you be certain I don't have accommodation available."

"You know I cannot disclose that information to you," Thurzo refused to play his cousin's game.

"Exactly how many castles do you have," Caesar inquired, tempted by the offer to travel a route that ensured they always had excellent meals, good wine and soft beds.

"Eighteen I believe. Sometimes I forget myself," she giggled, making that soft tittering sound that affected anyone hearing it.

"Well, we will keep that in mind," Caesar directed his response towards Count Thurzo, letting him know that not all decisions were to be made by him.

"And let us talk more about this beautiful young girl beside you dear Joseph. Look at her. Such delicate little fingers," The Countess reached across the table to hold Reisel's left hand in her own. "And so soft. Oh, how I would dream to have skin so soft again. She is like a little angel. And she looks so young Joseph," Elizabeth commented. "I'd swear she was still a child if I didn't know better. But a very beautiful child. I can understand why you are attracted to her."

"She is a child!" her father replied heatedly. "What kind of man takes a child from her family in order to bed her? God cannot approve of such a union!"

The Countess had begun to play her little game, satisfied that she had uncovered the Rabbi's weak spot, giving her an advantage that she could use to manipulate the Rabbi should it be to her benefit. But now it was time to demonstrate to Herr Lipmann who was actually in control. "Well if you must know, my dead husband would be one such man. I was only ten when engaged, fourteen when I was married. Your daughter I believe must be roughly that same age for her intended marriage. Am I not correct? I would like to believe that God did approve of my marriage and sanctified it."

"Forgive me," Herr Lipmann quickly apologized realizing that he may have affronted the Countess. "I did not mean to imply that your husband was in any way the type of man that Joseph Kahana is. Of course at your age it was perfectly fine to be married to an aristocratic, an educated and sophisticated man of such high bearing such as your husband was, but this Kahana, he is nothing more than a pretender, a charlatan, a pariah in my society."

"Papa, that is enough," the young girl raised her voice then quickly apologized to her hostess. "You will not speak of my future husband in that manner. If you ever wish to see me again, then you will learn to accept my decision. Is that clear, Papa?"

The rabbi crossed his arms across his chest, burying the fringe of his graying beard beneath a forearm as he grew silent. The Countess could see clearly that the threat of never seeing his daughter again was enough to silence him. It was his Achilles heal and it was just as clear that this pouting, petulant man had absolutely no love for Joseph Kahana at all. If there was any way he could prevent their marriage from taking place he would seize the opportunity. 'Oh Joseph,' she wondered. 'Do you even see the danger you placed yourself in by choosing this man's daughter to be your future wife?' But now that she had created a situation where everyone suddenly grew silent and no one wished to talk any longer, she knew it was her responsibility to repair and eliminate the dark cloud that had overtaken her dinner party.

Staring through the doorway into the anteroom off the dining hall, the Countess saw Wolf, laying down as he ate and drank from the bowls prepared for him. "Oh, what a lovely animal," she commented. "It is not often I see a wolf raised as someone's pet."

"He's actually my dog," Joseph corrected her. "He is often mistaken for a wolf."

"Because he is one, my dear," the Countess laughed. "We know our wolves in this part of the Empire, dear Joseph. Trust me, your dog is a wolf. Is that not so Valerie?"

Upon hearing his name, having been silent most of the night, the Captain entered into the conversation. "Yes, Countess. Most people only know about the gray wolf. After all, it is the one most commonly seen in this region. But if you know wolves, then you would realize that we can find six different kinds of wolves in Europe. Up north we can find a light coloured wolf that we call the Tundra wolf. In Russia they have even a bigger wolf that is distinguished by the whiteness of the marking around its eyes and mouth. To the east around the Black Sea there is the desert wolf, and to the west in Spain and Portugal there is the Iberian wolf. But to the south of us, in the Appenine Mountain regions of Italy, there is a particular wolf that the local farmers have often raised as pets and refer to as the wolf-dog. The fur is commonly brown and the cheeks and belly are a lighter tan. A kind of red wolf. Along the back, front legs and the tip of the tail one can see black bands. It weighs anywhere from fifty to a hundred pounds and usually a mere twenty inches at the shoulder. Your pet happens to be a bit taller. This Appenine Wolf as it is called, will sometimes come down our side of the mountains but it does not fare well, rejected by the wolf populations that are native to our countryside, and thus hunted by their own species."

Looking over at Wolf, Joseph could not argue that he fit the description of the Appenine Wolf that Captain Rodescu had just described. "You appear to know a lot about wolves, Captain," Joseph commented. "I can't help but notice the shawl and hood attached to your cape. Is it wolf pelt?"

"I wear it proudly," the Captain replied. "In my village we are sent out into the woods, with little more than a knife. We must find a lone wolf, track it and slay it with nothing more than our knife, our hands and our teeth. It is our right of manhood. Those of us that survive get to wear our adversary's pelt as a sign of respect and honour, not for ourselves but to honour the fallen in our primal battle with nature. We can then call ourselves 'omullup' signifying we are men."

As he told his story, the women gathered around the table held up their hands and covered their mouths both in horror and admiration of this epic battle to claim manhood.

"Well best then that I keep you and Wolf separate. I don't want to find out what happens next if the two of you find yourself in disagreement," Joseph made a little joke to the amusement of all.

"Your red Appenine wolf is truly a magnificent animal," the Captain praised Joseph's pet. "As I mentioned, many of the farmers in Italy raise them as dogs. Intelligent, extremely loyal and very protective of their owners. I doubt very much he would have stayed with me, even if I could have purchased him."

"But as you say, many have been raised as dogs. That is what Wolf is to me. He is my dog, and I would prefer if you don't mention to others that he might be a wolf. You know how people can get when they hear that word."

"Of course," the Captain nodded his head in agreement. "I fully understand."

"Now that we have settled that matter," the Countess concluded, "I believe it is time we send everyone to their rooms for a good night's sleep. But Gyorgy, I do think it would be in your best interests to tell me the details of your travels. I can make this journey far more comfortable for you and the others."

"I'm afraid I cannot reveal that information," Count Thurzo rejected her offer. "I think I speak for the others when I say we appreciate your offer but we must decline it."

Clearing his throat, it was obvious that Rabbi Lipmann was not of a single voice with the Count. "Countess, it would be my pleasure to take you up on your offer of hospitality," the Rabbi responded, "but sadly, I don't even know where this group intends to take my daughter and myself. They have disclosed nothing at all to me. As far as I'm concerned, whatever their destination, it is a fool's errand and if this man truly cared for my daughter, he would have never insisted she come along."

"Papa," Reisel chastised her father, "You know that isn't true. Joseph never wanted me to come along on this journey. I was the one to insist that he takes me. So if you need to blame someone, then blame me but stop casting blame on Joseph for everything!"

"Please, let us not quibble on such matters," the Countess insisted. "I'm certain I can assist in making the journey far more pleasant and comfortable for the two of you. Why don't I discuss this further with Gyorgy and see if we can find a compromise."

"Erzsibet, if you're trying to uncover the details of our mission and where we are going, then I'm afraid you are going to be disappointed. We must keep that information secret," Gyorgy Thurzo leaned over the table top as if to say that was his final word.

"Gyorgy," she responded. "You know I have my ways of finding out everything I desire to know. So why not save time and just tell me. You might just find out that I have valuable information that can in turn save you all a considerable amount of time and effort. Who knows more about these lands than I do? These are my lands, my people, and if there is anything happening within these parts then I am usually the first to know about it," she softened her tone to appear that she was begging to let him let her help.

"You are already involved Erzsibet. Two of your students from your finishing school are now dead and if we can't find out who is committing these murders, then who knows how many more there will be," Thurzo explained. "How much more do you need to be involved? Best you keep your distance from these matters."

"Did I hear that correctly?" Joseph inquired, having listened intently to their discussion. "Two of the girls from the aristocratic families attended your finishing school? Why wasn't I told about this before?" Joseph insisted on knowing.

In his own defense, Thurzo attempted to explain. "Neither girl was remotely close to the school which is located in Cachtice, in Slovakia. There are perhaps twenty girls in attendance there and when my men questioned them, they found nothing out of the ordinary. They mentioned that they may have have carried out their bullying of Maria Zapolya too far and may have even heard her mention committing suicide, but no one ever intended to actually harm her. And as for the Fogarasy girl, they all loved her. They said Nadia was like an older sister to them, fearless and very protective. She was also one of the more successful students at the school and admired by everyone. No, whomever committed these murders didn't have access to the school and that is why they had to wait for the girls to leave. Perhaps the misfortune of being the one to step down from their carriage at the wrong time and place where the killer happened to be waiting. This was all revealed to Senor Sarpi and Monsieur de Nostradame."

"But you never said it was Countess Bathory's school," Paolo Sarpi," tried to justify why they failed to disclose the matter to Joseph.

"Even more reason why you see we saw no need to take it further." Thurzo said.

"And did your men bother to ask the girls if they had seen anyone strange wandering around or near the school," it was apparent that Sarpi was still not satisfied with the level of investigation of the school girls by Thurzo's men and now had an opportunity to glean more information.

"Of course," the Count replied somewhat irritated. "My men are not fools. We do know how to conduct an investigation here in the northeast of the Empire as well as you do in the southwest."

"Technically, Venice is not part of the Empire," Sarpi refuted.

"And technically there was no one strange around the girls except for the hunchback that is in my cousin's employ. They complained of him making sexually rude remarks and occasionally stealing their undergarments. Hardly what I would classify as a high crime or misdemeanour."

"A hunchback?" The description of this individual had caught Paolo Sarpi's attention. "Did your men happen to question this hunchback?"

"They tried, but it was difficult. He is not in full retention of his faculties," Thurzo explained.

"And where is this miscreant now?"

"He remained behind at the Castle Cachtice," Countess Elizabeth Bathory answered. "Someone has to ready the rooms for the next semester and prepare everything prior to the girls returning."

"You said he was not in full retention of his mental faculties," Sarpi reiterated the Count's statement. "Why in the world would you leave someone like that in charge of preparations of your school?"

"Senor Sarpi," the Countess stated his name angrily, "Fizcko may be addled but that does not make him utterly incompetent. I'd swear you must be harboring a prejudice against hunchbacks."

Paolo Sarpi shook his head defensively. "Of course not," he denied. "That would be ridiculous. Forget I ever mentioned it. I'm sorry."

"Apology accepted," the Countess responded. "Now let's get everyone to bed."

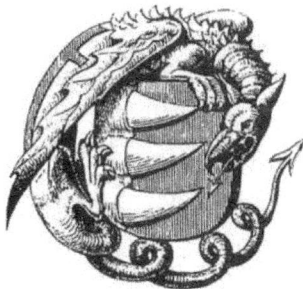

Chapter Nine

Hoia-Baciu Forest: February 1610

Watching from his bedroom window, Joseph was intrigued by what appeared to be a young boy gathering firewood in the distance. He was most impressed as he watched the lad chop down tree after tree with apparent ease and then briskly slice off the branches so that he could lash the logs together in a tight bundle. Then almost effortlessly, he hoisted the bundle of logs onto his shoulder and began the long march back to the castle, oblivious of the ankle deep snow that had fallen over night and now attempted to impede his movements. Very, very impressive, Joseph thought to himself. They definitely raise them to be strong in Slovakia. Most grown men wouldn't have been able to lift that bundle and here was a young boy doing it while hardly breaking a sweat. On a more insightful plane, it made him wonder why God apparently gifted some people with extraordinary powers, while ignoring the majority, leaving them to struggle from day to day. God only knows was the only conclusion he could arrive at, as he prepared his bag and then exited the room.

By the time he had assembled in the courtyard, everyone else from his party was already prepared and waiting. He looked around for the other carriages as only one of them had been hitched to a team of horses.

"So a slight change in plan," Count Thurzo informed Joseph upon seeing the confused look on his face "In response to the incessant urging by the Countess, Rabbi Lipmann has insisted that he and his daughter must be allowed to stay at my cousin's castle in Oradea, while we continue on our journey through the forests of the Bihor Mountains. They will then travel with a party of her men through the safer passes south of the mountains and wait for us at Bran Castle outside Brasov until we finish our mission. Once our mission is complete, we will reunite with them again upon our return journey towards Vienna."

"That is not what the Archduke intended," Joseph reminded the

Count. "He was very clear in that we were not to leave Reisel alone with her father or else he might find a way to steal her away back to Germany."

"All very well," Thurzo acknowledge, "But the path we are intending to take is fraught with dangers. I doubt very much it was Maximilian's intent to place your fiance''s life in danger."

"And how then will we prevent Lipmann trying to make his escape and take his daughter with him" Joseph was concerned.

"I've explained to Erzsibet, that at no time are they to be left unsupervised for that very reason," the Count explained. "She has agreed to have them under surveillance at all times."

"I presume it is for the best," Joseph reluctantly agreed. "I need Reisel to remain safe and that sounds as if it would be difficult as we proceed on our mission. It also sounds like you have revealed to Elizabeth all of our plans."

"Only our route and that the Lipmanns cannot be permitted to leave," the Count insisted in his defense. "Certainly nothing about our intentions once we reach our destination. But she is absolutely right. After she heard me mention that we would pass through the forest, it was obvious we would be placing the girl in grave danger."

Reisel was approaching Joseph when she overheard part of the conversation. "I certainly did not agree to this." she stated in a tone that was challenging to the Count's authority. "I still insist that I be able to accompany you wherever you go but now I overhear Count Thurzo is saying this is no place for a woman."

"I have always insisted from the start that this was not a trip for a little girl," the Count rebutted her accusation. "What I have just said is nothing new. But now more than ever I consider it is too dangerous."

"I am not a little girl," Reisel was indignant, feeling slighted by the overt insult.

"This journey has always been dangerous," Joseph was weakening under Reisel's stern look. Why suddenly now? What makes this more dangerous" Joseph wanted to know.

"Because the forest is haunted," Elizabeth's voice surfaced from behind where they were discussing the matter.

Turning, Joseph saw the Countess, as beautiful as ever, even for this early hour in the morning. "There is no such thing as a haunted forest," Joseph chastised her for believing in such nonsense.

"That is where you are very wrong, dear Joseph. The Hoia-Baciu Forest is very haunted. They say the souls of those killed in the forest are trapped in the trees, causing the trunks to be twisted and misshapen so that they resemble the tortured souls they contain. They say that the trees are dangerous!"

"That is nonsense," Joseph insisted.

"Is it? Then ask your seer if you choose not believe me," she insisted making reference to Caesar.

"Caesar," Joseph called out, "What is all this nonsense about a haunted forest? Why are they insisting that I ask you?"

"I'm sorry Joseph, but early this morning I had another visitation from my father. I'm afraid I told the others about it before you joined us. But it is all true."

"Let me hear for myself," Joseph insisted. "What did he say?"

"Century IV, Quatrain 82," Caesar responded to his request.

'A throng approaches coming from the land of Slavs,
The old Destroyer the city will ruin:
He will see his Romania quite desolated,
Then he will not know how to put out the great flame.'

"And you think you know how to interpret this one properly?" Joseph questioned.

"No, I don't think, I know. When I interpret this one, I'm afraid it is not good," Caesar explained. "We are that throng approaching from Slovakia where the two girls were murdered. You are the old destroyer, or more correctly, in this case the son of the old destroyer. It is suggesting that when we enter into Romania it could be your downfall. Not in the city, which is your natural domain but in the desolated area; in our case, the forest. It is saying being city bred, you have no survival skills to manage the wilderness."

"I possess the same skills that the rest of your possess," Joseph argued. "Which is practically none, but your father doesn't seem too concerned about the rest of you."

"Because like your father, you are the key to our success for this mission. Somewhere in this wilderness of Romania we will identify the source of these murders, that much I do know, but once we have discovered the answer it will consume everything and everyone like a fire that we can't put out. Everyone, including us, will be burned as a result of what we find."

"Or it could mean that we are on the right path, we will find our answers in Romania, which has suffered so much already from these atrocities that it is desolated and once we identify the guilty, there will be many that will pay the price for their complicity in these murders. Those responsible will be consumed in flames and it is not a threat at all to those that weren't involved," Joseph provided an alternative explanation. "That's how I interpret it."

"But are you willing to take the risk and put the one you love in danger by having her close to you on the mission in case you are wrong?"

'Love.' It was a strange word to hear pronounced out loud. Joseph had not really thought about it. When he first selected a daughter of his family's arch-nemesis it was primarily out of revenge. Yes, Reisel was beautiful but she was also very young and innocent. At first he felt guilty about his selection, making her pay the price for her father's sins. But now...now he realized he liked having her near. He enjoyed their talks, as limited as they may have been on this journey, but inwardly he felt as if he had found a soulmate. Someone he could talk to freely and who understood his thoughts and emotions immediately. At first, it may have been the fear that if they were apart her father would find some way to steal her away and take her to some far off place where he wouldn't be able to find her but now it was more a case that if she was not with him, he would feel terribly alone. He needed her. He needed her to be there when he wanted to communicate his anxieties, celebrate his happy moments, experience and share whatever life threw in his direction. This must be love, he realized. And because it was love, he knew the decision he had to make.

"Reisel," he held her tenderly by her shoulders. "You will listen to me now. What I say to you now may hurt but realize that I say it because I care for you deeply. I care for you more than I can ever explain in words. And when a man cares...a man loves...a woman the way that I do, he would never place her in danger. So you will do as your father says. You will stay safely in the Countess's castles until I return for you. We will meet again in Brasov. I promise you, it shouldn't be long. For the next few days we will travel together to Oradea but that is where we must part for the time being." Turning to the Count, Joseph wanted to know why they still couldn't travel all together to the next destination. Thurzo tried to explain that he had made the decision to separate now in order to travel faster as the other carriages slowed them down, but Joseph was not willing to accept the excuse, overruling the Count and ordering that the other carriages be prepared and their horses hitched as well. The Count had no other choice but to agree.

"I don't want to be apart from you," she became tearful.

"That will never happen. For the next few days we will travel together and once we separate, then you will always be here." Joseph tapped the left side of his chest.

Standing on her toes she extended her face upward so that Joseph could kiss her lips.

"Remove your hands from my daughter immediately," Lipmann came rushing in their direction only to be suddenly grabbed by the long hairs of his graying beard rather roughly by Paulo Sarpi who had been listening quietly to the two lovers.

"You know Rabbi, I have been stabbed seventeen times but each time God refused to let me die. I wonder if you would be so lucky."

"Are you threatening me," Lipmann pulled his beard from Sarpi's grasp, visibly shaken by the magistrate's words.

"Of course not," Paolo answered. "I'm just wondering how much your god actually loves you. If you continue insisting on interfering in permitting their love to blossom, then we might actually find out the answer to that question."

"You will be held accountable for this affront," the Rabbi insisted.

"Actually, I won't be. I'll let you in on a little secret. The Archduke said to me that if you become too much of a problem I'm to make you discretely disappear. Do you understand what that means?"

Looking horrified, Lipmann nodded his head and retreated a few steps from Sarpi. "But you're a man of justice."

"I'm a man that upholds the law," Sarpi clarified. "To a Venetian, love is the ultimate law that supersedes all else. Are we clear?"

Rubbing his chin to diminish the pain, Lipmann continued to nod.

"Good. I'm glad we have an understanding," Sarpi commented. "Now remember, not a word of our little discussion to anyone. I would simply deny it anyway but in the end, it wouldn't work out well for you. So while we are off on this mission, you will remain on your best behaviour and we will find you and your daughter waiting anxiously for our return. Do we have an agreement?"

Practically paralyzed with fear, Rabbi Yom Tov Lipmann began nodding but the uncontrollable shaking of his entire body made the nods hard to distinguish.

"Now stand here, say nothing, and let our two lovebirds have their moment," Sarpi grinned, baring all his teeth in a vicious grin as he did so.

It was already the second day and almost sixty miles from Oradea, when the lone carriage and its military escort reached the fringe of the Hoia-Baciu Forest. Count Thurzo suggested his men take a brief rest before they challenged the heavy darkness that spread out before them, oozing eerily from the dense rows of trees. Everyone dismounted and gathered around the small fire that Thurzo's men were fueling with dried branches from the surrounding area.

"I think it's best we review the next details of our journey gentlemen," Count Thurzo began the discussion. "The most direct route to reach Brasov as we know it, is through this forest. If we were to circumvent the mountains as the other carriages will be doing, it would add and additional two hundred and fifty miles to our journey. I don't believe any of us wish to spend another week traveling the countryside under these conditions simply because we believe in ghost stories. But I will warn you now that you will feel things, you will see things, and you will hear things in this forest that will upset you. That much I know to be true about this forest."

"What sort of things are we talking about Count Thurzo?" Caesar wanted to know in advance.

"Many have said that they become disoriented when they enter this forest," Gyorgy Thurzo began counting off the list of complaints people have had in the past that they attributed to this dark, foreboding place. "Others say they have even suffered burns or scratches from unknown origin. But I think they are just so frightened they easily forget about the thorns and thistles that line the paths that they probably brush up against unwittingly as they flee from the forest."

"That is all?" Caesar had been expecting to hear far more serious evidence.

"Not exactly," Thurzo continued telling the tales. "There are stories of disappearances. People that have entered the forest never to be seen again. There's one story of a shepherd boy and his entire flock that disappeared from the face of the earth. The locals tell you to look out for the black fog because it is seen as a sign of impending danger but exactly what that danger is, they never say. Then there are the stories of the lights that flash all about you, but the origins of these lights cannot be identified. Naturally they attribute these lights to the fairy people. Again, such things as fairies are nothing but childhood legends that no one should take seriously. Then there are the voices on the wind, the moving trees, but fear is known to make people see and hear what isn't there. Granted, the trees are strangely shaped and the vegetation is bizarre in its appearance but that just fuels vivid imaginations even more."

"Count Thurzo is correct," Fra Paolo Sarpi confirmed. "There are no poltergeists or ghosts or goblins my friends. They are merely stories to frighten young children. But we live in a wonderful age of scientific discovery, and our science tells us there are no such things, except in our imagination. So have no fear, we shall be fine," he reassured them.

"Just one more thing," Gyorgy Thurzo advised, "As you probably noticed, the paths through the forest are narrow. They were never intended for heavy travel. It won't be easy but the carriage should make it through the thirty-five miles of heavily treed land without a mishap. It will be slow going and will probably take us the rest of the day. But if something should prevent the carriage from reaching the other side, then we will unhitch the horses and leave the carriage behind. I do hope the three of you know how to ride."

Now they were scared. Not because of the hidden dangers of the forest but the fact that two of them had never learned to ride and Caesar hadn't been on the back of a horse in a very long time. Sensing their nervousness, Thurzo dismissed the issue by saying that the probability of their needing to ride was practically non-existent. He just raised it as a precautionary notice.

Speaking to his men, Thurzo warned them against becoming separated. "When we do enter the forest I need everyone to stay clearly in sight of the man in front of you. We will light the lanterns but in a fog they still may be difficult to see. Don't let yourself fall behind because if you stray off the correct path, you might not be able to find us again. Is that understood?"

"Yes Sir," the unit of twelve men responded in unison.

"Enough rest, let's mount up and be on our way," Thurzo commanded. "Dominic and Sergei, take the lead and scout out front around fifty feet. I will follow along side the carriage. The rest of you will follow behind. Pietro and Julius, you have the rear but don't fall behind more than twenty feet. The sooner we are through this, the happier everyone will be. Understood?"

"Yes Sir," came the reply from all the men in the unit.

"We are also in agreement," Paolo Sarpi responded on behalf of the three of them as they climbed into the carriage and quickly shut the door after lighting the internal lantern.

Riding up along side the carriage, Count Thurzo leaned in through the open window. "I think it would be best if you have your animal ride in the carriage with you," he suggested. "That way if there's anything unusual nearby, he'll sense it first and you'll recognize it immediately from the way he's acting. Then you signal me. I'll be riding right along side you. You may want to close the shutters on the windows. You know what they say, 'What you can't see, can't hurt you.'"

Taking the advice, Joseph opened the carriage door and whistled for Wolf to jump in. As soon as the wolf-dog had settled onto the cabin floor, Caesar quickly locked all the shutters in place. The Count signaled for the contingent of men to start moving into the forest, trotting his horse to a position several yards distant from the rolling carriage.

"Childhood legends my ass," Caesar commented. "The man is just as afraid as the rest of us. Why else would he ask you to bring Wolf inside with us to act as some kind of early warning detection."

"A mere precaution," Paolo tried to reassure his companion. "Don't read anything more into it than it actually is."

"If there's no such thing as the supernatural, then you will a very hard time explaining what the link is between myself and my dead father," Caesar both stated and challenged Paolo Sarpi to explain the phenomena with his scientific knowledge.

"I don't have an explanation at this time," Sarpi evaded answering, "But given enough time, I'm certain I could find one if you would like."

"Yes, it is called the inexplicable," Caesar decided to provide him with the answer. "There are some things in this world that defy explanation! We need to admit that. Even Giordano, for all his love of science had to admit that."

"Gentlemen, can we all please remain calm," Joseph urged both of them to settle back into their seats and just relax. "Trust me, if there is anything unusual out there, then Wolf will definitely let us know."

"As I said, the dog is merely a simple precaution. Nothing else," Sarpi restated. "By twilight we will have made it through the forest and you will both see that there was never anything to have been concerned about."

"I further suggest we all just take a rest, shut our eyes, and when we awake, we should be well on our way to the other side of this desolate forest," Joseph advised. "We all know it is unlikely to be haunted."

"Unlikely but definitely a possibility," Caesar pointed out the fact that even Joseph refused to say that the forest was absolutely not haunted.

"A poor choice of words on my part," Joseph tried to correct his error. "Let us all just take a rest and forget we are even here."

"An excellent suggestion" Paolo Sarpi agreed, hoping that would be the last word they shared in regards to the forest being anything else but a grouping of grotesquely twisted trees.

They three had no idea of how long they had been asleep when they were abruptly jolted awake as the carriage was brought to a sudden halt. They could hear the voices of men shouting excitedly, their hollers echoing back and forth between the trees, making it impossible to determine the direction the voices were actually coming from. Opening the shutter covering one of the windows, Paolo Sarpi tried to peer outside and see what was causing all the commotion.

"What do you see," Caesar asked nervously.

"Absolutely nothing," the magistrate replied. "This must be the black fog they talk about," he determined. "It is as thick as soup. You can't see more than a few feet in any direction."

"Something must be wrong," Caesar was certain. "They wouldn't be shouting like that unless there was a serious problem."

Looking immediately at his animal, Joseph noticed that Wolf did not appear overly agitated, responding to the loud noises much as any other dog would, showing more curiosity than fear. "Whatever it is," Joseph advised, "There isn't any threat to us."

"And exactly how do you know that?" Caesar questioned.

"Wolf says so," Joseph replied. "If he doesn't sense a threat then there isn't any."

"Maybe so," Paolo responded, "But there is definitely something wrong out there. Count Thurzo!" he shouted. "Count are you out there? Where in hell is he? I can't see anyone!"

They stared out the open window but they were lucky if they could even make out the faint outlines of trees. The light of the day could barely penetrate the fog, assuming that it was still day, which they could no longer tell and the light from the lantern within the cabin couldn't illuminate more than a few feet past the window. They kept staring into absolute nothingness when suddenly a face appeared in the window. All three jumped away from the window reflexively, only to laugh awkwardly when they realized that it was the Count staring in at them.

"What's happening?" they asked simultaneously.

"We've had a terrible accident," he informed them. "Sergei was riding up ahead, scouting out a clear path through this fog, when a tree fell just in front of him. His horse became startled, falling backwards and crushing Sergei beneath it. I'm afraid it crushed his chest. He survived for a short time afterwards but we lost him. Tragic. Terribly tragic! There was nothing we could do."

"We are sorry to hear that," Joseph responded. "As you said, a tragic accident. Right?"

"Nothing supernatural," The Count reassured them. "Trees naturally fall. But now it will take us some time to clear the tree from the path," Thurzo replied. Then we'll wrap the body and as soon as possible I'll have one of my men take him back to Budapest. His family deserves to give him a proper burial."

"Can we do anything to help?" Joseph offered their assistance in removing the tree.

"I fear that if you step out of this carriage you are going to get lost in this fog. Best you just stay where you are. My men will remove the tree and we will be on our way within the hour. This bloody fog has to lift eventually." Having said that, Count Thurzo pulled the reins in his hand to the left and trotted off into the fog, leaving the three within the carriage staring into emptiness.

Paolo knew what the others were thinking and decided that he better quickly put an end to it before their imaginations ran wild. "A perfectly normal event as the Count said. Tragic, yes, but trees in a forest do fall down all the time."

"Yes, but what are the chances that a tree falls in the forest, precisely at the time a rider would be beneath it? I've been to forests hundreds of times in my life, "Caesar continued, "And I don't believe I have ever seen a tree fall. I admit I would see lots of fallen trees but never actually see one of them fall."

"The chance of it happening when you are there I agree is slim but as you pointed out, you have seen them after they have fallen perhaps hundreds of times. It would therefore not be unreasonable that the next time you visit a forest, you would actually see one fall." Paolo Sarpi tried to explain the laws of probability as simply as he could.

"I have to agree with Paolo," Joseph rested a hand on Caesar's shoulder to calm his older companion. "Tragic but nonetheless a natural event. Living on the streets of Brody, one learns that life and death are doled out in unequal proportions. Not fair, but that's the way it is. We just wait and soon we'll be on our way."

Shortly after he felt the touch on his shoulder, it was as if Joseph hand shot a powerful current through Caesar's body. He immediately seized both sides of his head, pressing upon his temples as he writhed in discomfort, his face bearing an obvious mask of pain.

> '*The one whose face is splattered with the blood*
> *Of the victim nearly sacrificed:*
> *Jupiter in Leon, omen through presage:*
> *To be put to death then for the bride.*'

"Another Quatrain?" Paolo asked, already knowing the answer.

"Yes," Caesar barely could get the words out between anguished breaths. "Century II, Quatrain 98. We are under attack! One has already been splattered with blood. More to be sacrificed!"

"By trees? Seriously?" Sarpi ridiculed the warning, finding it hard to accept the prophecy at face value."

Grabbing the lantern, Joseph began pushing his companions towards the carriage door. "Get out of the carriage. Get out now!" he demanded they move immediately.

Sarpi initially objected to both being manhandled, as well as leaving the security of the cabin but had little choice after Joseph swung open the door and using his foot forced him through the opening. Grumbling his displeasure, Sarpi took a few steps from the carriage before they all heard the sharp snapping of splintering wood, like the crackle of a lightning bolt. As soon as the three looked upwards to find the source of the threatening noise, they found themselves tumbling backwards from the door of the carriage, as a massive tree limb fell across the top of their cabin, shattering the carriage in half as if it were made from balsa. Their carriage driver was not so lucky, buried beneath the colossal branch along with the remains of their transportation.

"You knew?" Sarpi turned to Joseph dismay.

"Either I heard the initial break, or just had this feeling, but I knew we had to get out immediately," Joseph responded.

"Is that enough blood for you?" Caesar asked, the croaking fear evident in his voice. "You can argue all you want about trees falling naturally but these 'wooden columns' as my father said are targeting us!"

This time the Venetian magistrate was silent, staring blankly at the huge branch that had obliterated everything where they had been sitting just moments before.

Thurzo appeared looking panicked as he emerged from the thick wisps of rolling fog. "Is everyone alright?" No sooner did he ask, he saw the carriage driver lying motionless, caught between the tree and the remains of carriage's jump seat. The force of the impact had snapped the central spar pole like a twig, so that only the harnesses and reins kept the four black horses from running loose in terror. "Everyone, just stay where you are and I'll get my men to clear this."

"You do that," Joseph commented, "But I have no intention to just stand here while being attacked by trees. This is no longer a mere coincidence. Caesar's father just told us that if we don't start moving out from here right away, then this mission is doomed and if we fail, then the Empire is doomed as well."

"So you're suggesting we just leave everything and run," Gyorgy Thurzo wanted Joseph to clarify his stance.

"We run, but we run towards our destination. We need to finish this mission more than ever. We can't turn back," Joseph commanded. "Take the dead back to Budapest, and have them send more men. I think we're going to need them. This was no accident!"

"I need to get my bag," Paolo Sarpi overcame the shock of having seen the carriage destroyed and moved towards it. "I need to write a letter to the Medical College in Budapest." Searching through the wreckage, Sarpi found his traveling bag and then rummaged through it to find a piece of paper and his writing utensils.

"Come with me Caesar, I need to check something too," Joseph instructed Caesar to follow as he went around the carriage with lantern in hand, nimbly making his way through the fog that hung to him like a second skin.

"What are we looking for?" Caesar was curious as to what Joseph was thinking at the moment.

"Anything," was Joseph's answer. "If it doesn't look like it belongs, then it must be a clue.

Closely examining the trunk of the tree from which the limb fell, there was nothing glaringly out of the ordinary. Though difficult to see through the fog, where the actual limb splintered from the trunk, nothing looked unusual at that point either. As much as Joseph didn't want to admit it, the falling limb was beginning to look like a natural occurrence. 'Rather than searching for answers above, perhaps there were clues much closer to the ground,' he thought. Joseph examined the earth around the base of the tree but once again, neither he nor Caesar could find anything out of the ordinary. Spinning away from the base of the tree frustrated and at a loss for answers, Joseph caught in the corner of his eye, a weak reflection of the lantern's light illuminated by a thin layer of snow that remained on the ground from the flurry that fell a couple of days earlier. Walking slowly towards the small patch of snow, Joseph knelt to get a closer look, mindful to avoid having the heat from his lantern melt any remaining evidence that might be there.

"Caesar, come here quickly!"

His older companion came quickly over, only to find Joseph's outstretched arm preventing him from moving forward another inch. "Careful, my friend. You're about to destroy the only evidence we have of this accident being suspicious. Bend down and look at this."

Getting down on his knees, Caesar scrutinized the patch of snow that Joseph was protecting. "Footprints," Caesar analyzed the impressions. "Very small footprints. Like those of a woman"

"Obviously someone else is here in the forest with us," Joseph speculated. "Probably watching us right now."

"How can that be," Caesar was still doubtful. "We saw no one and surely if there were other horses nearby, we would have heard them. How could someone else be here if they weren't riding a horse?"

"Not if they tethered their horses a distance from here and were waiting for us to pass this way," Joseph surmised.

"But they're the footprints of a woman," Caesar was still doubtful.

"Or a boy," Joseph added.

"It makes no sense for either to be out here in this wilderness. Unless you now are believing in hobgoblins," Caesar suggested.

"It doesn't make any sense now, but I'm certain we will start putting the findings together soon enough. Whoever it was knew that we'd be passing this way. We need to tell Thurzo about this."

"Tell him exactly what?"

"We're not alone," Joseph replied. "In some way, the person or people behind the murders are aware of our mission and they are determined to stop us."

Returning to where they had left Paolo Sapri and Count Thurzo, Joseph explained his findings but still could not provide any answer as to who would be trying to kill them. "I think your front rider was an accident. I think that first tree was designed simply to stop our progress and line up our carriage with this tree."

"You're suggesting that someone had designed a kill zone with the three of you as the target," Thurzo analyzed Joseph's hypothesis.

"Yes, I believe so," Joseph confirmed.

"But there was no guarantee your carriage would even be aligned with that limb," Thurzo countered.

"Paolo, would it be possible to cut into a tree in such a way that you can predict exactly when and where the branch will fall?"

"I'm a magistrate, a lawyer, and a scientist," Sarpi replied. "Not to mention a former priest, but what you are looking for is an arborist. That is not a job I recall seeing in my repertoire."

"But is it possible. As a scientist, what do you think?"

Sarpi shook his head. "I doubt it. Someone would have to force the break at the required time. As for the direction, yes, thy could make their cut in such a way that with the correct application of pressure at the right spot, the branch would fall where they want it to."

"So you are saying that the person responsible would have to be in the tree at the time the branch fell," Joseph extrapolated from Paolo's comment. "Not only to make certain it breaks off at the time they want but also in the direction they need."

"Yes, that is exactly what I'm saying," Sarpi confirmed.

"In this fog it would be incredibly easy to avoid being seen, even if the individual was mere yards from us," Joseph continued formulating his theory. "What about shearing the limb itself. Would it be possible to cut the limb free from the trunk and still make it look like a natural break."

"Well, if one is expert enough with an axe, then I guess it would be possible."

"Could a young boy do it?" Joseph began stringing his thoughts together.

"I doubt it," Paolo thought for a moment and then shook his head. "The weight of this limb alone would suggest it would take a very strong person to chop through it. Any child would have to have the strength of Hercules."

"A dwarf," Caesar blurted. "A dwarf could probably do it."

"I presume so," Sarpi agreed. "He would have the strength of a full grown man, even if he doesn't have the size.

"Certainly could explain the small footprints," Joseph connected Caesar's suggestion to the evidence they had found.

"All the fables talk about dwarfs that live in the woods," Caesar postulated. "He wouldn't need a horse if he lives somewhere in this forest."

"And why exactly would anyone live in this forest," Sarpi questioned Caesar's explanation.

"Senor Sarpi, you of all people I thought would have been familiar with the writings of Straparola or Basile. Were they not Italian's themselves? In their folk tales, the elements of evil always dwell in the forest because there they can live undetected." Caesar knew his folktales.

"Firstly, I am Venetian, Monsieur de Nostradame and secondly, those two are writers of myths, not reality."

"Behind every myth is some basis of truth," Caesar advised. "The same rules apply to them as they do to my father. Behind the words they write is an elemental truth."

"I'm not certain about that," Joseph rebutted Caesar's last comment. "I can't see why a dwarf living in a forest would be trying to kill us. If there is a dwarf involved, then there has to be more to this," Joseph argued. "There has to be a connection to our killer, we just haven't ascertained it yet. What about the letter you wrote, Paolo? Anything to do with identifying our killer?"

"Merely a feeling I had," Sarpi explained. "If I should get an answer, then I'll have more to say about it. But right now it is nothing more than an infinitely small afterthought that has been nagging in the back of my head for some time."

"Well don't expect that answer any time soon," Count Thurzo threw cold water on any expectations Paolo Sarpi might have had. "It will take my man some time to get the dead back to the city. Then we are talking at least a month before a fresh unit of men will be able to join up with us. I'll see to it that they carry with them any reply to your letter, but we might be getting closer to an answer to this mission's success and that is the reason whomever is out there is trying to stop us. Now gentlemen, I think our most pressing concern will be how well you can ride a horse."

Chapter Ten

Oradea; February 1610

Reisel sat in her boudoir, before the French Louis XII style dresser, while one of her handmaidens brushed her long chestnut coloured hair repetitively. Earlier that morning she had seen the carriage off that was carrying Joseph towards the reportedly haunted forest of Hoia-Baciu. Her normally sparkling emerald eyes were now red and swollen from the tears she shed fearing that he might not return. She had been unable all day to shake the feeling of dread from her mind, feeling the heaviness that pressed unrelenting upon her heart.

As her other handmaid searched through the wardrobe to find an appropriate night-dress, there was a knock on the boudoir door. Before either handmaid could respond, the door was already opened and the Countess Elizabeth allowed herself into the room. With a wave of her hands she shooed the handmaidens away, while taking the brush from the one and then proceeding to brush Reisel's hair by herself.

"Why is the little bird crying so?" she asked, inviting Reisel to speak out and unburden her heart.

"I'm so afraid that Joseph will not come back," she said tearfully, wiping away a droplet that was resting on her right cheekbone, her lips protruding in a heart rendering pout.

Picking up a linen handkerchief, the Countess carefully dabbed the girl's face. "Careful my dear," Elizabeth cautioned her, "You don't want to crease this beautiful face. What would your beloved Joseph think when he returns and sees your face all drawn and wrinkled?"

"But I miss him so much," Reisel contended. "I should have stayed with him."

"What foolishness that would be," Elizabeth dismissed her complaint. "How could he succeed in his mission if every minute he had to worry about your welfare. You would have placed both your lives in danger. Your sacrifice of staying behind permits him to focus on the mission."

"Do you really think so," Reisel turned her head to look directly upon the Countess's beautiful countenance.

"I know it to be so," Elizabeth stated confidently. "It was no different between my husband and myself. At first I insisted that I accompany him on every one of his military campaigns. I thought my presence would bring him good luck but instead it only hampered his ability to conduct his battles. Wherever I was stationed meant that he had to ensure the battle was fought in a location far away from me. That in turn limited his options and forced him to engage in battle in locations that weren't of his choosing. My husband would never say so, but I knew that he desperately wanted me to stay behind and way from harm. I eventually made that decision myself but not before it cost him both in lives of his soldiers and in our relationship. If only there had been someone that could have talked to me the way that I can talk to you now."

"I don't want to be a burden to Joseph," Reisel confessed to the Countess. "I want us to love one another for the rest of our lives."

"Oh to be so young again," Elizabeth sighed, "And to have such illusions of what love was meant to be."

"Why would you say it was an illusion," Reisel was curious.

"Because, like you, I was married to my husband at the age of fourteen. Ferencz Nadasdy was a man that every girl dreams of being married to. He was handsome, strong and a perfect gentleman. His voice sounded like a silver strung lyre, drawing you into every word as if he spouted poetry. I don't think there was a happier girl in all of Hungary when we exchanged our wedding vows. But as I grew into a woman, I learned that handsome, debonair and well-spoken young men are always surrounded by beautiful women. They cannot feed their appetite by catching only one fish. As much as I always tried to be one of the most beautiful women in the world, there were always other beds that he found his way in to. I learned that I had to be content with only possessing a part of him and never the whole."

"But Joseph is not like that," Reisel protested. "He will only love me. I can see it in his eyes. He only holds me in his heart."

"I hope so my dear," Elizabeth patted the back of Reisel's hand tenderly. "I pray for you that he is different from other men."

"He is; I know he is," the girl defended her future husband.

"I'm not certain your father believes so," the Countess was still curious about the animosity that existed between the two men.

"That is an issue that bears no relationship to Joseph's character at all. My father detests what Joseph cannot change; the past. Joseph's family represents everything that the Rabbis reject most in this world. Joseph's existence is seen as as an affront to them and a crime against the Lord."

"That is very serious," Elizabeth expressed her sympathy "If they resent that which can never be changed then you will always have their never ending battle raging throughout your life. Perhaps there is something I can do to change your father's attitude."

"Papa does not admit to being wrong easily."

"I never said he was wrong, my dear. The fact is that your life with Joseph will be very different from how you were raised. With his sister's marriage into the aristocracy of the Empire, he essentially has become one of us. You will move in different circles, no longer insulated within your own community as you have been in the past. Your father is aware of that and he probably fears that he is going to lose you."

"I wish it was that simple," Reisel closed her eyes as if reciting a simple prayer.

"There obviously is more between Rabbi Lipmann and Joseph Kahana than what meets the eye," Elizabeth realized. "Some secret from the past that you haven't told me?" The Countess ran her index finger teasingly down the girl's cheek, enticing her to reveal this deep, dark secret.

"I don't really understand it," Reisel revealed honestly. "There is something special about Joseph, something my father fears. I know that in some way the old rabbi of Prague was responsible for the death of Joseph's father but this loathing my father bears is beyond that. I see it every time he looks at Joseph but I don't know the reason behind it."

"Fair enough child," the Countess consoled her. "I will see what I can find out. After all, we can't have your father hating your future husband forever now, can we?"

"You will do that for me?" Reisel was appreciative.

"Of course my dear. Young lovers should be given all the help necessary to succeed. Life is hard enough without unnecessary obstacles being placed in your paths. You and I must find a way to help Joseph succeed in his mission so that you two can be together again. I would do all I can to see that happen but I do not even know the crux of this mission that has torn you apart. As much as I'd love to help, unless I know what task my cousin has assigned to your beloved, there is nothing I can do."

Apologizing, Reisel explained, "We are only to keep the details of the mission between ourselves. That we shouldn't involve others."

Stroking the girl's cheek with the back of her hand, Elizabeth smiled quaintly, acknowledging that Reisel must keep her word. "But I am already involved," the Countess tried a different tactic. "As you heard the other night, two of the girls murdered attended my finishing school. If that doesn't indicate that I am involved as much as anyone else, I don't know how else to prove it. If only I knew what the goal of their mission was, then perhaps I do have vital information available that could solve it for them."

Thinking about the Countess's explanation of why she should be included along with the others that were entrusted with the information, Reisel found it to be both rational and logical. "I guess it wouldn't do any harm," she agreed, "Considering in a way, you are involved. You might even know of some link between the girls that the investigators failed to uncover."

"A very smart deduction, my dear," Elizabeth congratulated the girl for being so astute. The compliment made Reisel blush, here face adopting a rosy complexion. "How absolutely sweet," Countess Elizabeth responded to seeing the reddening of her skin. "A little colour makes you even more beautiful than you already are. So tell me of the mission's supposed outcome and I can see where I can be of assistance."

"It's actually quite simple," Reisel explained. "They think they've identified the killings being related to some kind of ritual sacrifice. If that is so, then there may be a group of people responsible for the murders, rather than a single individual."

"How fascinating," the Countess cooed, "In the manner of a a secret society or maybe even a coven," she gasped.

"Perhaps," Reisel agreed. "Not necessarily dealing in black magic but more of an elder religion involving human sacrifice."

"How absolutely frightening," Elizabeth sounded appalled. "But what has that to do with going east into the forested area of the Carpathians."

"Nothing," the girl replied. "Their destination is well beyond the forest. Something about the Dacians that used to live in the southeast."

"The Dacians!" the Countess practically squealed with laughter. "There haven't been any Dacians in these parts for a thousand years. I could have told them that before they left."

"I don't believe its actual Dacians they're trying to find but to see if there are any reports about someone trying to resurrect the Dacian customs, including the one of virgin sacrifice."

"Why would anyone want to do something like that?" Elizabeth pondered the reasons anyone would attempt to revive an ancient culture.

"I don't know," Reisel laughed. "It sounds rather silly to think that they will find something in the area where the first of the murders actually took place that can actually tell them how this may have all begun."

"Your right girl, that does sound rather silly. Now get some sleep so you can stay young and beautiful and I will talk to your father as promised. Now not another worry about your handsome Joseph. I will see what I can do to help."

"Can I get you another glass of wine, Herr Lipmann," the steward asked as she approached the rabbi sitting on the sedan in the parlour.

"I would be most appreciative," he responded as he held out his cup so that she could pour another. "I must say, that the villagers in this area prepare a most delicious kosher wine."

"We are pleased that you are enjoying it," Erzsi Majorova responded. "It was not easy to convince them to sell it to us but as soon as we mentioned it was for the famous student of Rabbi Loew, Yom Tov Lipmann, they insisted that they give it to us as a present."

"I see my reputation has preceded me in this part of the Empire."

"Most definitely, Herr Lipmann. You are quite famous in these parts."

"Perhaps I should give consideration in the future to seek the Chief Rabbi position of these lands," Lipmann contemplated, having had his ego stroked expertly.

Descending the stairs from the upper landing, the Countess Elizabeth joined her other guest in the parlour. "And what a pleasure it would be to have you in charge of my Jewish communities, Rabbi Lipmann. I'm certain we could achieve great things together within your community if we worked together."

"I would be honored, Countess," the Rabbi was enticed by her offer. "I have thought about finding a more permanent home for my family. It would be good to have a jurisdiction I could call my own."

Moving to a position where she could sit across from the Rabbi, Elizabeth Bathory signaled for her steward to fetch her a cup of wine as well. "Something from my own stock Erzsi, I don't want to deprive Herr Lipmann of the enjoyment of his special bottle."

"Yes Mistress," Erzsi replied as she decanted from a different bottle, then handed the cup over to the Countess.

"I must commend you Rabbi on raising such a wonderful daughter," Elizabeth raised her glass in a toast to Reisel. "She is such a delight. So young and such vitality, you must be very proud of her."

"She has disappointed me of late," the Rabbi blurted out, then suddenly covered his mouth as if trying to stop himself from saying anything else. "I am not sure why I said that...I didn't mean to. But suddenly I feel so sleepy."

"Hardly time to go to bed Herr Lipmann," the Countess advised. "It still is so early. Perhaps a little more wine," she suggested as she winked at her steward to pour another cup for the Rabbi.

"Feeling so tired," Lipmann repeated.

"Plenty of time to sleep later," Herr Lipmann," Elizabeth prodded him lightly under his arm to keep him awake. "So why would Reisel disappoint you Rabbi? She is such a wonderful girl."

"Yes, wonderful but loves him more than me…" his words trailed off as he half closed his eyes.

"Love who Rabbi. Please continue."

"The Kahana. How could she love one of them…"

"I heard the Kahana were great men like Joseph's father," the Countess attempted to tease a response from the Rabbi as he teetered on the edge of sleep.

"Terrible men…So full of themselves…Think they are a gift from God…Terrible," the words stumbled from his mouth.

"Are they not a chosen family by God," Elizabeth challenged.

"Immortal bloodline…sceptre, staff never to fall…live forever."

The last comment peaked her interest. "Why immortal. How is it they live forever?" she pushed him for an answer.

"Family can never die out…never ill...all live above ninety years…not fair. Not fair," Lipmann spat as he silently cursed their name.

"How are they special," the Countess wanted to know.

"In the blood…in the blood," Lipmann repeated as he fell to one side and slumbered.

"How much nightshade did you give him?" Elizabeth asked Erzsi.

"Only a small amount of Devil's Breath," she answered. "He shouldn't have fallen asleep so readily."

"It doesn't matter," the Countess forgave Erzsi. "I got the answers that I wanted for tonight. Tomorrow you can give him a smaller dose. Obviously he is jealous of the lineage that Joseph Kahana possesses. Those born as peasants always want what they are not entitled to. He can't stomach the fact that Joseph's family has been gifted with an immortal bloodline. And with it comes longevity and a natural resistance to illness. Lipmann cannot even contemplate the fact that the same gifts would be bestowed upon his grandchildren. All he can think about is how unfair it is that he was given nothing from God, while thinking himself to be much holier than the Kahana and therefore far more deserving. Blind hatred from a foolish man."

"What is the next step Mistress?"

"I think I desire young Joseph Kahana for myself," the Countess smiled devilishly. "Tomorrow we start sowing the seeds in Herr Lipmann's mind. He will be a most useful tool in ensuring that I have Joseph returned safely to me. Then Joseph can share his immortal bloodline with me."

Chapter Eleven

Haiu-Baciu Plateau: February 1610

Moving between the trees shielded by the heavy fog was made even more tedious by the fact that both Joseph's and Paolo's riding skills were practically non-existent. Caesar still retained some ability from his younger days but nothing close to the expertise of Count Thurzo's men. It hardly mattered, since conditions made anything faster than a walking pace hazardous. Along the trail, no one escaped the sensation that they were being watched, as ridiculous as that appeared to be, since the mist made it impossible for anyone or anything to see more than several yards in any direction.

"Stay close together men," they could hear Count Thurzo shouting his orders, though most could not make out his position in the line. But along with his voice they could hear a cacophony of other sounds, a plethora of noise that was a blend of what almost sounded like laughter mingled with the snarls and growls of wild animals. "Keep moving follow one another," their commander continued shouting his orders, his voice a beacon to those in the rear to focus upon and not lose their way.

Looking up at the sky, the few times that the fog parted let them know that the day had already passed and night was closing in fast. Branches swayed above their heads ominously in the breeze but one could not state with any certainty whether the howling was the result of the wind rushing through the hollows of the trees or emanating from something else, something waiting and watching from above.

Lanterns swayed from the sides of saddles where they were hung, the candlelight casting eerie shapes on the passing landscape. The coronas of light providing the only rays of hope that they would manage to escape the grasp of the unseen danger lurking in the woods. Some of the men had already come to the realization that they should have been already through the forest having ridden for so many hours, which could only mean that they had been moving in circles, criss-crossing the same patches of forest even though they swore they had never strayed from the road. As frustrating as that may have been, they persevered, following the trail set by Count Thurzo, still convinced that they were heading in the right direction.

Another hour passed before they could hear their commander shout that there was a clearing ahead. A euphoric feeling of relief and salvation flooded across the unit as they emerged from the trees and strolled into the clearing. As quickly as that feeling of euphoria had surfaced, so to did the feeling of desperation when they realized that the clearing was not the other side of the forest but in fact a circular area deep in the centre of the forest where nothing grew. They could not help but notice that not even the fog dared to enter this clearing, as if there was an invisible barrier that held it at bay. There was not a single blade of grass or any other evidence of vegetation within the perfect circle measuring fifty yards across.

"Most strange," Paolo Sarpi commented to his companions. "This should not be possible. There is no reason that nothing should grow here."

"We are in the eye," Caesar commented.

"What are you talking about," Sarpi wanted Caesar to explain his observation.

"Just what I said. Just as there is an eye to every storm, this is the eye of the forest. The dead zone, where nothing happens, nothing exists."

"Well we exist and I'm just happy to be out of that black fog," Joseph commented. "I don't care what you call this place, I'm just happy to have the opportunity to dismount and sit for a while because right now my backside is the sorest it has ever been."

Moving to the centre of the clearing, Count Thurzo made an announcement. "Men, we will set camp here for the night. No use trying to ride through the other side of this forest tonight. With a little luck the fog will pass by morning and we will have an easy ride. See if you can find any dried roots and branches from the edge of the forest and get a fire going. I want it kept going through the night. Now if everyone is here, count off and let's make certain of it."

The men sounded off according to the placement in the line but it became obvious one was missing. "Where's Pietro," someone shouted.

"Damn it," Thurzo cursed. "I told you men to stay close and stay in sight of each other. Who had eyes on Pietro?"

"He was riding rear guard Commander," the second to last rider responded. "I saw him occasionally behind me but I was more focused on the rider in front, Sir. Sorry Sir."

"It's alright Julius. You can't be riding forward and looking behind all the time. Get that fire built as soon as possible. If it is bright enough, Pietro will have a beacon to find us. Let's pray that he is fine and not hurt."

With greater impetus, the men in the unit scrounged the edges of the forest, finding enough wood to start a fire. Within a few minutes, there were enough logs and dried out roots to build a strong blaze. Satisfied that the fire was large enough that Pietro would be able to see its glow, even through the fog in the forest, Thurzo ordered the men to begin setting up ground blankets and bedrolls.

"I think I hear a horse approaching quickly," one of the men shouted excitedly. "Pietro, Pietro," the men shouted repeatedly, encouraging their mate to ride in their direction. As Pietro's gray gelding popped its head into the clearing, emerging from the concealment of the fog, they knew immediately something wasn't right. The horses coal black eyes bulged from its skull in terror, as a thick frothy lather coated its mouth and tongue. The sweat was practically dripping from its head and shoulders, but as the rest of its body emerged from the curtain of fog, they all became aware that the saddle was empty, Pietro was nowhere to be seen.

"What in seven Hells," Count Thurzo said in astonishment as his hand snaked out and seized the runaway horse's reins in the blink of an eye. Dragged over a distance of several yards, the Count was able to concentrate the full weight of his body behind the tug on the halter, managing to turn the gelding's head and bring the terrified animal to a stop. The sweat poured down his face and ran down his arms from the Herculean effort of stopping the runaway. His feat was met with awe but it was nothing compared to the sheer shock of viewing the empty saddle and the series of claw marks that tore into the heavy leather and cut deep into the left flank of the horse. His unit immediately gathered around the animal to stare dumbfounded at the oozing wounds.

Joseph stepped forward as well to examine the horse's flank. "There are only two animals that can make cuts like that," he informed everyone, "You're looking at either a bear or a very big wolf."

"Must be a bear," one of the unit's members responded. "Bears stand up on their hind legs to attack. That puts the animal at saddle height. But a wolf will go after the horse's hind legs."

"Yes, but when have you ever seen a brown bear go after a horse," another of the squadron provided his own opinion.

"Look at the width of the claw marks," the first man to speak up argued. "That would take a wolf of incredible size to make marks that wide. It would be a monster, not just a wolf. Most likely in the heavy fog, Pietro must have encountered a bear by accident and the beast acted instinctively. Wouldn't matter then if it was a horse or a deer as far as the bear was concerned. It would only have in its mind that it was being attacked."

The debate raged back and forth between bear or wolf between the men gathered in the clearing. Whichever the case, it was unlikely that Pietro would still be alive. Count Thurzo raised the question as to whether any of his men were willing to join a search party to see if they could find Pietro's remains but he already knew the answer when he posed the question. None of his men were willing to step outside of the relative safety of the clearing and enter the dark, cold embrace of the black fog.

Settling back on the ground, it was not long after that they had their answer to the debate of wolf versus bear. From every direction beyond the circumference of the clearing, the howling of wolves rang through the twisted trees, causing even the bravest of Thurzo's men to shudder in fear. "It's an entire pack of the beasts," the Count cursed as he contemplated their next move. "If we let them into the clearing it will be too late for any of us," he advised. "Men, load your muskets."

Each man retrieved their long rifles hanging from their saddles and began the complex task of loading powder from the horn and inserting the wads before finally placing the pellet down the muzzle with wadding and then ramming the iron balls in place. As soon as they had completed the preparation ritual, Thurzo order them to take positions around the clock face. With only eleven men left, including himself, he turned to the three saviors he was charged with guarding and inquired if any knew how to shoot a rifle. Once again, only Caesar had any experience with firing a weapon and so he was instructed to make use of Pietro's rifle that was still hanging from the saddle. Once everyone was in place, the Count shouted his next order. "Everyone in kneeling position," he commanded. "Remember, we are not firing on soldiers this time. This enemy is much lower to the ground. When I say fire, you fire and afterwards you keep reloading and firing until I say stop. Do you understand me?"

"Yes Sir," came the reply.

"Fire!"

Twelve shots rang out blindly and everyone listened intently to the sounds carried on the wind to see if by chance they hit their targets. All that could be hear was the sound of splintering wood, as the metal pellets ricocheted off tree trunks and buried themselves into either the soft vegetation or clay of the muddied ground. Rifles were reloaded and fired off randomly as soon as each soldier had released the previous round. Sparks from the flints shot high in the air from different positions and at different times, making it totally unpredictable as to which direction was being targeted at any moment. It was exactly what Count Gyorgy Thurzo had wanted to achieve. The rifle fire would most likely cause the pack to band together, running in a single formation, coalescing their total body mass so that the odds of his men hitting a target actually improved. The randomness of the shots would prevent even the cleverest of animals from knowing when to lay low and when to run.

By the third round, the men heard it, a distinct yelp that signaled at least one of the wolves had been hit. Another shot and another yelp, but this time the tricks of the wind made it sound more like a pleading cry for help. The men kept firing, until Thurzo finally gave the order to stop. They listened intently. Nothing but silence emanating from the forest. The wolves were now gone and the men raised a cheer, celebrating their victory over an invisible but lethal enemy.

"Well done, Count," Sarpi was the first to congratulate Gyorgy Thurzo. "I must admit, I thought we didn't have a chance. I'm glad you proved me wrong."

"You were not the only one thinking our luck had run out. It was a desperate play but thank God, it worked," Thurzo replied.

"Keep it up, Gyorgy," Paolo slapped him appreciatively on the back, "And you just may have me believing in God again."

"We wait for the sun to raise and then we'll see what we my have hit," the Count ordered. "For now, I need you to take turns standing sentry while the rest of us try to get some sleep. Keep your muskets loaded by your side. They may be back tonight."

"Do you think that going to sleep is wise right now," Caesar questioned the Count in a hushed tone.

"I doubt anyone will be doing much sleeping," Thurzo responded, "But any rest we can get is better than stumbling around in the forest tomorrow because we're exhausted. We still have to get through the other side of these woods and there's no telling what might be in there."

"Well, that just killed any prospect of sleeping for me," Caesar joked halfheartedly. "No offense Joseph, but this is one of those times I truly wish your father was here. Yakov had this uncanny knack of knowing what to say and what to do at precisely the right time."

"No offense taken, my friend," Joseph nodded. "I too wish my father was here to advise us. All of this is well beyond my comprehension. Truthfully, I wonder why I am here. I certainly am not my father."

"I believe your are here for exactly one of the reasons your father was with Giordano and myself. Your father was the calm in the storm. He could unite people, persuade them to do what was necessary. No matter how bad the situation became, he could find the courage to move forward and he could instill that same courage into the rest of us."

"I don't think that describes me very well," Joseph argued.

"If I may be so bold to offer my opinion," Paolo Sarpi interjected. "I believe Caesar is right. Whether you recognize it or not, you have been instrumental in uniting us together. Without you, I doubt Caesar and I would have ever been able to cooperate. But you somehow bring out the best in both of us. And I don't just mean in having an ability to make sense of Caesar's babbling."

"Hey," Caesar sounded offended. "What do you mean by babbling. Those are my father's quatrains."

"Exactly," Sarpi smiled at his companion. "They are your father's quatrains but when you say them, they are babblings. Yes, whatever your ability, you do manage to say them at the right time and in the right situation, which I do admire, but often it is young Joseph here that has to interpret them. Agreed?"

"When you put it that way, I guess I agree," Caesar concurred.

"And when I might sound a little arrogant, or high-handed, it is you Joseph that manages to reduce the offensive nature my character might generate and thereby making me more tolerable to the others."

"I certainly agree with that," Caesar returned the slight insult in payback to Sarpi.

"And you have insights; insights into a world that is beyond my science, or Caesar's mysticism that manages to unite both extremes into a single focus. Now if you ask me, that is probably an ability that far exceeds any that either of us can do."

"I wish I had an opportunity to know my father the way that you did Caesar. How can I live up to the reputation of a man that I never knew."

"If you'd like, I can tell you about him."

"I would appreciate that greatly."

"Yakov Kahana was unlike any man I had ever known, or will probably ever know again. Everything that Paolo has said about you, your father also had that ability. To unite people, to somehow look into their hearts and bring out the best in each of us. I have never met a man so fearless and self-sacrificing. He gave up his life so that others wouldn't have to give up theirs. But what was most outstanding was his ability to know right from wrong, to see the world in black and white even though everyone kept telling him that he had to live in a world that accepted shades of gray. Where the rest of us would compromise, even sell our souls, that was never a possibility with your father. He was honourable, truthful and no one I know could have ever been more loyal. He never imposed his will on others, even though your lineage would have suggested that would be the natural thing to do. I would go as far as saying that had he been a Catholic, they would have called him a saint. But alas, he was a Jew and the world seemed to make a point of never letting him forget that. That is the man that Yakov Kahana was. And from the moment we met, I sensed that same man existed within you."

"I wish I knew that was true," Joseph sighed dejectedly.

"Trust me," Caesar confirmed, "It is true."

"I believe so too," Paolo Sarpi agreed. "Well let's try to get some sleep even though I doubt that will be possible." Using the bed rolls from the soldiers that were dead or missing, both Caesar and Paolo stretched themselves out in the clearing, attempting to seize any opportunity to rest, perchance even to sleep.

Before long, Joseph found himself sitting upright while listening to the snoring from both his companions. He envied them for their ability to sleep under such circumstances. As far as he was concerned, any chance to even repose was long gone, his mind dwelling on the events of the day and wondering what tomorrow might bring. All he knew was that somehow everything had to be related to the efforts to find the killer. Even the wolves he felt were in some way connected, though he could not exactly pinpoint what that connection might be. Why didn't his dog react this time when the wolves had surrounded the clearing. It should have been a natural response, yet, now that he was thinking about it, the only reaction displayed by Wolf was his dislike of the sound of the gunfire. Most perplexing. And now, there he was, stretched out along side Caesar, sleeping soundly as if he too hadn't a care in the world. In fact, looking about the encampment, everyone was sound asleep. Where were the sentries supposedly standing guard? He failed to understand how everyone could be sleeping when their situation was still so dire.

As his eyes swept around the clearing another time, he noticed the most peculiar light that appeared to be simply hovering above an area in the clearing. At first he thought it may have been cinders, ejected by the campfire and just floating in the air. But that made no sense, as a slight breeze was blowing, but the light never moved, never varied from its current position. Perhaps a firefly, he thought next, but then again, fire flies would naturally flit about and this one didn't. Rising from the small patch of ground he had claimed as his own, Joseph headed towards the light. Though he knew he was walking normally, his progress felt exceedingly slow. He compared it to walking through a bowl of 'galla', the thick gelatin his mother used to make from ground cow's hooves. The more he walked, the longer the distance covered as he approached that solitary light he was singularly focused upon.

It seemed to take forever to cross the clearing but once he did so, he reached out with his right hand trying to grasp the light but as soon as he was about to close his hand, he found himself standing in what looked like a grassy valley surrounded by hills with a river running through it. There was a man standing immediately in his path, not just any man but the one man he thought he had lost forever. "Father?"

He could not explain it, perhaps he was also asleep like his companions and dreaming this entire event. He told himself this was not real and he had to wake up, but no matter how hard he tried, he couldn't. He wondered why he would even be dreaming about being asleep unless he was actually awake. It was a conundrum he couldn't explain. "Father is that really you? How is this possible?"

"How is anything possible," Yakov Kahana answered. "Through the will of God, all things are possible my son. You must remember that and not ever give up hope."

As he stared at his father, he realized that in the intervening two decades, he remained exactly as he remember him, standing tall and erect, with his black spiked beard and long robes of an Eastern potentate. He even was wearing the same leather cap that he always used to wear, the cap reminding Joseph of the pictures he saw drawn in the Haggadah, depicting life in ancient Egypt. "This must be a dream," Joseph repeated to himself. "How else can you be here and looking exactly as you did before you died."

"It is no dream," Yakov responded. "You have entered a nexus point. A place outside time and space."

"I don't understand," Joseph replied.

"I will tell you something that you can repeat to your companions and perhaps then the one called Paolo can explain it to you."

"This must be a dream, otherwise how would you know about the companions I am traveling with."

"Because a nexus point is a window and I have been standing here at this window waiting for you to come," Yakov explained.

"You are saying that you have been standing there for almost twenty years," his son questioned.

"There is no passing of time as you understand time at the nexus point," his father responded. "Only the now. Your past, what would be my future, is currently only the now and the present."

"I still don't understand," Joseph tapped the sides of his head, confused and uncertain of the reality of this situation.

"Tell Paolo that he is partially right," Yakov attempted to explain. "The circle is the key to the universe. Everything from the beginning to the end is a circle. Everything from the smallest existence, less than a particle of dust invisible to the eye to the size of the universe is a circle. And even the universe is merely a circle within circles. At the point of contact where any of these circles meet, is a nexus point, a window as I have explained it. This place, where you now rest is one such nexus point in your world. Wherever I am, wherever that may be, is also one such nexus point. Through this window we can see and hear other worlds but we must never try to use the windows as crossover points."

"Why not Father? Why can't you come to me now."

"Because in your time and space I no longer exist, my son. As I said, where we now stand is a place outside of time, outside of space as you know it."

"Then I will cross over to you," Joseph suggested.

"To do so would mean that you could never return to your existence. You would be trapped in this world, which is not intended for the likes of you."

"I don't understand," Joseph shook his head wildly. "Why are you even here if I can't be with you. Why torment me so, if you cannot help me? Or are you merely a ghost that has come to haunt me?"

"Because I heard that this is what you wished for," his father explained. "The circle in which you and your colleagues are resting is essentially a mystical place, where you can state wishes, and if those on the other side of the nexus can make your wish come true, then it can happen."

"What did I wish for," Joseph did not recall making any wish.

"You wished for an opportunity to know me," his father recalled the event for his son. "I am here because that wish can be fulfilled. As long as this window holds steady you will have the opportunity to do so. And I will have the opportunity to know my son that has grown up without me into a fine young man."

"I have done things father, things you would not be proud of," Joseph apologized.

"And you have done far more things of which I am extremely proud of Joseph. We all make mistakes in life but the measure of a man is not by how many times he falls down but by the number of times he rises back up on to his feet."

Pinching himself, Joseph still refused to accept what he was being told. "This cannot be really happening."

His father laughed. "Then let my friend Caesar tell you that I am as real as you are, but not in your reality. Tell him to look at his own father's proverb in Century VIII, Quatrain 95 when the time is right."

"Century VIII, Quatrain 95," Joseph repeated. "What does it say?"

"It will be the ending to all you seek, so I will let him answer that for you. Tell him that I miss him, we who were one heart, one soul, one mind, we three of a kind. Let him know that he need not fear the end because it is nothing more than a new beginning. His father knew it and that is why the spirit of Nostradamus is always with him."

"What can you tell me Father of our mission. Do you know who it is we are seeking?"

"As I said son, this window is only at the present, in your case my future, in my case your past. I cannot see what has not yet transpired in your world. I only know that I am very proud of you, as proud as any father can be and I know that you will set your companions on the right path. You are the Kahana now and the Lord smiles upon you."

"I have so many questions," Joseph didn't know where to begin to ask them.

"Another time, another place perhaps," Yakov responded. "This nexus point I feel is about to close."

"Wait...wait, you cannot leave me yet."

"Joseph...Joseph, where have you been," Caesar's voice sounded muffled and far away in the distance behind him as Joseph felt himself being dragged backwards suddenly as if there was a rope tied about his waist pulling him through an opening no larger than a pinhole.

Angry and furious with his colleague, Joseph turned on Caesar, spitting out his words as he expressed his displeasure, "Why did you do that? Why did you pull me away from him?"

"What are you talking about?" Caesar considered that the forest had somehow driven Joseph to the point of insanity.

"My father...I was with my father," Joseph shouted.

"Calm down Joseph," Paolo Sarpi placed his hand on Joseph's left shoulder. "I don't know who you think you were with but you have been missing for several hours."

"What are you talking about?" Joseph didn't believe them. "I was right here. I was talking to my father for several minutes, that's all. I don't know what is wrong with both of you, but I have been no where else but here."

"Calm down," Caesar tried to console his colleague. "Look about you, it is morning already. We were breaking camp when we found you missing. We thought you may have gone into the forest to do your ablutions. It would have been a stupid thing to do but it was the only explanation we had for your disappearance."

"That is insane," Joseph continued to argue with them. "I have been here all the time. As I said, talking to my father for perhaps ten minutes at the most."

"I would say that was evidence of insanity," Paulo made a diagnosis, "If it wasn't for the fact that you just materialized in front of us out of nowhere because honestly, you weren't there a minute ago."

"It's true, we were looking everywhere, and one minute you aren't there and then the next minute you are," Caesar confirmed what Paolo had just said.

"Does the little rhyme, 'One heart, one soul, one mind, we three of a kind,' mean anything to you Caesar," Joseph asked.

Upon hearing the words, Caesar fell to his knees and began crying. Both Joseph and Paolo grabbed him under the arms and helped him back on to his feet. "It was him, it was really him," Caesar cried. "I can't believe it but your father was actually here. Why didn't he come to me too," Caesar wanted to know.

"How do you know it was him," Joseph questioned.

"That rhyme is something that only myself, Yakov and Giordano knew. It meant everything and was everything to us. It united us and no matter even if death separated us it tethered us together."

"That's impossible," Paolo Sarpi refused to accept the reasoning. "There has to be another explanation. Perhaps Joseph heard his father recite it when he was a young child."

"He had a message for you too, Paolo," Joseph continued. "He said you are right. Or more correctly, partially right."

"He did?" Suddenly Paolo was almost a believer, "What did he say," Sarpi was eager to hear this message from beyond.

He said, "The circle is the key to the universe. Everything from the beginning to the end is a circle. Everything from the smallest existence, to the vastness of the universe is nothing more than circles. And also there were several circular universes, or something to that effect."

"I knew it, I knew it," Paolo hammered his fist into the palm of his left hand. "I've been trying to explain that to Galileo for years and he has rebuked my thinking. His fear of reprisal by the Church is clouding his mind. Now I can tell him I was on the right track."

"Well I hope you can explain it to me," Joseph suggested, "Because he said where we are standing is a nexus point and that was why he could talk to me from my past to his future. Makes no sense but that is what he told me to say."

"This is so exciting," Paolo was practically jumping for joy. "Have you ever watched a magician do the trick where he has two rings which he holds one in each hand, then he taps them together and their conjoined and then he taps them again and once more they're separate?"

"Yes, I've seen it, but that's merely a slight of hand magician's trick as you said."

"Now imagine if it weren't a trick. Imagine that two separate rings could phase through one another and be linked, and then just as easily be parted once more. The point where they joined would be the nexus point. If you imagine that each of those rings represented a separate world, then when they were linked, however briefly that time might be, each world could see into the other world. There would be an actual bridge." Paolo attempted to make the explanation as simple as possible. "It is a theory I am working on but I have no proof."

"So in other words, wherever my father is now, it was temporarily joined to our world because of this clearing."

"Correct," Paolo confirmed. "His spirit world joined with our world. This is so exciting, But I need proof."

"Sorry to interrupt you three, now that we've found young Master Kahana again," Count Thurzo approached their conference, thus putting an end to their discussion, "But we need to take advantage of the fact the fog has lifted and see if we can find any remains of Pietro while we still have he morning light. Then we have to get to the other side of this forest as quickly as we can before we have any other problems. I expect you three to joint the search. And Master Kahana, at some point I expect an explanation of where you have been for the last couple of hours." Having given his instructions, the Count marched away, joining his armed men in looking for the body, ensuring his men did not go too deep into the forest in their search at the same time.

"He's not going to believe me, will he," Joseph stated the obvious.

"Not in a million years. Guess we better join in the search," Caesar suggested.

"Oh, one last message for you Caesar. My father said Century VIII, Quatrain 95. is important in the end. What does it say?"

"I can't recall," Caesar told them.

"What do you mean you can't recall?" Sarpi questioned. "Don't you bother to keep a copy of your father's books with you?"

"Why would I bother? The quatrains appear in my mind during a time of stress. As I explained to everyone before, they need a trigger in order to spring into my head. Without the trigger, I don't know what is written."

"So unless we find the trigger, you won't be able to recall what your father wrote," the magistrate complained.

"Correct."

"Don't worry about it," Joseph commented. "Yakov said that

when the time was right, you will hear it. Best we help look for the body along with everyone else."

"I have a blood trail over here," one of the soldiers was heard to yell.

Everyone quickly ran over to that location. Pointing at the trail of blood, they all followed the droplets as a tight group, afraid to separate. It wound back into the woods further than they wanted to go, but without the black fog swirling through the trees, the forest appeared quite benign. Following the trail, they could see that it led towards a mound that had been conspicuously overlaid with a thin cover of branches and leaves. The count ordered his men to clear the brush and check on the remote chance that Pietro was still alive. Upon clearing the brush, they gasped and took several quick steps back from the site.

"Who the hell is that?" Count Thurzo wanted to know. Standing over the body, they examined the face closely but it was not anyone that they knew; it certainly wasn't their fellow solider, Pietro. There was no evidence that could provide a clue either, as the individual was completely naked. The cause of death though was obvious as they quickly spotted the entry point of the lead ball mid abdomen.

"Any thoughts on this one?" the Count directed his question towards Senor Sarpi."

Before Sarpi could provide a comment, the men in the unit were uttering the word 'verfarkas'. Those that bore Romanian blood used the word 'varcolac'. Either word meant trouble for the Commander as superstition was clouding over the minds of his men.

"What is a varcolac," Caesar asked the Count, seeing that everyone had mentioned the word with such fear and loathing.

"Nothing but a stupid superstition for the feeble minded," he answered, loud enough for all his men to hear. There are no such things as werewolves." He could repeat that as many times as he wanted but Caesar could see that his men were far beyond believing anything their commander would say now. As far as they were concerned, they were standing over a werewolf and no one could persuade them otherwise.

"Well, let me see what makes a man into a varcolac," Sarpi suggested as he bent down, preparing to examine the body.

No sooner did he reach towards the corpse, when one of the soldiers raised his rifle and pointed it towards Paolo Sarpi's head, while repeating in a very threatening voice, 'varcolac'.

"What is the meaning of this," Sarpi shouted angrily as he stared up at the barrel of the rifle.

"This superstition says that lycanthropy can be transmitted from the werewolf to a man simply through contact. They don't want you to touch the body. Otherwise, they will shoot you before any transformation can take place," the Count explained.

"That's ridiculous," Sarpi exclaimed.

"No," Gyorgy Thurzo responded. "Ridiculous is getting a bullet fired into your head after being told not to touch the body. I might even call it being stupid."

Rising back up from where he knelt, Paolo Sarpi nodded his head in agreement. "Yes, that would be stupid."

"So what do we do now?" Joseph asked.

"We pack up and head towards our next destination," Count Thurzo instructed his men.

"But what about Pietro?" Joseph inquired.

"What about him?" Gyorgy Thurzo responded bitterly. "If he's merely wounded, and laying out there in the forest somewhere, then as far as my men are concerned, he will become one of the 'verfarkasak'. And if he was killed by werewolves, then they will assume there is not enough left of him to fill a bag. Either way they will not look for him any longer. As far a we are concerned, we leave now!"

Whispering into Paolo's ear, Caesar commented. "I told you we should have listened to my father and gathered some wolfsbane."

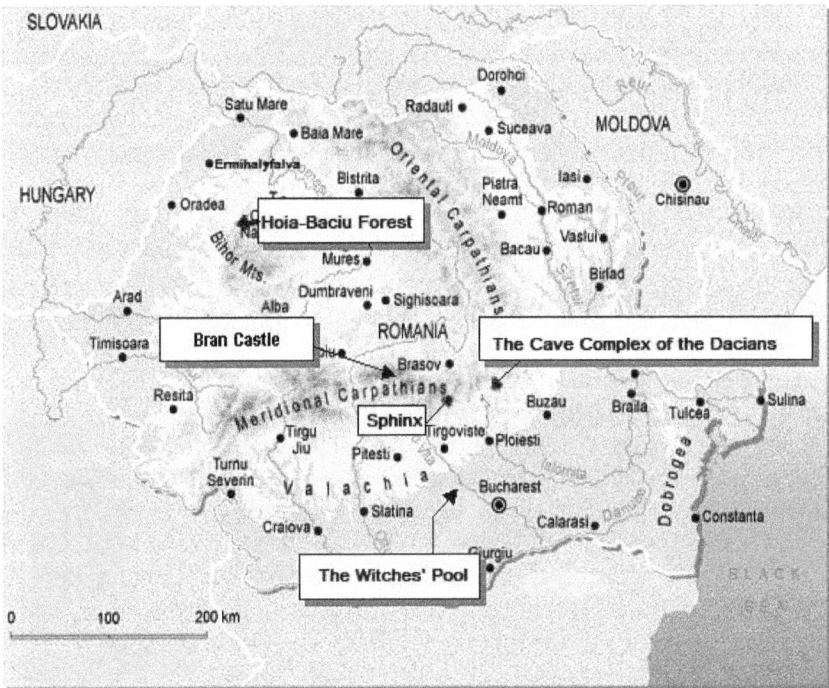

Map of Transylvania and Wallachia

Chapter Twelve

Tirgu Mures: March 1610

As his men rode through the grassed plains in the shadow of the Eastern Carpathians, they barely exchanged a word. Overall it took several days to traverse and emerge from the haunted forests of Hoia-Baciu, Count Thurzo sent his fastest rider along with two dead bodies strapped to the back of a pack horse to his garrison stationed in Budapest. With him the rider carried two letters, one from Paolo Sarpi and the other from the Count, seeking reinforcements. The passage out of the forest had been without incident but by then the damage had already been done. The loss of two men from the squadron as well as the carriage driver had impacted them severely, filling their minds with superstition and thoughts dwelling only on supernatural occurrences.

Knowing that this threat of the unknown would directly impact on the return of his rider with any reinforcements, as they would only travel the safer routes south of the mountains, Gyorgy Thurzo calculated that it would now be at least two months until they arrived. That meant two months of dealing with this current complement of men that had become frightened by their own shadows, jumping at the slightest sound in the middle of the night. Men who could mutiny at any time for the most minimal of reasons, simply because they were frightened by the unknown more than they feared to be court-martialled. Unless he could find the answers on their mission quickly and begin the return journey home, he considered it only a matter of time before the situation would become acute. He didn't bother to express his concerns to Joseph and his companions. No use adding to their own fears.

At times the four of them would sit together and review the facts as they knew them. The initial thoughts of a single killer being responsible for the death of the young girls had essentially been negated by those trying to kill them along the journey. Instead, they were now considered to be crimes committed by an ideological group that essentially believed they would attain some degree of power through virgin sacrifice. An organization large enough that it could dispatch a team of assassins over hundreds of miles, in an attempt to eliminate those attempting to expose its existence.

Whether or not this occult organization was in some way related to the ancient beliefs of the Dacians, they would learn very soon, once they discovered the actual site where the ancient rituals were conducted. Clearly, whomever they were, they were trying to shield their identity by preying upon populace by reinforcing the superstitious fears of vampires and werewolves.

As for themselves, they were convinced that such creatures of the night could not possibly exist, although Caesar wavered from time to time in that belief. But it was easy to see how others could be influenced and manipulated. At times they would overhear Thurzo's men, sitting by the fire, discussing such things as the 'strigoi' or 'elhalott', terms which the Count translated for them as meaning the 'undead'.

But knowing that there was a clandestine organization operating within the Empire, responsible for the murders of innocent young girls was very different from knowing the actual reason why. They knew that unless they could discover the motives behind the killings, it would be almost impossible to uncover the identity of the group's members. Count Thurzo still raised a concern that it was politically motivated, based on the identity of the girls selected from the aristocratic families but Joseph would disagree, reminding him of Thurzo's own points he raised against that possibility because originally the girls were all from peasant stock. No, these killers sought a different kind of power, he insisted.

The effect of the murders within the religious structures of the time had already begun, with Catholics and Protestants accusing each other of being responsible, and then both uniting at times to accuse both Jews and Gypsies of being the perpetrators. Reports of pogroms and death squads at various villages throughout the Empire were becoming routine. Thus far it was being contained but as far as the three saviors were concerned, Cardinal Melchior Klesl was correct in his assumption that they were living on the precipice of Armageddon. One spark and the religious leaders among the people would begin the battle to end all battles, as they burned each others holy houses to the ground. But how would anyone gain from such an event? The answer to that question eluded them. It was just another piece of the puzzle they needed to identify.

Paolo Sarpi repeatedly emphasized the fact that whoever was involved in this sinister organization must have connections within government or how else would they know the details and route of their mission. Only someone close to the Archduke or even the Emperor would have access to that knowledge. But the Count disagreed with his assumption, insisting that the palace was nothing more than a hotbed of gossip and there were rarely any secrets that actually remained secret for very long in Vienna. Using his cousin, Erzsibet Bathory as an example, he accused her of being a notorious gossip that for years had knowledge of almost every political, military and diplomatic mission that was undertaken within the Habsburg Empire. Once she possessed the knowledge, then it was easy to assume that everyone else would know the details because she could never keep a secret herself. That was why he was not surprised when she sent her men out to receive them on the road and invite them to the castle. Thurzo had been expecting it from the moment they left Vienna and would have been surprised if they had not been intercepted by her patrols along the way.

Caesar de Nostradame was more direct in his analysis. Arguing that once you eliminate political or religious motivation as reasons for this mysterious occult organization, then all that was left was a pursuit of wealth. The others argued against that option, noting that at no time did money appear to be an issue, since the peasant girls had none to offer, and the aristocratic girls were never held for ransom. Caesar still considered it a crucial factor, arguing that wealth does not necessarily equate to money. Something of value he stated is not always measured in silver or gold. What these men were accumulating held a greater value to them, he surmised, even though the rest of the world may think differently. He was still confident that once they found the Dacian holy place, they would have a better understanding of what this alternative consideration of wealth might be.

One thing they all agreed upon was that the mission had taken upon itself a life of its own, growing far beyond the initial scope as had been presented, possibly now involving people at the highest echelons of power. Such a thought was inconceivable when they first arrived in Vienna but now, considering all they had experienced, it seemed quite possible.

"Unless you do give consideration to the remote chance," Caesar would suggest from time to time, "That we truthfully are dealing with supernatural forces at play, and there really are nests of vampires and packs of werewolves."

"You can't really believe that," Sarpi dismissed his suggestion.

"I know it is hard to believe but remember there really was a Golem responsible for those murders in Prague. Sure, he turned out to be human after all, but he was far from being normal. He had a strength and agility that I can only refer to as extremely unnatural. Superhuman in fact. Furthermore, it is an undeniable fact that people still gather on occasion in covens, purporting to practice witchcraft and to worship Satan, so why couldn't there be people that do the same, believing in their own minds that they really are vampires or werewolves."

"Because witchcraft is a real crime," Count Thurzo tried to explain the legal issue. "Those people that practice witchcraft have existed since the dawn of time. Even the Bible mentions them as being a real entity that must be prosecuted and eliminated. Didn't Saul go to the witch of Endor? Why would the Bible mention witches if we weren't to believe they actually existed. But there is no mention of vampires and werewolves in the Bible, so therefore, they do not exist."

"Witchcraft was only knowledge that others didn't understand at the time," Sarpi disagreed with both their arguments . "What we can do as an alchemist and a scientist today would have had us burnt at the stake as witches just a century ago. Right Joseph?"

Having avoided the discussion regarding the supernatural thus far, Joseph felt compelled to participate, now that Paolo Sarpi left him no other option. "Yes, there are those with special gifts. To deny that would mean denying Caesar's father had talents and insights beyond most men. My own father reached out to me beyond time and space at the clearing and there is no denying of that by any of you. But I think what we must learn from this discussion is something that Caesar indirectly mentioned and thus far we never gave it a second thought. I ask you now, how could we not have thought of this before?"

"What are you referring to?" Caesar asked, surprised just as much as anyone else that he had said something illuminating.

"Think about it. What Caesar identified is that these people of like mind can only function and achieve their purpose if they can gather together. Call it a coven, a nest, or a pack, it doesn't really matter. You can call them a herd of sheep for all I care but what is important is that they must seek one another out, they must find each other in order to gather. We have been looking for an individual, much like your needle in the haystack you constantly refer to Gyorgy, and now we recognize we must look for a group, which would be more like a rock hidden in a haystack and that is something we should be able to find. But for a group to survive, it must have a leader. We must think of what would be necessary for an individual to not only originate such a group but to nurture it as well. That person we already know requires certain attributes in order to succeed."

The others nodded, realizing that Joseph was perhaps on to a significant change in strategy but needed further clarification.

"Perhaps the members of this group come from across the political spectrum, or they are from different religious backgrounds, or financially they range from being wealthy to extremely poor, but none of that matters because what unites them is this cult of sacrifice and whatever is the promise the leadership makes to its adherents outweighs their differences. The leader holds the key."

"Find the promise and we find the followers," Sarpi guessed at the message Joseph was trying to deliver.

"Not exactly," Joseph corrected him. "Find an unexpected gathering and we find the followers. If someone reported they knew of a few hundred people gathering in a building, and those people were from all different walks in life, we would all say that is strange, true?"

"And then what," Count Thurzo decided to throw some cold water on Joseph's deductions. "Are we to arrest them all without cause or reason, just on the suspicion that they may be doing something wrong. We need to catch them in the act of committing a crime."

"I'm not suggesting we can arrest them. But we could find out who invited them there. Or who owned that building. Because the person that made it possible for them to gather would likely be the leader that we'd be looking for. Identify the leader and then we might be able to identify what is the motive behind the killings. Establish a motive and then you can make the arrests."

"Perhaps it's a good theory," Thurzo conceded, "But unless Caesar can magically pull names from his father's prophecies of who might be holding an unexpected large gathering, we won't be any closer to finding those responsible."

"But we do have some basic facts we can work with," Joseph defended his statements. "We already know from their attacks against us that they have structure, they have organization, and that suggests there must be someone in charge of them that has wealth and power to pull them together. But that person at the top of this haystack expects to gain something more through the reward of performing the ritual sacrifices of these girls, since power and monetary wealth are meaningless to them. They already have that."

"You make this organization sound as if it is already in power," the Count was offended by the insinuation that it could be overseen by a highly placed government official, like himself.

"Maybe it is," Joseph insisted. "But what I do suspect is that it will take someone with the right amount of money, the right number of connections, and the right amount of land to support the gathering of people in this cult. They need a place big enough and secure enough where they can meet without being discovered. They need enough money to bribe the right officials to turn a blind eye. But most of all they need to be at the right level of power that people are afraid to suspect them or even if they do suspect, not to speak up."

"Then you must be suggesting we look at someone in the aristocracy," Sarpi contemplated Joseph's logical trail of thinking.

"Or as Caesar can confirm when he was with my father in Prague, someone as rich as an aristocrat but not a nobleman."

"Castles, palaces, perhaps even cathedrals or synagogues" Caesar listed off several of the places he and Joseph's father, Yakov, had to investigate.

"But this time I believe we need to look at remote places, well beyond public scrutiny," Joseph refined his thinking. "Places so large and far away that you would tire of opening doors before you find the one that leads to their sacrificial chamber. I'm afraid Gyorgy, if that means someone in the aristocracy, then that is where we must look."

"You are accusing the very people that have sponsored you to find the killer in the first place," Thurzo reminded Joseph that he was actually working for those people he was referring to. "Why would they bother if the trail was going lead back to themselves?"

"I'm not specifically accusing the Royal family of any wrong doing," Joseph was quick to point out, "But there are thousands of aristocrats in the Empire that are not directly related to the Habsburgs. We may be just looking for one out of that that thousand."

"Yes, and there are hundreds if not thousands of castles within the Empire as well," Thurzo was quick to add. "It would take a lifetime to search all of them,"

"Maybe we can get some help," Joseph had another thought. "Perhaps we can enlist additional support in our task."

"Are you suggesting who I think you might be suggesting," Thurzo was clearly unhappy if he guessed right in what Joseph was now thinking.

"As you said, your cousin is a notorious gossip but she also is a very sociable woman that likely is in communication with many of the lesser nobles in the Empire that constantly seek her favour. She may hear things and know things already that can point us in the right direction."

"And as one of the leading aristocratic families in the Empire, why would you think Erzsibet would betray any of the nobles if they did confide in her information that would assist us?" her cousin asked. "Let me explain something to you, Joseph, that you may not be aware of concerning nobles such as myself. We may have our disagreements, and our families may literally be at war with each other, but when an outsider, someone who is not of the nobility, attacks any of us, we will stand together despite our squabbles. Erzsibet has absolutely no reason to tell you anything she might know. It would be to her disadvantage."

"True," Joseph responded. "But I have this feeling that the Countess Elizabeth may be far more cooperative than you think."

"Then there must be something else you must know about my cousin," Thurzo instructed Joseph. "My cousin can't be trusted in regards to anything she might say. She can look you in the eye and lie to you just as easily as others tell the truth and you would never know the difference. She could give you a name of someone she had a falling out with, just to see them hang and then confiscate their property. Do you really want to trust someone like that?"

"That is a possibility," Joseph agreed, "But we can't afford to overlook any information that she might be able to offer, whether it be true or false."

"I still think this is a very bad idea," Count Thurzo expressed his concerns.

"I agree," Sarpi added his opinion. "I can't explain it yet but there is something telling me that she may not be all that she appears to be."

"And what do you think Caesar," Joseph wanted to know. "Do you agree with them."

"She definitely has some inexplicable affect on me whenever she is near, that much I can say. But clearly we need help. Twenty years ago we could turn to Emperor Rudolph for that help. He was our anchor. Perhaps the Countess is meant to be our anchor this time.

"I say that when we return to Brasov, we must tell her everything we learned regarding our mission and see if she can assist in making sense of our findings," Joseph expressed his opinion. "We need someone socially active within the aristocracy that can let us know when they hear or see something out of the ordinary."

"I doubt very much Erzsibet can be that someone but I will concede to your suggestion," Thurzo reluctantly agreed.

"I guess we have no one else to turn to," Paolo Sarpi accepted that the Countess Elizabeth could prove cooperative and beneficial.

"I'm hoping we can convince her, but before then, we still need more evidence that proves beyond a doubt that we are searching in the right direction," Joseph reminded them they still had much to do.

"Actually, I believe the only direction we need right now is to know where the Dacians had their sanctum," Caesar advised. "We can worry about the rest later!"

"And we must find it quickly," Thurzo cautioned. "I don't know how long I can keep my men in line. They are convinced we are dealing with monsters in the night. When men become that afraid, it's not long before they start thinking about desertion."

After several days of riding across the plain, the contingent of men under Thurzo's command came across a relatively small caravan of traveling gypsies. Though only consisting of about twenty wagons, they thought it best to give the nomads a wide berth, to avoid any direct contact. The Roma or Gypsies as they were commonly known, had no love for authority and Count Thurzo knew that any meeting between the two groups could easily turn into a confrontation. They were all in agreement to avoid an encounter until Caesar suddenly experienced another episode of his father's making contact. Practically falling from his horse, had it not been for Paolo Sarpi quickly riding to his side and catching him as he slipped from the saddle, Caesar might have been severely injured.

"Are you alright?" Sarpi asked deeply concerned at the sight of his stricken colleague.

"Yes, I am now that you caught me," Caesar smiled in gratitude. "But more importantly, we are not to let the Gypsies pass without speaking with them. It is important that we engage them."

"I'd ask how you know, but I guess I already know that," Sarpi responded.

"My father instructs us to pay attention to Century II, Quatrain 54," Caesar advised:

'By a strange people, and of these distant Romans,
Their great city after the water is much troubled,
Girls without very different domains,
Their leader, a blacksmith does not have order.'

Nodding his head, Joseph also knew exactly what Nostradamus was advising. "It's is clear that he wants us to talk to these Gypsies. Strange people and distant Romans could not be construed to mean anything other than the Roma. I didn't know they had a great city. I always considered them to be wanderers," Caesar commented.

"Once upon a time they did have a city," Sarpi informed the others. "Some say it was on the Indus river and after the city was destroyed in a great flood, they took to a life of wandering."

"Well, that certainly explains the second line. And the next line suggests they may know something about all the girls from different parts of the Empire that were murdered," Joseph reviewed the third line from the Quatrain. But what does the blacksmith have to do with anything?"

"I don't think we have to be surprised that is probably the main reason my father is requiring us to speak with them."

"We must approach them very carefully," Thurzo warned. "They will not necessarily welcome our presence."

"You mean the presence of your men," Sarpi confided in the others. "Considering you enslave their people, it is not surprising," .

Count Thurzo chose to ignore the comment, instead riding ahead so that the could extend greetings to those sitting in the lead horse-drawn *vardos*.

Speaking in a mixture of Hungarian and the Romani tongue the Count addressed the man he assumed to be the *bare-roma*, or chieftain. "*Sastimos Phral*. I wish no harm to your *tsigni vitsa*, myself and my men, we come in peace. May your *tsigni vitsa* remain strong and may you live for a hundred and twenty years," Thurzo provided the usual greeting between strangers.

"*Sastimos*. What do you wish from us *Gazho*?" the leader referred to Gyorgy Thurzo as being 'the other' and not as brother. "We have done nothing wrong," he quickly added as he watched the soldiers in Thurzo's unit approach. I am the *vaida vitsa*, the leader of this clan and I can attest we have done nothing to offend the authorities."

"I ask *phral*, my brother, only that I be granted permission to speak to those of your *kris*. It is a matter of great urgency."

"Since when do you refer to us who you consider *marime* as *phral*?" the caravan leader expressed his distrust of the Count's warm words.

"I have never considered the Romani to be *marime*. Your way of life is not offensive to me. I only wish to speak to your *kris*.

"There is no council that travels with our caravan. Only the *Dya-Bulibasha*." The leader referred to the elder-woman of the *vitsa*, that would act as judge, spiritual leader and shaman of their family.

"Then may we speak to the *Dya-Bulibsaha*," Thurzo requested.

"And why would she wish to speak to a bunch of *Gazhos*?" the man replied in refusing any access to the old woman.

"Because the *marturo* said she must speak with us. Or does she wish to offend the *mulo.*" Thurzo used the threat of being haunted by the spirit of the dead Nostradamus as the pretext for their meeting. After years of dealing with the Gypsies, he knew their worst fears derived from their superstitions.

"One moment. I will talk with her." The leader brought his wagon to a halt and then climbed into the back of the covered *vardos* to speak with the elderly woman.

Several minutes later he emerged from the covering of the wagon and addressed the Count with her response. The *Dya-Bulibasha* says that she can sense two men that ride with you are conduits to the spirit world. She is intrigued why men of such power would seek her out. Follow along with us and when we establish camp, then she will speak with you.

The Count and his men fell in behind the last wagon of the caravan, which kept a steady pace along the road heading south-east, not readying camp until the sun began to set. He knew it was custom that first they must partake in a meal together and only after that could there be any trust between the two parties. He instructed his men to do nothing that would be taken as an affront by their hosts. Eat whatever they served, drink whatever they poured.

Once they arrived at what they considered a secure location, the Gypsies quickly established a fire to keep them warm through the night and upon which they could cook their prepared food pots. They waved for the Hungarian soldiers to come sit by the fire and share in their meal. The *bogacha* or flat-bread was distributed to all, along with a wooden bowl containing *fusui eski zumi,* the traditional bean soup. Everyone from the Count's contingent were delighted to have something warm fill their bellies. Especially Joseph, who had been surviving thus far on dried beef and stale bread because of his dietary restrictions. Next came the *bokali*, thick pancakes stuffed with pieces of chicken and finally the *lovina*, gypsy beer, to wash it all down.

As the meal came to an end, the *bare-roma* approached Count Thurzo and passed on his message, "She will see you now." Signaling to the three others, he indicated for them to follow. They were escorted to the back of the *vardos*, pulling the heavy brocade curtain aside and climbing the two wooden stairs into the wagon. In the glimmer of the candle light, sitting on a stack of cushions behind a low table made from oak, sat the *Dya-Bulibasha.* Even in the dim light of the flickering candles they could see that she was ancient, an old and haggled crone that already had one foot in the grave. Through cataract eyes she gazed in their direction but whether or not she actually could see her guests was questionable.

"*Besh!*" she commanded in a frail, creaking voice, which the *bare-roma* immediately translated the term as meaning 'sit' in Hungarian, which Thurzo had to translate for the sake of his companions into German. They all found a comfortable spot, covered in cushions where they could fold their legs without any difficulty. Looking about the wagon, they were impressed by the wool carpets that covered the floor boards, and the thick drapes that covered the walls, keeping the draft from entering. Overall, the *vardos* was quite comfortable and decorated pleasingly to the eye in green, yellow and red objects. Even lacking her full eyesight, the old woman poured six cups of *chao* without spilling a single drop. "Tea" the leader explained as he placed a cup in each of their hands.

It was the old woman that spoke first, welcoming them with the usual expression of '*sastimos*'. *Sastimos* they all responded. She asked a question concerning the *koro Romni*, which she immediately answered on her own before it was translated.

"She asked if you were wondering why a blind woman would be sitting with candles lit," the leader of the caravan translated. "She responded that even the blind like the feel of the heat from the flames upon their skin."

"*Chindilan de lungo drom kasht?*"

"She wishes to know if you are weary from your long journey through the forest," the gypsy translated.

They were surprised that she knew that they had come through the forest wilderness. Thurzo was immediately suspicious that it may have been men from her caravan that had attacked them for how else would she know their route of travel.

"*Draburav tu humishagos kesali!*" the old woman responded as if she could read the Count's thoughts.

"She says that she knows because she can sense that you have disturbed the forest spirits," the *vitsa vaida* translated.

"Tell her I meant no offense," the Count claiming that they were '*mora*' or friends.

"She knows that," the chieftain said without bothering to translate, "Otherwise she never would have invited you into her home. She told me earlier before we ate, *mulengi djila bi lacho*, that she had heard the spirit songs of these three," he pointed at Joseph, Caesar and Paolo, "and they were not good. They are the Janus, yet they don't know which direction to look?"

"The Janus?" the Count looked confused as it was a word he was not familiar with.

"Yes, the Janus, the ancient three headed god that could see through time," the Gypsy answered. He pointed at Joseph and waited for the old woman to tell him what to say. "This one she says can see into the past; the memories and thoughts of his ancestors." Then he pointed at Caesar and waited for her to speak. "This one she says can see into the future, but his vision is not always what will be but what can be." Finally pointing at Sarpi, he had a much longer story to tell. "And this one can see the present," he continued. "He is the bridge between the past and the future, seeing what happens today in a new framework that is free from the prejudices of the past. Together they can be a formidable weapon but they still need to be forged into that singular sword. You need to find the *chokesarava*."

"In other words they need to find the blacksmith," Thurzo responded, recalling the quatrain that Caesar had recited earlier.

"Yes, a blacksmith" the Gypsy repeated now that Thurzo had provided the word in Hungarian.

"And where can we find this blacksmith?" the Count asked that the question be relayed to the old woman.

"*Varekai,*" she answered succinctly as if the one word would solve all their problems.

"Wherever," the chieftain translated.

"What exactly does that mean?" Thurzo needed her to explain. "Wherever is not exactly a place we can point to on the map."

"*So keres*?" she asked, not even waiting for the translation of the Count's question, knowing in advance what he had asked.

"She says, where is it that you intend to go next."

"We are looking for the holy place that the ancient Dacians used for their rituals."

"*Bi lacho, bi lacho,*" she responded as soon as the chieftain translated the location provided. "*Armaya bengalo.*"

"She says that place is cursed by the Devil," the chieftain translated. "It is not a good place."

"That's hardly a surprise to us," Count Thurzo laughed off the warning. "But if she knew why we had to go then she would understand we have no choice in the matter."

"*Me djan. Detlene*" the old crone's voice shuddered.

"She says she knows. You are called by the spirits of dead children."

The others were surprised by her ability to delve into their minds when the Count translated what she just said. How could she possibly know about the girls that were murdered?

"Not your minds," the chieftain explained once Thurzo retranslated their thoughts, "But your fortunes. My grandmother is what you would label as a *chovexani,* a witch, but like that one there," he pointed at Joseph, "She is gifted to see the aura that surrounds you, which let's her see short distances into one's past or near future."

"I have no such gifts," Joseph refuted the description. "I may know the things my father told me but that is all I have ever claimed to see." Gyorgy Thurzo translated Joseph's words into Hungarian.

At that moment the ancient raised her gnarled hand and pointed a crooked finger at Joseph. She raised her voice until it was shrill, angry and impatient. "Because you need the blacksmith to forge and then hone that sword. For so long he has denied the *chachimos*, truth about himself. He keeps himself hidden beneath the basket, but he has the *trushal odji*. There are hungry spirits within him. He cannot deny who he is. And that one," she pointed at Caesar next, "His entire life has been controlled by the *drane svatura*. He has let superstition and the supernatural control his life rather than take control of it himself. He is gifted far more than I am to see into the future, yet he denies himself the opportunity to do so." And this one, she then pointed at Paolo Sarpi, "Where is his *pakiv de Devel?* He has no longer any respect for God. In his effort to run from God and embrace his new found science he has forgotten that God is the supreme scientist of our world. He has abandoned his true calling and because of that his mind remains in confusion. Until he can reconcile what lies in his left hand with his right, he is as broken as the other two."

"What did she say," Paolo asked, knowing that she had just finished speaking about himself.

Waiting for the translation from the chieftain, Thurzo explained, "Basically she says all three of you are broken. The only way I'm guessing that we are going to solve these murders and survive this quest is having all three of you reach your potential and you aren't able to achieve that until we meet this person they refer to as a blacksmith."

Reaching into the pouch beneath her skirt, known as the *posoti* she removed a short belt from which hung a series of gold coins and told her son to give it to the Count.

"What is that for?" Caesar was curious about the strange markings on the coins.

"She says I must wear it at all times on my wrist. When the time is right, it will be payment for this mysterious blacksmith."

"First time I've ever seen Gypsies giving something valuable to someone else," Sarpi remarked, doing so somewhat condescendingly.

"She has heard the screams of the young girls for a long time, she says. She is hoping that she can buy herself some peace before she passes into the spirit world herself."

"But we still do not know where we can find this Dacian holy place," Sarpi reminded his companions. "If she fears the place then she must know where it is."

"Tell your grandmother this," Sarpi instructed the chieftain. "We are most grateful for this belt of coins and I promise we will do everything possible to silence the screams once and for all. But to do that we must know the location of the Dacian Holy Place."

In her response, Thurzo heard her use the word *armaya* over and over again, emphasizing how much the place was cursed. Her hands were quite animated as she provided the details to the chieftain. When she completed outlining the directions, her grandson then gave his best effort to translate her instructions, but even he admitted that some of what she said did not make sense. They were to continue towards the southeast until they came to place the Ialomita was birthed. On their left they would see the camel. Walk towards the camel's tail and look into the hollow in the tree. The hollow will show them the doorway to Hell. That is where they will find what they are looking for.

"Where will we find this blacksmith, she spoke of," Thurzo inquired.

Her answer was equally a cryptic. "When they find the secret of the Dacians, they will know where to seek the blacksmith. *Me dikh ruv*."

"She asks to see your wolf," the chieftain requested that they bring the animal into the wagon.

Joseph whistled for Wolf to jump into the *vardos*. No sooner had Wolf entered into the wagon, he immediately approached the old woman and lay his huge head in her lap. "Amazing," Joseph sounded astonished.

"What is?" Caesar immediately asked.

"That is most unusual," Joseph commented. "He never takes to strangers that easily. I've never seen him do that."

Relaying what Joseph had said, the *bare-roma* replied, "Because the wolf knows his own. My grandmother wast birthed under the totem of the *ruv*. This wolf totem made her one with their kind. That is how she knew there was a kindred spirit waiting outside her wagon."

The old woman began to talk again as she patted Wolf's head.

"She says that this one has been confused. As a dog he knew not his own kind. Like other dogs they associate with their human family and become individuals. That is why a dog will see other dog's as a challenge to their territory and first meet them fiercely. But of late he realizes that you are not his kind. He has caught the scent of his kind and recognizes that he is not part of your family but of theirs. As part of the pack he no longer has a sense of preserving his own territory because he knows it belongs to the others."

"Which would explain why he failed to alert us to the presence of other wolves in forest," the Count surmised. "What is she doing now?"

"She makes the *draba* to give him *zor*. A spell to have the strength to resist the call of the pack and maintain his individual identity. She says he will need to remember who is his family if you are to survive."

"Tell her we are most grateful," Joseph responded once he heard the translation.

"Now go and feast with the rest she says," her grandson commanded. "She is an old lady and needs her sleep."

Bowing deeply they left the *vardos*, taking Wolf with them.

"Time for *saviako* and more *lovina*," the chieftain slapped Count Thurzo on the back as they were welcomed back into the circle of the feasting gypsies.

Chapter Thirteen

Bran Castle: April 1610

It was almost noon when the first of them managed to wake, holding their heads in anguish and fighting hard the urge to vomit. Looking around, Joseph noticed that other than their small contingent of men, the Gypsy caravan was gone. Not a single trace of them having been there remained. Even the tracks from their horses and carts were barely visible as an indentation in the grass, suggesting that they had left several hours ago.

"What was in the beer?" Joseph asked as he held his head, feeling the after-effects of drinking all night.

"Wasn't the beer," Gyorgy Thurzo responded. "The fruit in the desert we ate is soaked in pure alcohol before they roll it together with the cottage cheese and raisins into a pastry."

"Well that explains why I couldn't stop eating them," Paolo Sarpi admitted, "But perhaps you can warn us next time before I go ahead and eat a dozen of them."

"Let's pray there's not a next time," Joseph muttered.

"Well, I feel fine," Caesar exclaimed to the others "Shall we think about finding this Dacian holy place now or are you all going to sit here moaning and complaining?"

"Why aren't you affected," Sarpi asked.

"I'm French," Caesar replied proudly. "Practically every desert we make is soaked in alcohol. That *saviako*, or whatever they called it, was nothing compared to the *chocolade mille feuille* my sister would make. So shall we go?"

"Yes...yes," Thurzo answered. "Give my men some time to break camp and we'll be on our way."

Shortly afterwards one of the soldiers alerted his commander to the fact that the two extra horses that they had remaining after they abandoned the carriage in the forest were no longer hobbled where they had left the others tied up. Asking if he should take some men to retrieve the stolen animals, Thurzo told him to stand down and let it be.

"It would appear our hosts demanded some payment for their hospitality," Count Thurzo informed his three companions. Holding up his left hand, he shook the gold coins tied around his wrist. "But in all fairness, I think we can call it a fair trade. Now does everyone still remember what the old crone told us about where we should start looking?"

"I believe she mentioned we should go to the place where the Ialomita is birthed. I am presuming that she is referring to a river?" Paolo guessed.

"That she is," Gyorgy Thurzo confirmed. "It lies where the two ridges of the Carpathians come together. Where the Meridonals conjoin with the Orientals."

"And how far is that," Sarpi asked.

"About one hundred miles as the crow flies," the Count calculated. "But it won't be that easy. We are on the north side of the ridge and the river actually lies on the south side. We have to cross over those mountains. I hope the three of you are prepared to climb."

"Is there no other way?" Paolo Sarpi was a bit reluctant to start mountain climbing at his age.

"The only way to circumvent the mountains is to travel the gorge of the Olt River as it cuts through the Meridonal Range."

"And what is wrong with taking that route?" Sarpi still pressed for an alternative.

"Besides adding another three to four days to the journey, the gorge is known to be treacherous for several reasons."

"And crossing over a mountain with two old men in tow isn't treacherous."

"I'm not that old," Caesar said in his own defence. "But just to be on the safe side, what are the dangers if went the way of this gorge?"

"In winter, the terrain can be dangerous," Thurzo began listing off the difficulties. "The ground can slip at any time. We'd never survive the fall from the paths. And secondly the paths can be narrow, barely enough room in some places for a wagon to pass. Should there be other travelers coming the other way at the same time, then it becomes a major problem, often resolved in a fight to the death. Third, the gorge tends to be the hideaway for numerous gangs of thieves. The considerable growth of tress and bushes on the slopes gives them plenty of places to hide. If they think you have something of value worth stealing, they will not hesitate to attack. As I said, the extra few days isn't the issue, it's the other problems that I'm concerned with."

"Well I vote that we take this pass through the Olt River Gorge,"

Paolo cast his vote. "What do you two say?"

"Somehow the appeal of climbing up and over a mountain isn't that appealing after all," Caesar slapped his knees as if to say they were making the decision for him.

"I guess you are the decision maker Joseph," the Count turned to his last resort to select the faster route.

"We've lost so much time already, a few more days is not an issue," Joseph crossed off the first objection. "Dangerous paths? Well we managed to survive a haunted forest. Can't be more dangerous than that. Narrow pathways don't concern me. I think there is enough of us here that it would deter anyone from challenging us. And lastly gangs of thieves? I doubt they will bother us for two reasons. It is pretty obvious that we carry nothing of value and we will have enough rifles on view that they would be foolish to attack. I also vote that we take the gorge."

"In deference to your decisions, that is what we will do gentlemen," Count Thurzo acquiesced. Then may I make another suggestion as well. Since we will be passing within twenty-five miles of Castle Bran when we are outside the village of Sibiu, that we send a couple of men to retrieve provisions from my cousin. It means adding one more day to our journey but we have already run low on supplies."

"Splendid idea," Joseph agreed. "But I would like to be one of those men retrieving supplies."

"It is too dangerous," Thurzo tried to discourage him. "There is no telling what could happen along the way."

"We are talking about an additional day, Gyorgy," Joseph argued. "I am accompanied by one armed soldier and one very intimidating wolf. What could possibly happen?"

"I am responsible for your safety," Thurzo refused.

"And I, from what I have been told by the Archduke, I am in charge of this mission. Therefore I am making this decision and I will bear full responsibility."

"Then I am sending two men to accompany you," the Count insisted. "See to it that you stay alive."

"I will try my best," Joseph remarked. "So let us press on to Sibiu, so we can get this over with as soon as possible.

The journey of fifty miles to Sibiu was uneventful. Setting up camp outside the village, they prepared Joseph for the short ride to Bran Castle in the east. Count Thurzo provided his men with last minute instructions, advising them that they were to protect Joseph Kahana at all costs. Calculating that it would take four hours for them to reach the castle, it would already be getting dark by the time they arrived. That being the case, they would stay the night and return early the next morning with the necessary provisions.

Joseph was excited by the prospect he would see Reisel again. With all the time they had lost in the forest, crossing the plains and drinking with the Roma, there was a good chance she would be there already. What was supposed to be a mission of only a few months in total had already been over two months without even reaching their intended destination. He wondered how he was going to explain to her that she would have to wait even longer for his return and even much longer before they could travel to Vienna, where they could celebrate their wedding. Not even formally engaged and he was already thinking of the excuses he would have to use to explain the postponement. He envied how simple everything had been for his sister's marriage to arrange. He began to think that perhaps their relationship was not meant to be but then he quickly dismissed those thoughts from his mind. Between being attacked by demonic trees and horrifying werewolves, once she knew of these events, how could she not forgive him for any delays they had suffered?

As soon as they could see castle Bran in the distance, Joseph could feel the cold sweat rolling down his temples. It was only then he realized that he was afraid. Afraid that this young girl whom he had fallen in love with would now reject him. That having been apart for so long, she had reconsidered and decided to take the option he had always left open to her, to cancel their engagement and return home with her father. In his conscious mind he thought of turning around and riding back to their camp outside the village of Sibiu. There had been no one encountered on the road thus far and he was certain there wouldn't be anyone on the way back either. But it was his subconscious mind that kept him from fleeing. It told him despite their age differences, regardless of their religious backgrounds, they were meant to be together. That in some way God had ordained it and he had nothing to worry about. 'It is meant to be' he kept repeating to himself and he rode forward.

Whereas the castle in Ecsed was considered sinister looking in its outward construction, Bran Castle was simply, for lack of a better word, daunting. Built in medieval times as a stronghold to protect the trade routes across the Carpathian Mountains, Bran Castle was expanded in the fourteenth century to withstand the surging forces of the Ottoman Empire. It was such a formidable structure, that even after the Ottoman Turks took the capital of Hungary, Bran Castle with its massive walls withstood the full force of the attack by Suleiman the Magnificent.

Joseph gazed upward to see it sitting on its rocky precipice, like a brooding giant with seven towered structures capped with blood red ceramic scales. Its brick walls the same colour as the gray storm clouds that dotted the sky above it; each walled section distinctly marked by their different epochs of construction as seen by the variety of bricks stacked one atop the other. It was clearly evident that Bran Castle was designed to keep out all those that were uninvited. One look at the formidable structure and it was no wonder that Suleiman the Magnificent could never lay conquest to its defenders. Small square windows dotted its walls, and as Joseph approached he felt that from behind each one there was a pair of eyes watching his every move. It made his skin crawl, but he pressed on, thinking only about Reisel who he hoped would be waiting eagerly for him inside.

Ascending the conifer lined road towards the base of the central tower, expecting to find the entrance gates set into the white stone wall, the riders were met only by impenetrable ashlars that comprised the first ten feet of the building. From the weathering of these stones, it was obvious that they had been there for at least four hundred years and would likely be there for four hundred more. The trail around the base of the castle was narrow, permitting only two horses to walk abreast of one another, as they searched for the entrance. Circling around the back of the castle, the edge of the precipice dropped dramatically, a fall straight down of at least fifty feet. They decided it was best to walk the horses along the edge single file, rather than chance a mishap if one horse accidentally bumped into another. Even Wolf stepped gingerly along the stone path, weary that if any of the horses kicked out intentionally, he would not survive the fall. Midway, on the back circumference of the castle wall, they found the stone portico that was sealed shut with a wrought iron gate. The sentries at the gate demanded to know who was requesting entry. Providing his name, they did not hesitate to raise the gate and let Joseph pass; they had been expecting him. Once in the plaza, the three riders dismounted and handed the reins of their horses to the two stable boys that were waiting patiently. The boys would see to it that the horses were watered and fed, as they led them to the stables.

Shouting excitedly in the manner that young girls do to express their joy, Reisel careened out the castle door and into Joseph's waiting arms. She had no reservations as she stretched on her toes so that she could kiss his dried lips. It was obvious she was trying to extend the kiss as long as possible before her father would appeared and make her stop. "I am so happy to see you," she expressed herself gleefully. "I was beginning to think you would never return. Papa tried to tell me that you were most likely dead and that we should return home but I knew you were still alive. I could see you in my dreams. I knew you were coming back for me." She could hardly control her enthusiasm, grasping Joseph's hands and dancing around him playfully only to have her joy suddenly interrupted.

"Have you no shame girl," her father yelled at her as soon as he exited the castle. "That is how a strumpet behaves! Dancing in front of men like some Jezebel. Stop it immediately, do you hear me."

She released Joseph's hands, but instead grabbed his left arm as she stood beside him. "Sorry Papa," she apologized. "It was just that I was so happy to see that my Joseph had returned to me. God had brought him back to me Papa."

"Bah," her father spat. "God had nothing to do with him," her father was still consumed with bitterness. "If God had anything to do with this then he would have granted my prayers."

"When will you learn Herr Lipmann, that God oversees everything that I do and he obviously wishes nothing to do with you?" Joseph could not resist antagonizing his future father-in-law.

"It is Reb Lipmann to you and you are nothing but a pariah in God's eyes."

"And you are merely an accident that gave life to the woman that will now share the rest of my life, so remember for that reason alone I will tolerate your poisonous attitude and let God take pity on you. But these past couple of months on the road I must admit have changed me somewhat, and although I may tolerate you now, it does not mean I will suffer your belligerence." At that moment Joseph made a decision. Speaking to the two guards assigned for his protection, Joseph instructed them to find out in which room Herr Lipmann resided, and to secure him within until such time that they left tomorrow.

"They won't hurt Papa, will they?" Reisel expressed concern for her father as he was forcefully led away, one guard under each arm.

"Do not worry my little lamb," Joseph reassured her, "They will not hurt him. But I hope you understand that I cannot have him interfering with us during the short time that I am here."

"What do you mean?" she sounded confused by his statement.

"I have not actually returned. My mission is still far from over but I prayed you would have already arrived here as I needed to see you to tell you that in person. I know it is longer than I said it would be but I need you to promise that you will still wait for me."

"You said it would be done quickly," she reminded him. "Now you say you need to go away again? How long am I to wait this time?" Tears welled in her eyes as she could not hide the fact that she was upset.

"I don't know," Joseph replied apologetically. "All I know is that I prayed all these weeks that you would still be waiting for me and now I will pray however long it takes that you will not forget me."

"Am I to become an old maid waiting for you?"

Joseph could not resist laughing at her question as he looked into the sea green eyes of a fourteen year old girl.

"What is so funny," she asked, stamping her foot as if to suggest she was furious.

"I promise you that I will not be that long," Joseph smiled. "Perhaps a few more months at best, maybe sooner. But I swear that nothing in this world will keep me from coming back to you. I will find you wherever you may be. You have my promise."

"You better, or I will never forgive you," she warned him.

"What is this I hear," the voice of Elizabeth Bathory interrupted their little spat as the Countess emerged from the front door of the castle and stood upon the wide stone stoop.

"Countess," Joseph turned and bowed.

"Ah, what did I say about calling me Countess," she shook her finger as if to discipline him.

"Forgive me. Elizabeth," he corrected his address, "I am surprised to see you here. I thought you were sending Reisel and her father on alone while you returned to conduct your finishing school."

"I must admit that had been my intentions but when we failed to see you returning as expected, I could not leave your lovely fiance' alone to face the unknown, especially with her father suggesting that you had met your demise on the road. It would have been cruel of me to let her suffer like that. So I decided that I must keep her company and raise her spirits. Plus I have enough household staff in Cachtice to operate the school efficiently in my absence."

As she emerged from the covered porch, she extended her hand. Joseph experienced that same strange feeling when he kissed her hand as he did back in Vienna. The desire not to release her hand was strong, but he resisted the urge, taking a deep breath and backing away.

"I am so grateful that you have cared for Reisel so diligently. I worried about her every day. Had I known that you were here to protect her and raise her spirits, I would have worried a lot less."

"Yes, the Countess has been very good to me," Reisel confirmed. "I don't know how we shall ever repay her kindness."

"Don't be foolish, Reisel" the Countess waved off any offer of repayment. "You have already given me more than I could expect. With my three daughters all married off and living in their husband's estates you have filled that hole in my heart that was left behind."

"Still, I can never tell you how much I appreciate you taking special care of Reisel," Joseph continued to express his gratitude.

"Now come inside," she invited them to leave the courtyard and follow her. "You must tell me everything that has transpired in your mission thus far. And where is everyone? Why are the rest not with you? I hope they are all fine."

"Of course," Joseph reassured her. "It is just that the mission has not gone exactly as planned and we needed more supplies if we are to continue it. I volunteered to retrieve them so that I could see Reisel."

Leading them to a small salon, Elizabeth reclined on a white satin settee, while offering the double seated couch across the onyx table for Reisel and Joseph to sit upon. At that moment, her steward, Erzsi Majorova entered carrying a silver tray on which stood an ornate cloisonne teapot and three exquisitely flowered china cups. Setting the tray down on the table, the steward poured each a cup of tea and then carefully handed it to them.

"Will there be any anything else, Countess," she asked.

"Erzsi, why don't you sit down with us. I'm certain that Joseph's unexpected visit today will require your attention."

"Yes Madame," the steward responded as she sat herself down in a large wing-back chair located in a corner of the room.

"So Joseph, what adventures have you experienced on your mission thus far," the Countess was direct and to the point as if this was one of her many book reading sessions she held regularly for the ladies of Hungarian society in her castle.

"Sadly, I must report that three of our contingent are now dead."

Placing their hands over her mouths, both Elizabeth and Reisel were in shock upon hearing the news.

"Oh my!" the Countess exclaimed. "Who were they? How did it happen?" she asked. "I hope my cousin and your companions are still alright."

"They are fine, Elizabeth," Joseph immediately soothed their fears, "But our driver and two of our guards were killed."

"How?" she asked again.

"This will sound very strange to you," Joseph took Reisel's hand in his own so that she would not be frightened by what he was about to say. "We were in the Hoia-Baciu Forest, which they say is haunted. And though I try not to believe in such things, I swear that forest came alive. Now we suspect there may have been some foul play, but those perpetrating the act appear to have been either children of the forest, the fairy people, or according to Caesar, dwarfs. I know this makes no sense at all," he looked into Reisel's eyes and could see that she was terrified by the story, "But that is not even the worst of it. Later on we were attacked by what we assumed to be a pack of wolves. We fired our weapons, we even heard them cry out when the bullets struck their targets but when we searched in the forests to find any of the dead bones, instead we found a man had been shot. Not a man they said, but a werewolf. I don't know what I actually believe now. As impossible as it seems, they might be right because not even Wolf reacted to them as he would do normally, because he thought they were wolves as well."

"My God," Reisel shuddered. "Do such monsters actually exist?" She could not stop her body from shivering uncontrollably. Joseph tried to comfort her by softly rubbing her hand in his but the trembling continued.

"That is terrible," Countess Bathory commented. "It is so hard to believe but clearly the Elementals are trying to stop your mission. What could you possibly be intending to do that would rile the spirit world so viciously?"

"You sound like the old Gypsy woman we met," Joseph compared Elizabeth's comment to those of the *Dya-Bulibasha.*

"Gypsies now!" Elizabeth Bathory couldn't believe what she was hearing. "How did you manage to encounter Gypsies."

"If you believe in coincidence then I would say that was how it happened but our meeting was already foretold by Nostradamus. Our mission has taken on these supernatural overtones that appear to be directing everything we do."

"So what did these Gypsies have to do with all this?" the Countess was still confused why it was so necessary to meet with a caravan of Roma.

Joseph cleared his throat, knowing that what he was about to say would sound very foolish. "Because when we parted company in Oradea, we had no idea where we were going."

"What!" Reisel suddenly snapped out of her terrified trance. "How could you have left with no destination in mind." Even for a young girl like myself, it sounded ridiculous.

Sheepishly answering Joseph tried to explain, "We had a general location in mind. Just not a specific one." Turning towards Countess Elizabeth, Joseph began to confide in her. "We have discussed the need for any information you might be able to provide. It was decided that we should reveal our mission to you, now that we have a little more clarity as to who might be committing the murder of these young girls."

"Why would you think I can help you," the Countess was quite surprised by this unexpected revelation.

"I need you to swear to me by an oath to God that what I'm about to tell you will go no farther than this room. I need your steward's commitment as well."

"Of course," Elizabeth replied emphatically. "I swear, I swear. And you do too, right Erzsi."

"Yes, I swear too," the steward consented.

"We think that it is not a single killer but a congregation of people gathered from all walks in life but led by someone with enough authority and power that they can remain hidden even when their actions might be so conspicuous. That would point to either someone in the aristocracy or else someone so wealthy that they can buy the silence of everyone else."

"And how do you think I can be of any assistance?"

"Because you know people that know people," Joseph said bluntly. "I suspect that if there's anything unusual happening among the nobles of Hungary that you would somehow know about it almost immediately."

"You flatter me Joseph but I don't really believe that I have connections as strong as you are indicating. I may hear a few things here and there but that is about all."

"And I believe you undersell you skills," Joseph countered. "I believe that when it comes to Hungary that you are the true ruler of these lands and everything of importance is funneled through you before the Habsburgs ever hear about it."

Laughing, the Countess was amused by Joseph's insinuation. "That almost sounds treasonous, dear Joseph. To suggest that I am in a position of authority that rivals my cousin Matthias would often be enough to justify the removal of my head."

"As I mentioned, Elizabeth, whatever we discuss stays within this room. I have no intention for you to lose your head."

"I hope so Joseph. I have grown quite attached to it."

Everyone relaxed, letting the tensions lower as they laughed at the Countess's joke.

"But seriously," Joseph continued, "Are you able to help us."

"If I can, I will," she responded. "But as to date, I have heard no one in my circle discussing anything concerning the horrible deaths of these girls."

"You may not even realize what they might be saying," Joseph indicated. "It could be something as simple as their talking about large groups of people suddenly meeting in their castles or villas, without any purpose mentioned. It is their ramblings that we need to pay attention to. What they say accidentally may be the key to unlocking this mystery and pointing us towards those responsible."

"I will definitely pay more attention," she assured him. "But what are you plans now? Surely you can provide me with more to grasp at than a hunch that someone in the aristocracy might be involved."

"Now that we have the location of our destination from the old Gypsy, we should have far more to work with, very soon."

"Where are you going now?" Reisel wanted to know, fearing that it may prove even more dangerous than what Joseph and his companions had already faced.

"Still the same place I told you before Reisel. From what we know, whatever is happening now, all began with the Dacians a long time ago," he explained. "But now we know where they were located."

"Dacians? What are Dacians?" Elizabeth wanted to know.

Reisel stared at the Countess wondering why she would suddenly deny knowing anything about the Dacians after they had already discussed it earlier. She said nothing, waiting to see if there would be an explanation.

"Not what but who," Joseph clarified. "They were an ancient people that once lived in these lands. They disappeared long ago, but the killers we are trying to capture may be adhering to rituals that the Dacians left behind. There must be a clue they left behind."

"How will you prove that?" the Countess was curious.

"We now know how to find their Holy of Holies, the place where they performed their virgin sacrifices. We expect that will provide us with a good understanding of any motives behind the actions of the killers. Once we know the motives then we can possibly determine who actually benefits from these deaths. The benefit is key to the mystery."

"I can appreciate what you think you will find, but drawing the connection from some ancient ritual then applying it to actions today seems unreliable at best. In fact, it sounds quite improbable to me." Elizabeth Bathory deliberately intended to sound discouraging, emphasizing how she failed to see any point to Joseph's reasoning.

"I understand the connection appears weak but we have every confidence that we will be able to establish it once we encounter a stranger that helps the three of us to see more clearly. The Gypsy referred to him as the blacksmith."

"Pardon my laughing," Elizabeth excused herself, "But placing your faith in an old Gypsy woman and relying on some stranger you don't even know exists, doesn't sound like a well thought out strategy to me. Perhaps it would be best for all of you to return to Vienna and just leave it remain with me to see if I hear anything unusual from among my fellow nobility. That makes far more sense."

"Yes, Joseph," Reisel encouraged her betrothed. "Let us return to Vienna and we can start planning the rest of our life. The Countess can now investigate on your behalf."

"As attractive as all that sounds to me," Joseph replied, "It is not possible. Our promise to the Emperor was that we will not return until we complete this mission and find the killer or killers." His response was directed towards the Countess. The next statement he directed towards Reisel. "His promise to me was that we will only be permitted to marry if I succeed. Otherwise I am certain they will place your father back in jail and you will regret ever having known me."

"That is not true," Reisel denied his conclusion.

"But it is," he refuted. "You will look at me and blame me for anything they do to your father. How could you accept to remain in a marriage with such a dark cloud hanging over it? How could I live, looking into your eyes and seeing the contempt that you will hold for me? I must complete this mission."

"I think it is best that my steward and I leave you two alone to discuss this between yourselves," Elizabeth Bathory suggested. Rising from the settee, she signaled for Erzsi Majorova to follow her out of the room.

Bowing his head, Joseph waited until he was certain both women were far enough away that they could not hear any of their conversation. Brushing away the tears that were beginning to stream down Reisel's cheeks, he tried his best to console her. "You know that I want nothing more than for us to spend our lives together but what kind of life would that be if it was always under a cloud. How would we survive if there would always be those trying to tear us apart?"

Curling into his arms she snuggled her head into his chest. "I don't want you to leave me again," she stated tearfully. "I'm afraid something bad will happen to you."

"I promise that nothing bad will happen," Joseph tried to assure her. "Did they ever tell you that those of the Kahana live blessed lives. We rarely get sick and where others would be in danger, God shields us and keeps us safe."

"Is that true?" she looked up at him with soulful eyes that practically made his heart melt.

"Of course it is true," he reassured her. "There are so many stories regarding the Kahana that you realize they must be true. I know your father will probably never tell them to you but why do you think he hates my family so much. It is because those stories are true."

"But I don't like it here," she revealed another secret that she had not disclosed while the Countess was sitting in the room with them.

"Why," Joseph sounded perplexed. "The Countess takes such good care of you. She treats you like a daughter. What more could she do for you?"

"There are noises at night. Terrifying noises that I can hear in my bedroom."

"Probably just the wind," Joseph speculated. "These old castles have no protection from the drafts. The wind rushes and races down the halls creating all sorts of strange sounds."

"No!" she objected to his treating her like a little girl. "I know the wind when I hear it. These sound like screams. I hear crying in the night. I don't know where they are coming from but it is not the wind. One night I was so frightened I left my bedroom to search for the source of these noises. I walked down the hallway and I heard strange sounds coming from the Countess's bedroom. There were moans and muffled screams emanating from her room. The door was partially opened and I looked in. She was in bed with her steward. They were making love."

"How do you know?" Joseph asked. "You are still young. How would you know what making love looks like?"

"Don't try to make me sound stupid simply because I am young," she lightly punched Joseph for his insinuation. "They were making love!" She was adamant.

"Well then," Joseph curled his lip. "At least you know now where all the strange noises were coming from.

"That was not the same noises I heard from my room," she refuted Joseph's explanation.

"I cannot tell you that their conduct was acceptable, but I still do not see that as an excuse for your wanting to leave the castle. The Countess is still very good to you."

"You don't understand Joseph." She unveiled the second secret. "Tonight the Countess denied knowing anything about the Dacians yet she already discussed them with me as being an ancient people that inhabited these lands. Why would she do that? I have this feeling that there are inexplicable strange occurrences taking place in this castle and it makes me afraid. Even my father's behaviour is very different when he is around the Countess. He has never looked at another woman other than my mother but now I sense he is being seduced by both the Countess and her steward."

"In what manner," Joseph pressed her for more information.

"I can't say exactly. It is just different. The way he talks to them. The way he looks at them. I know all my father's mannerisms and behaviors and this is different."

"I think you are letting your imagination run wild. You find yourself in strange surroundings, among people that are behaving differently from what you are accustomed to and that makes you very apprehensive. The Countess probably forgot that she knew about the Dacians. She does drink a lot of wine. The reality is, you are worried about me, you are worried about your father but most of the things we worry about never come to pass. I don't doubt you hear noises in the night. These old castles hold their secrets and as I told you, I have come to realize that the supernatural may be more common than we think. I'm certain Senor Sarpi can arrive at some logical and scientific explanation but until then, I certainly do believe you hear what you describe. All I can say is that you have nothing to fear because the blessings that protect my family have been extended to protect you as well. God has brought us together and only God can tear us apart."

She took comfort in Joseph's words, content that the blessing of the Lord would be sufficient to protect her.

"Be reassured that while you sleep tonight," Joseph clasped her closely against his beating chest, "I will be watching over you as well. If I hear anything unusual I will be up and guarding your door. You merely have to look outside your bedroom and you will see me there."

"Thank you my beloved. I will sleep much better tonight."

She found herself feeling her way through the cloister that ran between the castle walls. Her hands were tracing the face of the stones as if they had a life of their own. Finally she found the cleft between bricks and reached her right hand in and pulled the concealed lever. In response, the great stone slab rotated on silent hinges. She quietly strolled into the yawning stillness of the chamber. Faint images danced across the chamber's surfaces, created by the covered lanterns that hung along the walls. She lowered the straps of her gossamer-like gown, permitting it to slide slowly to the ground. Her skin was so smooth that it could be seen to shimmer and radiate a white glow as she passed close to any of the lanterns. She rolled her hands across her firm breasts and then down the sides of her torso, seemingly awakening her alluring body. Her nipples became erect, each surrounded by a ring of deep magenta. As she touched her skin, she felt her senses being flooded by a wave of emotion, energizing every sinew in her lithe body.

Auburn hair fell to her waist, wrapping her in silk-like splendour, billowing softly in the slight breeze that entered the room as she moved towards the bed. Raising one knee onto the mattress she deftly climbed into the bed without awakening her slumbering guest. Stretching herself out, she nuzzled into the full length of his body, while he lay undisturbed beneath the heavy woolen blanket. She placed the back of her hand to his nostrils, allowing him to inhale repeatedly the perfumed scent upon her skin. The unusual scent made him stir slightly, licking his lips as if he could taste the strange aroma. As he rolled over on to his back, she placed one of her nipples into his open mouth. His tongue immediately responded reflexively as he tasted another unusual essence, different from the first but just as intoxicating. As he began suckling harder on her flushed nipple, she could not prevent herself from moaning with excitement Her groans were loud enough to partially stir him from his slumber.

His first reaction was one of shock and surprise, followed by a simple question with an obvious answer. "What are you doing?" he blurted. He wanted to push her away but he found his limbs refusing to let him do so, his tongue still craving the unusual taste of her nipples. While continuing to suck, his mind still protested the intrusion into his bedroom, finally winning the battle and enabling him to turn his head away. "What is going on? Why are you here?"

"Oh, let's be honest with each other," she confessed. "Ever since I saw you at my castle in Ecsed, I have thought of little else. I'm a very candid woman, who always gets what she wants" she laughed enticingly. "Why shouldn't I? I am practically a goddess. Would you not agree?" She didn't wait for an answer. "Anything I want, I get. You understand? And right now I want you."

"I think you may have misunderstood any attention I might have paid you," Joseph winced, pretending that he did not actually comprehend the intimations of her words and blaming himself. He tried to keep his head turned away but the desire to suckle on her breasts was overwhelming.

"When I saw your face, the noble contour of your brow and the luscious curve of your lips, the radiance in your eyes, I knew that you were special. You were a gift being offered to me. Now I want to open that gift. I want to tear apart the layers of wrapping and take delight in my special gift. I want to explore why you are so different from the others," she purred.

"I think this is wrong," Joseph found his voice faltering as he tried to explain why she shouldn't continue talking this way or pursue the interaction any further but the more he inhaled the sweet scent of her skin, the more clouded his mind was becoming.

"Do you really believe this is wrong Joseph?"

"I…I can't think straight. I see…"

"What do you see Joseph?"

"Your indescribable beauty." Joseph tried to stop himself. "I'm sorry. I don't know why I said that."

Elizabeth moaned in response to the compliment. "How beautiful am I, Joseph?

"So very beautiful," Joseph could not stop himself from saying these things. "What is happening to me. Is this some kind of spell?"

Placing her finger in his mouth, she encouraged Joseph to suck each digit slowly as if each finger was a stick of sugar candy. He could not resist. There was a sweet and fragrant substance that he detected, different from the other tastes on her fingers, which made his entire body feel as if it was floating effortlessly high above the bed. An overwhelming feeling of well-being, coursed through his veins, flooding every cell with an awakened awareness of every sensation.

"Oh, I am so glad that you find me beautiful," she smiled devilishly. "More beautiful than you little lamb, Reisel?"

Closing his eyes, Joseph wondered what he could do now. He wanted to say that Reisel was the only woman in his life, but whatever was coursing through his system now, prevented him from doing so. His body was craving Elizabeth so strongly that he felt himself fighting desperately to resist and losing. He was trapped in her little game of cat and mouse and Elizabeth most certainly was a very hungry cat.

Sliding under the cover, she forced herself up against Joseph's quivering body. "Now isn't that much better?" she cooed. "I want you to relax and set your body free. Stop resisting Joseph. You cannot overpower the sexual stimuli. Ravage me like a hungry animal wanting to taste the pleasures of its kill."

Joseph continued to resist, his limbs growing rigid.

"Am I not appealing to you?" she drew her lips into a heart rendering pout

"This is too much." He felt panic stricken, knowing that whatever he had tasted was overpowering his resistance. "I shouldn't be feeling this way about you. I love Reisel!" He felt the tear rolling down the side of his face.

Reaching through the cloth of the cover, she felt the imprint of his genitals and then squeezed gently. It came alive in her hand, forcing itself fully into the cup of her fingers until it began prying them apart through the sheer size of the uncontrollable swelling. Elizabeth licked her lips, excited by the sheer enormity of his penis.

"This isn't right; you are my host. I am betrothed to another," he bleated but he no longer had any control of his body. Elizabeth was in total control and he was now merely a puppet having his strings pulled.

Elizabeth gave a wicked laugh. "It isn't a marriage until you actually exchange your vows. And even so, marriage is merely an institution created by men so that they cant take possession of a woman as if she were property. Tonight you are my property." She gripped his penis more tightly as if punishing him for even mentioning Reisel at that moment. He winced from the sudden pain but it only served to make him even more excited.

She put her head under the linen sheet and slowly licked the smooth glans of his organ. He heard her giggle from underneath the blanket. "So it is true," she smirked. "They say you Jews have so much that you have to cut off the extra and throw it away." Joseph found he could not even speak any more, his mind reeling from the combination of substances he ingested and the indescribable feelings she was generating as her tongue circled repeatedly around his shaft.

"Do you fear me?" she asked with a childlike innocence while she held his manhood as hostage. "You should!" Elizabeth laughed delightedly. Inserting his penis into her mouth she twisted her body and rolled her legs about his head so that her vulva was positioned over his mouth. She could sense his capitulation as he began sucking on the folded lips of her flesh. Another strange taste, Joseph realized, this one a mixture of herbs mixed with a musky odour.

Feeling the tingling sensations rising in her own groin, the Countess cupped her hands about her breasts and tightly squeezed her erect nipples, all the while working his shaft in and out of her hungry mouth. Joseph inhaled the intoxicating scent that flowed from her vagina and his hands were no longer laying limp at this side but became strengthened in their purpose as they raced to her breasts and he began squeezing her firm protruding nipples.

She laughed excitedly as she kneaded his manhood towards its maximum potential. Any trace of resistance was now long suppressed and Joseph released one of her breasts so that the fingers of his right hand could explore excitedly within Elizabeth's canal, searching, circling and continually moving into new recesses of unexpected pleasure.

Her mouth continued to roll upon the swell of the storm until she knew that the damn holding back Joseph's essence was about to burst. At that very moment she bit sharply into one of the throbbing veins of his penis, letting the mixture of warm blood and hot semen flow freely into her mouth, ingesting every drop of this sacred serum, while Joseph groaned at first in pain but then the intense and infinite pleasure.

Chapter Fourteen

The Witches' Pool: May 1610

The following morning Joseph and his two sentries began loading the packs of their horses with enough supplies from the Castle stores to keep their small platoon well fed for the next few months.

She did not know why, but Reisel had the distinct feeling that Joseph was avoiding her, as he managed to keep busy preparing for his imminent departure rather than paying her any of his usual attention. Wise beyond her years, she was not accepting his excuses that time was precious and he had little to spare. Marching into the stables, she finally confronted him as he was fitting the bridle to his horse.

"No more excuses. Is there something wrong Joseph?" she was blunt with her question, refusing to leave until he started talking.

"Of course not," he responded in his defense. "Why would you think that?"

"Because you have barely spoken a couple of words to me all morning. That's why."

"That's ridiculous," he attempted to dismiss her concerns. "Of course I've spoken to you all morning."

"No" she replied, "You said a word here or a word there but you haven't really talked to me. If there is something wrong, then tell me. Have I done something that has upset you?"

"Never," he reassured her. "You could never do anything wrong." He wrestled with the thought of telling her everything but knew that he would only lose her if he did. How could he possibly explain that he was under a spell and unable to break it? Dancing on the strings of a marionette and made to perform in a way that he was too embarrassed to even describe. The truth sounded even more ridiculous than simply saying he was ashamed that he cheated on her. He would never be able to convince her otherwise and he was smart enough to know that no woman would ever believe that a man could be forced to participate in a sexual act unwillingly.

"Then is there something you're not telling me?" she asked immediately following his denial.

It is as if they have some inner sense, Joseph thought to himself. He wondered how a woman could always tell when a man was hiding something. His sister used to use it all the time on him and here was Reisel having that same ability. But he realized this could be used to his advantage. Since she already believed it to be the truth, then he knew it was best to let her know it was true.

"Yes, I have been hiding something from you but only because I didn't want to frighten you. Forgive me but I thought it was in your best interest. Now I realize I have been acting like such a fool. By shutting you out I was hurting you, not protecting you. It was because I know how much you fear staying in this castle and I didn't want to unsettle you any further. I am so sorry."

"You saw something, didn't you," she pressed him for an answer. "You can't hide it from me. I need to know."

Looking sheepish, Joseph nodded his head. "Yes, I don't even know how to explain it. There are secret passages built into the walls of this castle. As I lay there, half awake, half asleep, one of those doors opened in the middle of the night into my room. I dared not look. I knew someone else was in my room but I remained beneath the covers. There were noises, strange noises, and it shames me to admit but I was paralyzed with fear, unable to move. I know that I had told you that if I heard or saw anything strange I would patrol the hallways and safeguard your door but I failed you. I am so ashamed. Can you forgive me?"

"Oh, Joseph, How can you even ask that? I don't need you to be a hero all the time. I am just glad you are safe. You were safe, right?"

"I am fine…" he lingered in his answer.

"Except?" Reisel jumped upon his slow response, sensing that he wanted to say more.

"It's embarrassing," he declined to answer.

"I will be your wife soon, you can tell me anything."

"I suffered a small cut, I bled a little bit. Nothing serious."

"Let me see," she demanded. "It may have to be treated so you don't get an infection," the concern in her voice was genuine.

"I can't," Joseph refused. "It is in a particular place I can't show you," he further explained. "Not yet. Not until we are married."

"A succubus!" she exclaimed with a horrified look upon her face.

"A what?" Joseph had no idea what she was talking about.

"A succubus!" The word practically leaped from her mouth. "My father has told me all about them. They come in the night attack men while they sleep. They are a form of demon like those mentioned in the Kabbalah."

"Demons?" Joseph scoffed at the idea. "This is what your father teaches you? Really? Then it is fortunate I don't believe in the Kabbalah. That is another thing you will learn that separates us Karaites from the Rabbanites. We don't believe in such nonsense."

"How can you call it nonsense when you freely admit that something came into the room last night and wounded you down there? Papa swears they exist. The succubus comes for the men, the incubus for a woman, forcing each to engage in sexual acts," Reisel repeated what she had been taught. "You didn't penetrate it, did you?"

"You mean intercourse? No, of course not!"

"Thank God," Reisel sounded relieved. "Papa said if you have sexual relations with the succubus then you are bound to her for the rest of your life. She will haunt you every night thereafter."

"Why would your father even discuss such things with his daughters," Joseph protested. "This sounds so wrong to me. You are fourteen and you are discussing issues of sexual relations with demons. That is just not right."

Reisel was surprised by Joseph's reaction. After all, this was the seventeenth century. People were far more open minded about these things. She was unsure how he would react to her next question. "Does that mean that when we are married during the year we will not be having a sexual relationship because you think I'm too young."

"That's completely different," Joseph waved his hands frantically. "You will be my wife. Of course we will be having intercourse." He realized that didn't sound right either, as he looked around the stables to see that no one else was listening.

"So I'm old enough to have sex with you but I'm not old enough to talk about it?"

"Your twisting this conversation out of context," Joseph complained. "I only meant that I don't believe a father should be discussing demons and sex with his daughters. Especially the two together. I don't believe in it and I certainly reject the Kabbalah."

Reisel could see how flustered he was becoming with the conversation and she was actually enjoying his discomfort. She decided to tease him some more. "So it is okay for a father to have a conversation regarding sex with his daughters as long as he keeps the discussion of demons separate."

"No, no. That's not what I'm saying either. I just think those types of conversations have their right place and time."

"Well, you were the one that told me something came into your room at night and afterwards you had a wound down there." She pointed at his groin and laughed.

"Yes I did," Joseph conceded. "You are having fun with this, aren't you?"

"I didn't want you leaving me today and regretting that we didn't have an opportunity to talk like we always do," she explained. "If it takes making you laugh, even if it means laughing at something that frightens us both, then that is what I had to do."

"You never cease to amaze me Reisel Lipmann. Here I am thinking that I'm protecting you and in truth you are the one protecting me. But let us agree not to discuss this further. I don't quite understand everything that happened to me last night but I never want to think anything more about it. I was only concerned for your welfare. You told me you think there were mysterious events and sounds taking place at night and I guess what I'm saying is that after last night I am agreeing with you. I need you to stay safe until I return. I was worried that by my leaving today, it will place you in danger."

"And I only wanted to ensure that you will always talk with me. You never have to feel that you can't talk to me, my beloved."

Moving towards his fiance', Joseph embraced her, holding her tightly in his arms. "How did I ever deserve to find someone so smart and beautiful."

"You got lucky," she joked, planting a big kiss on his cheek.

"I certainly did," Joseph replied. "I am thinking that perhaps I should leave Wolf with you while I am away."

"That would never work," she didn't give it a second thought. "He doesn't really know me and I'm guessing not too long after you leave he would find a way out of the castle to follow you. Furthermore, it sounds like you have been facing a lot more danger on your mission than my noises in the night. It is obvious that you will need him more."

"As usual, you are right. I guess I am going to have to get use to saying that a lot."

"You better," she warned him. "Now go solve these murders and come back to me soon."

Climbing into the saddle, Joseph blew a kiss towards Reisel and then snapped the reins so that his horse cantered slowly out of the stables.

"Come back to me soon," Reisel shouted after him once more.

As the three horses with their riders passed through the castle gates, followed closely by Wolf at his master's heels, their departure was being closely observed from one of the upper windows overlooking the castle courtyard.

"So, did it prove to be everything that you expected?" Erzsi Majorova asked her mistress.

"It was exquisite," the Countess responded. "So powerful. So stimulating. My body felt energized for hours. I crave more of it."

"Exactly how shall we arrange that," the steward inquired.

"He said they are heading to the Dacian holy place. That means he will be passing through Wallachia. Do you think they will help us?" Elizabeth wondered.

"It is a possibility. I will send word and see what my sisters will do for us," Erzsi responded.

___

By late afternoon, Joseph and his two guards rode into the encampment situated not far from the village of Sibiu. After unpacking his saddle bags and hobbling his horse, he joined his companions that had been enjoying a relaxing day sitting around a fire and telling stories of past adventures.

"So, did you manage to explain to your fiance' why you are still on the road and unlikely to see her again for months," Caesar immediately peppered Joseph upon his return.

"Yes, I did and she fully accepts the explanation."

"Amazing," Paolo responded. "If I was younger, I'd probably want to marry that girl myself. Certainly different from any of the woman I have known."

"She certainly is," Joseph confirmed. "But don't go getting any ideas, either of you. She's mine. Not that she'd be interested in two old goats like yourselves."

"Oh, and what are you in comparison to her, a spring chicken?" Paolo joked, poking fun at the fact that Joseph was twice her age.

"I'm just a goat, not an old goat," he replied.

"Anything out of the ordinary?" Caesar inquired.

"No," Joseph answered with strong conviction. "Why are you asking?"

"No reason," Caesar responded. "Just thought I'd ask."

"Absolutely nothing unusual happened," Joseph repeated.

"I do think the man protests too much," Paolo commented which made him and Caesar laugh out loud.

"Two lovebirds locked in a cage," Caesar drew a comparison. "What else can you expect?" Both of them laughed even more.

"Not funny," Joseph objected to their mirthful insinuation. "I'll have you know her father was there, the Countess was also there, and so were a household of her people. So you can laugh all you want but nothing happened." No sooner had he made his statement, the pair of them were laughing wildly again.

"Ah, the Countess," Paolo closed his eyes to take in the heavenly image of how he last saw her. "Now there's a woman worth her weight in gold for any Venetian.

"And why would she want the likes of you, you old goat," Caesar emphasized the words that were used by Joseph to describe both of them. It served to bring on another burst of laughter from the two men.

"Me, what about you," Paolo shot back. "Here you go telling us all that you have no interest in women and the next thing I see is you drooling over her fine tableware."

"Yes, that is true," Caesar admitted. "Don't know how I'm going to explain to Mademoiselle Claire that I actually came across a woman that put some life into my loins," Caesar laughed at his own inadequacy.

"Claire?" Joseph was intrigued by the woman he just mentioned.

"Yes, I believe I mentioned her when we were in the Palace meeting with the Emperor. She's my housemaid, secretary, confidante, and any other job that I require assistance for lady. Don't know how I'd ever get on without her," he admitted. "Really should send her a letter so that she knows I'm alright," Caesar realized that she might be worried about him after all this time.

"Right," Joseph nodded his head. "I do now recall you mentioning her. Your everything you need lady except a paramour. So how do you explain all those years you spent with her without any desires being unleashed, and yet one sniff of the Countess and you're feeling like a dog going after a bitch in heat."

"I can't explain it," Caesar admitted. "Never happened to me before."

"Strange don't you think," Joseph pursued the matter. "What do you think about it Paolo?"

"About Caesar finally putting some wood into his codpiece?"

"Yes, not that I would have said it like that but yes, why do you think it happened?"

"Well, she is a fine specimen of womanhood," Paolo concluded.

"And so is Mademoiselle Claire," Caesar informed them. "You would fill your codpiece too Senor Sarpi if you met my Claire."

"Any other thoughts, Paolo," Joseph pressed him for an answer.

"Perhaps like you said," Paolo Sarpi began to analyze the problem. "If she was to give off a scent like a bitch in heat, then the response by the dog would be autonomic, and it wouldn't require Caesar to even think about her at all. A purely autonomic reaction."

"But that works for dogs," Joseph disputed the example, "as humans we don't react that way."

"Only because we humans have lost much of our ability to smell, which all other animals have retained," Sarpi elaborated on his suggestion. "But for everything there is a balance. If we only have one percent of our ability to smell, then that loss can be offset by increasing the odour by one hundred fold."

"So you're saying if there was a way for a woman to increase her natural scent by some means, then something in Caesar's brain would receive messages that would cause him to react automatically and there was nothing he could do about it."

"Exactly," Paolo confirmed. "But no one knows how to do such a thing, thank heavens. Could you imagine if a woman actually possessed that power. We'd all be putty in her hands. We must be grateful that we lost our sense of smell or we'd be no better than animals."

"And you say no one has ever been able to formulate these scents."

"Not that I am aware of," Paolo assured Joseph that such things did not exist.

"It is funny but you seem so nervous when you are talking about it. You are even sweating." Joseph pointed to the beads of sweat appearing on Paolo's brow. "You certain it can't be done?"

"Hey, I would certainly know! Why are you so suddenly interested in Caesar's arousal?"

"Yes, why are you so interested," Caesar thought it was an interesting question to pursue.

"No reason, just curious," Joseph shied away from telling them anything further. Fortunately for Joseph, Count Thurzo came over to where they were resting and his interruption prevented Caesar or Paolo from questioning any further on the matter.

"We still have a few hours of daylight, so if you don't mind getting off your backsides and getting on your horses, my men would like to get on the road already," Thurzo advised them in his usual gruff manner, typical of his years of soldiering.

"So where do we plan to get to today?" Caesar inquired.

"With any luck, we'll be camped outside the village of Pitesti by tonight. Think I'll give the men a little break and let them go into town for a little recreation."

Leaning towards Joseph, Caesar provided the official translation. "Military language for alcohol, women and ribaldry."

"I heard that," the Count turned on Caesar, "And you're right. Time to raise their spirits. The mission thus far hasn't been what you would label as a glowing success."

"I'm certainly not against a little fun," Caesar was quick to defend himself. "I'm all for happy soldiers. Probably even share a pint or two with them"

"Good, I'll let them know you're buying," Gyorgy Thurzo nodded his approval.

"Wait...I didn't exactly say that," Caesar's voice trailed off but it was too late as the Count had already left to tell his men.

"Very generous of you," Sarpi commended his companion. "I'll accept your offer and have a couple of drinks as well.

"Me too," Joseph let Caesar know that he intended to go too. "Better saddle up. The sooner we get there, the sooner we can start drinking."

"But you told us you hardly every drink after you recovered from that night with the Gypsies," Sarpi reminded Joseph.

"I'm starting to make exceptions," Joseph answered. "Let's get going.

Riding into Pitesti, they were met by suspicious stares from everyone they passed.

"Not exactly a warm welcome," Joseph commented to Thurzo.

"It is a trading town," the Count explained. "Serves only one purpose and that's for merchants and traders to bring their goods from East to West. So the only real population comprises Vlachs, Slavs and any of the Armenian traders that set up shops here. So to them the appearance of Imperial soldiers can mean only one thing; tax collection. I probably should mention that they preferred their Turkish overlords to us, so whatever you do, avoid any discussion of politics tonight."

"No worries," Sarpi piped in. "I'm here to drink, womanize and sing some songs like a true Venetian."

"Well, the womanizing should be easy," Thurzo commented. "Tends to be one of their major industries. So make sure you keep a hand on your purses or you won't have them for very long."

Finding stalls where they could hitch up their horses, the Count flipped the stable boy a couple of thalers, telling him to make certain all fourteen horse were fed and well watered, offering another thaler if they were all brushed out by the time they returned.

Thurzo led his men towards the Armenian quarter of the city, relying on instincts and the fact that he had spent a few nights in the past in Pitesti. Less chance of finding trouble in an Armenian inn that sitting with the Vlachs, where there was definitely no love loss. He searched at the intersection of the two main streets for a hanging sign, pointing to it once it was spotted. "The Golden Goose, my friends, probably the only place in town where they don't water down the beer." It was an old mud brick building, showing the ravages of time after two hundred years of standing unprotected from the elements, but the lights from inside were burning bright and the music of the balalaikas filled the street. As they were entering, a beautiful young girl escorted her client for the night out on to the street and towards her apartment.

"As I said gentlemen, better hold on to your purses, if you can," the Count laughed. It was one of the few times they could remember him laughing at all.

As he was talking, several young girls, as pretty as the one that just left strolled into the inn. "No shortage of fun tonight, if you want it," Caesar mentioned to Paolo.

"Unlike our good friend, Joseph here, I'm more into an older, more refined and genteel woman."

"Sure you are," Caesar taunted. "At your age you happy to take whatever comes along."

"Not true, not true," Sarpi protested as Caesar gave him a playful shove on the shoulder to move him along into the building.

As the group of fourteen men moved into the ale hall, a few of the patrons that had been drinking alone and occupying one of the long tables, quickly moved out of the way. They wanted no trouble with soldiers, especially those still wearing their swords on their belts.

No sooner had they sat down, when they heard "Gyorgy, you old bitches' whelp," shouted from the back of the hall. "How long has it been?" The bald headed owner of the inn limped towards the Count and embraced him.

"Ilan, you donkey's arse, I can't believe you are still here," Thurzo exchanged salutations as he hugged his old friend in return. "I thought you'd be retired by now."

"No can do," Ilan explained, "Have a new wife. Wants everything the old one had, so I can't ever stop working."

"I warned you about chasing after those young foxes. Nothing but a basket full of trouble, I told you!"

"But Gyorgy," Ilan groaned, "Look at them," as he pointed to the girls that had passed by the Count's men when they first entered. "How can anyone resist that?"

"One day it will fall off and you'll have nothing to offer any longer," Thurzo warned him.

"Until that day, live, love and be lucky. So what can I get your men?"

"Several jugs of ale to start. And is that flat-bread I smell in your ovens."

"Of course," Ilan stated proudly, knowing that his garlic flat-bread was the best in town.

"Then enough flat-bread to feed this table," the Count ordered.

"And here I thought you had forgotten me after the passing of the years," the innkeeper mentioned.

"What do you mean?" Thurzo was surprised by the comment. "Why would I ever forget you. As I told my men, you have the best drinking establishment in all of Pitesti."

"You mean the only one that still gives you credit," Ilan responded. "I'll have to check my records to see if there is still an outstanding tab."

"You know I would never pass through town without coming here."

"And that is exactly what I said to those women that came into the place earlier today. They asked me if Count Gyorgy Thurzo had been here and I told them that you hadn't but if you were to pass through Pitesti, then you definitely would be coming here."

"What women are you talking about, Ilan?" Thurzo was confused by the statement.

"Must have been about six of them all together. I just figured you got yourself in trouble with one of them, you old dog," the innkeeper winked as he said so.

"Could you identify them if you saw them again?"

"Of course, but I don't think they will be coming this way. They were heading east. Probably to take part in that festival they hold in the forest each year."

"I have no idea what you're talking about," Thurzo admitted that he was lost in the conversation.

"At the new moon, each Spring, they gather at the pool in the forest where Vlad Dracul the Impaler was beheaded a hundred and fifty years ago. Story is his head still lies at the bottom of the pool," Ilan explained. "Apparently they dance around naked and do all sorts of weird things. Never had the chance to go find out for myself."

"And you say they asked for me."

"Yes," he was confident in his answer. "Asked for you by name. Said they have answers for you. That's why I figured you must have fathered a child on at least one of them. Only type of answer I could think of when a woman comes searching for a man."

"Sorry to disappoint you my old friend but that's not the case here." the Count replied. "But this pool. Where can I find it."

"They say if you draw a straight line from here to Bucharest then it is forty miles from here on that line. It lays in the Boldu-Creteasca Forest. You plan on going?"

"You know me," Thurzo slapped his friend on the back. "I can't pass up the opportunity to watch naked women dancing around a pool of water. That's my kind of entertainment."

"And while you are here, shall I arrange entertainment for your men as well?" Ilan asked.

"Been a rough couple of past months," the Count commented. "I'm pretty certain they would enjoy a little recreation."

"And what about the other three?"

"Well that one is soon to be married," he pointed and referred to Joseph, "Pretty much a virgin himself I think, so I wouldn't pressure him on it. As for that one," he pointed at Caesar, "He pretty much has sworn off sex completely, so don't bother. But the last one I'm certain would be happy to partake but wants an older, more sophisticated woman. Got anyone like that?"

"I'm certain I can find someone."

"Good. See to it that my men are happy tonight. Who knows, could be the last time."

Count Thurzo repeated the following morning the reason why they needed to go to this pool next. The explanation was sounding a bit desperate when he mentioned mysterious women having come into the beer hall and asking for him by name and then leaving a message that they have the answers they were looking for.

"It's a trap," Sarpi was the first to give his opinion.

"Of course it is a trap," the Count agreed. "Who would ever think it wasn't a trap. But it is also an opportunity to get some answers as well. Whomever they are working for will lead us back to the killers of these young girls."

"Presuming that they are working for them and not some other enemy that you have made along the way. It seems you are well known in this part of the Empire. Could be that someone else wants you dead."

"I don't think so," Thurzo responded.

"But you don't know either," Joseph filled in the gap.

"I guess it is possible but with all the other craziness, forest dwarfs and werewolves, it seems only natural that a witches coven would somehow be connected." The Count provided his explanation of how he was trying to connect the dots.

"A witches coven does sound more feasible," Sarpi commented. "How do you know they are a coven?"

"A group of women walk into an ale house together and then leave behind a cryptic message. What else could they be."

"Certainly doesn't say they're witches nor that they are intending to go to this pool," Sarpi pointed out the flaws in the statement.

"Yes, I agree, but it was the way Ilan mentioned the Spring festival that the witches hold at the Calends of this month each year. It made sense that was where they were going."

Caesar was about to argue why he considered the connection that

Thurzo was trying to make as being too abstract when suddenly his arms reached upward to hold his head, his temples throbbing as they had done so many times before.

> *'The tenth day of the April Calends,*
> *Calculated in Gothic fashion is revived again by wicked people.*
> *The fire is put out and the diabolic gathering*
> *Seek the bones of the demon of Psellus.'*

"Your father again," Joseph didn't need to ask.

"Yes, Century I, Quatrain 42."

"Well, out with it," Thurzo demanded. "Sounds like your father is only confirming what I said."

"Yes, it's my father's way of saying we have to go to this witches' pool. He is telling you that you were right. Ten days after the Calends of April is when they will start their festivities, and these aren't the good witch variety either. Their intentions are evil."

"Does he say what they want," Thurzo asked next.

"He says we have to put an end to it but I don't know why they wanted us. From what he says, it is some demon they're trying to raise and take control of by the name of Psellus. What that has to do with us I don't know."

"Everything," Joseph answered somewhat reluctantly.

"How so," Caesar inquired.

"That demon they're looking for is me."

The others were stunned by Joseph's answer. "What in the world are you talking about," Sarpi could not see how Joseph could connect himself to the prophecy.

"It is because you don't know my genealogy," Joseph explained. "Psellus was the cognomen of one of my ancestors. Not exactly a direct ancestor but a cousin of my ancestor Alcimus. Bottom line is that both lines of the family were demonized by both the Christian and Jewish worlds."

"But why would they want you?" Sarpi could not see the connection.

"It doesn't matter why," Thurzo answered on behalf of Joseph. "What matters is that we now know this must be connected to our mission to stop the murders. How else would they even know of Joseph. So if we capture these women, we'll be a huge step closer to solving the murders. Agree?"

They all agreed to the presented strategy though they freely admitted that none of them had any idea on how to capture a witch. As they rode towards the witches' pool, the details of how they were going to perform the task became wild and varied.

"All I know is that if you make a circle of salt around them then they can't cross over the line of salt," Caesar repeated an old folk tale that he once overheard.

"That doesn't make any sense," Sarpi ridiculed. "It is only salt. I'm sure they put it on their food like everyone else when they eat. Perhaps you throw it in their eyes and then they can't see for a few minutes, giving you the opportunity to wrestle them to the ground and then bind them. At least that makes more sense."

"I'm just telling you what I heard. I didn't say it works," Caesar didn't try to rationalize the suggestion. "But you have to admit, it wouldn't hurt for us to have a couple sacs of salt available just in case."

"Well I have heard that iron burns their flesh when it makes contact, so I'm guessing our swords will do very well against them," the Count commented as either a joke or very seriously. The others couldn't tell at the moment he said it.

"I thought you wanted to take a witch prisoner," Sarpi sought clarification of what Thurzo was actually intending.

"I do, Senor Sarpi, but I need only one. The rest we will deal with as we normally would in regards to witchcraft."

As a magistrate, Fra Paolo Sarpi was not entirely pleased with the answer he just heard. "Even those accused of practicing witchcraft have their day in court, Count Thurzo."

"Senor Sarpi, do you really believe that those bent on killing you, that are connected to these ghastly murders of the young girls, that according to Nostradamus's own words want the bones of our young friend, Joseph Kahana, should be given their day in court? I have lost two men already, you have lost your driver, who knows how many more will be lost until we end this nightmare, and you wish to speak to me of the rights of these witches to have their day in court. Justice is only deserving by those that actually deserve it. These monsters have given up that right a long time ago."

"But these are merely some misguided women that believe they have unnatural powers. It is not true. Scientifically it is unproven. How can we murder these women in cold blood."

"Have you ever known a witch before?" Thurzo asked Sarpi.

"No," Sarpi replied. "I don't believe they actually exist."

"Have you ever known anyone that ever claimed to have been attacked by a witch's spell before," the Count continued his line of questioning.

"I have tried cases where someone has accused another of being a witch and every time it turned out to be a lie. It was merely a vendetta of one neighbour against another," Paolo defended his conviction that there were no such people as witches.

"Well welcome to Transylvania, Senor Sarpi because I guarantee that when we find this pool you will see things that will definitely change your mind." Unbuttoning his high collared khaki shirt, Gyorgy Thurzo exposed his left breast for everyone to see three five inch scars that stretched from sternum to nipple. "You know what did that?" he questioned them.

"I'm guessing some sort of knife," Sarpi concluded.

"Guess again," Thurzo said angrily as he recalled how he had earned his scar. "That was a gift from one of your imaginary, non-existent witches. She was trying to rip out my heart with her bare hands. They weren't even hands, they were talons. Her strength was incredible and I can still feel her claw like nails burying themselves into my chest. If it hadn't been for one of my men putting a bayonet in her back while she was straddling me, I wouldn't be here today to talk about it. So don't try to tell me how these are misguided women that falsely believe they possess supernatural abilities. You believe that and it can very easily cost you your life."

"Well, I have no reason not to believe in them," Caesar concurred. "When you have a father that can stare into a bowl of water and gaze into the future, you quickly learn that anything is possible."

"Whatever the case," Joseph tried to ease the tensions that were raised between the Count and Paolo, "I have no desire to have my bones ground up into whatever magical powder or potion they think they make from them. I say maybe we capture one to see if they can shed any light on our investigation, but as for the rest, I'd sooner see the world rid of that kind of evil."

"So if we are all in agreement now, then the next town we come to, we pick up whatever trinkets, traps and all the salt we think we need to ward of their evil and we get the job done," Thurzo informed everyone.

Gaesti was more of a village than a town built at a crossroads that most travelers would pass right by. As they rode towards the town square, it was obvious that all eyes were clearly focused on their approach. If they had not known better, they would have sworn that the townspeople had been expecting them, but that was impossible. Thurzo carefully scanned the windows and doors of the two or three floored buildings that lined the street. Behind half closed shutters, and doors only open a crack he could see pairs of eyes staring at them from the darkness. Thurzo instructed his men to keep riding towards the town square as if they had noticed nothing unusual. Considering the less than warm welcome they were receiving, no one was surprised when they found the path blocked by a throng of angry townspeople. Some of his men began reaching towards the hilt of their swords but their commander barked an order to stand down. Until he knew exactly what was happening, there would be no bloodshed.

"Another attempt to assassinate us," Sarpi provided his assessment of the situation.

"I don't think so," the Count answered. "If they wanted to do that, they could have done it easily from behind shuttered windows. They wouldn't bother to gather in the street. These people want to talk about something."

"Definitely not here to celebrate our arrival," Joseph commented.

As they approached the assembly of townspeople, one distinguished looking man from the congregation emerged from the crowd and held up his hand urging the troops to stop. "I am the Mayor of Gaesti," he announced.

Not bothering to step down from his saddle, Thurzo introduced himself. "I am the Palatine of Hungary. What appears to be the problem here?"

"Are you the one the legislature in Bucharest sent for?" the mayor wanted to know.

"I do not know what you are referring to," Thurzo remarked.

"In response to our complaint. They said they would contact the territorial authorities and they would look into the matter immediately."

"Wallachia isn't under my jurisdiction, but tell me what your complaint was and perhaps I can help," the Count offered an olive branch to ease the tension.

"They promised that they would deal with it this year," the Mayor sounded distressed, which only made the crowd of people more restless and aggressive in their body movements.

"I have had no contact with your legislative body in Bucharest, but if you tell me the problem, I promise, if I can help, I will."

"It's the witches," the Mayor shouted, which was answered by several shouts of "Death to the witches," from some of the townspeople. "Every year at this time some of our young girls disappear and we never see them again. This year two girls have already gone missing. We know it is them. We need the authorities to get our daughters back. We have had enough of their doing nothing year after year."

"Are you certain it is the witches?" Thurzo wanted confirmation of their accusation.

"Who else could it be. Every year they hold their spring festival at this time and every year some of our daughters disappear. They want us to believe that it must be animals in the forest attacking them and dragging them into their dens but none of our girls would ever go into the forest alone. It has to be the witches taking them!"

Looking from one to the other, the three colleagues on the mission agreed with the Mayor's conclusion. It wasn't a coincidence, but they still couldn't establish how all the pieces of the puzzle fit together.

"I promise you, we will put an end to this," the Count made a commitment. "But I will need your help. We need you to lead us to this pool where they gather. We have word that they are there now. Any men from your community that have a rifle, let them come with me. If they see the girls there, then they can help us rescue them. We end the scourge of these witches tonight!"

Thurzo's statement was met with cheers from the townspeople. They had suffered for years and finally the felt the nightmare would be ending. It didn't matter that the Palatine of Hungary hadn't been the authority they had been expecting. All that mattered was an end to the kidnappings.

Some of the townspeople had reassembled with their weapons, swelling Count Thurzo's troops to about twenty-nine armed men in total. He was confident this number would be sufficient to eliminate the coven. No more than three men abreast, he gave the order to 'forward march." Not long afterwards, Joseph and his colleagues gazed upward at the ebony sky dotted with little bits of ivory. Lost in discussion, it had not been their intention to keep marching as long as they did, though they were positive that it hadn't actually been that long since they left the little village of Gaesti. At some point they had been oblivious to the sun setting, and now only darkness lay ahead of them. Thurzo tried to estimate how far they may have traveled. The surrounding trees provided no answer other than they had already entered into the forest which stretched out for miles and miles. Had it been seconds, minutes or even hours that they had begun passing under the shadows of the tall trees; no one seemed able to recall. There was no immediate clearing visible, where they could take a rest. The only decision now was whether they should continue deeper into the forest, or whether they should turn around and see if they had already passed a suitable area in which to have a respite. It was decided that they would travel for perhaps another half hour to see if there was a break among the trees, and if not, then they would turn back. But the further they rode their horses into the forest, the more intense the darkness became.

Caesar was the first to complain how hot and stifling the air was becoming, making it hard to breathe. There was a deafening silence that they all noticed next. The breeze appeared to pass through the trees but there was no rustling of the leaves, no sound from the bats or birds flapping their wings, and not even the sound of insects chirping from their hiding places within the bushes that filled the gaps between the trees. Only the sounds of their own hearts thumping upon the inside of their eardrums assured them that they had not gone deaf. The ghostly play of the shadows, stretching as they were given life by the occasional beam of moonlight penetrating the leaves brought to mind the past encounter with werewolves and the men in Thurzo's unit shuddered at the thought of reliving that nightmare.

Before the half hour deadline closed, everyone in the Count's band of witch hunters heard the cry from a baby goat, but none were quite certain in which direction the sound originated. But the townspeople had no doubt it was coming from the direction of the witches' pool. Some of the people quickly checked their pockets for their charms and glass witch bottles before taking a deep breath and marching on. The bleating of the kid was now joined by the sounds of rhythmic chants and crazed shouts, but in spite of their mounting fears they pushed forward, through the thickening trees until they reached a point where Thurzo and his men had to dismount because the bramble and thicket made it impossible for the horses to press on any further. Pushing the thorns aside, they suffered scratches wherever their skin was exposed, rivulets of blood making red tracks across their hands and arms. They could see a light ahead, flames dancing about a small clearing, but at the same time they realized that all they could hear now was the goat bleating, as all the other noise from the chanting suddenly fell silent. Holding up his hand, the Count signaled for everyone to halt in their tracks until he had a chance to assess the situation characterized by a disturbing lack of any other sounds.

Tied by one hind leg to an oak stump along side the pool, the little goat pulled desperately to free itself. From his position concealed behind a tree, Thurzo could not make out anyone or anything else in the vicinity of the pool other than the bleating kid. It made everyone start to doubt whether they had actually heard chanting at all or whether it was just the forest playing tricks in their collective minds.

Caesar felt every hair on his body bristle and stand erect. He knew something was wrong. As his eyes adjusted to the low light, and the glare from the torches that were planted into the ground at several positions in the clearing, he could make out the edges of the dark pool. He was surprised by how small it was; only fifteen feet across at best. There wasn't any evidence of a stream or creek feeding it, which meant it must be fed from an underground river. Like Gyorgy Thurzo, he was wondering where had all the witches gone. He looked at the bag he was carrying containing the salt he had purchased and he wondered how was he going to manage to encircle the entire clearing.

Fumbling with the rifle in his hands, Joseph required assistance from one of the soldiers assigned to guard him to load it properly. He had to caution Joseph not to ram the wad and pellet so hard, or else he might actually ignite the powder in the barrel. Far from confident, Joseph raised the rifle to his shoulder, looking through the forked site for any suspicious targets. As he scanned the clearing from left to right, he realized how completely absent the pool surroundings were of any evidence of life other than the goat. No toads, nor frogs, or even the usual insects that one would normally see gathered near a standing pond of water. Even though the goat had enough length to its binding tether to reach the water's edge, it showed no interest in drinking from the pool. So very strange he thought, wondering what it all meant.

Performing a quick calculation of the time it took them to reach the clearing, to the time the chanting stopped, and the normal speed of movement exhibited by humans, Paolo Sarpi attempted to determine the approximate position where the witches might currently be. He determined that that lack of sounds meant they had to have stopped and were no longer moving through the forest. If that were true, then he calculated they could not have moved more than twenty feet from the clearing, which meant they should be almost at the precise locations that they, themselves, along with the troops and the townspeople were located but that would be impossible. They would be practically on top of one another, yet he could see no one. No sooner did that comment register in his mind, did the ramifications of his calculation take root and he looked straight up into the trees. "They're right above us," he screamed.

The warning came too late as they fell like rain upon the band of witch hunters. Like wildcats possessed by demons, leaping from high concealing branches providing covering foliage and pouncing upon their petrified prey, the fell upon the Thurzo's men. It had never occurred to anyone to ask how many witches attended the spring festival at the pool. But then, anyone who may have ever seen the coven by the pool probably was never heard from again. If they had been thinking there would only be a handful comprising a coven's number then they were sorely mistaken. Easily, there must have been three dozen, as every villager and soldier found themselves engaged in deadly conflict with either one or two assailants.

Any illusions that these were merely misguided women masquerading to be in league with the devil were quickly swept away as these harbingers of evil tore into skin and muscle with the razor sharp metal talons they wore upon their fingers and small throwing blades tinged with a quick acting poison that if hit with enough blades caused those stung to fall into a catatonic state. Once down, they would sink their pointed teeth deep into the fleshy throats of their victims, tearing through cartilage and vessels with a rapid flick of their heads. Their onslaught was vicious and brutal, with no intention of letting anyone survive. Having used the element of surprise to quickly gain the upper hand the situation looked grave for the witch hunters.

In such close quarters, the soldiers of Thurzo's squadron never had the opportunity to raise their rifles. Finding the enemy within arm's length, they had to rely on their knives that they could swiftly pull from their belts, stabbing frantically in the hope of making contact before they became buried beneath the falling body of another attacker from above.

Caesar found himself unable to move, as one witch, screaming like a banshee, crashed into his chest as she fell from her perch on top of him. He could do nothing but watch, momentarily paralyzed with fear as she descended like a giant spider, arms and legs waving wildly, her deadly talons flashing in the scattered light from the torches like bolts of lightning skittering across the sky. Her naked body was painted in spiraling circles of blue and red from head to toe, with curved lines of colour streaking her face as if they were ancient tattoos. Black eyes orbiting in yellow seas, with chiseled cheekbones over charcoaled lips, her appearance would be the source of nightmares for years to come if he was able to survive. She straddled Caesar while he tried to catch his breath, his chest feeling as if it had been crushed by a one ton weight. Her tongue flickered across her lips from side to side as she prepared to deliver the final blow.

Caesar reached behind his head, his fingers desperately searching for the bag of salt. When she saw his hand dig into the bag and clutch a handful of salt, she laughed hoarsely, speaking in a slithering serpentine voice, "Silly man, salt only works on demons, not witches." Caesar didn't care what she had to say, flinging the handful of salt into her face as a last resort. She screamed as she felt the salt burning her eyes. She leaned backwards, using her hands to desperately rub the grains from her eyes. Having shifted her weight, Caesar could suddenly breathe again. He quickly looked to either side to see if there was anything he could pick up and use to defend himself. To his left lay a dead soldier who had not been quick enough to use his knife but fell with his hand holding the weapon within reach of Caesar's fingers. He snatched the blade and swinging his arm in an upward arc he plunged it into the side of the witch's head by her ear. She unleashed a horrific scream that was over almost as soon as it started, falling forward on top of Caesar and covering him with her lifeless body.

Having sidestepped his attacker as she fell from the tree, Count Thurzo had sufficient time to draw his rapier and run it through his assailant. She died before she even had sufficient time to pick herself off the ground. Never forgetting his past encounter with a witch, the Count fought like a man possessed, slashing and hacking through several of his attackers before being hit by the poisoned throwing blades that they were very adept at using. He tried to keep on his feet but the strength in his limbs was vanishing quickly as he sunk to his knees and then he collapsed head first into the ground.

When Joseph first heard Paolo Sarpi shout out his warning, he already had his rifle in his hands. Almost reflexively he pulled the trigger as his assailant fell from above. The shot caught her in the abdomen and she lay writhing on the ground while Joseph began loading his musket for another round. Before he even had a chance to insert the second wadding he was surrounded by three of the witches, snarling and cursing, preparing for the attack. Wolf placed himself between Joseph and the three assailants. But the witches showed no fear, reaching into their headbands to withdraw several throwing blades and hitting Wolf squarely along his back. Within seconds the animal was laying paralyzed, unable to help his master. "Wolf!" Joseph yelled, concerned for the safety of his animal. He then grabbed his rifle by the muzzle, attempting to use it as a club, swinging it angrily at their heads in the hope of making contact. Not willing to give him the chance, they drew out another set of their little throwing blades from their head bands and flung them in his direction. As the third blade penetrated his skin, he felt the rifle fall from his hands and watched as the world began to swirl before his eyes. Several minutes later he sensed that he was moving, being dragged by a number of his assailants but he could not move a muscle to resist. He was trapped within his own body and there was nothing he could do about it.

The battle was going poorly for the Count's men and the villagers. Most of them had already fallen and those that were still fighting were severely outnumbered. It was only a matter of time until they all became the victims to the coven of witches. Whether they died quickly or slowly was the only situation they were still in control of. These women were like wild beasts, swarming over each man as they fell, tearing them to pieces with howls of delight. It was the fear of seeing these subhuman creatures rip the flesh from their comrades that pushed any remaining troops to continue the fight. Those men still standing on their feet formed a circle, back to back, readying themselves for the onslaught that they knew would eventually come as the witches reorganized and divided themselves into several groups, preparing to attack their defensive ring from different angles.

In all the confusion, no one paid any attention to Paolo Sarpi, whom was the first to sound the alarm of the witches' arboreal attack. Sarpi reached up and tore a canteen from one of the saddle bags.

Fumbling with the cap, he managed to remove it and pour the remaining water on the ground. Down on all four limbs, he crawled over to the body of one of the soldiers, desperately searching through his leather pouch for any remaining lead pellets still in his possession. Rolling the pellets into the mouth of the canteen, he then ran his fingers across the surface of the ground, gathering any of the small rocks that would fit through the canteen's neck. He looked up from his position to make certain he had not been spotted, then quickly set about gathering two powderhorns from the corpses of Thurzo's men and packed the gunpowder tightly into the remaining space within the canteen. Using the tip of a knife, he punched a hole in the cap and sealed the cap tightly in place. Tearing a strip of wadding that he then meticulously coiled and braided, he fed it through the hole in the cap and into the belly of the canteen. Using his flint, he lit the strip of wadding that protruded from the metal water bottle and flung his creation in the general direction of where close to a dozen of the witches had gathered into a single group.

The device landed at their feet, and their immediate reaction was one of surprise rather than fright, as they quizzically gazed down at the contraption not exactly certain what it was intended to do. In the seconds it took to determine its purpose, it was already too late The explosion knocked them off their feet, shrapnel from the canteen burying itself into their legs and bellies, while the stones and lead pellets sprayed across a much broader area, striking eye sockets and lacerating temples of anyone in their path. The sound of the explosion, followed by the anguished screams of the victims caused everyone to stop in their tracks.

It was all the time and diversion that Paolo required as he had already filled another canteen and was in the process of threading the wick. The group of witches that had been dragging Joseph towards the forest, released their grip, letting him fall face down on to the ground as they began running towards the shelter of the trees. It was too late. Paulo had already tossed his second grenade, landing between themselves and the sheltering forest. As it exploded, the force was enough to shatter kneecaps and femurs when the stones hit, killing some instantly and leaving others writhing in pain on the blood soaked earth.

The tide had turned in the battle as those witches still engaged in the hand to hand combat, preparing to attack the remaining soldiers and townspeople they had surrounded, watched as their stricken comrades poured out the last of their life's blood. Paolo's deadly attack eliminated over half of their number and those remaining were quick to realize that unless they retreated and raced to the forest immediately, they too would be likely captured or killed.

Between the remaining soldiers and the surviving townspeople, several were able to reach their rifles quickly, load the shot and fire in the direction of the escapees. Several more fell under the hail of bullets and the small remainder they were content to let go, having no reserves of strength left with which they could pursue. Caesar rolled himself from underneath the dead witch and tried to rise to his feet but needed the support of one the guards to steady himself. He looked down at the woman in whom he had plunged his knife. Without the horrible mask of terror with which she concealed her true face, she actually was quite attractive he thought, her features now calm and serene. He was almost sympathetic, wondering how she ever managed to involve herself in witchcraft, but he quickly got over his feelings of being sorry when he noticed how she had torn through his vest and left trails of blood oozing from several wounds scattered across his body.

Sarpi was already kneeling over Joseph's body, examining it closely for any serious wounds. He recognized their use of a curare like substance, and knew it was only a matter of time until it wore off. He shouted over to Caesar. "Tell Thurzo's men he's going to be alright. The effects should wear off in a few hours." Satisfied that everyone still alive would recover, Paolo Sarpi then went over to examine the bodies of those witches that had borne the brunt of his explosive devices. Some of them were still alive, if just barely, but still able to talk. He sat down by one women as she groaned in torment but her injuries didn't appear life threatening. "You may live, if you cooperate," he suggested to her.

"Go to Hell," she coughed up blood.

"That's some place you will soon wish you were," Sarpi informed her, "Because when that man over there," he pointed towards Thurzo, "Finally gets control of his body back, he will do things to you that will make Hell feel like a pleasure palace. So if you cooperate with me, I may be able to save you from him. Now, did you kidnap those girls."

"What girls?" she pretended to know nothing.

"Don't play stupid with me," Sarpi warned her. "He will torture you to get the answer. I'm saving you that pain. Now, did you or didn't you kidnap those girls? And where are they now?"

"Sold," she responded.

"Sold to whom?"

"We don't know. We receive instructions as to what they want. We get it for them and then they meet us by the gorge."

"Surely you can tell me something about who they are. They obviously have money because curare from the New World isn't cheap. You would need a lot of money to buy it. So who is your rich benefactor?"

"Don't know any curare," she answered.

"Oh yes, you probably call it strychnos," Sarpi provided its Latin name. "So tell me about your buyer."

"Only know they have a fancy carriage when they pick up the girls. Never see the face of the driver."

"A carriage, not a wagon. You're certain of that."

"Yes a carriage," she was firm in her response.

"Any markings on this carriage you can describe.

"Just a black carriage," she groaned.

"And what about him," Sarpi pointed at Joseph. "Why were you trying to kidnap him. He's not one of your little girls."

"Immortal blood," she replied. "They wanted him alive."

"What do you mean immortal blood?" Paolo Sarpi had no idea what she was talking about.

"Just know he has immortal blood."

"Was it the same buyer," Sarpi wanted to know.

"Yes, now you will help me," she demanded.

"Yes, I will help." Removing her headband, Fra Sarpi pulled eight of the tiny blades from the band and proceeded to jab her in the neck with each one. "I'm guessing if three will paralyze, then eight will push you over the edge."

Before losing her ability to speak she cursed at Sarpi. "You pig sucking bastard. You said you would save me from him."

"And I just did," he reassured her. "This is far more painless than what he'd do to you just for his personal pleasure."

Rising back to his feet, Paolo Sarpi went to look at the other witches needing his attention.

Chapter Fifteen

The Dacian Caves: June 1610

It wasn't until almost two weeks later that both Count Thurzo and Joseph felt well enough to continue the journey. In the meantime they remained guests in the Mayor's house, sleeping in warm comfortable beds and having their meals fed to them by the Mayor's twin daughters.

The Count continually apologized to the village elders that kept coming to his room to visit, bringing him baskets of food and gifts of their own handicrafts. They would have no part of his apology, instead praising him for his heroic stand against the witches that had plagued their countryside for as long as anyone could remember. He hardly considered it a victory having lost seven of his own men, nine villagers and never retrieving the missing girls, but somehow the people of Gaesti were willing to forgive him all that. Burning the corpses of thirty-one witches provided them the satisfaction of knowing that the coven had been broken and would never likely be reformed. In any war there would be casualties but they considered that this time they had achieved a great victory.

Meanwhile Joseph lay in another room, with Wolf remaining at the foot of his bed during his entire recovery. His mind dwelt on the information that Sarpi had obtained from the dying witch. "Whomever has been killing these girls for the past two decades was now after Joseph's immortal blood." He scoffed at the misinterpretation of the family's credo, explaining to Sarpi that it came from the Book of Zechariah, in which it said the sceptre and rod wood never be swept away, indicating that it was two immortal bloodlines that were being referred to, not immortal blood. But the discussion soon switched to who would have even known about the history of his family. It was obvious that the Habsburgs rulers knew about it, and that was why they had requested both he and his father be involved on these missions. It was also known by the Catholic Church, but they too were responsible for requesting that Joseph and his father stop these monsters, placing their own Holy See in jeopardy to see that the Kahana succeeded. But lastly,

Joseph had to admit that the Jewish elders also knew of his family traditions and that concerned him because as with his father, they had already proven that they were willing to do whatever was necessary to see his family destroyed. What they could not identify is any benefit that would be derived by the Jewish community in having young girls from its own communities kidnapped and killed. Having ruled all these out, it meant there was a fourth entity that had somehow come to know of his lineage but in so doing had misinterpreted it. To Joseph this suggested that they had to have received their information second hand, and in so doing it had been mistranslated as it was passed down the line.

Before readying for their journey to take place the following day, the four of them sat around the table in the Mayor's house trying to solve the ever evolving riddle. Caesar had experienced another of his father's clues and it indicated that time was slipping away on them. They needed to act faster if they were going to stop the murders.

"This one was easy," Caesar explained, "But I don't think you are going to be happy with what it says in Century II, Quatrain 82."

> *'Through hunger the prey will make the wolf prisoner,*
> *The aggressor then in extreme distress.*
> *The heir having the last one before him,*
> *The great one does not escape in the middle of the crowd.'*

"Well for those of lesser ability, would you mind explaining it to us." Thurzo requested. "God, I hate these riddles," the Count muttered under her breath.

"It is simple," Caesar repeated his previous comment. "It's a retelling of what just happened. The prey, that being the killers that we are trying to stop, become greedy. They no longer want just the girls but they want Joseph as well. He's the one with a wolf, so he's the wolf. So they try to take him and in their attempt they practically lose the entire coven. We've broken their supply chain which causes them extreme distress. They still think if they can get this immortal blood from the heir, that being you Joseph, then it will all be worth it because they won't need the girls any longer. You will be the last one they ever need. In the end, we will find the leader of these evil deeds and he will not escape. No matter how many witches or werewolves he throws at us, we won't lose sight of him. We will get him."

"I'm obviously the bait," Joseph analyzed the situation. Therefore, if we're going to catch the 'great one', their leader, then we have to use that bait."

"Too risky," Thurzo refused to accept the advice. "We almost lost you once, we're not prepared to do that again. If it wasn't for Senor

Sarpi and his quick thinking, you'd be already in their possession. At some point in time you are going to have to show my men how you made those throwing bombs, Paolo. They will come in very handy I suspect in the near future."

"I'm just glad it worked," Paolo replied graciously. "I had no idea if they would. In principle they should but…"

"Can't you just say thank you without giving us an entire dissertation," Caesar interrupted. "I just want to say thank you too. If it wasn't for you, none of us would be here. I know it wasn't easy for you to do that."

"I had a choice between you or them," Paolo stated. "The decision was easy.

"Well these two may get more recognition because of their injuries, but to me you're the real hero of the witches' pool Paolo. I salute you," Caesar crossed his right hand over his chest and struck his shoulder.

"Hear, Hear,' both Gyorgy and Joseph saluted.

"Finally we are all in agreement on something," Thurzo commented. "This day really is historic. But I'm afraid I don't have many men to protect us any longer and reinforcements won't be coming for some time, so I won't blame any of you if you think we should turn back now."

"What are you talking about," Joseph dismissed the suggestion. "We have survived a haunted forest, werewolves and witches. There's not much else out there that we haven't faced and won. I say let's head onward to this Dacian holy place and start putting an end to this."

"I have to agree," Paolo piped in. "We know they want Joseph or at least parts of him for some ritual they perform and the answer to what that ritual is lies in those Dacian ruins. I think we're close to the end. I say we go forward."

"My father would never forgive me if we quit now," Caesar opined. "We head onward."

"Then it truly is a historic day," Thurzo announced. "Two unanimous decisions in a row. Let's mount up and move on," he commanded.

It took three uneventful days to travel the sixty miles to reach the birthing place of the Ialomita River, high in the hills of the Meridional Carpathians. It began as nothing more than a small spring flowing out through the rocks, and yet from this small beginning eventually it would become a mighty river that flowed into the Black Sea.

"So what do we do now?" Caesar asked Thurso who had inscribed the Gypsy's words into his memory.

"We look to our left and find the camel," he replied.

"But which left?" Caesar raised the issue that depending which direction they faced, left would always be pointing to a different location.

Thurzo thought about it and then answered, "If this is where the river is birthed, then if I stand higher up on the mountain, then that would be where it doesn't exist. I would then have to look down the mountain to see the river be born. Which would mean my left is here and the camel must be there…" moving in to position as per his instructions, the Count pointed to a location on the mountain ridge that was approximately north-east. They aligned their eyesight to the approximate location that he pointed. Sure enough, they saw the ridge resembled the back of a two humped camel. "Now we just have to decide where is its head and where is the tail," Thurzo instructed them.

"Head is on the left," Sarpi concluded.

"How do you know that?" Caesar asked for an explanation.

"Because it is higher on the left side of the humps than it is on the right side," Paolo explained. "And since a head is always higher than a tail, then it makes sense that the tail is there." He pointed to a specific location on the next ridge.

"We need to get over to that ridge and find this hollowed tree next," Thurzo provided the next instruction.

The distance to the next ridge was actually further than it looked and it took the rest of the day to reach it. When they approached the location of the camel's tail it was not difficult to find the hollowed tree as there was only a solitary tree standing where the old gypsy woman had described. Thurzo approached the tree excitedly, a feeling that their journey was finally coming to an end. He could see that there was a hollow in the trunk of the tree and when he looked into it, there was a small hole on the other side. But when he aligned the holes to see where they were pointing, all he saw was the rock face of the mountain, exactly as it appeared everywhere else.

"What do you see?" Joseph asked.

"Nothing," he replied disappointingly. "Absolutely nothing."

"Let me look," Joseph insisted. The Count stepped aside and Joseph peered through the aligned holes. He too saw nothing but the rock protrusions of the mountains. Then he had an idea. "Caesar, I need you to go to the location I'm looking at. I'll look through the tree and then tell you exactly where you need to go. Maybe we can only see what we need to see when we are actually standing there."

Following his instructions, Caesar would move so many feet one way or the other until he was perfectly aligned with the line of site projected by the holes in the tree. "What do you see," Joseph shouted to Caesar in the distance.

"You won't believe me until you come here and see it for yourself," he shouted back.

"What is it?"

"There's a cave."

The rock projections of the mountainside had concealed the entrance from view, making it almost impossible to see unless standing right at the cave entrance itself.

The others raced excitedly to where Caesar was standing, the three soldiers still remaining from the unit following behind and carrying the supplies.

They had to bend down to pass through the entrance but once inside, the cave was huge, permitting them to stand up freely with plenty of head space to spare.

"Where do you think it goes?" Joseph asked in shock and awe as he lit a torch and saw the series of tunnels that radiated off in different directions from the main entrance.

"There's only one way to find out," Thurzo answered. "There are seven of us and three separate tunnel. I suggest we split up and that way we can explore the caves faster. If you find anything, you come back and get the others. Agreed?"

"Agreed," they all responded.

"I'll take one of my men, Joseph, you take another, and Caesar and Paolo can go together with the last guard.

"What if the tunnel we are in, starts to branch out. What do we do then," Caesar inquired.

"Rule of thumb," the Count replied. "Always take the branch to the right. That way you know that in order to come back you always take the one on the left."

"Makes sense," Caesar agreed. "Let's start."

What they had not anticipated was that the tunnels continued on for miles, branching, crossing, and splitting into rooms and chambers along the way, each with several extensions. The complex was actually a city built into the side of a mountain, one time housing thousands of the Dacians that chose to live there. All three groups searched for hours, but other than the bats and other creatures that now called the tunnels home, they could not find any clues that revealed the ancient Dacian culture.

Dejected, after searching for a couple more hours they met up at the entrance to decide on what they should do next.

"This isn't right," Caesar was clearly upset. "My father would not have sent us here if it wasn't important."

"Perhaps we misinterpreted the quatrain," Count Thurzo suggested.

"I don't believe so," Paolo Sarpi agreed with Caesar.

"Somehow we missed the evidence. Perhaps we should just rest the night and then search again tomorrow." The Count was exhausted and hungry and had enough for the day.

"These tunnels stretched for miles," Joseph recapped their experience, and I'm sure we walked everyone. I can't see how we missed one."

"Somehow we must have," Caesar objected. "I'm telling you, Michel de Nostradame does not make mistakes. He wanted us here to find a specific clue."

"We will look again tomorrow then," Thurzo repeated his suggestion.

"Anyone see Wolf," Joseph inquired.

"I thought he was with you," Thurzo commented.

"He was, but he must have taken off on me when I wasn't looking and I just assumed he was following me." Joseph started walking partway along the tunnel he had been searching, calling out Wolf's name as he did so. "Wolf, where are you boy? Come here Wolf?" Joseph Kahana called for his animal but he couldn't see him anywhere down the tunnel. Returning back to the entrance, he was surprised to see Wolf emerge from one of the other tunnels. He was even more surprised to see what he was carrying. "You better grab that Paolo, I can't touch it if it is what I think it is," Joseph requested the favour from his colleague.

Taking the bone from Wolf's mouth, Paolo turned it over several times as he examined it. "Your right," he informed Joseph. "Human thigh bone."

As soon as Sarpi had delivered the results of his examination, Caesar was bent over in pain, holding his head as they've seen him do before but this time the pain appeared to be far greater.

'The bones of the feet and the hands locked up,
Because of the noise the house is uninhabited for a long time.
Digging in dreams they will be unearthed,
The house healthy in inhabited without noise.'

"Well I certainly don't have trouble translating that one myself," Thurzo, congratulated himself in finally being able to understand one of the Nostradamus quatrains.

"Which one is that one,"Sarpi asked.

"Century VII, Quatrain 41," Caesar replied, still bent over and feeling the pounding inside his head. "Almost get the feeling he was mad because we started doubting him," he wrestled with explaining why it hurt so much this time. "I think he was punishing me."

"Guess we never should have doubted him," Joseph comforted his friend. "Let's go find where Wolf found that bone. Come on Boy, show me where you got the bone. Let's go Boy. Show me Wolf."

As wolf started down the tunnel, the rest of them followed as best they could, trying to keep up while they ran with torches in hand. Half way along the tunnel, Wolf darted through a small opening that was barely eighteen inches high and about the same measurement across.

"No way we are getting through that," Thurzo commented.

Sarpi bent down and examined the opening. "I could probably squeeze through, but I don't know about the rest of you. But maybe you don't have to." Scratching at the surface of the rock, Sarpi put the finger in his mouth and analyzed the taste. "Just as I thought." He stood up and kicked at what looked like rock but it crumbled easily. "Limestone and clay powder mixture. Someone covered up the doorway to hide whatever is on the other side."

They all took turns at kicking down the weak cement mixture until they had exposed the entire doorway. Stepping inside they found themselves in a massive chamber that was dimly illuminated through a series of portals in the arched roof that permitted natural light to enter from the outside. Along another wall they could just barely see a similar area that had been patched with the limestone mixture and a small opening by which Wolf must have entered the first time from the other tunnel.

"I'm guessing all the tunnels connected to this main hall," Sarpi speculated. "But someone went to a lot of trouble trying to conceal it. Which means there are answers we are seeking in here if we look carefully."

"It looks like there are torches braced on the walls," Thurzo pointed out. "Lets get some more light in here," he ordered his men to light the torches. What they saw once the room was full illuminated horrified them.

In the centre of the room was a large table cut from granite stone, standing on a solid base that was three steps higher than the rest of the room. The top surface of the table was concave, leading to what appeared to be a chiseled channel starting in the center and then exiting out one side. They speculated that it served the purpose of draining the blood and debris from the table top, where the effluent would be gathered into a pail or drum that would sit below the exit hole. The granite had been masterly carved, polished smooth, and probably looked exactly as it did back in the days when the Dacian used it to sacrifice their victims. Along the rim of the table and the edge of the platform were words carved deep into the stone but in a language and script that none of them could read. It didn't matter that they couldn't decipher the language, the table spoke for itself, but still held the secret of how many victims over time had actually been slain on its cold sleek surface.

"Commander, come quickly," one of the soldiers that had been lighting the torches at the far end of the hall called out to Thurzo.

"What have you found, Ivescu?" the Count asked for a report.

"I think you better come see for yourself."

They began walking towards the area of the room where Ivescu was standing but as they approached, Count Thurzo turned to Joseph and warned him that he better step back and go no further. Joseph knew that the warning could mean only one thing. There must have been a dead body still laying in that part of the chamber.

"My God," he overheard Caesar saying. "This is unbelievable."

Once Joseph's eyes adjusted to the partial lighting in that area he saw what Caesar was referring to. It wasn't just one body, it was dozens of them; all either decomposed or partially decayed, suggesting that they had been piled there at different times.

"Wolf, get away from there," Joseph shouted at his dog. It was obvious this pile was where Wolf had pulled the bone from when he returned to the entrance of the cave. Reluctantly, the animal listened to his master and shied away from the bodies, coming to rest by Joseph's feet.

They were forced to loosen their neck scarves, retying them over their mouths and noses to reduce the malodorous scent of rotting flesh. Sarpi methodically looked over the bodies, examining as many as he could, while not actually touching them. Overcome by the disgusting sights and smells, one of the soldiers had to run to one corner of the room where he started to retch. Even standing so far away, Joseph could feel the reflux in his throat and began gagging, finally turning away and walking back to the sacrificial alter to avoid further discomfort. Only the Count and Sarpi appeared to be immune to the noxious vapors rising from the corpses.

"How can these bodies still be here after so many generations," the Count questioned Sarpi, as the magistrate found a metal rod nearby that he then used to prod and move various parts of the dead bodies, exposing body cavities that permitted him to view what remained of the victim's internal organs.

"They wouldn't be," Paolo Sarpi replied. "Any victims of the Dacians would have turned to dust a very long time ago. From the various states of decomposition, I would determine these girls have been dead between five to ten years at most."

"Are they all girls," Thurzo asked next.

"Every one of them," Sarpi replied. "And everyone a teenager just about their time of puberty."

The Count was amazed by the accuracy of Fra Sarpi's determination. "How can you be so certain?"

"By the width of their pelvic girdle," the Magistrate replied. "It's actually quite an easy means by which to determine a girl's age. You have to appreciate, that before puberty, there is very little difference between the bone structures of boys and girls, but once a girl enters puberty, the joint of the two pelvic blades relaxes and she begins to develop what we refer to as 'womanly hips', the feature that we find so attractive and by which some cultures judge a girl's fertility."

Paying attention to the explanation, Count Thurzo examined the skeletal structures more closely and realized that Sarpi was correct in his assessment. None of the bodies had what would be referred to as 'womanly hips' but they were no longer like a boy's either, beginning to show the signs of early feminization. "Amazing," the Count commented on the finding. "I did not know that. What else can you tell me?"

By this time Caesar had enough of inhaling the putrid scent from these dead girls and was definitely put off by the calm and composure by which Paolo and Gyorgy were discussing these victims of a horrendous crime as if they were merely a science project. Ambling up to where Joseph was standing, far enough away that the scent was barely perceptible, he decided to leave the investigation to those that were clearly enjoying it.

"Had enough?" Joseph questioned his friend.

"More than enough," Caesar responded. "I think Paolo's getting the answers that we were all looking for but I'm afraid we are far too late to help any of those poor girls. They've been butchered, Joseph. Cut up, disemboweled, left to rot like vermin. I don't know how much more of this I can take."

"We made a promise Caesar to stop these killings. We can't go back until we finish what we started."

"It's way beyond us," Caesar felt depressed and disheartened. "We've been attacked by trees, wolves, witches and now this. We are way over our heads. This is nothing like what I had to deal with when I was with your father. That was about stopping a solitary killer. Yes, there were others involved but they were relatively easy to deal with once the killer was identified but this…this is immense. This is insane. This truly is evil beyond anything or anyone has ever tried to deal with. There are forces of darkness involved here, I'm telling you. I feel it; I know it. I would not even hesitate to suggest that whomever we are after are in league with the Devil."

"I agree this is far bigger than we anticipated," Joseph attempted to calm him down, "But don't you think we owe it to all those dead girls laying over there to give them justice. Only we can give it to them. Imagine their final screams while they were laying on this alter, seeing that knife hovering above them, about to plunge into their hearts. They were praying for a saviour that never came. We can't give them their lives back but we can perhaps get justice for them and their families." Joseph finished his defense of what they were doing with a hammer like blow of his fist on the top of the sacrificial alter. The blow reverberated through the hall, followed by what sounded like a series of clicks. He looked at Caesar momentarily surprised and then realized they were hearing the sound of several latches opening. "Quick Caesar, check everyone of these stones. There's some kind of door built into this platform."

Pushing and pulling every stone that was exposed, Caesar was finally able to slide one of the platform stones outward a few inches. "Not a door but a compartment," he informed Joseph. He grasped the stone at the opened edge and forced it to slide a further ten inches, fully exposing the interior of the hidden vestibule. "Well, well, well, what do you think these were for?" He carefully raised the first pot on to the alter, careful not to damage any of the components attached to it. The clay pot was quite large, capable of holding three of four quarts in volume. The tight fitting lid provided a perfect seal except for the small spout in the centre of the lid that extended upward about an inch. Attached over this spigot and tied with thread was a brittle thick twine like material that was then coiled across the top of the lid three and a half times. At its opposite end, the thick twine was carefully fitted over a small hollow needle made from copper about a quarter inch in diameter and approximately three inches long. Where it was connected to this needle it was also tightly secured by fine thread. "There's another," Caesar started to remove the second pot but in doing so, the heavy twine like material they saw on the first began to crumble. Placing the pot beside the other, they could see that this one was different. About half the size of the other, it had not only the spout on the lid as did the other, but there was also one extending from the side of the pot, very close to its bottom surface. It was from this lower spigot that the twine like material had broken off. He didn't try to remove the brittle material, instead describing it to Joseph as being about the same length and having an identical copper needle tied to the other end. But what he did remove next was a small bellows that had a brass nozzle that would fit perfectly over the spigot in the centre of the lid. "What do you think they were doing with this," Caesar asked.

"I'm not the scientist in our group," Joseph replied. "If you want an answer to that question, then we need to ask Paolo."

Calling out to Paolo, the Venetian magistrate, waved his hand in a downward motion, indicating they would have to wait. What ever he was investigating at the time, he considered far more urgent of his attention.

"Well, obviously he's still enjoying himself," Caesar commented.

"If he's finding answers, then let him take as long as he wants," Joseph responded. "If ever we are going to find the answers we seek, then this has to be the place."

"I'm just afraid of the answers we're going to find," Caesar cautioned.

"So am I," Joseph agreed. "It doesn't make sense how something this big could have remained hidden for so long."

"What do you mean," Caesar asked Joseph to elaborate

"Dozens of girls taken and then slaughtered here. From the size of this chamber, you can only guess that their rituals were attended by far more than just a handful of people. It's obvious that those villagers taken by the witches a decade ago ended up here. Why didn't the local authorities bother to interrogate any of the witches, or even tried to investigate the crimes. Back then, when they were using this place, the police could have easily used dogs to find the cave. But they didn't. Why didn't they? There's a reason and it has nothing to do with fear of superstition. I am certain that they intentionally failed to investigate. We need to find out why."

"Interesting theory," Caesar admitted, "But if it is true, then we can expect no help from any of the local authorities in providing us any information."

"It also means we have to be very careful with whom we share our information," Joseph insinuated that even those they thought close may not be trusted.

Sarpi took about another hour searching through the bodies, checking their remains, examining loose bones that appeared to have been tossed into the corner of the hall for no apparent reason. When he was finally done, both he and Thurzo, undid the scarves covering their face and walked to where Joseph and Thurzo had been patiently waiting.

"Quite a remarkable system for air exchange," Paolo commented. "It would appear that the air is drawn in from those same portals above letting in the light, and then it is drawn over to the far end of this chamber to where the bodies are located, and escapes through that hole in the wall, right there." He pointed to what appeared to be a circular hole carved into the stone wall at about a ten foot height. "That vents out the air to somewhere above the ranges, where it is diffused by the circulating winds. Considering this was built by the Dacians over a thousand years ago, their knowledge regarding ventilation is truly remarkable."

"And what about this," Caesar pointed to the clay jars he had assembled on the alter.

"Definitely not Dacian," Sarpi replied immediately. "I'd say they are most likely from some local potter. The Venetian magistrate began closely examining the containers with all their connection and attachments. "Most interesting," Sarpi hummed and hawed as he delicately touched the thick twine like material, only to have part of it crumble practically to dust under the slightest pressure. He continued to make the same noises as he fingered the copper needles, noticing how at one time the points were probably razor sharp.

"Enough with the noises," Caesar grew impatient, "What do you think it is?"

"I think it is our vampire," he answered cool and collected.

"Our vampire?" Joseph responded incredulously.

"Yes," Paolo replied with certainty. "Quite an astounding invention," he heaped praise on the contraption. "Absolutely fantastic. I must make note of it later. I think it could prove very useful in the future."

"Forget the future," Caesar's impatience grew, "What about now?"

"This is how they removed the blood from the girl we saw in the mortuary and why there was never a trace of the blood at the site where they found the body. It's because they collected it and carried it away in a pot just like this one." Sarpi tapped the pot that only had the spigot on its lid.

"What does the twine have to do with it?" Caesar inquired.

"It isn't twine," Sarpi indicated. "It is made from small intestine. "Perhaps a cat, or a puppy," the magistrate suggested. "When fresh, it would have been quite flexible and able to extend to a good length. It would conduct fluids between the needle to the pot or in the other direction as well. "This one," he held up the needle attached to the single spouted pot, "They would have inserted into the carotid artery Quite easy to do when it was sharp. The girls heart would keep pumping the blood into that pot until the volume was so low that there wasn't enough blood pressure to keep it flowing. That's when they'd insert the other needle into the jugular vein. That second pot would be filed with some kind of solution, and they'd use the bellows fitted to the top to put downward pressure on that solution, forcing it to flow through the intestinal tube and into the vein. This would build up the volume of liquid in the circulatory system, so the heart would be able to pump out the last of the actual blood through the carotid artery. Quite ingenious." Sapri continued to compliment the technology behind the equipment.

"This doesn't sound like a crazed killer attempting to revive some ancient rituals from a lost civilization," Joseph deduced from Paolo's explanation.

"Not at all," Sarpi concurred. "But they actually took it to a much higher level. The revival of the Dacian rituals was probably used to bind the adherents together through the cult like activities, creating a brotherhood of sorts. But the sacrifices had nothing to do with trying to appease or gain the pleasure of some wolf god to gain immortality. To take the reference from what they said about you Joseph, they considered this blood they gathered to be the key to immortality. This was their immortal blood."

"How do you know that," Joseph was curious as to how Paolo came to that conclusion.

"They told me," Paolo pointed back towards the pile of corpses. "The dead do speak if you only take the time to learn how to listen."

"Alright, so what did they say," Caesar asked, pushing Sarpi to get on with his narrative.

"There may have been some ritual involved in the killing of these girls but as I mentioned, it would be used to create the cord that binds a secret society together. But the girls were actually being harvested for their blood and certain organs."

"That certainly wasn't the case with the girl in the mortuary. They only took her blood. Considering how decomposed these bodies are, I'm surprised you were able to tell if anything was missing or not." Caesar looked for an explanation after pointing out the differences when they examined Maria Zapolya.

"They took her blood, but I agree left her intact otherwise. That suggests to me they either didn't have time or they didn't have need of the rest."

"The rest of what?" Joseph interjected at that point. "What exactly was it they were harvesting?"

"Most had the brain case opened from the bottom of the skull. There's a small gland there we call the pituitary. It looks like they were particularly interested in that. There's a break of several ribs on the right side of the chest in most. My guess is they were taking the spleens and gall bladder as well."

"Anything else," they asked.

"It was hard to say because most of the soft tissues were already too decomposed, but of the few uteri I could find, it looks like the ovaries were missing."

"And…"

"Particular attention was paid to long bones. Many were cracked in half suggesting they were spooning out the marrow."

"Can you think of any reason anyone would be wanting those particular organs," Joseph struggled to make sense of Paolo's findings.

"I don't have any idea," Sarpi admitted. "But they obviously had a purpose for them in this pursuit for immortality. Take a look at what we now know," Sarpi recapped their findings. "These aren't barbarians practicing some ancient god worshiping ritual," he stated, "It took a scientific intellect to build that contraption. It takes individuals with medical knowledge and a foundation in human anatomy to know where to find the organs and glands they were harvesting. We can no longer assume that the people perpetrating these crimes are the scum of the earth. Some of them are clearly at the top of the social ladder and they may have been here for years, building their secret society but just over half a decade ago, for whatever reason, they decided to move west."

"Caesar and I were just discussing how the authorities in Wallachia must have known more than they were willing to admit. When all those girls from the villages were disappearing, there was a reason they didn't go after the witches that took them. Either it was highly likely some were involved themselves in the kidnappings or else they were being told not to investigate by someone of a higher authority that they took orders from."

"I fear you may be right," Thurzo confirmed what he had already been suspecting himself. "As much as it pains me to think that some of my friends in the nobility are responsible, I can no longer dismiss that possibility."

"But until someone actually confesses, there is no way for us identify who they are," Joseph bemoaned their situation.

"Not true! We find out what happened here five or so years ago and we will know exactly who is responsible," Paolo Sarpi disagreed. "I now know why Nostradamus wanted us here. The evidence says if we find out who used this cave several years back, then we will know who our killer is now. The people that know their identity are still around."

"And how do you presume that?" Thurzo wanted to know what magical skill of deduction Sarpi would use to make the leap from a decade old ritual to identifying the individuals responsible.

"Because someone tried to seal off the horrors of this chamber by cementing closed all the openings. It wasn't those performing the killings. They wouldn't have cared less if anyone discovered the grizzly aftermath of their slaughter. Whoever sealed those walls did so as an act of compassion. They couldn't bare to let the families of these victims find their daughters in that condition. In their minds the best way to protect the living was to conceal the dead."

"How can it be compassionate to not let them find their children?" Caesar could not accept any justification to deny families that right. "Protect them from knowing what exactly?

"There was a reason those bodies were disposed like refuse at the end of the chamber. The cult could have easily just burned the bodies if they wanted to. But they had another use for them. There were other marks on the long bones that weren't from someone breaking them."

"What are you saying," Caesar already feared the answer.

"Those bones that we saw in the corners and scattered about, didn't just happen to fall from the bodies in the pile and land a good distance away. They were dragged there. The same way Wolf decided to drag one to the entrance to show us."

"You are suggesting they were feeding the corpses to their dogs," Joseph connected to what Paolo was trying to say indirectly.

"Would have been very big dogs. More like wolves from the marks I witnessed engraved into the bones. Remember, these may not be Dacians, but they are performing the ritual of the Wolf god, to unite their brotherhood. It only makes sense that they had their own wolves, so they would all be part of a pack. The Dacians were called the wolf warriors and these men considered themselves to be worthy of inheriting that title as well."

"And if there were enough of these 'wolf warriors' with their pet wolves still around today, then they easily could have been responsible for attacking us in the forest," connecting all the dots, Joseph was speculating exactly what Sarpi and Thurzo had already discussed when they were sorting through the bodies.

"Don't refer to them as pets," Sarpi warned him. "They're not like your animal. These have already fed on human flesh. They will be more wild than domesticated. Far more dangerous than Wolf could ever be."

"Point taken," Joseph agreed. "So if you are right, then we have to find whoever it was that sealed the caves and he will be able to tell us everything about what happened here. Problem is we don't know who that person was, and I doubt anyone in the villages knows his identity either."

"Not true," Sarpi blurted in response to Joseph's statement. "I know exactly who sealed the caves."

"So you are a fortune teller now too," Caesar scoffed at what he considered Paolo's unfounded statement. "Are you going to tell me the dead told you who it was?" he asked.

"Actually, they did tell me," Sarpi smirked but which grew into a broad smile as soon as he saw the surprise on Caesar's face. "The majority of these girls still wore beads and charms with Arabic engravings. They were from the Muslim villages further east. We can find who was responsible for sealing the caves if we go south."

"You're not suggesting what I think you are suggesting," Thurzo fretted.

"We will find our man in Turkey.

"Probably along with our deaths as well," Thurzo spat.

Chapter Sixteen

Turkey: July 1610

"This is a terrible idea" Count Thurzo complained as they crossed the Danube River that ran the border between Wallachia and the Turkish Empire.

"Why so worried," Paolo Sarpi could not understand the Count's concerns. "We've had a peace treaty since signing it in Zsitvatoraok four years ago."

"No, you've had a peace treaty," Thurzo corrected him. "You Venetians along with the French have had an accord where you can take advantage of the treaty, sending your merchants into the Ottoman Empire and practically dominating the trade in every aspect. What we in Austria got was a break from paying them their annual tribute money and they've resented that loss to their coffers for the past four years."

"Well perhaps if you and your men took off their military cloaks you wouldn't be so obvious and you'd worry a lot less," Joseph suggested.

"No, the cloaks stay on," Thurzo insisted. "We could be riding around the countryside for days trying to find a unit of Ottoman soldiers. But by wearing our Austrian uniforms, Paolo and I are calculating that we won't have to look at all; they'll find us."

"Good plan," Caesar was sarcastic. "What if they decide to shoot us first and then ask questions afterwards."

"They won't," the Venetian sounded positive.

"And you know that because...?" Joseph wasn't so positive as his companion.

"Because of human nature," Paolo explained.

"You are assuming they'll be curious as to why four Austrian military men are riding through the Turkish province of Bulgaria," Caesar attempted to interpret Paolo's explanation.

"No," Sarpi shook his head. "I'm counting on human greed. They'll see a big fat reward for catching a few Austrian soldiers this side of the border."

"I'm glad you're confident in this plan of yours," Caesar still did not think it was a good idea.

"You sure you are right about this," Joseph asked Paolo in a hushed voice so the others wouldn't overhear.

"It should work," Paolo responded, which was hardly reassuring.

"I heard that," Thurzo let them know he was listening.

"Perhaps we should have sent one of the men ahead as a messenger," Joseph began second-guessing the plan.

"That definitely wouldn't have worked," Paolo dismissed his idea outright. "A lone rider in this land wouldn't have made it a few miles at best before being attacked and robbed. We stay together; we stay protected, we stay alive."

"Definitely not sounding reassuring," Joseph muttered.

"We keep heading south on this road," Fra Sarpi insisted. "Sooner or later we'll come across an outpost.

"I'm placing my life in your hands, Senor Sarpi," Count Thurzo admitted, "So try not to lose it for me."

"It shouldn't be too long," Sarpi replied. "A few hours at most on the road. Trust me."

Paolo Sarpi had actually overstated the time frame. It wasn't even an hour later that they found themselves surrounded by a squadron of Ottoman cavalry. The commander of the Turks was direct and unforgiving in his manner. Perhaps nearing thirty years of age, he was already a seasoned warrior from numerous encounters on the battlefield against the continent's Holy Roman forces before the signing of the treaty. As far as he was concerned, the humiliation of signing at Zsitvatoraok was a grave mistake that dishonored the glory of the Ottoman Empire. He had no difficulty in letting the group of stragglers know his true sentiments. He was just as unforgiving as he was proud, which meant this group of seven travelers needed to be humiliated in the same manner he felt his empire was. Outnumbered four to one, the Europeans were quickly stripped of their weapons, knives, swords and muskets, then forced to step down from their mounts and walk without the benefit of any water from their saddle bags.

"Where are you taking us?" Thurzo asked his captors.

"Quiet dog!" the commander shouted. "You will speak when I command you to speak."

"Is that any way to speak to your guest?" Fra Sarpi piped up in the Count's defense.

"You are not my guests, you are spies and therefore my prisoners," the commander had already sentenced them in his mind. The penalty for spying was death, treaty or no treaty.

"Your Sultan will think differently when he finds out that you have treated Fra Paolo Sarpi in this manner."

The name definitely registered with the commander. They could see the moment of confusion he experienced, contemplating what he should do if Paolo was speaking the truth."

"You lie," he refused to believe Sarpi, raising a fist in his face as he leaned over in his saddle, but then hesitated when he saw that Paolo showed no evidence of fear. "Why would the Magistrate of Venice be wandering through these lands with such a pathetic looking escort.

"I assure you, my escort was much larger when I started out but we have been attacked repeatedly since we left Vienna. And now all I have left is what you see."

"If you were the Magistrate then you would have sent word you were coming. We've had no such instruction. You cannot be him."

"I assure you, I am him, just as I assure you that it was never our intention to come to your Empire, but matters have arisen that requires your support."

"And who is this then," the commander kicked out his foot in the direction of Count Thurzo."

"Just a military man that led my escort. But as you can plainly see he has only three men remaining and therefore you would be hard pressed to justify him as being any manner of threat."

"And these others?"

"Merely a Frenchman and a Galician that are my traveling companions. Under the terms of the agreement, men from two of the countries that are to be considered trading partners and not enemies."

"Why should I believe any of this," the commander's distrust of foreigners clouded his thinking. "You could very well be spies and this is the cover story that you were instructed to repeat if caught."

"You could be right, Commander, but are you willing to gamble with your lives in case you are wrong.

"We could cut you down right here and leave your bodies to be eaten by the birds. No one would be the wiser," the commander threatened.

"And then no one would know the urgent message I bear and when the Sultan finds out what you have done, you and every one of your men will find their heads on a spike. *Bize zarar verin ve padisahiniz baslarinizi diken diken gorecektir!*" Sarpi repeated his warning in Turkish while moving his right arm in a circle from left to right, his index finger pointing at everyone in the platoon to let them know their fate if any harm came to himself or his companions.

The Ottoman cavalry unit began chattering nervously, fearing that their commander's behaviour could result in all of them being punished.

"So give me your message and I will carry it to my government's officials," the commander ordered Sarpi.

"And who are you," Sarpi questioned the commander, as if he was of little consequence.

"I am Rashid Kartal, Captain of the 1st Bulgari Unit."

"Then you are an officer of no consequence," Sarpi responded. "I will not give my message to you. Take me to someone of more importance."

The response from the Venetian Magistrate infuriated the officer but there was nothing he could do but comply. "Give these men back their horses to ride," he instructed his men. "But do not give them their weapons." He then turned back to Paolo Sarpi and threatened him again. "You want someone of higher authority. You are in luck. The Sultan himself is in the province reviewing the administration. I swear by Allah, if he does not recognize you, then I will kill you with my own two hands."

"Lead on, Captain Kartal," Sarpi replied with a smile upon his face.

The Commander gave orders for his men to begin riding towards the Sultan's court being held outside Shurmen, sixty miles away.

As they were getting back on their horses, Thurzo leaned over to speak quietly to Sarpi. "Remind me to never play cards with you," the Count said jokingly.

"You should have no worries Gyorgy," Paolo winked, "I never bluff."

Looking down from the hills ringing the plain, the Sultan's encampment consisted of over two hundred colourful tents, the predominant colors of the striped canvas being green and deep orange. Wherever the Sultan went, his entire court would follow, and as they approached the city of tents it was apparent that a large proportion of the civic employees of Konstantiniye had made the journey. They could not help but be impressed, witnessing the nomadic nature of the Ottoman government, a concept extremely foreign and the antithesis to the European fixation with bricks and mortar as the only place where governments could rule and make policy.

As they descended the hill, they joined the serpentine string of caravans descended upon the plain outside the city of Shurmen, originating from those territories in the west under the suzerainty of the Sultan. Princes, governors and ambassadors of these territories, flooded past the inspection of the Sultan's elite guards looking eagerly to their audience with the ruler of the empire to make their petitions.

Moving towards the center of the encampment they passed malls of shops, offering a wide variety of goods from across both the Ottoman and Habsburg Empires. The festival atmosphere of the encampment overwhelmed their senses as they approached. Dancing girls, jugglers, acrobats and magicians competed for their attention. Children from the small city of Shurmen sat entranced listening to the story tellers providing tales of fantastic quests of magical lamps and powerful jinn. Once again in their minds they contrasted this with the practically dreary atmosphere of the European courts they were accustomed to.

Ahmed, son of Mohomaad III, savored the pageantry and succored the success of his early reign. Having come to the throne at the age of fourteen in 1603, Ahmed was the youngest to ever become Sultan. He considered himself a ruler for the people, liberal in his thinking and choosing to put an end to the long wars that were raged against the Europeans for over a hundred years.

There were long lines of dignitaries eagerly awaited their chance to proclaim their loyalty and adherence to this newly established order. As it came to their turn to appear before the Sultan, they would bow low, practically touching their heads to the ground, just before they would hand over their gifts of coins or jewels into the hands of the Vizier, whom announced their names and from whence they came.

Sultan Ahmed accepted their gifts graciously, welcoming each entourage and then inviting them to sit and join him later at his table beneath the huge dining tent. By day's end, the pile of offerings began to obscure the platform.

"The emissary from Venice, Chief Magistrate of the City State, and his companions," the Vizier announced after Rashid Kartal whispered into his ear whom he was escorting.

Much to the disappointment of the Ottoman captain, the Sultan immediately recognized Paolo Sarpi. "Senor Sarpi!" the Sultan held up his outstretched arms in a sign of warm welcome. "I am so surprised to see you here. I had no idea that the Venetians were sending anyone to greet my presence here in the western provinces. This is quite unexpected but a most happy occasion."

"It is a great honour to see you once again, Excellency. You have matured into a fine young man since we last met."

"But still not able to grow a proper beard," Ahmed laughed as he rubbed the straggly growth of hair on his chin."

"Everything in its time," Paolo assured him.

Those accompanying Sarpi were surprised when they saw the Sultan. Here was one of the most powerful men in the world and he was hardly beyond his teenage years. The high white turban with its jewelled peacock feather adornment gave the impression that Ahmed was much taller than his five and a half foot frame.

"So what has brought you here," the Sultan quickly turned to business. I thought you had already taken everything you wanted from me in the treaty. Are you back for more? You can turn me upside down and shake me but there is nothing left for you to take," Ahmed joked, his response immediately met with laughter from his surrounding councilors.

"Let us be honest with one another, Excellency. You have done very well from the treaty too. There are European goods flowing through all your markets and you even get to charge a tariff on them to fill your tax coffers."

"Yes, but when do I get control of the territories promised to me. It is now four years and they have not been transferred to me. I should be sitting in Wallachia, not south of the Danube as I am now."

"Which lands are those you are specifically referring to, Excellency?" Sarpi asked to be reminded of where they had defaulted on the treaty. "As far as I know, nothing stops you from being north of the river."

"The agreement stipulated that in exchange for the Austrian Empire no longer having to pay its tribute, I would have the sole right to reign over Transylvania. Was I not named as Suzerain of Transylvania within the treaty. Did I not propose that Gabor Bethlen would be my governor over these lands and he should be installed immediately. Why are none of my officials administering in the province? Why are soldiers only loyal to the Habsburgs, policing the territories? Why is there this man Gabriel Bathory calling himself governor and prince over the lands."

"I do recall that these items were all part of the treaty," Paolo conceded. "I do not exactly have the ear of the Austrian Emperor and as you know there is currently some confusion as to who actually has the right to call themself the Emperor."

"Are you suggesting that the treaty made with Emperor Rudolph is no longer valid and I will need to renegotiate with his brother Matthias? I know for a fact Matthias is already challenging my right to the lands. These Bathorys are like weeds, cropping up everywhere."

"No...no, not at all Excellency. The Emperor Matthias is pleased to honour the agreement as it stands but perhaps a reminder regarding Transylvania needs to be brought to his attention."

"You were one of the chief negotiators for the Europeans, Senor Sarpi. If you cannot deliver on your promises, then I am seriously disappointed in you."

Seeing the Magistrate squirm under pressure, Rashid Kartal who was still standing along side the Vizier was excited by the possibility that he might still have a chance to exact some form of punishment against the Venetian and his companions if the discussion with the Sultan continued to sour.

"And who do you suggest will deliver this message of my disappointment to this Emperor," clearly the Sultan wanted an answer.

Thinking quickly, Paolo had an idea. "Excellency, may I introduce to you the Palatine of Hungary, Count Gyorgy Thurzo. If anyone can capture the ear of Emperor Matthias, it will be Count Thurzo. We have already discussed the need to sit down with the Palatine in Wallachia on our return journey because of other matters. We will represent your concerns as well."

Thurzo stepped forward and bowed with dramatic flair, swinging his left arm in a wide sweeping flourish as he did so. As his arm moved, the gold coins tied about his wrist sweetly rang as they jangled like a tambourine.

The ringing coins immediately caught the Sultan's interest. "Where did you get that?" Ahmed demanded to know, his tone sounding angry as he asked the question. Thurzo was concerned by the Sultan's apparent displeasure upon seeing the coins.

"I came by it honestly, Excellency," Thurzo explained. "An old Gypsy lady gave it to me and told me to wear it in order to guard my safety. I know nothing more about the coins than that."

"Come closer, let me see it," the young Sultan urged, grabbing Thurzo's arm as he approached. He looked over each coin as if he was familiar with them. "And the old Gypsy, she is well?"

"That she is, Excellency."

After concluding his examination, he smiled. "She is a wise lady that one," Ahmed admitted. "I gave her that belt of coins to show everyone she was under my protection if she was ever threatened. Obviously, she knew the two of us would meet. She has that ability to see things," the Sultan stated, a fact that they were already aware of. "A good thing too," the Sultan smiled wickedly. "Otherwise I might have mistaken you and your men here as spies, but hardly very good ones if you could be captured so easily. So tell me Count, as Palatine of Hungary, why have the lands not been restored to me as promised under the Treaty of Zsitvatorak?"

"It is a matter well beyond my level of authority and outside my territory," Count Thurzo explained. "If I had any information in that regard, Excellency, I would certainly tell you but sadly I don't."

"Surely you must have some explanation to offer," the Sultan insisted. "My understanding is that this Gabriel Bathory still takes direction form the matriarch of the family because of her marriage to the

Nadasdy family. So how is it that they are holding on to the reins of power in Transylvania against my wishes?"

"Excellency, the Bathorys are my cousins, but even so, they confide nothing in me. But I assure you that will not stop me from taking your complaint to the Emperor."

"You mean your Emperor who is severely in debt to the Bathory family and will not dare to take any stand against them lest they cut off his funding." The Sultan was still flashing his wicked but now threatening smile. "I may be young, and thousands of miles away, but I still have my sources of information within your Empire."

"Yes, you are clearly well informed Excellency of the matters in the Austrian Court," Gyorgy complimented the Sultan on his level of knowledge. "But then you also know that it was your great-great-grandfather Suleiman that appointed the Bathorys to first govern Transylvania on his behalf. They've exercised that authority for over forty years. They consider themselves the actual rulers of the lands under appointed authority of the Ottomans."

"Clearly a mistake that I wished to rectify by appointing Gabor Bethlen as my representative. I expect the terms of the treaty to be honored and I will accept no less. Even your clergy is dissatisfied with the Bathorys. From what I was told, it was under their direction that the attempted assassination of Gabriel Bathory took place in March."

"I promise you Excellency that I will act on your behalf to ensure the Treaty is honored," Thurzo swore. "I am a man of law and order, and I uphold the law above all else. Justice will prevail."

"And I will express your sentiments to the Court when I have the opportunity to do so, Excellency," Sarpi promised as well.

"I have my utmost faith that both of you will keep your word to me," Ahmed accepted their commitment. "That belt of coins binds you to me," the Sultan explained. "If you should go back on your word, then the consequences are upon your head. As I said, I may not be ruling those lands currently as I should be but I do have my agents buried well within your systems. Let that be a warning to you." The smile on the Sultan's face clearly resembled a serpentine mask.

The look of disappointment on Rashid Kartal's face was obvious. He would not have the opportunity to remove the heads of the Count and his men either at this time. That might be a task given to others should the Count fail to uphold his promise. Kartal could only find solace if perhaps the other two would prove to be more offensive to the Sultan.

"So who is this man, Senor Sarpi?" the Sultan inquired, looking directly at Joseph, recognizing that his features were clearly non

European.

"May I introduce Joseph Kahana to you, Excellency. Prince of the Jews, from the ancient Houses of Aaron and David."

The Sultan looked momentarily confused by the introduction. He looked at Joseph more intently, studying him as his gaze traveled up and down, absorbing every feature. Joseph felt uncomfortable under his stare. Ahmed then looked closely at Wolf sitting calmly at Joseph's side. His eyes went back and forth between the animal and the man.

"And the Prophet said unto them, 'Lo! The token of His kingdom is that there shall come unto the ark wherein is peace of reassurance from your Lord, and a remnant of that which is the House of Moses and the House of Aaron left behind, the angels bearing it. Lo! Herein shall be a token for you, if you are believers.' The truth is in the words" the Sultan concluded.

"Forgive me Excellency," Joseph apologized, "I am not certain what you quotation refers to."

"Greetings brother," Ahmed rose from his throne to extend his arm toward Joseph, an act that few had ever seen a sultan do before. Joseph reached out and together they clasped forearms in a universal sign of brotherhood. "I recited to you a quote from the Qur'an. The two hundred and forty-eighth verse of the second Sura Baqarah Ayat."

"I am afraid I am not familiar with the Qur'an, Excellency."

"It says that your coming here is the sign of peace in our time. You are the remnant of the House of Moses and Aaron and you are a sign that the glory of the Holy Ark has come to rest upon my reign. Clearly you walk with the beasts of the field and they have come to know the peace which you bring."

"You mean my dog?" Joseph pointed at Wolf.

"If you choose to believe that the wolf is a dog, that is your choice. We all have two wolves within us. One which is loyal and protective, the other which is deceptive and predatory. You display the wolf within you outwardly. I am honored by your presence. Mahoza waits for your return," the Sultan advised Joseph.

"Mahoza?" Joseph was unfamiliar with that word.

"Are you not aware of the city in Mesopotamia where your family ruled?" the Sultan was quite surprised.

"Alas, Excellency, my father died when I was young and many of the stories of my family's heritage were lost to me."

"A tragedy, but as your city lays within my Empire, I can tell you many things about your family. Even though it has been six centuries when your family was forced to flee from their throne, the people still sing the praises of the Kahana as being a golden age for Mahoza."

"I will look forward to hearing the many stories during our time here with you Excellency."

"And I hope you will consider fulfilling the Sura and accept my offer to live within the boundaries of my Empire. I will make you a governor of my Eastern provinces. I will restore your birthright. I will shower you with wealth beyond your dreams if you say you will remain with me and bless my kingdom."

"You honour me Excellency, more than I could ever express, but there are those that still need me in the west."

"Then at least give consideration to living in the western provinces of my Empire if you will not accept your birthright. The House of Aaron must return to the lands where Allah is supreme. The Lord has ordained it will be so. I will give you lands in Transylvania or Wallachia if you so desire. Swear to me that you will give it consideration."

"I swear to you Excellency, when all that I must do has been completed, I will give your kind offer its deserved consideration."

"Come home brother, it is time," the Sultan pleaded as he sat back in his throne.

Growing restless, Rashid Kartal dug the toes of his boot into the ground, sorely disappointed that not even this Jew was going to have his neck stretched beneath his curved blade.

"And finally we have this last one in your party, Senor Sarpi. Of such a varied group of travelers as I have ever seen, will you still be able to surprise me with this last man as you have done with the others?" Ahmed challenged Sarpi to surprise him even more.

"I think that will not be difficult at all, Excellency," Paolo Sarpi laughed. "Without doubt you know of the famous seer, Michel de Nostradame, the man that the entire world has come to know as Nostradamus. A man that has provided the fortunes and futures for kings and queens. Several hundred prophecies that have been proven thus far to be beyond questioning, beyond dispute. But what most do not know is that there is a cipher to understanding what Nostradamus wrote; a key to interpreting exactly what was said. Excellency, I present to you Caesar do Nostradame, the son of Nostradamus, and the living cipher to his father's quatrains."

Clapping his hands together, the Sultan was definitely excited about this last man introduced by Paolo Sarpi. "How in the world did it come about Senor Sarpi that you would have assembled this phenomenal group of men to see me?" Before Sarpi even had an opportunity to answer the question, the Sultan had already moved on to his next request.

"Did your father speak of me at all," The Sultan hoped that Nostradamus had described his rule within the quatrains. Little did the Sultan know that his request was going to be the trigger to another of Caesar's spontaneous migraines

Bending over in pain, Caesar simultaneously began spouting one of his father's rhymes.

> *'The Blue Turban King entered into Foix,*
> *And he will reign less than an evolution of Saturn:*
> *The White Turban King Byzantium heart banished,*
> *Sun, Mars and Mercury near Aquarius'*

"Is that how you do it," the Sultan didn't look overly impressed. "I thought you prophets had to look into a fire in front of a mirror, or something similar. This was so…so banal."

"My father would stare into a bowl of water in a candle lit room, Excellency," Caesar admitted.

"That would have been more impressive," Ahmed confided. "A little more showmanship is necessary if you want to be taken more seriously."

"I don't actually create the quatrains, Excellency," Caesar explained. "That was Quatrain 73 from my father's Century IX. I just merely interpret them."

"Well then, tell me what he said."

That was the moment both Joseph and Paolo were dreading. They had already interpreted the quatrain in part as Caesar spoke it and it did not bode well for the Sultan. Shaking their heads rapidly back and forth, they tried to catch Caesar's attention to warn him not to translate it exactly as written but it was too late. He had already begun the explanation.

"The Sultan that has made a pact with France and is sending his trade ships to France's Southern Ports, that being indicated by the town of Foix, will not live longer than a single revolution of Saturn around the sun."

His companions continued to shake their heads, knowing that the Sultan wasn't going to take this well once he heard all the details.

"I presume that is me," Ahmed determined, "That is true, I did open the trade routes with France. But tell me, how long does it take for Saturn to revolve around the Sun?"

"I'm afraid you won't see your twenty-ninth birthday, Excellency," Caesar answered.

"And my death, I'm guessing this banished white turbaned king is responsible for my death in some way."

"It is possible," was all that Caesar could say.

"Well, I guess that is my fault in part," the Sultan mentioned nonchalantly. "You know, all my advisers begged me to put my brother to death when I took the throne because he was plotting against me, but I pardoned him. He was my brother after all. What kind of ruler would I be if I killed my own brother? And what's the meaning of the planets ascending into Aquarius?"

"Though you brother may take your crown after you die, he won't wear it for long. He will be deposed twice between the time it takes for Mercury the first time and Mars,the second time to revolve around the sun. After each deposition, the two sons of Jupiter will wear the crown."

"And Jupiter is...?"

"It is you of course, Excellency," Caesar had no doubt about the identity of the two princes.

"Do you know, my court astrologer almost said the exact same thing to me," Ahmed recalled. "I thought he was a charlatan, so I had him imprisoned. Guess I was wrong. Make a note that we should release him from the prison," Ahmed instructed his Vizier.

"Sadly Excellency," the Vizier apologized, "He was executed a few months ago."

"Terrible pity. He obviously was a better astrologer than I thought. They are hard to find, you know," Ahmed eulogized. "I have an opening if you are interested Caesar de Nostradame."

"I'm afraid Excellency that my services are sorely needed by the Austrian Empire right now to resolve a terrible situation that plagues the country. It is why we have come to you."

"Is this True Senor Sarpi? Is this terrible situation he speaks of the reason you have all come to me?"

"Yes, it is Excellency," Paolo Sarpi confirmed. "We believe you have information that will save the world."

"You make it sound so dramatic and ominous," the Sultan reflected on Sarpi's words. "Sultan Ahmed, the first of that name, saves the world! Though I must admit I like the sound of that, I seriously doubt the ramifications you speak of could be so dire."

"I would be downplaying the situation if I said it were any less, Excellency. What I am about to tell you is the reason that we were initially brought together by the Emperor Matthias. They fear that if we do not solve this threat to the Habsburg Empire it could mean an end to the Church and to the monarchy."

The Sultan listened intently but once Sarpi had finished explaining the potential of the threat, Ahmed was confused as to why he should be involved at all. "Not to lessen the impact of the threat that you are obviously concerned about, but why should I care. I pray to Allah that your institutions should be eroded so that in His name I can bring all the people of the world under His law and rule. What you talk of would be a good thing for me. Do you not agree, Murad," he sought the opinion of his Vizier."

"Most definitely, your Highness," the Vizier agreed. "It would be a great day for Allah and His Prophet."

"Exactly," the Sultan confirmed. "You really haven't told me why I should want to help you Senor Sarpi. Somehow, I remember your negotiating skills were much better than this six years ago when you were taking advantage of my negotiation team."

"I have not yet mentioned what fills the void, if our institutions in Europe should collapse. What I am about to say is attested to by the words of Nostradamus and it does not bode well for your empire either. We all will suffer terribly if we are to let this happen."

"Much better. You have caught my interest, continue," Ahmed bade Paolo to continue explaining the extent of the threat.

"I believe you already had some interaction with those that are intending to destroy our world. From what I have seen, I know that they were kidnapping dozens of young girls from your own villages and towns and were sacrificing them in the Dacian caves. I think you know of where and what I am talking about."

The Sultan's face was quite solemn looking, his eyes narrowing as they focused on Paolo Sarpi, and several beads of sweat appeared on his brow. That place is no longer spoken of," Ahmed warned. "We put an end to it and we swore never to speak of it again."

"Except it was not the end Excellency. It was only a new beginning. You merely forced them to move westward but they are still terrorizing the people and killing even more young girls," Paolo Sarpi informed the Sultan. "They are rising in power. They are gaining more adherents and threaten all of us. They may have moved away from your borders but they still have every intent to extend their control into your lands as well."

"And you believe that the four of you are strong enough to oppose them," Ahmed scoffed at their hubris.

"Actually just the three of us," Sarpi corrected the Sultan. "Count Thurzo was only assigned to us in order to provide protection."

"Then I can only tell you that what you are involving yourselves in is way over your heads and unless you mend the tears in your souls, you are doomed to failure," Ahmed cautioned him.

"We have already been told that we are broken," Sarpi confessed. "It was foretold that we will find someone that will forge us into a steeled weapon. You say that we have a tear in our souls, Excellency, but we need to now how to repair the damage, not just repeat that we are broken men. If you have insight into our deficiencies, will you not also share your insights into how we can resolve them."

"Do you even know of what deficiencies we speak?" Sultan Ahmed questioned. "You ask for solutions without even admitting that you have a problem."

Paolo Sarpi wished to protest that last admonishment. "We can't fix what hasn't been disclosed to us."

"How is it that the writing on the wall can be so obvious to the rest of us, yet none of you can read it?" Ahmed wanted to know.

"Forgive us, Excellency, but we are blind and need your help to see," Paolo Sarpi begged for the Sultan to explain.

"Brother Yusef, are you also asking me to explain?

"I would be most grateful for your insight Excellency."

"And what of you Caesar de Nostradame? Has your father not already indicated to you what ails you or do you need me to point it out as well?"

"Like my colleagues, Excellency, I would appreciate any light that you can shed on our ailments."

"Come with me then," the Sultan rose from the throne and signaled to them to follow as he climbed into the sedan chair which was then raised onto the shoulder of four hulking servants. "Murad, let every know that the audiences are over for now." Ahmed instructed his Vizier. "And you," the Sultan turned to Captain Rashid Kartal, "Give my guests back their weapons. I hardly think they are a threat."

"But your Highness…" Kartal was reluctant to comply.

"Do not worry Captain. If they should attempt to assassinate me, I will not hold you responsible," Ahmed laughed as he made his little joke.

Leading the procession to his private tent, the Sultan's guards pulled aside the flaps allowing them to enter inside. As Wolf was about to stride inside the tent, the servants became visibly flustered by the presence of the wolf. Realizing it was not permitted, Joseph instructed his animal to sit and stand guard. Much to the discomfort of the guards standing at the tent flap, Wolf took up a position beside them.

Inside the tent, the ground was covered by a multitude of colourful hand knotted carpets, so that not a square inch of grass was visible. The tent was separated into several rooms, the first being his living quarters, where the Sultan would entertain and dine with guests. Behind this large room was a series of smaller bed chambers for his wives and then the larger bed chamber which was his own.

The furnishings in the living area were extravagant, trimmed with gold and silver, and embedded with precious jewels. Precious silks lined the canvas walls, along with intricate tapestries recording many of the Sultan's own hunting trips. In one corner of the room stood a large machine that they recognized immediately as a very complex telescope.

The Sultan invited his guests to make themselves comfortable on the low standing cushioned divans, while servants entered the living area carrying an array of fruits and sweet meats. The Sultan then clapped his hands and instructed them to bring refreshments. Once they all had an opportunity to eat and refresh themselves, Ahmed felt it was time to educate them as to their deficiencies.

"So when did you lose your faith Senor Sarpi," the Sultan immediately challenged the Venetian Magistrate.

"I'm not certain what you mean, Excellency."

"You know exactly what I mean," Ahmed responded. "You who were once a man of God, now find it impossible to believe. You still say you believe in the Lord to others but your words are hollow. You have walked away from the Almighty, and He in turn has cut you free."

"You can tell this, Excellency?" Sarpi was surprised.

"Allah tells me many things," the Sultan admitted nonchalantly.

Paolo Sarpi was not aware that his loss of faith was so obvious. As he thought about it, he grew angry. "Well He abandoned me first," Sarpi declared. "How could a Church built in his name be responsible for so much death and destruction? How many times would they attempt to assassinate me before it became obvious that God was merely an excuse for men to do evil? I didn't walk away from God," Sarpi snapped. "I merely realized that there was nothing to walk towards."

"So now you believe in nothing?" Sultan Ahmed provided a brief summation of Paolo Sarpi's statements.

"I believe in science," Paolo responded. "I find all the answers I need there."

"And yet you have more questions than answers," Ahmed guessed. "Am I right?"

"Science is still in its infancy. It will take time before we have all the answers," Paolo defended his stance.

"But is it not true that every question you ask only results in further questions," the Sultan began lecturing the scientist on science. "One hypothesis, leading to another, and then another, only to find that in the end you know far less than what was your original belief. I am not criticizing you, my friend, I am only describing the every increasing hole that you find growing in your own mind. You begin to doubt yourself and that will lead to failure in many ways."

"And you're suggesting that there is another way to find the answers, Excellency," Paolo was challenging the Sultan more than asking.

"You think science is the answer but science is merely a tool. Just like my telescope. It is a tool of science but it is not an answer. Merely a device that helps me look for the truth. And during the night-time we will use it and I will show you what the truth looks like."

"I'm not quite appreciating how looking through a telescope is going to answer all my questions, Excellency."

"Not all your questions but most of them," Ahmed replied with a sly smile upon his face. Your soul is torn my friend, and not until you see the truth for yourself will you ever be able to repair it. Tonight you will see God and you will repair that rend."

"You believe you can see God through that telescope?" Sarpi had to hold back his laughter.

"Most definitely," the Sultan replied. "It is unique, one of the first refractory telescopes produced and I can see things you couldn't even imagine. You will see them too."

"And what does he look like, Excellency?" Sarpi could not resist asking as he scratched his head in disbelief.

Bending down, the Sultan picked up an ant that he saw walking across the knotted wool carpet. "He looks like this," Ahmed held open hand and showed them the ant. He then took one of the flowers out of the ceramic vase that stood beside his chair. "And he looks like this," holding out the flower for all to see,

"Those are merely things that exist," Sarpi rejected the explanation.

"Exactly," Ahmed replied. "Allah is existence. He is the ultimate scientist, creating from himself all that we see and feel. Within every creature, flower, human is the divine spark provided by Him. And the proof is that he built the entire universe on a singular design; the circle. The perfect shape that has no beginning and has no end. Allah is that perfect circle and everything in our wold is a repetition of that design."

"You are suggesting in some way, I am nothing more than a circle," Sarpi was still reluctant to accept the Sultan's theory.

"In more ways than you can appreciate," Sultan Ahmed schooled him. "You are a man of medicine Senor Sarpi. Describe to these others how blood moves through our bodies."

"There are loops that interconnect at the heart," Sarpi answered. "The blood is red as it leaves from one side of the heart, turning gradually blue as it eventually returns to the heart to begin the cycle once again."

"A series of circles that have a nexus point, would you not agree? That bein the heart. Why can you not see that Allah is the heart of our existence."

"Yes, but its not that simple," Sarpi tried to argue.

Joseph remained silent but realized that all this was beginning to sound very familiar and it could not be a coincidence.

"What about the solar system Senor Sarpi. I'm certain you've taken the opportunity to review the findings of Copernicus."

"Not proven as yet," Sarpi argued.

"But generally accepted, even by your friend Galileo though he is reluctant to admit it. So, how does he describe the planets."

"Spheres that revolve around a central sphere being the sun," Sarpi admitted.

"And the moons?"

"Spheres that revolve around other spheres being the planets."

"And just recently William Gilbert has just shown that the Earth itself revolves on an axis, while generating an electric current that creates the magnetism looping from pole to pole. Tonight, once we can use my telescope, I will show you that even our solar system is nothing more than a circle moving around an axis along with the stars. Circles around circles around other circles. And where some of these circles are conjoined, we have can see their origin and their end. Such is the Law of Continuity as proposed by Kepler."

"Granted, there is a basic design that seems to repeat itself throughout existence," Sarpi conceded. "But that is not proof of God."

"But you would like to believe it is still coincidence. Is that what you wish to say to me Senor Sarpi?"

"I don't know what to say," the Venetian could no longer find an appropriate answer.

"Yes you can," Joseph answered for him. "It is exactly as my father tried to tell you. You even said you always knew there was a universal design."

"But I never said there was a God," Sarpi defended his stance.

"And what would you call a universal design then," the Sultan pressed the Magistrate for an answer. To have a universal design, there has to be a sentient power to ensure that design is replicated. Otherwise if left to randomness, there would never be this common element but only an occasional replication. Agreed?"

"I need to think about this," Paolo reflected upon Ahmed's words.

"And what of you, brother Yusef," the Sultan picked his next target. "Where is your faith? Why is there this hole in your soul where Allah normally resides. How can a son of Aaron be so bereft of the Holy Spirit?

"Because He cursed me and then He abandoned me," Joseph tried to restrain his anger. He took my parents from me and then left my sister and myself to live on the streets. There were days we starved, months we struggled, years we shed tears, praying only to be met by silence. People scorned us, laughed at us, saying, there is the family beloved by God. See how He spits upon them."

"And you believed that what they heaped upon you was scorn?" the Sultan asked.

"What else could you call it? Scorn, hate, ridicule, it all adds up to the same."

"I call it fear," Sultan Ahmed redefined Joseph's and Tanit's experiences. "If only you had known your family's histories. The things your ancestors had done to change the world. Yes they were scorned and detested by others, but only because those that tried to put them down feared what they could do. God gave them gifts so that they could rise above other men. They became great warriors, tearing down empires, possessed great wisdom and in so doing became viziers to the early Caliphs, and teachers that possessed knowledge that could bind all the people of the world through their words."

"Then why did he abandon us, why did he take my father away and then my mother," Joseph felt the tears welling in his eyes.

"None of us will even know the will of God. Allah acts in mysterious ways but trust me when I say everything he does will have a purpose. I was just told I will be dead before my twenty-ninth birthday. I do not fear it, I embrace it. It means I have seven more years to make my kingdom great, to ensure my people are happy, and prepare a glorious future for those that will come after me. You must recognize that whatever flames Allah makes you pass through, it is not unlike raw iron passing into a fiery furnace so that it can become steel. The trial and tribulations you consider as suffering are merely a device to make you something and someone greater than you were."

"You shame me Excellency for my failure to see that behind my misfortune, there always has been opportunity. I let adversity tear me down, rather than use it as a vehicle to strengthen my resolve."

"Now you sound like your father," Caesar shouted jubilantly. "You asked me what your father was like, and now I think you know. In the darkest night, he could find the light of the moon. He mastered his fears and molded them into an armor that shielded him from the missiles launched by his enemies. I was there those last days of his life, and never could you have me a braver man, knowing full well that he had to sacrifice his life in order to save the lives of so many others. He talked of the Shekinah. He knew he was going to join God and his ancestors but he did so gladly. His only regret was that he would not be there to see his family again but he knew because of his sacrifice you were going to be fine. And in spite of all the bad things you may have suffered, you are fine Joseph. Your sister has a life better than most. You have a young girl waiting for you to shower you with love, and you will restore your family to its past glory."

"Well said, Caesar de Nostradame," the Sultan congratulated him. "But what of you. You mask your emptiness, there is a hole in your soul, but I can see that inside you are a very much a broken man."

"I am fine, Excellency. I live a good life, I have my personal wealth, and I have my work that keeps me busy. I would not say that my life is empty."

"Yet you have no one in your life, is that not so," Ahmed questioned him. "Because you feel you have no life of your own to offer anyone else. They have told me you are the key to deciphering your father's works, but that has only served to blur the lines as to who you really are. You live and work in shadows, never trying to find out who the man known as Caesar de Nostradame truly is. Yet the life you chose to lead is your decision, it always has been, so how is it you can deny God access into your life?"

"Why would I give Him access?" Caesar challenged the Sultan for an answer. "If my father proved anything to me it is the hypocrisy of the Church. His prophecies have proven all those that say they are the spokesperson of God are nothing but liars and charlatans and God let's them be so. He painted all religions with this broad brush and left me with no reason to believe in a God that is loving an merciful. And if God cannot love man which He created, then how can I find true love myself?"

"So it is not that you reject God or do not believe in God, it is only that you see us as nothing more than chess pieces to be moved along the board for his entertainment. You have come to resent God because He manipulates us to do as He pleases and those that are his standard bearers only further manipulate His words for their own advantage. How sad."

"I did not ask for your pity, Excellency."

"And I did not offer it," he was immediately advised by Ahmed. "Such a wonderful gift you and your father possess, with so much potential to do good. What do you do with it? You squander it, dwelling on all the negative projections and failing to see all the good that could be achieved by attempting to steer the world in a direction to avoid such calamities. You feel safest when you can deliver your message of doom and gloom when the event is about to transpire and unavoidable. But what if you actually attempted to raise a particular prediction in advance of its occurrence so that you could prevent it? God gave you the ability to manipulate the lives of so many for the better and you have squandered it. You have wasted his gift to you!"

Caesar was dumbfounded by not only the Sultan's directness but by the clarity with which he was able to determine his failings. He was right. All his life he only saw the inevitability of the predictions of bringing sorrow and misery on those they involved. Only on a few occasions was he ever able to use them as a source of intuition to prevent disaster and that was only through the encouragement and optimism of Yakov Kahana. Even then, he was unable to use his powers to prevent the death of both his friends Yakov and Giordano. Was the true purpose of the quatrain to actually prevent what they predicted rather than convince people of the inevitable? Had he been misusing his gift all his life? The Sultan now had him questioning his entire existence.

"You denied the existence of God," he pointed at Paolo; "You felt abandoned by God," he then pointed his finger at Joseph; "And you saw God as being petty and malicious," he pointed lastly at Caesar. "And together you think you are strong enough to go up against the evil that once dwelt in those caves? I will tell you directly, you will not stand a chance of defeating the entity that is behind these killings. You will fail and you will die in the process."

The words terrified Caesar, not because he would die, but once again two others that were entrusted to his care would also die because of his failure to use his power to save them. He felt the blood vessels pounding within his skull once again.

'The antichrist very soon annihilates the three,
Twenty-seven years this war will last.
The unbelievers are dead, captive, exiled;
Blood, human bodies, water and red hail covering the earth.'

No one appeared surprised that Caesar had experienced another of his revelations. The emotional stress of having Sultan Ahmed hammering at the hole within their souls was enough to leave them all predicting their untimely deaths.

"Century VIII, Quatrain 77," Caesar identified his father's words. "Do you see Excellency. All I ever see is the doom about to descend."

"Because you think you know how to interpret these prophecies but you're blind to the meaning of the words," Ahmed enlightened him.

They could not believe they were being reprimanded by this twenty-one year old princeling but clearly, in spite of his age, the boy was blessed with the wisdom of Solomon and was gifted with an insight beyond their understanding.

"Your father was right," he continued. These deaths of the young virgins did begin in the year of 1593 which means you will either end this terror very soon or it will end you. This is the twenty-seventh year. Do you need to die as it says? I say it is so, for it is clear the three will die if you remain as you are. If you remain unbelievers. But if you choose to place your faith in God, then he will deliver you, and it will not be so. Restore your faith and you will survive. Nostradamus has only said what will happen if you refuse to change. Which in turn means that it will not happen if you pledge your service to the Lord. That is how we were able to defeat them six years ago, by letting Allah be our strong right arm and our shield in battle. You can do the same."

"How I wish that were true," Caesar bemoaned his fate and the fate of the others.

"Believe and it will be so," Ahmed encouraged them. "You father's quatrain only rings true if you remain as unbelievers. He says as much himself." Shouting to one of his bodyguards, the Sultan instructed him to find and return with General Ibrahim al-Naziri.

"Who is that?" Paolo Sarpi asked, after overhearing and translating the command that was in Turkish.

"That my good friend is the man that was in charge of finally putting an end to the kidnapping and torturing of our young Muslim girls. I think it is important that you hear what he has to say."

Within minutes, the bodyguard had returned, escorting General Naziri into the tent. "Your Highness, you have summoned me? " The general bowed and took to one knee, slowly rising after being bade to do so by the Sultan.

"General, these men have recently been to the caves that were used by the Dacians. They have been witness to all the bodies that remain. They fear they are dealing with a repeat of what we had experienced so many years ago. I need you to explain what happened there."

"That is impossible your Highness, we sealed all the entrances to the inner chamber."

"Apparently age has taken its toll on your sealing of the doorways. The enemy still exists and is now terrorizing the Austrian Empire. I need you to tell them everything you were up against. Magistrate Sarpi speaks the language so do not hesitate to tell him all that you know and all that you saw."

"It was back in the days when Mohomaad was Sultan. Our lands were being raided by the wolf-warriors that came out of Wallachia and crossed the river. They called themselves the Omullup."

"We have heard that word," Paolo Sarpi interceded, reminding the others that it had been used by Captain Rodescu.

"It means the men who are wolves and the wolves who are men," the General explained. "They would attack the small towns and villages, slaughtering everyone they found but taking the girls between twelve and fourteen years with them back to their hideout in the Carpathian Mountains. They were not soldiers, they were animals. They were savage creatures sent by Shatan. The people had no defense against these men that ran with their wolf packs." The General took a look at Wolf who was sitting patiently by the tent flaps. "Big wolves, not like that one," he pointed at Joseph's animal. "Blackish-brown wolves with yellow eyes and huge teeth that tore a person to pieces in minutes. They caused such fear among the people that soon they dared not venture far from their homes, afraid to tend their fields. If they did not grow food, then they could not eat, and people were beginning to starve.

When I first arrived with my men in the Bulgari Province, I had no knowledge of the enemy. Some of the old villagers described them as evil Jinn, able to transform between human and animal shape. I dismissed their stories as nonsense but when we first encountered the enemy it was easy to believe the stories were true. The men wore skins from wolves draped over their shoulders and covering their heads. They moved liked the animals themselves, running and killing in packs, so that it became impossible to distinguish between animal and man as they spread themselves across the field of battle.

Our horses were terrified of the wolves which would tear at the tendons, crippling them so that both horse and rider fell to the ground. Once you were toppled there was no hope of survival, as they swarmed over you, slashing, ripping, tearing with teeth and knives. I lost so many men in those first few encounters. I shudder to think of how many brave lads I lost during those first years. And still the girls were taken, and the villages ravaged but we could not give up. I sent out sentries to find where they were encamped but they were like ghosts, disappearing off the landscape as if they never existed. We never found any remains of the girls, so it was still our hope that they were being kept alive as slaves and we would be able one day to return them to their families.

One day while on a scouting mission I came across a large caravan of Roma. They too had been terrorized by these Omullup that would appear and disappear, making their raids impossible to predict. These Gypsies had stories of the wolf warriors that inhabited the land hundreds of years ago, speaking of a wolf god that they served and prayed to and how the girls would be used for human sacrifice to appease their blood thirsty god. The Omullup sought immortality and they believed this could be granted by their wolf god if they drank the blood of their victims and sent one of their own soldiers to deliver the spirits of the stolen girls to him as a gift of fidelity and servitude. At first I did not want to believe in the stories they were telling me but then they brought out one of their own, a young girl that had escaped from their holding pen. She told a horrific tale, but still I did not believe her. But then she showed me her scars and then there was no doubt that it was true. In her panic to escape, she never attempted to look for any identifying signs of the landscape where she was being held, simply running until she became exhausted and collapsed when she could run no further. Thankfully she was found by the caravan of Roma that were passing by. They nursed her and restored her to life. She did remember she was caged within in a cave that stretched for miles. Once she found a path to the outside, she was high on a mountainside. That was all she remembered and all she could reveal.

I prayed to Allah to grant me the intelligence to deal with an enemy that could disappear without a trace. Allah told me to see from whence they came rather than to look as to where they've gone. So I had my engineers make topographical maps of the southern Carpathians, showing all the mountain routes that we knew of. My top aides prepared possible models of where this cave system might be located. I sent men up into the hills with no other purpose but to keep hidden and survey the possible locations for any evidence of movement. Every few days I would rotate new spies into the locations in order to keep fresh eyes on these potential locations. Months passed and still we could not find this hidden lair. I began to doubt the wisdom that Allah had given me. I felt that Allah had failed me.

More years had passed and by this time Ahmed was now Sultan and he made it imperative that we finally end these attacks on the villages and the loss of their young girls. I was desperate. I had received no further word from Allah. He had abandoned me. I began to doubt my faith but then I thought perhaps it was my fault. That I had misinterpreted what God had told me. So I prayed to Allah to grant me even more wisdom on how to defeat an enemy that fought in such an unconventional manner. For ten years I had been unsuccessful, chasing ghosts that appeared and vanished by the time I could assemble my men and reach the attack site. This time he sent me a dream in which I saw the wolves scattering in panic as they were pelted by a driving rain. Allah had forgiven my lack of faith and trust by answering my prayers. The mistake I had made was only having men waiting in the hills to see where they may have come from. But once they were already outside their lair, they were free to do as they pleased because I only reacted to the sightings after they had done their damage. I would send out my troops to engage the enemy in battle when they were already returning to their hideouts. By the time we got there, they were gone.

Allah was not telling me only to have men in the hills. He was saying the key to defeating them was never letting them get close to the villages in the first place. To be proactive rather than reactive. Instead, I needed to prepare a kill zone where my men were already waiting for them in concealment soon after they crossed the river. So I recruited a company of over two hundred musketeers. I had them dig in to the hillsides along the routes that I calculated were the most likely for the enemy to traverse on their raids. We waited in these ditches. Days turned into weeks but still my men waited, concealed in the dens they had dug into the earth. Eventually the Omullup came down from their lair and approached the border at the location where my men were waiting. As soon as they were in range, my musketeers rained down upon them with a hail of bullets. Each rifleman had another soldier preparing a second musket, so that there was never an interruption in the firing. The bullets poured down as a torrential rain, exactly as I had foreseen in my vision. We sent them back from where they came after inflicting a terrible slaughter. It was difficult to estimate how many had been killed but the plain was blanketed with the bodies of both wolves and men.

I thought it was over, but I was wrong. It should have been the beginning of the end but they came back in a second wave, almost as strong in numbers as in their first attack. But this time they were not alone. There were cavalry and infantry soldiers with them. Now that they knew where my musketeers were positioned, they circumvented the hills in which the riflemen had dug in, directing their attack at my main body of men which I had held back in reserve.

That is when I saw their leader. Covered in black armor from helm to heel, he charged into the battle like a man possessed, slashing and stabbing relentlessly. The winged serpent on his helm meant that we all knew who he was. We all feared him for he was the devil incarnate. We had been fighting his regular army for a decade in Moldova. I had no idea that he would be in some way connected to the Omullup but now it all made sense. Count Ferencz Nadasdy, the most fearsome of all the Transylvanian warlords, a man with no honour, a crazed killer that was in league with Shatan. A demon in human disguise, that was seen to drink his enemy's blood in the field, spreading fear among the enemy and his own troops alike.

In the distance I could see a woman standing on a hill, wailing into the wind. This was his personal witch that was seen casting spells over the enemy as her master rode to victory after victory. My men began to suffer from mysterious symptoms where they felt their arms suddenly growing exceedingly heavy and they could barely swing their swords. Not long afterwards, the tide of battle began to turn in their favour. Most of my musketeers had already left their dug-in positions and were firing on the enemy from behind their lines. I knew if I was to call a retreat at that time, it would have meant sacrificing all my remaining riflemen who were now separated behind the enemy. But in doing so, my infantry and cavalry would live to fight another day, though the enemy would be wise to this tactic and I would not be able to use it again. It meant I could be looking at several more years of fighting against an unstoppable enemy. Every voice in my head told me to sound the retreat. All my years of studying warfare and military training said to sound the retreat. My officers looked to me and in their eyes I could see them pleading for me to sound the retreat. It was what any other general would have done and no one would have blamed me for the decision. But I could not do it. I could not let it end this way. I looked towards heaven and heard Allah tell me clearly to 'charge'.

It made no sense. My men were in disarray, scattered to the four corners of the battlefield. Attacked from all sides by beasts and demons, praying only for an opportunity and a chance to escape. But I told my signalmen and trumpeters to sound the attack. I would never doubt the word of Allah again. I had my signalmen give the order to charge through the centre of the enemy. They all looked at me as if I had gone mad but I ordered them again to sound the charge. They had no choice but to obey. And then it happened; it was a miracle. My men must have assumed we had the advantage because without hesitation they charged the centre of the enemy line. The fierceness of their attack split the enemy and cleared a path so that my army was reunited and now stood between Count Nadasdy with his army of men and beasts and their only route to return safely to their camp. We had completely switched sides on the battlefield. His men wheeled about and for the moment stood there in stunned silence.

I immediately ordered my musketeers to fire and keep on firing. Their numbers had been markedly reduced but at such close range, every bullet hit a target. I saw the Count double over in his saddle which sent his men into a panic. The sight of their commander suffering a mortal wound must have made them second guess everything they believed, destroyed their false sense of immortality, because suddenly it was their turn to scatter in every direction.

My main concern remained with the Omullup. I ordered my cavalry to remain on their tail and only pursue those men with their wolves that looked to be heading in the general direction of where our models suggested their hidden lair might be located. We followed them across the river and into the mountain ranges. No matter where they went, we followed. Those that ran into the forests to the west we let escape as my men focused solely on finding the lair. The escape of a handful to the west I considered a small price to pay.

Some of my men shouted that the Count was escaping, but it did not matter. Only the Omullup mattered. Nadasdy's days were clearly numbered. Perhaps weeks, even months but eventually the lead shot would fester and he would die in agony. I only prayed he would suffer as much as the pain and grief he had brought to my men and the people of Moldova. Others shouted that the witch had fled, but she did not matter either. Once again, only the Omullup mattered and that meant finding the caves and ending the curse upon the land once and for all.

As expected, both animals and their handlers only knew of one safe place, overlooking the fact that once they entered into their lair they had sealed their doom. This time my men that I had spying in the hills were able to pinpoint exactly where they entered into their cave. This was the day that Allah had been showing me all along but I failed to listen to Him, blinded by my own arrogance.

We saw them disappear under the camel humped mountain, where I knew their plan of defense would be to order their wolves to attack anyone coming through the passages. I countered by having six men move through at a time with locked shields. Three men low and three men high, swords protruding though spaces between the shields. The beasts never had a chance. Wave after wave of these six man shield units moved through the tunnels until we eliminated all resistance. We now stood at three different entrances to the central chamber. There may have been about fifty of the wolf warriors still gathered in the hall. Their high priest stood behind the alter that was at the eastern end of the chamber. We had eliminated almost all of their wolves, there were only perhaps four or five remaining. Their remaining men had gathered in a circle, back to back, rapiers held in a defensive posture but you could see on their faces that they knew their situation was hopeless. The priest was reciting some strange chant in a language I had never heard before. As soon as he finished his words, he plunged the knife into his own chest, falling face down upon the alter. My men were startled by his self sacrifice but that hardly compared to the anger that fueled them when they spotted the pile of dead bodies at the western end of the hall.

I'm guessing you saw what we saw when you entered the chamber. I feared that my men would slaughter every last one of the Omullup and I could not allow that to happen. Yet at the same time I recognized that I had to let them seek revenge against these savages.

The frustration of fighting these barbarians for over ten years taxed my men's souls heavily. Many of my men had lost friends within the units over those ten years. Some of them had relatives that lost their young daughters during the raids. I knew I had to give them their pound of flesh. I asked my first question of the surrounded wolf warriors. 'Who knew how to speak Turkish?' Seven raised their hands. I then said to them, if they wanted to live then they should throw down their weapons and walk towards me. Four of them did so. It was enough. Once my men had secured the four, I told them to slaughter the rest. They did so without hesitation.

When all was done, I had my men drag the dead bodies of the Omullup and their wolves out of the cave and toss them down the side of the mountain. I wanted their bodies to experience the same shame as their victims, to be eaten by the wild animals of the forest and the birds in the sky. As for the corpses of the dead girls I had to make a decision as to what I should do with them. To return them to their families was not an option. We must bury our dead entire. As we come into the world, so must we leave. Most of these girls as you probably saw were no longer entire. I could not cremate their bodies as that would prevent their souls from reaching heaven. So I had only one option and that was to seal the chamber and make that their tomb for eternity. I prayed that no one else would come seeking the caves."

The General stood erect, having completed his story and awaiting his next instructions from the Sultan.

"General, the four wolf warriors that spoke Turkish. I presume there was a reason for selecting them," Sarpi asked.

"Yes, you are probably wondering what I learned from these four Omullup that I had taken prisoner. Like the Dacians before them, they had adopted the belief that the blood of these virgins would grant them immortality but the witch, she was convinced that immortality did not reside in the blood. That blood was merely the carrier. She was of the belief that there were parts of the body that secreted special potions and humors that if harvested and blended correctly, she could not only achieve immortality but cure diseases, increase strength and even change the size and structure of the human body. Apparently, all these organs that she harvested would be prepared into powders, pastes or solutions that she would then pack onto a wagon, which two or three times a year would take them to another destination somewhere to the West. But none could say where that was.".

After I learned everything there was from these men I had them executed. There never could be any forgiveness for their sins. I had truly hoped that we had ended this evil practice once and for all, but now you tell me that it has arisen once again. I pray that Allah gives you the wisdom and strength to finally put an end to it."

"It would appear that we have encountered the remnant of these wolf warriors that escaped," Senor Sarpi updated the General as to what happened to the Omullup that had fled to the west. "They attacked us in a forest in Romania. Fortunately, they are no longer in the numbers that you describe, otherwise we would not be standing here today."

"As long as any of them still remain, they will always be a scourge on both our peoples."

"It is our intention to do so," Sarpi concurred.

"May Allah guide you and protect you," the Sultan prayed for them.

The Two Empires

Chapter Seventeen

Bran Castle: August 1610

"I'm telling you, they know what we've done," the Steward sounded panicked as she paced back and forth about the room.

"Nonsense, they know nothing," the Countess reassured her. "They have no idea what is happening or why. We don't even know if they are still alive."

"Why else would they have entered into the Turkish Territories unless they have already put the pieces together?" Erzsi Majorova voice dripped with trepidation.

"Because they knew nothing. If they had known, then there was no reason to seek out information from the Turks. Now sit down and be quiet. I need to think. Just remember, we are more clever than they are." Elizabeth Bathory tried to remain calm as her collaborators tried to assess what their enemy might already know.

The room they sat in was a large study, filled with endless rows of book cases lining the walls. It was located in a wing of the castle, far away from the bedrooms where the Countess's guests slept. The harsh illumination from the several candelabra situated about the room played with the worried features of the anxious men and women sitting nervously around their mistress who sat behind the large wooden desk that was one of the room's main attractions.

"If the Turks haven't already killed them, then whatever they're up to cannot be good," Captain Rodescu provided his opinion. "It's been weeks since they crossed over the river, which suggests to me they are either dead or they have had the time to learn every little detail regarding our past and present operations." In his frilled white cuffs and laced collar, it was clear that the Captain had been spending most of the time in the castle and very little time on the road to investigate his claims.

"So, even if they do know everything now, what of it?" the Countess analyzed the situation. "They can't prove it without real evidence. What occurred years ago in the East cannot be tied to anything they have discovered about the girls here. Yes, there may be some similarities but that is all circumstantial. Their hands are tied."

"I say we kill all of them when they cross back into Transylvania," the Captain suggested. "After the altercation with the witches, there are only four left that can fight. We can take them easily and once they are gone, so are all our problems."

"Did you not hear what my sisters said!" Erzsi screamed at Valerie Rodescu. "That man Sarpi was able to create a weapon of mass destruction out of thin air. With one explosion he could kill a dozen within my sisterhood. And you want to discount him as a threat!"

"You and your witches were weak," Rodescu responded. "I can practically blow you over if I wished to. Your only advantage was surprise and fear and once you lost that, you were easy to pick off. My men are not as susceptible as your legion of frail women with their spells and hexes."

"Most of my family are dead now because you and your men couldn't do your job in the forest. Don't tell me about weakness. Your men ran as soon as they heard the sound of the muskets firing. We took down most of the soldiers and the townspeople before they prevailed over us, but your men and animals just ran like the cowards they are!" the Steward screamed in defense of her sisterhood.

"My men were not cowards!" Rodescu defended his own troops. "The gunfire surprised the wolves and they panicked. My men had to retrieve them. That's all."

"Valerie, I can assure you, all men fear death. It humbles the bravest of men. Don't pretend that your wolf warriors are any different. They're not!" Elizabeth Bathory commented.

"That's a lie," Rodescu blurted angrily. "My men are the bravest there are. What other soldiers would dare to engage in battle with nothing more than a knife against men with swords and rifles?"

"Only fools!" Erzsi expressed her opinion forcefully.

"Oh yes, and a group of naked women with knives attached to their fingertips and some bottles of poison are playing the role of fools any less!" The Captain resented anyone attacking his men unfavorably.

"Everyone relax!" Bathory ordered her associates. "If they are still alive, which we all agree is highly unlikely, then all they are on is a fishing expedition in a sea without fish. They are trying to make a connection between events six years ago and now. No one even cared about all those peasant girls disappearing years ago and it is unlikely that anyone bothers to care even now. Now, everyone calm down and let us discuss this rationally and come up with a plan just in case they do return." Bathory motioned with her hands for everyone to sit and be calm.

"Those men have powers," came a voice from the corner shadows of the room. "Men knew branch was going to fall on to carriage. Men have supernatural powers?"

The Captain turned in his chair to stare down the diminutive creature sitting in the corner. "Hey Fasz, They have no powers! You were just too slow in breaking off that branch. How many times do I have to tell you that."

"My name is Fizcko," the diminutive hunchback shouted in his defense, resenting having his name turned into a Hungarian expletive. "Fizcko was not slow. They knew."

"Listen, you ugly little monster, if you had done your job right, they'd be dead and we wouldn't even be worrying about what happens next! It's all you fault."

"Not Fizcko's fault!" the imp shouted in his own defense.

"And how many times do I have to repeat myself," Elizabeth Bathory stopped their endless banter. "I want Joseph Kahana alive. If I find out any one of you is responsible for his death then I will kill you myself. Are we clear? And you, Captain, don't you ever underestimate the powers these three might have. That is why you have failed so miserably because you believe we are dealing with ordinary men. Why do you think they were even recruited in the first place if there wasn't something special about each one of them?"

"My apologies, my Lady. I admit we may have underestimated their abilities for survival but I will not take back my comment that the dwarf is useless when it comes to strategy. His mind is too slow to comprehend the speed at which things must be done."

"Fizcko not slow!" he exclaimed in his own defense.

"It is alright, Janos," the Countess calmed her servant by referring to him by actual name. "I am glad they escaped. I must have the one called Joseph captured alive."

"And what makes him so special anyway," Rodescu wanted to know.

Elizabeth Bathory donned an alluring but dangerous smile which she had used often to bend men to her will. "You know nothing about this Karaite Prince," she taunted the Captain, "But having forced the fool of a Rabbi to divulge everything he knew about the Kahana, using a little nightshade, I now know everything there is about him. He is the rod and the scepter combined in one. That means whether you agree with Janos's conclusion that he has powers, the truth is that he is protected by this ancient covenant from God."

"See, told you!" Fizcko shouted. "Magic man!"

"It is also said that the blood line cannot be extinguished. Erzsi looked into her crystal and it said he can provide us with the final ingredient. Do you know what that means? There is a gift of immortality in his blood. All we need to do is to get his blood, unlock its secrets and we can obtain that immortality for ourselves. Imagine it, longevity, immunity from disease, we will be like gods!"

"I thought this Rabbi, his own future father-in-law described him as an insignificant ant that needs to be squashed," Rodescu reminded her. "Hardly a solid recommendation for proclaiming this Joseph Kahana is anything special."

"The Rabbi is a fool but it is clearly evident he fears the power that the Kahana possesses. Whatever action we take, I need you all to swear, no one will lay a hand on Joseph Kahana."

"As long as he remains alive, then he is a threat because he still knows too much, even if he does not know the full story," the Captain protested. "If he should ever manage to convince the Emperor of our complicity in the disappearance of these girls, we are doomed."

"That is why we must not wait for the next battle to come to our doorstep. We must strike first while they are still weak in numbers and before they have any time to recruit more men," Bathory advised her collaborators.

"We've already stopped that possibility when my men intercepted their rider," the Captain reminded her. "There won't be any reinforcements coming."

"Not now," Bathory agreed, "But given enough time my cousin Gyorgy will recruit reinforcements from the local villagers. He is quite resourceful, unlike the rest of my worthless relatives. I don't want him given that much time. You need to have your men ready to remove him and his men at the first opportunity."

"What about the Venetian and the Frenchman?"

"What about them?" Bathory laughed wickedly. "I'm certain your wolves will enjoy a couple of exotic treats. Make certain there isn't a trace left of either. But the Jew, you make certain you bring him to me unscathed or else I will feed you to your own animals."

"So what is it that you intend to do?" Rodescu was hunched over the table wondering if there was any backup plan.

"Because I can't be guarantee that you will be able to carry out my simple instructions, I'm going to make a trade," she grinned wickedly. "If you can't defeat them physically, then you have to do it mentally. That is how you finally beat these men with their lofty ideals. You bring out the hero in them so that they are bound to fail as a result of their own arrogance. I will outsmart them at their own game."

"Exactly what are you planning?" the Captain wanted to know.

"Best you don't have all the details," the Countess declined to answer. "I'd rather have you focus on succeeding in the field rather than wondering what will happen next if you should fail. Don't let me down, Valerie."

"They will not escape from me this time, my Lady. You have my word on it."

"No Valerie, I will have your head on it."

Reisel woke to the sound of what sounded like muffled screams in the night. At first she thought about Joseph's warning to remain safe until he returned but she refused to do nothing if someone was in urgent need of her help. Donning her night coat, she walked about her bed chambers, seeking that point where the sounds appeared to be loudest.

When she came to stand in front of the tall wardrobe, that stood beside the vanity, she was confident that was the location where the sounds were the most intense and unmistakable for screams coming from a young girl. She remembered that Joseph told her there were hidden passages in the walls, which meant there had to be hidden levers, so she began looking all around the wardrobe, feeling inside every crack and crevice for any indication of a handle but there was nothing.

She thought about simply exiting her room and traversing the many staircases and hall ways until she found a clear pathway leading to the screams but she knew as soon as anyone saw her walking around the castle they would swiftly escort her back to her room. She quickly dismissed that idea and restarted her search for the hidden lever. Still nothing, but then she had the notion that if there was nothing on the outside of the wardrobe, then perhaps she would find something inside it. Climbing into the wardrobe, she knocked on the back panel, and was met with a hollow reverberation, just as she had hoped. She pulled on everything and everything she could find within the massive cupboard until she reached for a protruding peg, that was situated high above her head. It was an automatic impulse to push the peg rather than pull on it. As soon as she did, the back panel of wardrobe slid open and she found herself standing on the landing of a hidden staircase.

Descending the stairs in the dark was dangerous, the stones slick with moisture and moss but with time her eye began to adjust, and she could see that every so often there was a small fraction of light slipping through the cracks and crevices of secret doors from other landings and other rooms. She kept descending the stairs, her hands reaching out to the stone walls for support to aid her balance. The further she descended the more intense and violent the screams became. But now she could also hear the ripple of laughter from several people, following shortly after each one of the screams.

From the moment she entered into the staircase, she began counting the steps to ensure she could find her way back to her room. She was now at step sixty-four and the screams appeared to be coming directly from the other side of the wall. She presumed she must be well below ground as her breath misted as it met the cold air. Her bare feet felt like they were walking on ice, the stones of the stairway freezing to the touch. She listened, but the screams had now stopped and she questioned whether she had imagined it all, her subconscious mind urging her to return up the stairs and back into bed. She had almost convinced herself that it was her imagination when the screams started anew but this time a different voice, a different girl.

Wherever the doorway was, it had been fitted so well that there were no cracks that she could peer through. There was no other choice but to find the lever that operated the door and enter the room if she was to see what was happening. Her hands felt around on the surface of the stones for anything unusual. Up, down, from side to side she searched frantically, telling herself to calm down and think, it had to be there. Being on the secret corridor side, she recognized that it would not be necessary to hide the mechanism that opened the passageway. Therefore, it would be something obvious directly in front of her. In the dim light she could make out an iron brace for holding a torch bolted to the wall. She instinctively pulled on it and as she did so, she could hear the mechanism click, followed by the column of stones swinging outward into the room, wide enough to easily pass through.

She poked her head around the stone doorway into the room only to find it wasn't occupied. Both light and sound streamed in from an adjacent room but there was no clear view into it. She had to leave the safety of the stairway if she was going to see anything. Reisel knew the risks but of all the daughters of Rabbi Lipmann, she had always been the most daring and the one they referred to as a tomboy because of her love of climbing trees and taking risks. She decided if she was going to be the wife of Joseph Kahana, the man already risking his life to save the Empire, then it was only fitting that she be willing to put her life equally in danger.

She crept stealthily inside the room, at first hugging the wall in case she had to make a hasty retreat to the stairwell. The screams came more rapidly, one after the other, mixed with the laughter of several voices. She knew that unless she crossed the room and peered around the next doorway, she wouldn't see anything but it also left her fully exposed if anyone entered this room from the other side. It would be a tremendous risk and she knew a fatal one if she was to be discovered. Every fibre of her body attempted to pull her back to the safety of the stairs and back to her room, but her mind resisted the urge, determined to prove she was a fitting wife for the family of the Kahana. Silently, she began a prayer. It was Psalm 23, with subtle modifications.

"The LORD is my shepherd, I only want to make my husband proud. Lord you have always made me lie down in green pastures, and have led me through quiet waters, but now my soul is in peril and I need you to guide me along the right paths, so that I will be deserving of the name Kahana. Right now I am treading through a valley of shadows, and I'm trying not to be scared, so please be with me Lord, so that I will be here when my Joseph, the rod and the staff of your choosing will be able to hold me in his arms and comfort me. You are bringing me to the threshold before my enemies, I need you now more than ever to anoint my head with holy oil and fill my cup with goodness and love for the rest of my life. I promise Lord that if you see me through this, I will dedicate my life to living in the House of Aaron forever. Amen."

By the time she had finished reciting the Psalm, Reisel was standing beside the doorway that opened into the brightly lit adjacent room. She was relieved that no one had entered behind her, and now all she had to do was look around the door frame and witness what was happening. The moment she extended her head, she had to bite down on her lip and stop herself from screaming aloud. It was as if she had opened a gateway to Hell and all the torments and tortures that were ever attributed to Gehenna were all suddenly true. She reminded herself that she was marrying a Karaite and that meant there was no Hell, only the sick deviant behaviors of mankind on Earth. She forced her eyes to remain open and her lungs to stop breathing, fearing that she would be unable to remain silent if she took another breath.

There were already several naked bodies of girls, none any older than she was, laying motionless on the stone floor, their flesh covered in cuts from which they had bled profusely. None of them appeared to be breathing, no rising and falling of their chests to even suggest they were alive. Reisel studied the bodies and recognized they all had one thing in common, they were all pubescent, just becoming women with budding breasts and the first evidence of hair growth between their legs.

Hanging from the ceiling was a metal cage, a young girl trapped within its narrowly spaced bars, while several women and a deformed man gazed upward and laughed, poking and jabbing her with long poles with spiked ends that easily pierced her body. The terror on her face was gut wrenching, and Reisel wanted to reach out and help but knew there was nothing she could do but watch. Each time a spike penetrated her skin she screamed in excruciating pain and in response they would laugh, enjoying every moment of the torture they inflicted. She recognized some of them. There was Ilona and Dorottya, the Countess's two hand maidens. Another girl she knew as Katarina, that often made up her bedchamber. And the hunchback they all called Fizcko, who along with his spinal deformity was barely five feet in height. Beneath the cage was a large white porcelain pan in which they collected the blood as it dripped from the girl's body and fell to the ground.

As much as she wanted to turn away, Reisel knew she had to watch. She needed to record every detail in her mind if she was to tell Joseph that she had uncovered the source of the mystery of the dead girls. She watched as Fizcko grabbed another pole but this one was different. It was all metal and on its tip it had what looked like a shining brass rose bud the size of a large plum. The hunchback held it high so that it hovered in front of the girl's face. He wanted her to see this metal contraption and the intricacies of its working mechanism. Twisting the knob at the other end in his hand, the rose bud bloomed, spreading its razor sharp petals gloriously. Fizcko laughed almost hysterically as he closed the petals so it resumed the perfect shape of the rose bud once again. The three women tightened the ropes that were tied to the girls wrists and ankles, so that the girl was spread-eagled as she stood within the cage. Fizcko continued to laugh as he ran the brass bud downward, along her chest, her belly, and then let it rest momentarily against her pubic area. The girl closed her eyes, knowing what was to come next. Reizel's eyes opened wide as she watched the rose bud disappear within the girl's vagina. As the hunchback moved the pole back and forth, up and down, then rotating it slightly, the hapless girl could not help but respond to the stimulation applied. In spite of her tears and all her fears she could not help herself from groaning in response to the subtle manipulation of the contraption. In response to her moans, her torturers became even more excited, cackling like fowl, encouraging the hunchback to probe her faster and deeper. Uncontrollably, the girl's sinews and muscles tensed and relaxed repeatedly as she submitted to the intense stimulation of her groin but the moment she reached the peak of her reflexive response, Fizcko turned the knob, releasing the razor sharp petals and resulting in a series of screams the likes of which Reisel had never heard before.

With tears in her eyes she refused to watch any longer the girl in the cage, who fortunately fell into unconsciousness, while the blood poured down her legs and into the pan below. All that mattered now was returning safely to her room undetected. If she managed that, then she would plan on how she and her father would escape from the castle. She pulled herself back from the door way, petrified that she would be discovered at any moment. Her feet felt wet and she realized that the sheer terror of witnessing the torture of the young girl had released her bladder. There was nothing she could do about it, except pray that no one passed this way and discovered the puddle on the ground.

Edging her way back along the wall, she slipped by the open stone column and then felt the relief of having returned to the relative safety of the stairwell wash over her like a wave. She quickly figured out if pulling down on the brace for the torch caused the column to swing inward, then pushing it up would seal the column in its closed position. She counted the sixty-four steps back to the landing of her wardrobe, exhausted by the climb but deliriously happy that she had returned undiscovered.

Having escaped detection, she now only one thought in mind, that they must escape from the castle, She quickly dressed into her clothes and headed directly to her father's bedroom. She tried to open his door but it was locked from the inside. "Papa, Papa, she whispered as she banged softly on the door, desperate to wake him without alerting anyone else to her presence in the hallway. Her standing in the hallway seemed to last an eternity but finally she heard her father's voice from the other side.

"Who's there?" he asked, still half asleep as he cleared his throat repeatedly.

"Papa, open up. It's me."

"Go to bed Reisel," he told her. "It is still night time. You should be sleeping."

"Papa, please! Open your door," she pleaded.

"Alright, alright," he answered gruffly, obviously upset at being woken while it was still dark outside.

As soon as the door opened, Reisel raced past him, urging him to lock the door quickly behind her.

"What is this emergency?" her father asked, "That it can't wait for the morning."

"We have to leave now Papa. We have to get away immediately," the tears streamed down her cheeks as she spoke.

"What is this nonsense, Reisel? Do you know what time it is?"

"Listen to me Papa, they're killing young girls! I saw it! There is a room below the castle where they were torturing all these girls! We must go! We have to leave now!" Reisel was practically hysterical trying to get her father to listen to her but she could tell by looking in his eyes that he wasn't believing a word of what she said.

Folding his arms across his chest, Rabbi Yom Tov Lipmann had heard enough of this nonsense. "You had a bad dream Reisel. Nothing more, do you understand. Now go to bed and not another word of this!"

"But Papa…"

At that instant her father grabbed her beneath her armpit and forced her out from his room, locking the door behind her. Leaning her head against his door she wept. "Papa, you have to listen to me. Please..." Her fists barely knocking against the door, becoming weaker with each blow until she could barely lift her arms any longer. She slumped against the wood, bracing her body within the heavy door frame, crying until she finally surrendered, and began the lonely and desperate walk back to her own room.

Once back in her room she locked her door and then wrestled with the vanity, pushing, then pulling and then pushing it again until it was siting in front of the wardrobe so that the cupboard doors were barricaded. Curled up in her bed, still fully dress in her everyday clothes, she pulled the covers over her head, trying to block out the noises still floating into her room from far below.

The next morning Reisel ran to her father's room hoping to talk to him again before he went down to the breakfast room. It was too late, as she opened his door, she stared into an empty room. as he had already gone down for his morning eggs and tea. She ran downstairs, hoping that she still had a chance to convince him of the danger they were in. Perhaps if she provided all the details he would realize that it couldn't possibly have been a dream and then he would follow her back to her room where she could demonstrate the secret passageway in the wardrobe. Surely then he would believe her.

She found him sitting alone in the breakfast room, sipping slowly on his cup of tea. There was no one else around. Sitting in the chair next to him, she spoke softly so anyone in the kitchen would not be able to overhear what she said. "Papa, I know you do not want to believe what I told you last night but I need you to believe me. I have never lied to you before and there is no reason in the world why I should lie about this. There is a room beneath the castle where they commit these murders. There is a doorway in the back of my wardrobe that leads to this underground crypt. If you come with me I can show it to you. I need you to believe me because we are in danger here. We need to leave immediately." Finishing what she needed to say, Reisel checked around the room again to insure that no one overheard her conversation.

Slowly placing his cup onto the matching saucer,her father took the napkin from the table and patted his lips and beard to dry any droplets from the tea. He didn't bother to look at his daughter, preferring to stare at the tea cup as if he was talking instead to this inanimate object. "I don't know why you are saying these things Reisel but this is not how I raised my daughters, to tell such stories about people they do not know.

Countess Bathory has been very nice and cordial to us all these weeks that we have been staying with her. In fact she has taken better care of us than we deserve, being strangers that have taken advantage of her hospitality. She has even talked with me about providing her support for me to become the Chief Rabbi in Moravia. It is an important position and it would be foolish for me not to give it consideration."

"Papa, she is not who you think she is. She is not doing any of this out of the goodness of her heart. You are dealing with the Devil. If she is offering you something it is only because she wants something of greater value. You must believe me, these are evil people."

Her father still refused to look directly at his daughter, preferring instead to let his gaze glance over the tabletop. Reisel recognized that look. It was what her father always did when he felt guilty about telling his daughters anything that he might have done.

"And this is why I think you have fabricated this story because you somehow found out that there were conditions attached to her offer that you object to. And I forgive you for that. I can understand that you feel hurt and think I must be the cruelest man in the world but what I do is for your own good. I'm your father and I do this because I love you."

Reisel was completely confused by her father's words. She had no idea what he was talking about but now she knew for certain that he had apparently made a deal with the Countess of which he felt somewhat ashamed. "Papa, what is for my own good? What are your referring to? You are scaring me Papa!"

"The Countess has expressed to me that she has deep feelings and desires for Joseph Kahana. And she also believes that she has seen in him a desire for her as well but she would dare not interfere with a betrothal, especially one that was made under the direction and authorization of the Emperor. But she is right, I have also seen how he looks at her and I know it to be true. You know it yourself that Joseph Kahana is more suitable to live in her world than he could ever be in ours. These Karaites are essentially no different from the nobility of these Goyim. They have intermarried with them for generations. Yes, they call themselves Jews, but when you take a serious look at how they live, how they look, how they act, then you recognize that they are no different from these aristocrats. You would never be able to make him happy Reisel, but the Countess Bathory could certainly do so.

I promise that in time, when you are ready, I will find a far more suitable husband for you. You must learn not to harbour this hatred against the Countess and manufacture these false accusations as a result of your hurt feelings. All she asked was that I find a way to break the betrothal and in return she will use her influence to help our family. She will practically guarantee my appointment. As a Chief Rabbi, all the brightest and best Rabbis from around the continent will seek your hand in marriage. You will then be able to pick whomever you wish and not be forced to marry some man in order to buy my release from jail.

I know you probably think I am terrible for agreeing to this but in time you will see it is the best for all involved. So you can be mad at me now all you want, but there was never any need for you to fabricate this horrible accusation against the Countess. She is not to blame for my decision. I need you to act mature and recognize this right now!"

Reisel's head was spinning. She did not know whether she should scream, shout or feel pity for the level of gullibility her father had demonstrated. Not only had he betrayed his own daughter but Joseph and the Emperor as well. If he thought that the Countess Bathory had enough authority to protect him from the Archduke's vengeance, then he was even a bigger fool than she considered him to be right now.

"Papa, I don't know what you have been doing or saying to the Countess, but I am telling you right now, there is a torture chamber below this castle, in which I witnessed them torturing and murdering a young girl no older than I am and may God find some way to have mercy upon your soul if He finds you have aided and abetted this woman's crimes. She is the Devil and I believe she is the one responsible for all the deaths of those innocent young girls that are being investigated. God will not forgive you if you listen to her over the truth!"

"How dare you! How dare you preach to me about what God wants! You are behaving like a ridiculous child! You know nothing about God!" Rabbi Lipmann finally turned towards his daughter, raising his hand as if he was prepared to slap her. "You dare to invoke God's wrath against me, your own father! How dare you!"

"Did I miss something here," the Countess's voice interrupted the Rabbi's tirade before he had the opportunity to strike his daughter. "I do hope that you do not intend to hit a child, Rabbi. I definitely do not approve of such behaviour." Entering the breakfast room, the Countess took a seat at the table, followed by her steward who chose to remain standing. Reaching across the table she attempted to hold Reisel's hand but the girl quickly withdrew it as if the offering was poisonous. "My, my, someone is very angry this morning," Elizabeth Bathory commented.

"Forgive my daughter Countess, but she is distraught with me this morning and she needs to be disciplined."

"Rabbi Lipmann, you should know that at my finishing school we do not practice any form of physical punishment. We have found that there are much better ways of discipline without resorting to such unacceptable practices. So I beg you to please refrain yourself and perhaps let Madame Majorova and myself deal with the issue with more civility."

The Rabbi nodded his acceptance, willing to let the Countess Buthory resolve the matter.

"Dear, dear Reisel, you must believe me when I tell you that withholding your anger against you father will only disturb the balance within your body. You must be willing to express your angst and discuss the matter as adults do in order to find a mutually acceptable resolution. So please, my dear, tell me what troubles you so much." Once again, the Countess reached out her hands towards the troubled girl, hoping that she would take hold and find comfort in the hands of another.

Reisel withdrew more dramatically, her chair audibly scraping against the stone tiles of the floor as she put even more distance between herself and the Countess.

"My, my," Countess Bathory tutted as her tongue reflected off the roof of her mouth several times. "It appears that you are mad at me as well. What could I possibly have done to anger you so?"

"I'm afraid it is all my fault," Rabbi Lipmann apologized. "Somehow my daughter has become aware of our conversations and she is only acting out because she interprets my having her best interests at heart as interference in her marriage to Joseph Kahana?"

A brief flush of anger washed over the Countess's face before she quickly resumed her calm demeanour. "I thought we had discussed this thoroughly Rabbi?" the Countess shook her head in disappointment. "Didn't we say we would work out a strategy together on how we would break the news to your darling daughter so we could avoid causing her any distress and anguish?"

"I am so sorry, Countess," Rabbi Lipmann apologized. "I have no idea how she found out. She must have been listening to our conversations at night from some place where we did not notice her. But I promise you, in time she will come to realize that we are only acting in our best interests."

"This has become so awkward now, my dear," the Countess Bathory addressed Reisel. "I think you may have only overheard parts of the conversations your father and I had but I'm certain if you knew everything you would understand and agree with our reasons for wanting what is best for you."

Reisel covered her ears, trying to block out the Countess's voice with its melodic rhythmic pacing designed to capture her attention.

"It is best you listen to me Reisel, as one woman to another. Sometimes fate brings two people together that were never meant to be. It is as if day wanted to lay down with the night but there is never a time that the two can be together. Or the fish in the sea looks up and sees the bird circling high above the waters, but no matter how much they may be attracted to one another, their worlds will never be united. You are young, vibrant, ready to enter the world of adulthood, whereas Joseph has travelled well beyond that bridge many years ago. The world in which he engages is much like that of the bird soaring to new heights, flying across not only the sea but the mountains, the cities, the plains, unfettered and unlimited. Whereas, the fish is just beginning to emerge its head above the waves, taking that first breath of air before it immerses itself back into the waters. How long before the birds realizes the fish is nothing more than an anchor that prevents it flying to new destinations. I know that you would never wish to be that anchor, causing Joseph to only resent you in the future for tying him down."

As much as she struggled not to engage in the conversation, she felt compelled to tell the Countess how wrong she was about their relationship. "Joseph would never see me as a burden. Even now, he saw how I would go anywhere with him. Face any danger with him. I embrace his life fully and there will never be any restrictions. That is what love is all about."

"From a young girl's perspective, you believe it to be so," the Countess continued undaunted by Reisel's refusal to accept her initial comparisons. "Love is far more than sacrificing your own wants and desires for the other person. That only succeeds if both are willing to do the same for the other. But when has Joseph ever said to you that he would abandon his senseless quest in order to make a home for you. To spend all his time with you and raise a family. No, he has never done so. Joseph Kahana is an adventurer, a dreamer, chasing after one quest and then another. Is that what you truly wish for your life, to be chasing after the man you think you love for the rest of your life, never settling down, never fulfilling your own dreams of marriage and family. You are a young woman craving what all young woman desire Reisel. Joseph Kahana is not a man that can be tied down. He is like the wind, scattering himself to the four corners of the world."

"Then he would never be there for you either," Reisel challenged the Countess, thinking that perhaps there was still a way that she and her father could leave the horror of the castle without the Countess being aware of what she had seen. She only needed to make Elizabeth Bathory see the futility of trying to take Joseph away from her and then they both would be dismissed from her protective custody, ejected from the castle, as she would have no further use for her father.

"You fail to appreciate dear Reisel, I've already had those things that you still crave. I've had children, I have always dealt with a husband that was never present, and I certainly have already done my fair share of travelling across the countryside in pursuit of the man I love. The lifestyle that Joseph Kahana would offer to you is one that I have already fully embraced. Whereas to you it would be considered a hardship, to myself it is liberation."

"You see my darling Reisel, they are meant to be together. His world and that of the Countess are the same," her father agreed with the Countess's explanation.

"Stay out of this Papa!" she shouted at he father, angry that she still had not found a weakness in Elizabeth Bathory's argument against her relationship with Joseph. "He can never love you!," her voice furious and unyielding. "He has told me things and shared with me insights into his life that he could never share with you!"

The Countess saw an opportunity to drive a wedge between the two lovers, the more Reisel became frustrated. "You may be right," she agreed. "He may never open up to me and discuss his world as he does with you. Because he would know that I could never understand his background or his beliefs because they would be foreign to my own. But unlike yourself, it is not my intent to engage in boring conversation with my lover. That is a characteristic of domestic life that holds no interest for me. What Joseph and I share is lust." The Countess noticed how those words turned like a knife in the pit of the girl's stomach. "I desire him and I know he desires me equally. I see in his eyes the lust in which he craves my body. Every time we meet he undresses me and ravishes me within his mind. It is a hot, searing passion that can never be quenched and one which sadly I have never seen him show when he looks at you."

"That is a lie," Reisel screamed, pounding her fists against the breakfast table.

"Is it?" Elizabeth Bathory fired back. "Why then did he invite me into his bed chamber and lay with me. Even now I can feel his tongue exploring every inch of my body!"

"You're a liar," Reisel accused her, though in the back of her mind she knew now where the story of the succubus had originated. "If you did enter his bed chamber it was only because you used the secret entrance in the wall. He never invited you in!" No sooner had Reisel made the accusation, did she realize she had committed a grave error.

"What is this about secret entrances?" the Countess demanded to know forgetting completely about her plan to drive a wedge between Reisel and Joseph.

"It is nothing," Rabbi Lipmann attempted to reduce the temperature that was quickly rising within the room. "Just some foolish dreams of a frightened girl," he admonished his daughter at the same time trying to appease the Countess. "She claimed that she used some hidden corridor last night to secretly move through the castle."

"Papa, be quiet," she pleaded with her father.

"It is alright Reisel," he responded. "The Countess will tell you how ridiculous this dream of yours was and you will see that it is best she takes that sinner away from you. Already he commits adultery and he hasn't even married you yet."

But the Countess wasn't listening at all to what the Rabbi had to say, focusing only on Reisel's admission that she knew of the secret passages. "What did you see girl?" she demanded an answer.

"She saw nothing," the Rabbi answered for his daughter. "It was only a dream. Forgive her, he knows not what she is saying," the Rabbi begged for forgiveness on behalf of his daughter.

"Shut up you old fool!" the Countess roared at Lipmann, her face twisted with rage. "What did you see girl, I need to know?"

Reisel cowered before her, holding up her arms defensively in order to shield herself from the Countess's verbal attack.

"Tell me what you saw now," the Countess was practically crawling across the table, seething with anger.

"I don't believe it is necessary to talk to us that way," the Rabbi intervened.

Picking up one of the saucers, Bathory hurled it at Lipmann, striking him across the side of his face, just below his right eye. As the saucer disintegrated into pieces it left a deep gash that bled profusely. "I told you to shut up. Another word and I'll cut your tongue from your mouth."

"Papa," Reisel screamed as soon as she saw the blood flowing from his face, tears streaming from her own eyes.

"What did you see", The Countess was already across the table screaming like a banshee.

"I saw that he could never love a murderer like you," the girl defended her betrothed.

"Love?" the Countess cackled with a vicious laugh. "I never wanted his love, you foolish little girl, I only want his blood," she divulged her real reason for wanting Joseph, seeing no reason to hide the truth any longer. "See to it that they're locked away," she ordered her steward. "Summon everyone, we have to make some new plans!"

Chapter Eighteen

Bucharest: September 1610

"How will we ever thank you Excellency for all that you have done for us," Paolo Sarpi bowed before the Sultan.

"Thank me first by putting an end once and for all to this nightmare that has plagued both our Kingdoms for too long," Ahmed replied. "And then secondly, see that Bethlen takes his rightful place as the governor of my lands."

"I promise you Excellency, it will be done." Sarpi swore. "We have answers now that will lead us to the perpetrators of these horrendous crimes. If we can hold the Bathorys responsible for the first, then the second of your requests should follow automatically."

"You have answers but you do not have teeth," the Sultan let the Venetian Magistrate know that it was not enough. Turning to his Vizier, Ahmed instructed him to see if the commander of the border patrol was still present within the camp. If he was, then he was to be placed under Count Thurzo's command until such time that the crisis was ended.

Explaining to Thurzo what had just taken place, the Count asked Sarpi to relay his response. "Excellency, although I appreciate your consideration in this matter, I don't believe this is going to be well accepted when we return across the border. It would be considered most unusual and the Emperor might even consider it as interference in an internal matter."

Sultan Ahmed was not impressed by the Count's attempt to refuse his most generous offer and he let them know his displeasure immediately. "You say that you are a man of honour, Gyorgy Thurzo, yet, you choose to dishonour me when I exercise my authority over my own lands that have been placed under my jurisdiction by a treaty that your own leaders have signed. Prove to me that you are this man of honour as you believe. You have only three men under your command and that tells me that none of you will live out the week after you return to Transylvania. I am gifting you a company of thirty men that will not only guarantee your survival, they will ensure you win the battle. Do not think that myself and my generals do not know why there has been no justice as yet for those murdered for more than twenty years. The name Nadasdy strikes fear in the hearts of those that govern your Empire even long after his death. Prove to me that you are the man I believe you think you are. End this once and for all. Restore my lands to me. Raise Gabor Bethlen to the governor's seat. Restore honour to your family."

The Count saluted the Sultan by striking his left chest with his right hand, accepting Ahmed's criticism completely after it was translated. "I will not fail you, Excellency. I am a man of honour and although I may serve a different master, as God is my witness, truth, dignity and veracity will govern my actions."

The Sultan nodded, accepting the Count's words at face value and having no doubt he would live and die by them. "And you my good friend Senor Sarpi, I pray that Allah has opened your eyes finally to the glory of His universe these past few days that you have been here."

"Excellency, God, with your assistance of course has shown me things I could never imagine. Looking through your telescope, I now see how small and insignificant we truly are in his overall plan. For so long I have demanded that the Lord prove himself to me, and now I realize it was myself that had to prove my value to Him. In so many ways He has communicated with me and in my pettiness and self-absorption I chose to ignore His words. I saw the attempts on my life as an indication there could be no God but now I realize the reason I survived every attempt was solely because there is a God. The universe is ordered and structured to show that nothing happens without His involvement."

"It pleases me my friend that you have finally learned this valuable lesson. It is never too late to let Allah know that you were mistaken and now embrace his universal laws without question."

Paolo Sarpi bowed, displaying his gratitude and admiration to this young potentate, wise well beyond his youthful years.

"I can only pray that one day the Kahana will recognize that his destiny lies within my kingdom. He and his descendants will never be accepted for who they truly are in the western world. It is time for him to forgive Allah and understand that his ancestors willingly chose this path in order to be His instruments on Earth."

Listening intently to the translation, Joseph Kahana felt as if a heavy burden had fallen from his heart and the scales had dropped from his eyes. "Excellency, there is much I need God to forgive me for. I recognize that I have failed Him in the past but will not do so in the future. God willing, the Kahana will return to your lands and we will rebuild the glorious age where all men can live freely under God's rule."

The Sultan appeared satisfied with the response. "And what can I say about this one?" he referred to Caesar de Nostradame. "A man gifted with such powers and yet he fears to accept the responsibility with which Allah has entrusted him. Accept the mantle of God and recognize you are not unlike the prophets of old. It is not your role or purpose to comment after the events have taken place but to prevent them from ever happening. Prophecy is and always will be about steering the people in the correct direction in order to avoid the terrible events that will take place if they fail to heed God's words."

"I have dishonored my father, I have dishonored myself, and most of all I have dishonored God," Caesar admitted in a confession to the Sultan. "I will do so no longer. There is so much that I have withheld from my companions and I can do so no longer. I will be the prophet whom God wants me to be."

Ahmed waited for the translation of his words, then clapped his hands in appreciation of all that he had heard. "Now you are ready to face the demons that plague our world," the Sultan celebrated their awakening. "Allah had brought me mere rock from which the ore had barely been extracted. Now he has forged a weapon of hardened steel that will strike terror in the hearts of His enemies. Go forth in the name of the Almighty. You are Allah's soldiers now and he will fortify your right arms and give you the strength to overcome all adversity. Today you are sanctified in his holy name. All praise be to Allah."

Once shuttled away from the Sultan's presence, the companions prepared their horses for the long journey back to the world from which they came. As they tightened the girths on their saddles, contemplating all that they had experienced and now understood in regards to their mission, Paolo felt the urge to speak.

"I need to apologize for my failure to trust in you. I have made you suffer and endure far more than was necessary if only I had confided in you earlier. I realize that now."

The others looked at one another, not certain of what Paolo was actually trying to say to them. "What are you talking about Paolo," Joseph questioned him. "You did nothing that harmed us."

"But I did," he confessed. "You think that only now that we know Ferencz Nadasdy was in command of the Omullup and behind the initial murders that began decades ago that we have our important link to implicate those that his rule over Hungary and Transylvania in his name. But that is not true. I think I had already made the connection when we were at Ecsed. I never told you about the letter I sent back with the rider. It was to be delivered to an old friend, a professor at the medical school in Budapest. Not to ask him for help but to confirm something I already suspected. I let all of you down by not telling you then. At the castle they mentioned the loss of their attending doctor Anna Darvula. I knew then that they must be speaking of someone that I knew very well, many years ago. Her name was Annise Darvolya. She was a medical student at the university. She had an exceptional mind, years ahead of anyone else in the profession. Her professors feared her exuberance but most of all they feared her level of knowledge that apparently surpassed them all.

Annise was convinced that there were specific organs in the body that secreted substances that controlled every other function in our body. She theorized that there were substances to tell us when to become a man or a woman, another to make us older or younger, even one to make us stronger or weaker. Her professors warned her to abandon such ideas and recognize that the traits we possess were nothing more than gifts from God and that we were not able to control any of our characteristics. She refused to accept that all these things were merely the will of God, that a cripple had to be cripple simply because it was preordained. She assumed that if she could determine which of these humors controlled a particular function, then she felt she could correct afflictions by determining whether quantities of these humors had to be increased or decreased when they entered into the blood. She even said if she could find the right combination of humors she could unlock the secrets to immortality. The University warned her to stop pursuing her bizarre theories but she worked clandestinely on corpses that were brought into the morgue, stealing body parts and preparing potions and pastes that I believed she tried out on patients in the poorer parts of the city. When they discovered what she was doing, they accused of her of being a witch and she was forced to flee from Budapest in order to save her life."

"How is it you know so much about her?" Caesar was curious. "Was she one of the young doctors you were trying to entice and recruit to come to Venice?"

"This was years before I was even the city magistrate," he shook his head. "No, back then, I was her lover. I was only a young student in the clergy, doing my post-graduate medical studies at various institutions throughout the Empire when we met. I could not resist her passion and enthusiasm for medicine. It was infectious and the more we worked together, the closer we became."

"And then you found out later what she was doing?" Caesar guessed. "That must have been difficult for you."

"No," Sarpi set the record straight. "I was the one that turned her in to the authorities at the University. She fled, knowing that I was the one that betrayed her. When the general told us the story of the Omullup and I saw the procedures that were performed on those dead girls, I knew then where she had gone. She was that witch he mentioned with

Nadasdy. She was the doctor tending to Elizabeth Bathory. So you see, I could have told you months ago what I knew and we could have put an end to this mission long ago. It is exactly as your father, Joseph, tried to tell me, and what the Sultan finally did show me, is that God has designed our universe, our world, our lives based on circles, even to the point that our past will eventually catch up with our future. I tried to ignore the sins of my past, I still hoped it wasn't true. My betrayal of her actually made this all come to pass. Hence my delay and I used the letter as an excuse to delay it even further, but now I can finally admit before God that I was wrong and I am responsible for all we have suffered as a result of my procrastination and denial."

"Don't go taking all the credit for our failures, Joseph considered it his turn to talk. "So what if it turned out that the doctor administering to the Countess was this woman you knew from the past. It still didn't connect the Countess to the crimes but I hid from you events that did exactly that. In my misguided belief that God has been punishing me all my life, I denied the evidence he laid in my lap so I would not have to acknowledge his hand in guiding me. I am the one you need to forgive because if I only told you these things we would not even be here."

"What nonsense are you talking about Joseph," Paolo was not willing to share the blame for their failure thus far.

"Not nonsense," Joseph was not willing to excuse himself from being to blame. "When we escaped from the carriage, I guess I already knew the Countess was somehow behind the murders. There were no little fairy people chopping tree branches so that they would fall on us. The reason I was late joining our party as we were leaving Castle Ecsed was because I was looking out the window of my bedroom and watching what I thought was a young boy chopping trees at the edge of the forest. I marveled at how he could fell a tree with only a few blows and how incredible his strength was when he effortlessly hoisted the bundle of boughs onto his shoulders and began carrying them back to the castle. When I saw those footprints in the snow around the tree that crushed our carriage I had no doubt that it was him. But I said nothing. It was as if I wanted God to keep trying to kill me. I could have stopped it then but I didn't."

"That still proves nothing," Caesar exclaimed. "There could be hundreds of small people with amazing strength. It doesn't mean it was the same one you saw at the castle. You had no way to prove it."

"Yes, that may be right but there is more I didn't tell you. The night I stayed at Castle Bran, the Countess used a secret passage to break into my bedroom. She drugged me, I couldn't resist her advances and then she took advantage of me. But more than that, she made me bleed and then she drank my blood."

The others looked at each other, not with shock, but a look that almost appeared to be envy. "Well I can understand how that certainly makes her a murderer," Caesar quipped. "Yes, most definitely," Sarpi agreed. "A death most welcome I can assure you. If I must go, that is the way I wish it will happen."

"You don't understand," Joseph insisted. "The drugs she used, they had a certain aroma, a very distinct taste in my mouth that I will never forget. When I was drugged and being carried away by the witches, they had the same smells on their bodies. In my mouth I could taste some of the same substances from their bodies that were present on the countess's body. They were unmistakable. I knew then she was connected in some way to these witches. And when the one told you, Paolo, that they wanted my immortal blood, I also knew that it was for her. She had tasted my blood and she wanted more. I'm so sorry I have not revealed any of this sooner to you."

"Nothing to be sorry about," Caesar felt it was his time to speak. "I knew long before the rest of you that the Countess was involved and I said nothing to you. I am exactly what the Sultan said I was. Only willing to reveal the prophecy when it was already too late to do anything about it because I was too afraid to say anything in advance when I had the opportunity to change the future."

"So what are you exactly saying," Sarpi questioned him.

"I knew the day she walked down the stairs at the palace in Vienna that she was the one responsible for all the murders but I couldn't bring myself to say it. I've let you all believe that in order to envision my father's prophecies I have to suffer terrible pains in my skull for them to be revealed. That's only partly true. I think that is the way by which my father punishes me if I don't tend to be proactive. When those prophecies are revealed it is usually at the time the event has actually just passed or is presently occurring. Rather than stopping anything, I am just confirming that which was predicted to happen. But there are other prophecies, ones that I receive well in advance of the occurrence. Ones that if I acted upon immediately we would have been able to prevent what followed later. Those prophecies never present themselves as severe headaches. But as Sultan Ahmed said, I was afraid to act, I was afraid to say or do anything just in case I was wrong. I had the ability and the opportunity to take action well in advance and I did nothing. People died because I did nothing and therefore if there is anyone guilty of failing in our mission, it is me!"

"You said you knew when you first met her, how so?" Joseph inquired.

"As in Century X, Quatrain 10 so," Caesar answered then delivered the quatrain.

'Stained with murder and enormous adulteries,
Great enemy of the entire human race:
One who will be worse than his grandfathers, uncles or fathers,
In steel, fire, waters, bloody and inhuman.'

"I didn't mention it to you because I convinced myself that because my father used the word 'his', he couldn't possibly be talking about the Countess. I knew I was lying to myself but I couldn't help it. Something about her clouded my senses. As you said Joseph, there were smells, tastes that were exuding from her skin that managed to make me feel like I had never felt before. Maximilian even told us that she was an adulterer and I chose to ignore it. Now we know her husband was guilty of performing the same inhuman acts and who knows, if we looked at her family tree, we could possibly find they were all guilty of these horrendous crimes."

"I've learned to trust your father's predictions," Sarpi admitted, "So I have to accept that you may have known right away, but again, how can you accuse someone of a crime without the proof. You can't make a prophecy from a dead prophet hold up in a court of law. I probably would have been just as skeptical too, if I were you."

"And do you think I should have been skeptical about this one as well?" Caesar then recited another of the quatrains.

'Of land weak and parentage poor,
Through piece and peace he will attain to the empire.
For a long time a young female to reign,
Never has one so bad come upon the kingdom.'

"That was Century III, Quatrain 28," he informed them. Are there any doubts after that one. The Bathorys had lost much of their territory they ruled through the war between Hungary and the Ottomans. It wasn't until they started playing both sides against one another, switching allegiances repeatedly, gaining land and wealth with every double dealing that they were able to amass land and wealth beyond the possessions of most kings. Since 1604 Elizabeth Bathory has been the one solely in control of their princedom and as a result, my father was saying she also brought the evil upon the land."

"When did you manage to gain all this knowledge about the Bathorys," Sarpi was curious.

"Shortly after she was introduced to us. I was actually following up on the history of the Nadasdy family when we were in Vienna since that was the name by which she was introduced to us. But both families have been so intertwined by incest that they are inseparable."

"Was that all?" Joseph asked, now convinced that they all had been guilty of concealing truths that would have made the entire mission easier if they had trusted in themselves and in one another.

"Not exactly," Caesar admitted. "There may have been one more. It was Century III, Quatrain 41."

'Hunchback will be elected by the council,
A more hideous monster not seen on earth,
The willing blow will put out his eye:
The traitor to the King received as faithful.'

"Let me guess," Sarpi thought he could establish when this one revealed itself. "You heard this when we were sitting at the dinner table and I started asking the Countess about this hunchback she left in charge of her school."

"You are right," Caesar told him. As soon as she said he was in charge, that's when I heard my father saying 'elected by council.' But at the same time, the quatrain was saying he would be eventually held accountable and put to the axe by the Emperor. So once more I said nothing. I can't express to all of you how sorry I am. I hope you can forgive me."

"You don't need our forgiveness Caesar," Sarpi concluded. "It would appear that all of us were guilty of concealing vital information. The very reason the three of us were brought together, because we all had specific strengths by which we could have put the pieces of the puzzle together and brought this to an earlier conclusion, ultimately became our Achilles heel. Our own doubts and insecurities were our true enemy. I only hope that you, Gyorgy can forgive us for our failures."

Count Thurzo had remained absolutely silent throughout the confessions made by his three colleagues. They hoped that he would not be too judgemental when he finally spoke but they were willing to take a tongue lashing as a well deserved punishment for their failures if he thought it was merited. They had not accounted for the possibility that his opening words were going to be his own personal apology.

"If anyone needs to apologize, it is myself," Gyorgy Thurzo began his explanation. None of your oversights even comes close to my total failure to uphold the law and the honour of my family. I let pride and false loyalty cloud my judgment and for that reason I alone deserve to bear all the guilt for the deaths of these young girls. You think a few months of turning a blind eye makes you responsible for what has transpired. Perhaps if I tell you of eight years of ignoring what was right in front of me, then you will know what real responsibility feels like. The Sultan was correct, a man must uphold truth and fidelity and his commitment to God, if he is to consider himself righteous and honourable. Alas, for eight years I have not practiced any of those godly acts and I can only pray that the Almighty forgives me for what I have done. Eight years ago a Lutheran priest named Istvan Magyari sought me out, thinking I was the only one he could tell of the crimes his parishioners had witnessed but were afraid to bring to the attention of the authorities. With their own eyes they had seen servants from the Nadasdy household kidnap young girls that were never to be seen again. He said he even talked to several victims that managed to escape that spoke of how the Count and his wife had done terrible things to them, sticking them with pins, sodomizing them, burning them with hot irons, just to mention a few of the tortures they had suffered. But these were mere peasant girls, servants of gentry households, how was I to take their word against members of the aristocracy.

The Nadasdys had power, they had influence and unlimited wealth, and I was merely a poor cousin to the family, a Count in name only and having to work for my earnings in order to take care of my family. So I did nothing; I said nothing; and because of that nothing changed, no one was arrested and innocent girls continued to die. Would any of you like to take the blame now?"

None of them could say a word after hearing the Count's confession. It was actually a full minute before Joseph extended his right arm with a clenched fist. "Enough of the past. From this moment onwards, we pledge to rectify mistakes we have made, bring penance to those that have escaped it, and bring justice to those that have cried out for so long. So help me God!"

Caesar extended his right hand, fist to fist, "So help me God!"

"So help me God," Paolo's fist joined with the other two.

Laying his hand over the other three, Gyorgy Thurzo added a few words of his own, "We are the right hand of God. Let all those that have done evil in His eyes beware of His mighty fist. Vengeance is the Lord's!"

Count Thurzo trotted towards the Turkish border patrol which had been assembled by order of the Sultan Ahmed to accompany the foreigners on their return mission. It was obvious from the expression on Rashid Kartal's face that he was not happy with the situation. There was little trust from Thurzo's remaining men, seeing themselves vastly outnumber by by the Turks, ten to one. The Count wished to defuse a situation before it had a chance to ignite.

"Captain," he addressed Kartal by rank, "Are we aware of the chain of command on this mission?

"I am aware Commander," Rashid Kartal responded by addressing Thurzo as his superior but it was if it left a foul taste in his mouth.

"Are you men aware of it as well," Thurzo wanted to ensure that there would be no conflicts arising.

"Yes Sir," Kartal replied. "It has all been made very clear to us by our Sultan, Sir."

"Good," the Count replied. "I want you to know that I will safeguard the men from your unit as if they were my own. I will not abuse my command in any way by sending them into a dangerous situation the I would not enter myself. I will not tell them how to fight, only who to fight and when to fight. From that point on, they are under your command when they engage the enemy. Are we clear?"

"Yes Sir," Kartal accepted the instructions, satisfied in part that the actual fighting would be left up to his orders and commands.

"So Captain, I've noticed that you've equipped all the man with lances. As I said, the method of engagement I leave up to you, but I must admit I am mystified. Why lances?" Gyorgy Thurzo had only read about the lancer units from medieval times in history books on warfare. With the invention of muskets and crossbows, he hadn't encountered any army that still relied on a lance.

The Captain was more than happy to explain. "General Naziri provided you with his account of how he could take on a pack of wolves with two hundred musketeers under his command. Other than your muskets and my own, we don't have any musketeers and even if we did, we certainly don't have two hundred. With that many rifles being fired, the probability of hitting a good number of the wolves was pretty high. You don't have to be an expert marksman when all you are doing is firing blindly with a couple of hundred shots heading in the same direction. Those of us assigned to border patrol know that meant there was a high probability of encountering all sorts of dangerous animals in the wilderness. Bears, wolves, foxes, even a water buffalo are all real threats that we faced all the time. My men have no muskets and even if we did, our chances of hitting one or two animals concealed in the tall grass and foliage would be slim to none. But none of those beasts is a match for a good horseman with a lance."

"Then I'm glad to leave that choice of weapons with you Captain. I intend for us to find the last of these wolf warriors and to eliminate them completely."

"We will do what needs to be done Commander," Rashid appeared to relax, now that he knew that there would be very little interference from Count Thurzo. "So where to first, Sir?"

"Have your men ever been to Bucharest, Captain?"

"No Sir."

"Well, I hear it is very beautiful this time of year. Let's see for ourselves just how beautiful it truly is. You may take the men out, Captain."

Kartal gave the order for his men to start the procession north. It would take several days to reach Bucharest and once they were across the Danube, most of the land would be heavily forested. A perfect setting for an ambush. Everyone remained alert, posting at night no less than six sentries that rotated every four hours to safeguard the encampment. Though they encountered no challenges along the way, no one could escape the eerie feeling that they were being watched. All of the Turkish soldiers were eager for the opportunity to fight but by this time, Thurzo and his men had seen enough death and wished only to reach the gates of Bucharest without incident.

By the start of the seventeenth century, Bucharest was already a thriving urban centre situated on the Dambovita River, and handling most of the commercial activity between Wallachia and the Ottoman Empire. It was a dramatic revival, since only sixteen years earlier much of the town had been set to the torch in a battle against the Turks when Michael the Brave decided they should be free of their Ottoman overlords. Thurzo was concerned that the presence of his Turkish soldiers was not going to be received very well, even though according to the treaty, all of this land had been returned on paper to the Turks. The closer they got to the city, the more concerned he became.

"Do you hear that?" the Count asked his three companions.

"We don't hear anything," they all replied.

"Exactly," he concurred. "This is a city with over a hundred thousand people. "Why don't we hear anything? Something is definitely wrong."

"I have something to say," Caesar responded at that moment. "Or I should say my father does. He's telling us to pay attention to Century VII, Quatrain 16:

> *'The deep entry made by the great Queen,*
> *Will make the place powerful and inaccessible;*
> *The army of the three lions will be defeated*
> *Causing within a thing hideous and terrible.'*

"So I'm presuming this time you are forewarning us Caesar," Thurzo surmised because none of them saw any signs of the usual distress he would suffer when Caesar delivered the message. "Because otherwise I certainly don't like that part regarding the defeat of the three lions."

"Yes, my father is saying that Bathory already controls everything and everyone in this city. We have to expect that she's turned the entire city against us. If we try to fight, by attacking the city we will lose. The three kings, being Joseph, Paolo and myself will surely die."

"So, does he give us a solution," Thurzo didn't care about how they would fail, he only wanted to know how they would succeed.

"From within, just as he said," Caesar stated.

"Nostradamus is telling us to simply ride in to a city which has been turned entirely against us and wants to kill us as if we don't have a care in the world. That's what you are saying. Just go in."

"Yes."

"Have you gone mad?" Thurzo wanted to know.

"Not at all," Caesar replied calmly. "I just have faith. I know once we are in there, it all will become clear. Trust my father, trust me!"

"I need to discuss this with the others first," the Count was still reluctant to accept the prophesy. "What do either of you have to say about this," he asked Joseph and Paolo.

"I believe what he believes," Joseph answered. "If Caesar says we are to ride straight in to the city, then that is what we do."

"And what about you," Thurzo hoped at least Paolo Sarpi had come to his senses.

"I agree with them. We ride in to the city. They don't know that we know they are waiting for us on the other side. That gives us the advantage."

"You think riding into a city that could have an execution squad waiting on the other side of that wall is to our advantage." Thurzo couldn't believe what he was hearing.

"And I suppose you're going to agree with them as well," he questioned Captain Kartal.

"My Sultan has told me these men have the hand of Allah resting upon their shoulders. I do not doubt it is so. I will ride into the heart of the city with them because Allah will protect us."

Thurzo was ready to capitulate. "I guess if everyone is so ready to commit suicide today, then I might as well be the one to lead this madness. We'll ride in slow. No one make any sudden movements that could be mistaken as being threatening. Stay close together and we'll head to the centre of the city. In the city plaza we will have more room if we need to manoeuvre. We can't let ourselves be cramped into any small alleys or lane-ways. Once we get to the city centre, God willing, we'll find a way to stay alive."

Rashid Kartal relayed the instructions to his men.

"Be ready for anything. Rashid, I'll need you to stay close to my side. You have to be ready for my orders at any moment. Do you understand?"

"Yes Sir," Captain Kartal knew exactly what was at stake.

"I think we need a code word for when I'm instructing you to take independent action," the Count suggested to Rashid. "Something like 'Zow'."

"What is this 'Zow', it makes no sense," the Captain complained.

"Exactly," Thurzo explained. "It is not supposed to make any sense. That is why it is called a code word. Only you and I will understand it."

"So what should I do when I hear this 'Zow'?"

"Whatever you think you should do," Gyorgy Thurzo was trying to explain. "Do what you think is best. Don't hesitate. I trust you will know from instinct exactly what to do."

"I will listen for this word Zow from now on," Rashid confirmed that he understood and was prepared.

"Well, I think you may be hearing it very soon," the Count advised him. "We are definitely riding into the lion's den this time."

As they passed through the open gates of the city, Thurzo noticed the two signal men posted on the parapets, Each held flags, one in each hand that they used to signal other units stationed throughout the city.

"Well they know we are here now," Thurzo informed the rest.

The passage to the center of the city was completely clear. No barricades, traps or obstacles had been set up of any kind. It was the first sign that Count Thurzo interpreted as circumstances might actually be turning in their favour. Clearly they had underestimated their strength. Either that or they were so overconfident in their superiority, that they weren't even concerned that they had just let an armed enemy waltz directly into the heart of their city.

Both Thurzo and Kartal checked all the upper story windows of the buildings they passed. A clever opponent would have posted archers or musketeers in high positions to take them out easily. Either the enemy didn't have any or else once again their adversary had seduced himself into believing they weren't necessary. Thurzo counted two points in their favour now.

Up ahead he could see the wide plaza with its fountain that marked the city center. The fountain would provide a good battle position he calculated. With their backs to the fountain his men would be able to perform a protective radius that their enemy would have to break through in order to reach them. With thirty lances pointed directly at their bellies, that wasn't going to be easy for the enemy soldiers to do.

There was a contingent of the enemy stationed on the east side of the plaza, perhaps thirty in total, all equipped with rapiers but no other weapons. Once more, Count Thurzo was relieved to see that they didn't have anything that fired a bullet or a missile such as a crossbow. Riding around the plaza's centerpiece, the Count instructed Captain Rashid to distribute themselves uniformly around the fountain, positioned at each hour point so that wherever the hour hand would be they were three men deep.

Time proceeded very slowly as everyone shifted into position, preparing for the next step. Cutting off any means of escape, units of the opposing army poured down every spoke road that fed the central circle of the city. All of them were infantry, another advantage Count Thurzo chalked up in his favour.

Their new unblooded rapiers shone in the afternoon sunlight, along with the bright polished brass buttons on their tunics and the rings on their tall fabric helmets. "I don't recognize these uniforms," the Count commented as more and more men formed a solid perimeter around the city plaza.

"It doesn't matter," Rashid dismissed the observation as unimportant. "They are the enemy no matter what they wear. All uniforms turn red when we give them the point of our swords."

"Doesn't look like a single one of them has ever seen a real battle," the Count observed.

Surrounded by the city's defenders, Gyorgy Thurzo searched for their leader, knowing that he had to be watching from somewhere just beyond the perimeter. It took a minute or two, but eventually he saw him concealed in the shadows, the old graybeard mounted on a dappled stallion that looked more like a parade horse than a military animal. He knew immediately from his stature that this must be their supreme commander, a typically pompous, overly ostentatious, puffed up peacock of an aristocrat that probably knew little of governing and far less about military matters. Shouting in the direction of the man he assumed to be their leader, he introduced himself. "I am Count Gyorgy Thurzo, Palatine of Hungary, on a mission for the Holy Roman Emperor Matthias and I demand to know the meaning of this unacceptable welcoming. Your formation by which you encircled my men can only be interpreted as being a hostile act.".

"I know very well who you are," the leader responded. "You and your contingent of Turkish soldiers are certainly not welcome here."

"By whose order?" Thurzo demanded to know.

"I give and take my own orders, the graybeard in his military uniform decorated with a chest full of medals responded.

"And who exactly are you?" Thurzo asked, not recognizing the man at all.

"I am Brigadier General Laszlo Nadasdy," the man proudly stated his name as if it was intended to send shivers down the spine of his enemies upon hearing it. As far as Thurzo was concerned it was just another useless cousin.

"I'm sorry," Thurzo smiled, as he excused his ignorance, "But I don't know any General Laszlo Nadasdy in His Majesty's army."

"I am the Brigadier General of the Wallachian army," he informed the Count, "And the acting Palatine of Wallachia."

"Oh, I guess I'm sorry once again," Thurzo apologized. "I had no knowledge that there was a Wallachian army in His Majesty's service."

"I serve at the behest of the Principality of Transylvania," the General responded as if his authority came from a higher power.

"Aha, I see, the Principality of Transylvania," Count Thurzo rolled his eyes a few times as if he was giving the notion of a principality due consideration. "And I presume that as a Brigadier General, this must be your brigade then. This is everyone under you command."

"This is the finest army in Wallachia," the general bragged about his men.

"I have no doubt. But this is it; this is all of it?" Thurzo wanted to make certain that he fully understood the extent of the General's command and that there was no other opposition force being hidden.

"It is far more men than you have," the General reminded the Count.

"Yes it is," Thurzo agreed. "You must have at least a hundred men here by my estimation."

Turning towards Sarpi, both Joseph and Caesar were concerned that the Count was simply antagonizing the General and thereby placing their lives further at risk. "Is there any sense to this," Joseph asked.

"How should I know," Sarpi was equally as concerned. "I think we have to trust his instincts and let him do what he thinks is best."

"Well, I think we better be prepared to fight because this doesn't look like it is going to end well," Joseph was growing nervous. "Surely Caesar you must be stressed enough by now that there's something else your father would like to say to us in addition to telling us to place ourselves in this situation in the first place."

"No, I can't think of anything. My minds gone blank," Caesar responded. "I'm guessing my father has nothing more to say about this event."

"This is hardly the time for Nostradamus to go quiet on us," Joseph rebuked Caesar's father. "Keep your hands on the hilts of your swords gentlemen, this could get a little bit messy."

"So I'm assuming this is the point where the commander's sword is handed over and the troops are surrendered," Count Thurzo provided the General with the suggestion of what usually would be the next move.

"That would be my expectation," the General agreed.

"Well then, I guess there is no other option but to submit and yield the sword. General, if you would be so kind as to approach." As Thurzo withdrew his rapier from its scabbard, he held it laterally, balanced in the palm of his hand in order to present it pommel first. As he held out his arm, he smiled and winked at Rashid Kartal, passing on a silent signal to be prepared.

Emerging from behind his lines, the General paraded towards the centre of the circle where Count Thurzo had remained steadfast. He was accompanied by his second in command, another highly decorated, arrogant looking nobleman wearing an absolutely spotless uniform as if it had never taken part in a battle from the day it was sewn.

Halting his horse within arm's length of Count Thurzo, and alongside Captain Kartal, the General began his acceptance speech for the sake of his men, in order that they would have a fabulous story to tell their grandchildren of how their brave and fearless general defeated the invading forces from the Turkish Empire. It was typical of these paper generals and Thurzo had already anticipated it would take place.

"In the name of the Principality of Wallachia, I Brigadier General Laszlo Nadasdy, Palatine of Wallachia, hereby accept you offer of surrender..."

"Wait...wait, I think you made an error there," the Count interrupted the speech.

"What are you talking about?" the General looked confused. "There was no error. Now let me continue."

"If I recall properly, this land is under the sovereignty of Sultan Ahmed of the Ottoman Empire. Zow! That would make you a traitor."

At the moment he heard the word 'Zow', Rashid had unsheathed his sword and in a smooth, practically imperceptible motion, sliced through both flesh and bone. At the same time Count Thurzo had immediately flipped in reverse the position of his rapier, knuckles safely beneath the bow loop, and plunged it deep into the chest of the General's second in command, making a bloody mess of his tidy, unsoiled uniform. "I never did say exactly who would be handing over their sword," the Count addressed the man in whose chest he wedged his rapier. By the time the Count had completed his thrust, the assembled troops of the

Wallachian army could be heard to groan in horror as they watched the Brigadier General's head slide from the stump of his neck and fall to the ground. His body remained upright in the saddle for what seemed an eternity as blood spurted upward from his collar, squirting into the air, until it too slid sideways and fell to the dirt road where it was trampled under the hooves of his startled horse.

"Well, that worked well," Thurzo could be overheard commenting to Captain Rashid.

"You know," the Captain joked, "You talk too much."

"Then you should be the one to give your men the next command," Thurzo acknowledged.

"Attack." Kartal shouted to his men in Turkish.

Leaderless and untried in battle, the army of Wallachia proved an easy rout for the seasoned warriors of the Ottoman Empire. Without losing a single man, the Turks impaled almost half of the opposing force before the rest of the city's soldiers threw down their weapons and begged for mercy.

The survivors of the routed army were stripped down to their undergarments and then locked inside one of the large wooden warehouses that were situated on the banks of the Dambovita River. These massive structures of commercialism were ideal for transformation into a temporary prisoner camp. Their names, residence details, and next of kin were all recorded. The interrogation process was about to begin.

"So what are we doing now," Caesar questioned Gyorgy Thurzo.

"It was my first intention when I said we had to come to Bucharest to find the traitors in the government that were in collaboration with the Bathorys. They were directly responsible for permitting the witches and the wolf warriors to run unchecked across the territories for years. I thought it would be a matter of bringing a number of bureaucrats to justice. But now, just as your father indicated, I see that she has installed an entire military government and equipped this rebel army beneath our very noses in Vienna. The crime of treason supersedes the killing of those girls and one which I believe even the Emperor can't ignore. But to prove it we need to gather as much evidence as possible. Someone in that warehouse is in a position of knowing exactly where we can find that evidence. Documents, papers, sales invoices, anything that we can use to pin her with this crime."

"Perhaps my father can help you with his latest quatrain," Caesar suggested.

"You received one from him just now?" Joseph asked. All of them were curious that they had not seen for a second time Caesar's usual behavior when the headaches would occur, indicating that a prophecy had been revealed while it was still possible to make a decision.

"As the Sultan said, if I start using my gift in advance of a problem materializing, then perhaps I don't need to suffer any longer. I needed to accept who I am and what my true purpose in life actually was. So now that I am beginning to accept that, then I think this one is everything you need to know about Elizabeth Bathory in regards to an accusation of treason."

'The author of the evils will begin to reign in the year six hundred and seven,
Without sparing all her subjects who belong to the leach,
And then afterwards she will come little by little to the Frank country to relight her fire,
Returning whence she has come.'

"So six hundred and seven years after the millennium will be the year when she began making plans to take over the Empire," Joseph interpreted the first line. "And obviously she has no intention of giving up her blood thirst either, as expressed by the leach, but she hardly can expect to conquer France as well. That is definitely an over exaggeration."

"You missed the use of the preposition," Caesar was confident he could now interpret his father's quatrains better than anyone else. "She only conquers as far as the border with France which means she intends to reign over all of the Austro-Hungarian Empire."

"And that part of returning whence she has come," Sarpi was confused by that line.

"She truly believes she is entitled to rule over it all. Her bloodlines already make her the most powerful person in Hungary, Slovakia, Morovia, Transylvania, Wallachia and Moldova. Why wouldn't she think that Austria should belong to her as well? This is her birthright or from whence she sprang," Caesar explained."

"It should be noted that I cannot actually bring the testimony of a dead prophet into the courtroom," Count Thurzo bemoaned the fact that he probably couldn't use any of the quatrains as evidence, "But just in case, what number of the prophecies was this one?"

"That's the strange thing," Caesar sounded reluctant when recalling the number. "It was Quatrain 21 from Century XI."

"I thought there were only ten centuries in total," Sarpi drew on his memory for the exact number from Nostradamus' books.

"There were only ten," Caesar admitted, "But as strange as this might sound, I think my father is still writing them. Or perhaps there a missing books I haven't found yet."

"From the other side, you mean," Thurzo questioned how that was even possible.

"If my father could pay me a visitation from the other side, then I don't see why it wouldn't be possible," Joseph came to Caesar's defense. "I think we've all seen too much, experienced too much to start doubting it now."

"As your father said," Sarpi was supporting their argument as well, "Time and space are just circular events that are bound to repeat at some point. Joseph spoke of nexus points where these circles actually meet and can transfer information between them. What if Caesar is himself an actual nexus point and his father uses him to transfer all these quatrains from whatever time he is existing. It could be endless if outside of our understanding of time. Reality is what God chooses it to be. Which means at this very time, Nostradamus could very well be writing more prophecies because in his time-frame he still exists." Fra Paolo Sarpi appeared far more willing now to extend his scientific mind beyond the framework of his world now that God had reentered his life.

"That is far too confusing for me to even attempt to understand," Count Thurzo expressed his current state of mind in trying to unwind this entire concept of circles within circles. Let's do some good old fashioned interrogation and find some hard evidence of my cousin Erzsibet Bathory's plan to take over the Empire."

Chapter Nineteen

The Olt Gorge: October 1610

It took several days to amass all the material concerning the political ambitions of the Countess Bathory to depose the current monarchy with its power base in Vienna, but once all collected, Gyorgy Thurzo was convinced that it would be enough to force Emperor Matthias to take action. Even so, it was still going to be a difficult argument as the Habsburgs were so indebted to the Bathory family that their normal inclination would be to pardon all the crimes just to insure the financial security of the Empire. The money trails didn't just lead to Erzsibet but to her cousin Gabriel and uncle Stephan as well.

Thurzo also knew that it wouldn't be long before the other ruling family in Hungary brought charges against him for the murder of one of their own. Laszlo Nadasdy had died in a most unbecoming way. Some may even suggest that Gyorgy had used subterfuge. Someone soon would begin demanding from the Emperor blood for blood. It didn't even matter which family would make the demand. The Bathory and Nadasdy families were practically inseparable, with so many cousin to cousin marriages that they had become indistinguishable. As a Thurzo, his was considered a minor aristocratic family with the occasional marriage into the higher ranks of the nobility, but no where even close to being blue blooded enough to be forgiven for shedding Nadasdy blood. Therefore it was imperative to find documents that would provide sufficient evidence that Laszlo Nadasdy was guilty of treasonous activity. All that he could find in the General's office was a letter from cousin Erzsibet thanking Laszlo for swearing allegiance to her and her cousin and to the princedom she inherited. Whether it would be enough to convince Matthias and Maximilian of intent to partake in treasonous behavior, he didn't know.

Other dispatches that they had uncovered provided clear evidence that Countess Elizabeth Bathory had established and armed her own militias across the Romanian territories, with definite instruction that they would only take orders from her. She never even bothered to use cousin Gabriel as an intermediary to shield her from a direct connection. Established in the same manner as the battalion that had been stationed in Bucharest, there were similar units entrenched in most of the other big cities across Transylvania, leaving Wallachia solely to be militarized by her cousin. As the governing prince, Gabriel Bathory could make an argument for having his own armed forces, but those tied directly to Erzsibet were in clear defiance of laws that restricted her to possessing only a personal guard, solely created for her own protection and to be based only at her places of residence. As for the territories under Bathory jurisdiction, they did require that a policing force loyal only to the crown and under the direct supervision of a Palatine would be provided but it was evident that Laszlo's men were never employed to perform any such policing function. Clearly she had breached this statute, and Gyorgy was confident that at least Maximilian would see it this way.

Convinced that all this should be enough to demonstrate to the Emperor that Erzsibet was at least preparing at some point in the future to challenge for the throne, he was still concerned that the Habsburg indebtedness would overrule sound judgment. The discovery that Bucharest was being used as the repository for the money with which to make payments to all the military units within the principality, sweetened the pot nicely. Seizing the large stash of thalers and ducats, Thurzo made a sizeable donation to the royal coffers by confiscating all of it in the name of the Crown. As extra insurance, the Bathory accountant stationed in Bucharest with all the records of payment was also dispatched to the palace in Vienna to confirm everything Gyorgy had written in his letter to the Archduke.

Trusting only his three remaining men with the task of escorting the secured wagon containing the cash boxes, documents, ledgers, letters, the accountant and several of Laszlo's junior officers in chains, Count Thurzo sent them on their way, along the road to Vienna. They would take the longest route possible, first heading south towards Slavonia, then across Croatian and into Carinthia. In that way they would avoid any of the lands where Countess Bathory held any influence.

The next few days the townspeople of Bucharest were entertained by a display of military prowess. Seeding an offer of enlistment into the policing force of the Palatine of Hungary, it was only a short wait until a number of the prisoners saw the advantage of accepting the offer over the possibility of further incarceration. Some were young boys that had only enlisted into the Brigadier's unit because of the opportunity to earn money. Now they had a second chance. Others saw it as as act of clemency to avoid charges for their participation in some of the General's illegal activities. The last group were the few career soldiers that had been transferred from the previous policing force into the brigade without any choice in the matter. But the one common feature of all of them was they had very little practical experience, especially the youngsters that had received no military training at all. The lack of battle experience was readily attested to when some of their comrades made the fatal mistake of resisting Rashid Kartal's force of elite border guards during that first encounter. They paid for that inexperience with their lives.

From the close to sixty remaining in the Bucharest unit, Gyorgy Thurzo managed to select twenty-four that he considered the brightest and the best. Whether that was true or not he left it to Captain Kartal to determine through an intense training regime. Kartal had one week to whip them into an effective fighting force, which on the first day he said could not be done. Nevertheless, he still accepted the challenge after Thurzo made the comment that Western training produced superior soldiers. Knowing full well that he was being baited, Rashid Kartal was unwilling to back away from such an obvious challenge.

From hand to hand combat, to fighting with wooden swords, the newly enlisted men were put through their paces for five continuous, unrelenting hours in the morning, followed by a half hour rest and then a further five hours of the same muscle aching exercises. At night they were given a typical army gruel to eat with a stick of bread and a jug of water to wash it down, very different from the stews and wine that General Nadasdy had provided. Thurzo had to tell them to stop their bellyaching, when they began complaining of the harsh treatment, informing them that once they were out in the field, the gruel would be a welcome delicacy compared to the reality of what they'll have to eat when scavenging from the neighbouring farms. By the time the week's training had completed, Kartal handed over twenty that he considered had the best chance of surviving in combat, returning four to the holding pens by the riverbank. They were still a sorry looking bunch, but appeared much better once Thurzo permitted them to wear their old uniforms into battle.

"At least they look like soldiers now," he commented to Captain Kartal once they were dressed.

"Appearances can be very deceiving," the Captain joked as the two of them watched as the soldiers continued their practice, except now they used their actual swords.

"With any luck, appearance will be all we require. If we can intimidate the enemy through appearances, they might surrender before they test our men."

"A wish that is fated to die a quick death, Sir," Kartal responded.

"How can you be so certain, Captain," Thurzo was curious as to why he thought there was no other choice but to do battle.

"Because I was there Commander, six years ago when we fought the Omullup. I was only a junior officer in the general's cavalry but I will never forget what I saw that day. The enemy are not soldiers as you would like to believe. They are savage beasts dressed as men accompanied by other beasts dressed as wolves. Even as our musketeers took down row after row with their lead shot, the Omullup would not stop coming towards us. They have no fear of death. They believe they are immortal and if they should fall in battle then they will be miraculously reborn on the battlefield at a later time. When men no longer have fear, they do not know the word surrender."

"Yes Captain, but when we engaged them in the forest and fired our rifles, they did run away. They were scared. So I don't necessarily agree."

"Because they could not rely on their senses any longer," the Captain was quick to explain. "Wolves rely on sight and hearing above all else. At night, in the dark, their sight is no better than ours. If they can't see the enemy well enough, then they rely on hearing in order to compensate in order to know where the enemy must be. A snap of a twig here, a hushed breath over there, they can isolate the sounds so easily. But in the woods, when the sound of your shots ricocheted among the trees, diffusing the sound as if it was coming from every direction, they were no longer able to pinpoint the locations of your men any longer. And once they heard the cry and wail of one of their own as you described to me, then they ran like any predator would if they thought an even bigger predator was coming their way."

"What could a pack of wolves possibly be afraid of," Thurzo tried to think of an animal that would send shivers down the spine of a wolf.

Kartal didn't need any time to answer. "Bigger wolves."

"Wolves attacking wolves."

"Not very different from mankind," the Captain drew he comparison. "Except we talk about bigger armies but the wolves are purely about size. That wolf of Joseph's wouldn't stand much of a chance against most of the species we find around here. We call it a red wolf and the red wolf is afraid of the steppe wolf. The steppe wolf is afraid of the tundra wolf. The tundra wolf is afraid of the arctic wolf and the arctic wolf fears the gray wolf."

"Let's pretend I know nothing about wolves," Thurzo suggested which was met with laughter from Rashid because it was obvious he didn't, "What are the wolves we are talking about that belong to these Omullup?"

"They are only steppe wolves, which they would have captured from the other shore of the Black Sea and brought here as young pups. Smaller, much easier to train and handle. But these wolves also know this is not their natural territory. These lands belong to the gray wolf, so I'm guessing that when they could no longer hear properly and able to identify where the sounds were originating, and then they heard the cry of pain and terror from one of their own, they naturally assumed they were being attacked by gray wolves. It is their natural fear. So they ran. Their masters had no other choice but to flee with them."

Nodding his head, Thurzo appreciated the lesson. "One more thing Captain, you said your lancers have taken down all sorts of wild animals while patrolling the borders. What kind of wolves did you encounter?"

"Gray wolves," the Captain fired back the answer. "They don't fear much, but they do fear me."

"Good to know Captain. Let's get all these men some wolf training. We still have a few hours of daylight, let's take advantage of it," Thurzo instructed. "Find Joseph and see if we can put his 'dog' to some use. Maybe if you point out the weak spots on a wolf, some of them will actually have the courage to fight back. Then afterwards get them packed into the wagons and rolling out of here. The less time we stay in Bucharest, the better."

"Yes Sir," Captain Rashid snapped a salute as he walked away to make preparations.

Days rolled by with the newly formed army under Count Thurzo making slow progress as they traversed the same route they had taken when they first came south of the Carpathian Mountains. The Count hoped that the enemy would not try anything now that news of what transpired in Bucharest had been spread through gossip to most of the cities but Captain Rashid continued to throw cold water on that hope. Claims of their having an army from anywhere from one hundred to over a thousand soldiers, Thurzo still thought would be enough to make most reconsider trying to attack them along the open road.

Once again they would take the gorge through the mountains created by the Olt River, from just west of Pitesti all the way to Sibiu on the other side. Twenty-eight miles of sloping ground, covered in brush and trees, rising from each bank of the river and providing the ideal terrain for setting a trap. It wasn't difficult to see exactly what both Gyorgy Thurzo and Rashid Kartal were thinking. They knew the best way to take advantage of the gorge was for the enemy to divide its army in two, the first half letting their men pass by and then following, while leaving about a mile in between. The other half positioning itself in front of Thurzo's men, using the higher ground as an advantage for an attack. They would then drive the Thurzo's men back knowing that the normal reaction by the Count would be to withdraw and regroup in order to prepare for a fight. But that would be impossible because as soon as they would retreat, they would find themselves being attacked from the rear. The two prong attack on a narrow fighting field would eliminate any advantage a larger army might have in numbers. It would only be a matter of time till the force caught in the middle was reduced to a level where it would have no choice but to either surrender or die. This was the ideal strategy they decided these wolf warriors could use, and upon this model they devised their own plan to counteract. They still knew that it would be difficult to successfully defend against such an attack, but they were relying on the enemy's inability to implement such a complex strategy properly. Every mistake the enemy might make, the better the odds became in Thurzo's favour. Regardless of how the battle went, both the Count and Captain knew that the enemy's total disregard for life made them far more unpredictable.

Aware that they would be riding into a trap and running short on time, Gyorgy Thurzo needed to talk to the three civilians that were at the center of this entire mission. As hard as it was going to be, he had to prepare them for the worst case scenario. Time for them to express their thoughts and ideas before they committed to entering the gorge.

Thurzo began by giving them fair warning. "As a military strategist, it is not hard to determine where they will attack us next," he began. "This canyon is the only way through the mountains. The terrain is in their favour. It provides them with the perfect cover in which they can attack us from two directions. We will be passing along a road that has a steep mountain on one side and a drop to the river on the other. We won't be able to run and if they pick their spot correctly, they could trap us in a position where we won't be able to move at all. Captain Kartal and myself have discussed this situation at length and we have no viable alternative but to march directly into the hell that awaits us. That is why I asked you here. If we are about to lay down our lives attempting to make a mad dash through the canyon, then it is best you agree, knowing that our chances of survival are very poor."

"Except for one thing," Caesar thought it time to correct the Count. "It is not the only way through the mountain," Caesar advised to the surprise of everyone.

"Yes it is," Thurzo countered. "It is the only road which exists through the southern ranges in these parts. The other two routes are well west of here and would take us days if not weeks out of our way in order to return to Brasov and Castle Bran if we were to use those. I don't think any of us want to lose all that time and furthermore, we are just as much at risk on either of those other passages once they determine where we have gone."

"That is very true," Caesar did not dispute what the Count was saying, "But there is another way across."

"Well don't just sit there telling us there's another way, spit it out!"

"I don't know where it is exactly but my father suggests we use this other way in Century II, Quatrain 27. He says:

'The divine word will be struck from the sky,
One who cannot proceed any further:
The secret closed up with the revelation,
Such that they will march over and ahead'

Considering that we all know that Joseph is the one that is recognized as carrying the divine word, then he will not survive the first wave of the attack," Caesar explained the first and second lines of the quatrain. "They will descend upon him from their hiding places on the hillside above and they will kill him. But that won't happen if we find the secret path that takes us over the mountains and we gain the advantage by getting ahead of them."

"Another needle in a haystack," Thurzo retorted. "How are we going to find some secret path that no one even knows about?"

"Not exactly," Joseph wagged a finger indicating that he had already thought of a solution. "We will never find it but those that use it already know where it is. I think the people of Gaesti will be happy to show it to us."

"How can you be so certain that they even know where it is?" Gyorgy still did not know what to make of Nostradamus's revelation.

"Considering they are the only town around here, which lies near the foothills of the mountains, then it only stands to reason." Joseph explained. "One tends to know his own backyard."

"I know we shouldn't doubt these prophecies but this one is very vague. A secret passage that no one knows and could place us in even greater danger. It is a risk," Thurzo repeated.

"The one certainty is that I am going to die if I go through the gorge," Joseph emphasized. "That was not vague at all. I'm willing to put my faith in this prophecy that it exists."

"Well dying would certainly ruin my day as well," Thurzo was in agreement. "The three of you and myself will ride in to Gaesti. I don't want the townspeople frightened if they start seeing an Ottoman cavalry unit and soldiers dressed in some fancy uniform from Bucharest rolling into their town. As much as they appreciated our delivering them from the witches, I don't know if they'd tolerate what they might view as an invasion. Captain," he shouted towards Rashid Kartal, "Set up camp here and keep the men ready to move out upon our return."

"Yes Sir, Commander," came the reply.

"Okay gentlemen," Thurzo announced. "We have a couple of hours ride ahead of us. Let's get started. I want to be in and out of there by noon."

Mounting their horses, they started heading east, covering the twelve mile distance in just a little under two hours.

They were warmly welcomed by the townspeople who had not forgotten all that they had done for them. Escorted by cheers and fanfare, the horses were steered towards the Mayor's residence, a home that both Gyorgy Thurzo and Joseph Kahana were very familiar with.

Once again they found themselves sitting on the padded couches of the Mayor's living room, being served cakes and teas by the Mayor's wife and his two single daughters. He made a point of emphasizing that his daughters were still single and that either would be a wonderful catch for any man. The four visitors could do nothing but smile and nod their appreciation to each daughter as they were handed their cup of tea.

Once they had eaten the delicious pastries, the Mayor politely asked, "What has brought you back to our town?"

Clearing his throat, Count Thurzo took upon himself the role of spokesperson for their group. "A favour Lord Mayor."

"Whatever is within our capacity to give is yours," the Mayor responded, still grateful for what they had done in the past, even though they never were able to retrieve their girls that had gone missing.

"We seek knowledge of a way through the mountains that does not make use of the Olt Gorge." Gyorgy hesitated after he posed the question, afraid that he was going to be met with a denial that such a path even exists.

The Mayor took his time, thinking on the matter before he bothered to respond. "I will have to get old Caspari to lead you on the trail," he finally answered. "You'll never be able to manage it on your own. It's an old goat trail, been there forever but no one but the shepherds use it. They say that Caspari is so old that he was there the day they first laid the trail. Most of it is only a few goats wide but it is passable and relatively safe."

"Is it far from here," Thurzo asked.

"Not at all," the Mayor shook his head. "In fact it extends right to the stockyards at the edge of town that are between here and Pitesti. "All the shepherds bring their goats and sheep down from the hills and straight into the paddocks when they come over to this side.

It's only once you get higher up in the hills that it gets a little treacherous, from what I've heard, but only in the sense you can get easily lost. Unless you know the right paths to select in order to get to the other side, you could be wandering up there for days."

"And where does it open to on the other side?" the Count was curious to know.

"Like I said, I never used it myself," the Mayor began excusing himself. "Always been more of an entrepreneur and politician than a farmer," he defined himself, "but from what I recall being told, it opens out less than a mile from where the gorge would take you. But don't worry, Caspari knows all the details and I'll have him take you across. Slip him a bit of coin and he'll be happy. Is there anything else you need from us?"

"Now that you mention it, three more horses."

Rubbing his chin, the Mayor contemplated what he could do about that request. "Most of the farmer's around here aren't very wealthy. Majority only have their one plough horse and if they give up that then they don't have a means to continue farming."

"I will pay them for their animals?" Thurzo interrupted the Mayor.

"How much?" Now the Mayor sounded keenly interested.

"Two ducats for the horse, another three if they throw in a saddle and reins."

"Five ducats all together," the Mayor rubbed his hands together. "Fifteen in total."

"Yes, but we'll need them sure footed to go over this pass."

"I will personally take charge in securing these horses for you," the Mayor was pleased to offer his services.

"Can we do it quickly," was the Count's next question.

"As soon as you hand me the money, I can be out the door and finding you these horses," the Mayor informed him.

Reaching inside his vest, Count Thurzo removed a leather money pouch. Loosening the string he reached inside and pulled out a small pile of gold ducats, laying them on the tea table in front of him. He counted out the fifteen ducats and handed them over to the Mayor, who was true to his word and out the door as soon as the money was in hand.

It only took the Mayor three quarters of an hour to arrange the purchase of the three horses, each provided with a saddle girthed around its belly and a bit with reigns in its mouth. The farmers he spoke to were more than happy to accept the offer even after the Mayor had taken his commission off the top for making the sale.

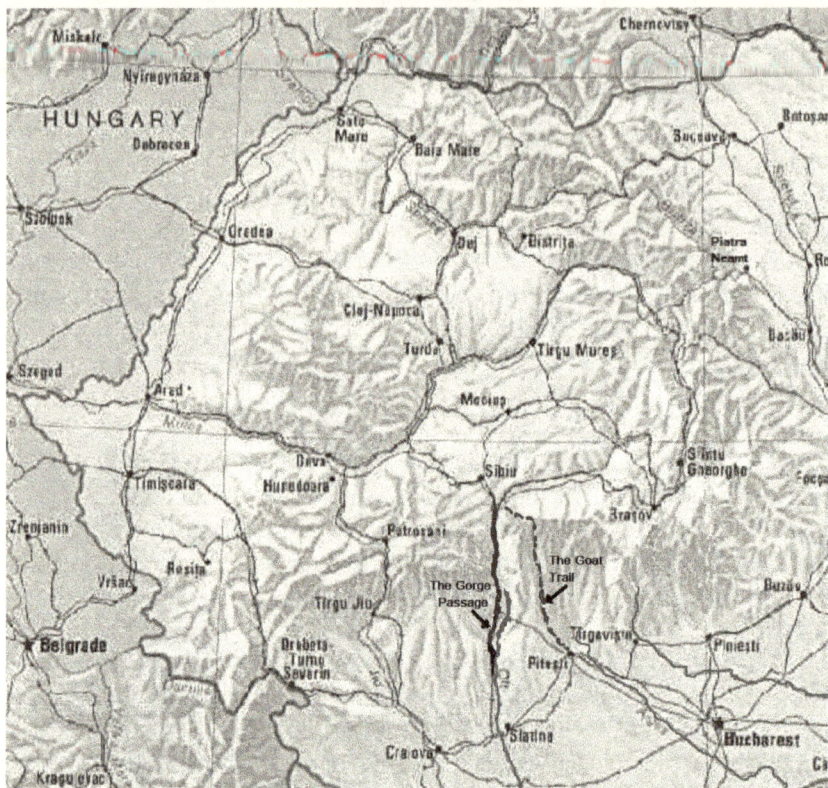

Passage Through the Carpathians

While waiting, Gyorgy requested that the three others be escorted to one of the bedrooms where they could strip out of their outer garments. At first they were confused by the request, thinking that perhaps Count Thurzo had come under some strange affliction that was having him make irrational requests.

"Is there some logical sense to this request," Paolo Sarpi asked.

"Of course there is," Thurzo replied. "Now take them off."

"First tell us the reason and then maybe I'll comply," Sarpi was reluctant to give up his clothes."

"Listen, I don't need to wait for the mayor to return but I do need to prepare everyone for the next phase of the plan. I'm going to take your three horses you rode here with along with your clothes back to the camp, where I am going to find three soldiers from Bucharest that are roughly your size. They will put on your clothing and ride your horses through the gorge passage. In the meantime, I will send Captain Rashid and his men back here with the three uniforms the men have removed. You will put those on. Make certain when Rashid arrives you steer him clear of the centre of the city take him directly to the sheep yards where you will tell the Mayor to send this guide he mentioned."

"Ah, now I get it," Sarpi understood. "You want the three men in your unit to pretend to be us. Meanwhile, we will be disguised as three soldiers on the goat path."

"If Nostradamus is right, then Joseph, or someone that looks like Joseph dies as we try to make it through that passage. I'm guessing that is the real secret that is not revealed to the enemy."

"I feel guilty that someone has to die in my stead," Joseph bemoaned the fact.

"Trust me, you'll get over it," Thurzo advised him. "Now all of you get out of your clothes."

"But how will we meet Captain Kartal out by the yards if we don't have any clothes on," Sarpi was offended by the thought of appearing in public in his undergarments

"I'm sure you will think of something," the Count couldn't be bothered to respond to his complaint. "Put on one of the daughter's dresses for all I care. Just be out there."

"Wait a minute," Caesar was thinking of something completely irrelevant to the conversation. "Where did you get all those gold ducats?"

"You don't think I'd be foolish enough to give all the money from the coffers we found in Bucharest over to the Emperor, did you?" Gyorgy laughed. "It's not as if we haven't encountered expenses along the way trying to complete this mission. I'm just ensuring that it doesn't all come out of my pocket."

"What about us?" Caesar wanted to know where their share was.

"Hey, we get through this, the Emperor has already said he is going to reward the three of you handsomely. As for me, somehow putting my life on the line was always considered my patriotic duty. Do we have a complaint if I should happen to think otherwise"

Looking back and forth between the three of them, they all shook their heads. "Perfectly fine with us," Caesar announced.

Joseph signaled for Captain Kartal to take his men to the outskirts of the village until they reached the yards where the others were already standing in borrowed pants from the Mayor, several sizes too large. Their guide easily looked to be on the far side of eighty, using his shepherds staff more for support than for herding animals. It really didn't matter that they were all mounted on horses, considering they would not be able to go any faster than old Caspari could walk.

Donning the military uniforms provided by three of the infantry men within Thurzo's unit, they stopped to admire how they looked in the attire.

"I think I would have been a fairly dashing soldier had I been in the French army," Caesar commented, giving himself a good look.

"Isn't that what the French army is all about," Sarpi scoffed at the man from Provence. "Looking good rather than knowing how to fight. When was the last time they ever won a battle? No one knows because they've been fighting nine religious wars for thirty-eight years now and we still don' know who won after these nine major conflicts."

"That is the French way," Paolo. "Let everyone win and there is no more need for further war."

"At least we Venetians know how to look good and how to fight at the same time," he said half jokingly.

"I think we might as well enjoy the moment my friends," Joseph intervened. "Once we engage in battle, these suits will no longer look as pristine on us."

"There is no need to worry about that Joseph Kahana," Captain Kartal informed them as he walked beside them. "None of you will be engaging in the battle. I will be keeping you well concealed at the point we descend from the goat track. It is my responsibility is to keep you safe and alive. I would be irresponsible to let you get close to the battle."

"And while we are left hiding in these bushes, have you considered that we may be of use to you and Count Thurzo if the battle requires some insight from our specific skills."

"Between myself and the Commander, I believe we have enough skills with which to engage the enemy. Without wishing to be offensive Joseph Kahana, if we had to rely on the fighting abilities of the three of you in order to win against this enemy, I would be afraid the battle may already be lost."

"No offense taken," Joseph replied. "We are not fighters but we are thinkers. Even though none of us are brilliant military strategists, shouldn't you enlighten us by telling us at least, what is your strategy?"

Rashid was more than happy to explain the tactics. Both he and Gyorgy had roughly estimated that it would take approximately one and a half times the number of hours to traverse the goat path as it would to roll the wagons through the gorge. That being the case, whereas they could expect the gorge to be completed in five hours, it would be almost eight hours for Rashid's men to cross over the goat track and then ride the short distance to the mouth of the gorge on the north side. That being the case, they saw little point in moving out the infantry in the wagons until the next day since it would already be nightfall before Rashid's cavalry could reach the battleground. Therefore, he would take his men and escort the three of them across today and they would set up camp immediately on the other side of the goat path. That way, there was only the short distance between the goat track and the gorge path to make up the next day. Anticipating that Count Thurzo would begin moving the wagons at around the ninth hour in the morning into the gorge, the infantry would just be visualizing the exit from the gorge around one thirty in the afternoon. That would still leave about half an hour to reach the exit, equating to about three miles. That's when he anticipated those concealed in the hills would start trailing behind Thurzo's men preparing to engage in an attack on the rear, waiting until those Omullup that were concealed in the bushes ahead of Thurzo's men would give the signal that they're preparing to attack. Once they had exposed themselves, Commander Thurzo would attempt to put a greater distance between himself and his attackers in the rear by racing for the gorge exit. The horses pulling the wagons would be tiring after the first mile. By the second mile they would be slowing down to nothing more than a fast walk. That's when they both believed the second wave would be launched by the waiting Omullup with the intent of using the last mile of the gorge as the battleground. If they were smart, they would block the wagons' exit and close in with a classical pincer movement, squeezing Commander Thurzo's men from both sides.

So, my men need to be ready in the hour past noon to lead a charge from our end of the gorge and pounce directly on the rear of the Omullup positioned ahead of the wagons. That will let Count Thurzo pay full attention on the force that is attacking his rear. Yes, he will likely take heavy losses but in the end we will win."

Captain Rashid had described the anticipated battle in such detail that the three of them were awed into silence momentarily.

Finally snapping out of their trance, Sarpi critiqued the strategy, "As long as your timing is precise. You go in too early and they'll be able to attack behind your cavalry as well and trap your men. You go in too late and Thurzo's men could very well be eliminated by then."

"There is no denying that timing will be everything, but we have to rely on Allah giving us wisdom to perform our strategy properly,"

"You will succeed," Caesar sounded confident. "According to my father you will end these Omullup once and for all."

"He said that," Rashid was eager to know what was said.

"Century II,Quatrain 33, he describes your role in the battle.

"Please, let me hear." It was evident that Rashid Kartal believed.

'In the city where the wolf will enter,
Very near there will the enemies be:
Foreign army will spoil a great country.
The friends will pass at the wall and Alps'

"You are that foreign army," Caesar pointed out. "All their plans to take over the Empire will be destroyed as a result of your intervention. And as you will notice, the three of us, we three friends," Caesar winked at his two companions, "Will pass through this mountain range unharmed, waiting safely where you have left us."

"I thank you my friend Caesar. I will pass the good news on to my men. Every soldier wants to know that when he goes into battle, his side will be victorious. You have given us that confidence that we will succeed and not fail. Allah be praised, your are truly his servant."

"Not to be a pessimist," Sarpi had one final question. "If you don't survive, what are we supposed to do?"

"If you see the sun going down behind the mountains in the west and I have not returned for you by then," Kartal responded, "Then ride as fast as you can in the other direction!"

Aware that the most fatal mistake he could make was at any point to halt the wagons and have his men take to their feet, attempting to engage both wolf and man in hand to hand combat on the ground, Thurzo's final instructions to the wagon drivers was never look behind to see what was happening, but instead just whip the horses and race forward as fast as the dirt road would permit.

As for the infantry seated in the rear of the wagons, his message was also simple; preventing the wolves leaping from behind the bushes and trees by impaling them on their steel rapiers as they flew through the air was never going to happen. Rather than take any immediate aggressive action, he advised them to stay low, keep their knives in hand, let the wolves and the warriors make their leaps, and don't move until they actually landed in the carts. For their strategy to work, they needed the beasts and their masters thinking that leaping into the wagons was not only achievable but their best option for success.

With three wagons, each having a single driver, that meant two had five men sitting in the rear, while the last one only had four. That provided plenty of space on the platform to attract both the wolves and their masters to sufficiently time their leaps into the air perfectly so that they could land squarely on the wooden slats. Captain Kartal's training had already prepared his men for such an event. Once they landed, the key was using their knives, which they already had firmly in hand to strike as one coordinated attack.

Kartal trained them to find the weak spots on both animal and man. Go for the throat first, the eyes second. Stabbing anywhere else would not immediately disable the threat, allowing sufficient time for them to retaliate and inflict terrible wounds of their own. Thurzo did a quick calculation in his head, determining from the time of making their hard landing in the wagon, then gaining their balance, to actually being able to directly attack one of his soldiers would be roughly three seconds, more than enough time for each of his men to have stabbed the adversary once or twice.

And he calculated, that in order to avoid colliding in mid air, the wolf warriors and their animals could only attempt leaping into the wagons one at a time. A sufficient delay that meant his men would rarely have to deal with multiple threats simultaneously in the back of the wagons. It appeared as if they had anticipated all events wisely.

The only misjudgment was they were mistaken on exactly when the first wave of attacks would begin. Thurzo had not anticipated that those hidden along the mountainside waiting for them to pass would attempt to launch their attack immediately, rather than follow from above and then take to running behind the wagons until the rest of their pack blocked the road up ahead. The early attack provided a short-lived advantage to the Omullup, as Thurzo's men were not expecting to be engaged in conflict so early, but it also meant that their enemy was at their weakest, split in two without the support of those that were over a mile or so ahead and unable to help.

The first of the wolves came flying into the cart in the lead, casting a large shadow as it passed over the heads of the huddled soldiers. Landing heavily on the moving platform, the impact forced its legs to splay, its body dropping to the cart floor as it snarled and gnashed its teeth, in a menacing display of bone crushing aggression. The first of the soldiers dived onto its back, plunging his knife into the side of its neck, followed by the second and third infantry men, burying the animal beneath their swarming bodies. From above they heard the ferocious scream of the wolf's master as he barreled through the air, watching haplessly as his beast was stabbed repeatedly. The moment his body fell into the wagon, he was set upon by those soldiers that had not been involved in the attack on his wolf, only to be joined by the others after they tossed the carcass of the beast over the side. It was a pattern that would repeat over and over again, in a never-ending cycle of violence. A second wolf, another of the warriors would successfully land in the rear of the wagons, righting themselves while Thurzo's men were still busy dispatching a previous attacker. But again the soldiers managed to deal with each threat one by one.

Riding between wagons while simultaneously defending himself from attackers on the ground, Thurzo knew that all that stood between his men panicking and subsequently embracing a horrific death was the sound of his own voice, encouraging them to resist, to fight on, to never surrender. But in all his years of combat, the Count had never seen an enemy like this. Wolves with yellow eyed fury, dripping saliva from one inch fangs, men crazed and consumed by their own blood-lust madness, attacking in waves that seemed as endless as the oceans.

Some of his soldiers were swept back against the wagon-rails as they were impacted by the first body blows from either man or beast. Thurzo could only watch as one soldier was under attack by both man and wolf. In a matter of seconds his man's throat was ripped from his neck, the blood spurting in a heavy spray that momentarily blinded his attackers. Long enough for one of the other soldiers fighting bravely beside to lunge at the wolf without fear, digging and twisting his knife through the left eyeball, so that the animal fell down instantly much to the dismay of his master, who was then dispatched by another of the soldiers standing directly behind. Thurzo listened as he heard the teeth of another wolf clamp down tightly on the leg of an infantry man, the bone loudly crunching as the animal began to twist its head from side to side. Its jaws were unyielding as the soldier screamed, desperately trying to strike the wolf in the head with his knife wielding hand. At that point a wolf warrior leaped upon the crippled soldier, slashing his throat with a quick flash of steel.

Thurzo slew a frothing adversary with his rapier, plunging it down through the back of its head as it attempted to sink its teeth into the forelimb of his horse. The intensity of battle excited both sides to greater fierceness. No sooner had one of his soldiers killed one of the enemy before they were already flinging themself upon another, until it finally became evident, which way the battle was swaying.

Those that would survive the battle would never forget the sight of either animal or man sinking teeth or knife into the soft flesh of one of their comrades in arms. The screams that men make when they felt their bones being crushed in powerful jaws of blood thirsty beasts would haunt them for the rest of their lives. They would remember the sight of death making one or two of them hesitate but not all as one of their mates would come to the rescue in the nick of time. Conquering their own fear was key to their survival but knowing that as long as there was at least one of their comrades willing to leap onto the jaws of death without concern for his own welfare, kept their spirits high. To be willing to ride the back of these killing machines, pummeling them with knives and fists, gave them hope and inspiration.

This was a fact that Gyorgy Thurzo had observed after years on the battlefield but his men did not have the luxury of time on their side to learn the same lessons. In the heat of their first battle they had to learn that bravery was a commodity, which under the proper conditions became infectious and immunized men against the worst fears that paralyzed others. When the Commander made his selection back in Bucharest, he only took those under his wing that had a certain look in the eye that said these men would likely not wither in the face of danger. Only now he knew that he had selected correctly.

Though many of the wolves and Omullup managed to land in the wagons, far more were unable to make the leap and instead took to the ground, running up the rear in pursuit of the wagons. Thurzo noticed that those on the ground were far more focused on himself and the other three riders on horseback. He watched as one wolf managed to catch one of the horses on the tendon just above the fetlock of the right hind leg. The horse reared up in pain, tossing its rider dressed in the clothes of Joseph Kahana high into the sky, only to land heavily on the road where he was immediately savaged and stabbed by both beast and man. It almost appeared as if they had specific orders that he was to be killed first, before anyone else. Clearly someone was working contrary to Countess Bathory's instructions. Someone that didn't like the fact they were being told how to conduct the conflicts by the Countess.

Not long afterwards, a pack of three wolves running together brought down the horse ridden by the counterfeit Paolo Sarpi, two attacking the legs but the largest of the wolves going for the horses unprotected neck. Both horse and rider went down, screaming in terror as skin, muscle and sinew were torn from their appendages.

Looking back over his shoulder, Count Thurzo made a quick count of what remained of the enemy from the first wave of attack. Approximately four wolves and six warriors were still in pursuit. It was less of a concern because by then all the wolves and their masters that had successfully breached the wagons were now dead and could be seen littering the road behind all the way into the distance. He had no doubt there would be more up ahead but he was relieved to see that he still had fourteen men remaining, including the lone rider dressed as Caesar de Nostradame. The odds were now definitely in his favour.

The exit from the gorge could be made out in the distance ahead of them. Another misjudgment by the enemy. They had set their second trap too close to the end of the gorge. They never took into consideration the possibility of being attacked by a secondary force entering the gorge from the north and only being minutes away from where they were stationed. Salvation was no more than a mile in the distance, when the first of two thickly truncated trees came crashing down heavily from where they were felled along the hillside.

Thurzo ordered the drivers to pull up sharply, bringing the wagons and horses to a skidding stop. He had always expected them to block the road and he was prepared. "Swords ready," he shouted to his men as he waved for them to leap from the backs of the wagons. The men all knew their instructions from the talk they received prior to the battle. Ignore what may be coming down the road from the other direction, concentrate only on the enemy they see before them. Those instructions had been impressed into their minds. The Palatine's soldiers formed a wall of bodies across the road so that the enemy that had been trailing them was forced to stay front of them at all times. They were to avoid engaging in single battle, conceding that the advantage was not theirs in that situation. Instead they were to pair up so that there would always be at least two taking on either a single beast or man at any time. Standing in the centre of their formation, Count Gyorgy Thurzo, challenged the enemy to attack, roaring like a lion as he cursed and heaped obscenities upon them.

"Eyes front," he yelled to his men. "Today we make history and put an end to this foul evil. Today we are Victorious," he shouted, the mantra taken up by his soldiers as they bellowed his words in a thunderous wave of repetition. Their shouts actually forced the enemy to pause momentarily, second guessing their own ability to defeat their adversaries, which now outnumber them. Their pause turned into seconds of hesitation and Thurzo knew exactly what was happening behind him. He could see it in the reflection of his enemies' eyes. He didn't have to turn his head to know that the panicked screams and yelps coming from behind meant that the Ottoman lancers on horseback had arrived and were dispatching the Omullup that had concealed themselves up ahead to the hell from where they were spawned. He wished he did have the opportunity to turn and witness the slaughter but he had to remain focused on eliminating the remaining enemy that were suddenly beginning to turn and run.

"Attack!" Thurzo screamed his order, sending his men on a wild pursuit. "Don't let them escape!" he screamed. But it wasn't until Kartal's cavalry unit was able to leap over the fallen trees and charge through the gorge, passing by Thurzo's men, that they were finally able to catch and kill the last of the Omullup. Not a single man or beast remained alive. Checking the string of bodies that littered the gorge track, Kartal's men took extreme pleasure in stabbing each wolf and warrior, ensuring that the dead remained dead. By late afternoon, on a warm October day, in the year of the Lord 1610, the existence of the Omullup legion from Hell became nothing more than the substance of myths.

Chapter Twenty

Castle Bran: October 1610

From the fields surrounding the plateau it was obvious that the Countess had withdrawn all her forces inside the walls of her fortified castle. Once they left the gorge and crossed the plain, they failed to encounter a single patrol along the way, which could only mean that they all must be waiting behind the castle walls. There they could wait patiently, secure in having every advantage provided by their fortifications and superior elevation. As far as Joseph was concerned, it looked no different than it had the first time he visited, except perhaps a little colder and a little more foreboding in the dim afternoon light, but whatever feeling of dread tried to manifest in his mind, he was driven by only one desire and that was to free Reisel, He tried not think of what they might be doing to his betrothed behind those impenetrable walls. His frustration grew more obvious with each passing hour because he couldn't understand why the Count was taking so long to make his decision on how best to storm the castle.

Thurzo was well aware of the castles history and how it had resisted falling to the Turks when so many of the other castles and strongholds in the surrounding countryside had been taken. If Suleiman the Magnificent couldn't seize the castle with all his siege engines and his vast army, there was very little that a thirty strong cavalry along with fourteen infantry were going to achieve. As far as he was concerned the narrow trail that wound itself around the base of the castle, completing half a circle before they could even approach the entrance was nothing more than a death sentence. From any point on the parapets or the towers, they would be easy targets for an archer with even limited skills. The narrowness of the path meant Bathory's men could easily roll boulders down the track, bowling horse and rider over the edge. And even if they had the good fortune to make it to the sealed gates, the iron bars would prove to be a formidable obstacle since they had no equipment to tear them down. The analysis of the situation provided only one possible answer; there was no way of breaching the castle's defenses. It was a message that Joseph did not take well.

"I need you to think this through logically," Thurzo urged Joseph to calm down.

"How can I be calm when they could be torturing the woman that I love right now while we are having this discussion?" Joseph sounded practically hysterical.

"That's what they are counting on," Count Thurzo revealed their plan to Joseph. "They are assuming that your love for the girl will overpower any logic and you will somehow manage to convince me to launch an assault on the castle. That gives them every advantage and us none. We will all be dead before we can breach the walls. You understand that don't you."

"But we have to save her," Joseph pleaded. "I must find a way to save her."

"And we will Joseph. You just have to trust me. Charging up that road is the worst option we could ever consider. So if I tell you the best thing we could do for her now is to leave, it is because it is the one thing they don't expect us to do."

"What if I offer myself now in exchange," Joseph contemplated riding up the path on his own. "She said she wanted my blood, therefore she must consider me more valuable as a hostage. We can make a trade."

"That my have been her thinking in the past before we recognized that she has been responsible for all these murders. Now she only will have once concern and that is staying alive. The only way she can do that is kill everyone that possibly knows her secret."

"How do you know that?" Joseph questioned him.

"Because that is what I would do!" the Count explained, raising his voice. "Everyone of us is marked for a dead man right now. With us out of the way, she can continue to do what she has been doing for years without fear of being caught. That means anyone associated with us, anyone that might ask questions, would also have to be eliminated. The only thing that will keep everyone alive for now is if she thinks she can use Reisel as a bargaining chip to get us all to surrender. You go up there now and you will be signing a death warrant for you both. After that she is one step closer to killing the rest of us."

"So you are saying we have to defeat her guard and take her prisoner in order to save Reisel but we don't even know how to make our way into her castle. So how is it you think we have an advantage?"

"I'm being honest with you Joseph, we don't have one right now but we do have a stalemate and that buys us time. That is our advantage. Trust me, she won't do anything until we've played our cards and that in turn will also buy Reisel time. We go away now, and that provides us with even more time because she won't know what we are planning. She won't make her next move until she thinks she knows ours. Do you understand?"

"This is a very dangerous game of cat and mouse you are playing," Joseph warned the Count. "The real problem is I cannot tell which one of us is the cat and which is the mouse."

"Let us ride back to the camp and talk to the others. I am certain that if we put our minds together we will arrive at a plan. There are times you need to realize you cannot do everything on your own and you have to trust in your friends."

"Are we all friends now?" Joseph was not certain that they had reached that outcome.

"We are something," Gyorgy Thurzo assured him. "I may not know exactly what, but having done the things we have done together, I think we definitely share a bond of some nature. Perhaps friend is not the right word but whatever it is, it is just as strong and just as durable."

Returning to the camp, while sitting around the fire, on which they cooked the evening meal, Count Thurzo described the fortifications he saw at the castle, much to the disillusionment of his companions.

"We are not equipped to storm a castle," Captain Kartal stated the obvious.

"Unless we could obtain some cannons," Paolo Sarpi suggested, only to be told that the only cannons in the territories all belonged to armies under the control of the Bathorys. It was unlikely any would be willing to supply weapons to be used against one of their own.

Around and around the discussion went, for over two hours before the makeshift council fell into a numbed silence, absent of any further ideas and sharing only in the hopelessness of the situation. At this point, Joseph could only think once again of surrendering himself with the hope that Elizabeth Bathory was capable of some modicum of mercy and would release his beloved Reisel.

"I have it, I have it," Caesar shouted gleefully, causing everyone to shake off the morose cloud that had descended and enshrouded them in a feeling of utter despair.

"It's all clear to me. Century II, Quatrain 75," he clapped his hands together. We can do this, I know it!"

"Unless you tell us what it is," Joseph reached out his hand laying it on Caesar's arm, "There is nothing we can do.

Caesar began reciting his father's quatrain:

'To pass beyond the mountain,
On the pipe of the air-vent floor:
So high will the bushel of wheat rise,
That man will be eating his fellow man.'

"It's simple," Caesar couldn't contain his excitement. "We find this pipe of which my father speaks of and we are inside the castle."

The others did not appear to immediately share in Caesar's enthusiasm.

"How are any of us going to fit through a pipe, even if one actually existed," Paolo challenged the literal nature of the quatrain. "Are we magically to transform into snakes that we can slither up this pipe and suddenly find ourselves in some room where our enemies just happen to be eating one another?"

"This is not the time to start doubting the words of Nostradamus," Caesar admonished him. Turning to Joseph, he was determined to convince him that this was the answer. "You have to believe Joseph. We only have to make sense of what my father is saying and it will all be clear. You better than anyone know how to interpret his quatrains."

But Joseph had given in to his melancholy. "A pipe Caesar. What can we possibly do through a pipe," he bemoaned what had been written. "Paolo is right, even if we find a pipe, what are we to do with it. There has to be another way but I fear it is not that way."

Like a bolt of lightning, the answer came to Gyorgy Thurzo and he started laughing to the point that the others feared he had lost his mind.

"This is one of the oldest castles in the land," Count Thurzo recollected upon the early history of Transylvania.

"And what of it," Joseph asked as if it mattered little.

"I happened to love exploring all the old castles when I was a boy," he recalled. "Not that my branch of the family had a castle of our own, but I guess that was why I was so inquisitive when we received invitations to attend family celebrations."

"Is there a point to this," Paolo wasn't interested in hearing stories about Thurzo's boyhood explorations.

"That's the problem with you self-proclaimed scientists," Gyorgy jabbed back at the Venetian. "With your modern minds, you can only think about the present and the future. Yes we have our plumbing today with the luxury of small clay pipes that carry water from one end of a city to another. But that was not the case in the old days and this castle is one of the oldest there is."

"So you are saying things were different back then," Joseph was now intrigued by what the Count had to say.

"In the old days, the Lords did not bury their dead in graveyards as is customary now. What if the line about man eating his fellow man is just simply about death and burial. Back then, they had huge catacombs carved into the rock below their castles. They would lay the dead in stone sarcophagi with ornate statues carved upon the lids. You can imagine how fetid the air would become with these rotting corpses all contained in windowless rooms, beneath a mountain of stone, and illuminated by the burning of torches producing thick smoke. Yet, it was the responsibility of these Princes to honour their dead, and to make ceremony at certain times to pray for attributes to be delivered by a past ancestor that possessed that trait. These catacombs in the past were actually quite active places where people gathered regularly."

"There is a point to this, I take it Gyorgy," Joseph was growing impatient with his delay of getting to the matter at hand.

"I'm getting to that part," the Count patted the air as if to say 'just wait'. "Knowing that they could get consumption from breathing foul air, they had their engineers build a means of bringing fresh air through one vent and using the natural air flow to exhaust it through another. They could only achieve that by creating a cross wind, pretty much at the same level as the burial chambers, which means…"

"Which means, there has to be two vents built into the sides of this particular hill," Joseph concluded the statement the Count was about to make.

"Exactly," Gyorgy Thurzo confirmed.

"But will they be big enough to get through?" was Paolo's concern, his mind still fixated on the clay pipes he was familiar with.

"You have to remember that when they made these ducts, it was done by men with hammers and chisels. It had to be big enough for them to carve through the rock every inch of the way from the inside to the outside," the Count explained.

"But they probably sealed the ends of these ducts," Paolo surmised. "They couldn't risk any animals getting in."

"One problem at a time," Gyorgy suggested that they'll find the answer to that issue once they find the ducts. "Now these catacombs could be many floors below the actual castle. In between there could be the jail cells, the kitchens, the infirmary, God only knows what. We will have no way of knowing where we will come out inside the castle and who or how many men might be waiting there for us."

"It does not matter Commander," Rashid Kartal dismissed any concern regarding the battle. "It would be an honour to my men if we can go in first."

"I will grant that to you but, you cannot kill everyone you encounter. We will need answers from some of these men, especially where they are keeping the girl. Are we clear on that?"

Rashid smiled back, "We will kill perhaps half then. By then your men should have made it into the castle," he laughed.

"We will worry about the details of how many encounters my men will engage in versus your men once we are there, Rashid. Remember, my men engaged in hand to hand combat with the wolf warriors and their beasts while your men used your extremely long poles to do their killing," he taunted in return. Both men laughed in good spirits regarding the challenge yet to come. "Once the sun has set we will go on foot to the base of the plateau and then start climbing the hillsides until we find those vents."

"It's a big hill," Joseph was concerned they would not find these vents quickly before dawn broke.

Do not worry Joseph, we will get your fiance' back for you, I promise. I believe Nostradamus gave us a clue where to look as well. I don't know how many bushels of wheat one could stack upon the other, but I'm certain it can't be that high before they would fall down. So we pay attention to the lower levels of the hill. Rashid will take his men through the first vent we find, I will take the rest of us through the second. That way, if something goes wrong, we all won't be trapped in one place."

"Sounds like a good plan, Commander," Rashid Kartal agreed.

Under the cover of darkness, the units split in two searched every crevice and crag of the hillside looking for these openings that Count Thurzo had spoken of. Needles in haystacks Magistrate Sarpi had referred to them but then quickly added that after all this time, they had become masters in finding such needles. From the initial description of holes carved into the side of a hill large enough for a man to crawl through on all fours, it didn't sound as if it would be possible to easily disguise such apertures. It wasn't until they were actually standing at the base of the hill in the dark hours of the night did they realize that across the entire surface of the hill there were these dark patches that matched that description. The only clue that the Count could provide was that if they thought they were higher on the hill than one could stack bushels of wheat, then they were probably too high.

"All we have to do is find one," Thurzo muttered to his companions. "Then we will know where to look on the opposite side of the hill and roughly how high." It was just a matter of finding that first damn vent he cursed.

They had already lost an hour before they heard one of the men say to the one beside him, "Hey, did you feel that?"

Thurzo jumped on the question immediately. "Who said that?" he asked.

"I did sir," one of his recruits from Bucharest answered.

"What did you feel soldier?"

"It was like a breeze wafting over me," he described the sensation. "It didn't last long. Stopped almost as fast as I noticed it."

"Don't move a muscle," Thurzo instructed him. "Stay exactly where you are. We'll come to you."

Gathering around the soldier laying flat against the hillside, Thurzo ordered the others to strip away all the vegetation in the immediate vicinity. The reason they couldn't see it was obvious. After so many hundreds of years the layers of scrub and brush had covered over the vents and hid them from direct view.

"I have found it Sir," one of the men alerted his Commander, not trying to make too much noise as he expressed his obvious joy, fearing his voice would be carried on the wind to the sentries posted above.

The vent looked exactly as Thurzo had described it would. A hand carved hole,wide and high enough to permit a kneeling man to hammer a passage, with a metal grill to protect against anything from gaining entry. The grill-work after several hundred years had become corroded and brittle, shattering easily after a few swift kicks.

"As promised Rashid, this passage is yours. Good luck, and may Allah be with you and your men," Thurzo sent them into the darkness, as he took his men to the other side of the hill to find the other shaft. Now that they knew the relative height and location on the hill face, finding the other opening would not be difficult.

It took only another quarter hour to find the other vent and clear the opening. Thurzo indicated he would go first, followed by his men and then the three companions would follow last. It wasn't until they were actually within the carved rock tunnel that they could appreciate just how long and dark the passageway actually was.

"Did I ever mention that I'm claustrophobic," Caesar announced his fear to the other two.

"This is hardly the time to let us know," Sarpi was sharply critical of Caesar's timing.

Caesar began to hyperventilate, feelings of panic and fear filling his head so that his body became frozen to the spot, with Joseph ahead and Paolo behind.

"Caesar," Joseph stated his name calmly. "I want you to close your eyes and listen to my voice. Do you have your eyes closed?"

Caesar nodded his head but in the darkness of the shaft, no one could see.

"I am assuming you said yes," Joseph continued. "Now, I want you to reach forward with you right hand and find my ankle. Can you do that?"

Joseph waited until he could feel the vice like grip around his ankle. "Just try to relax your grip a bit." Joseph couldn't feel much difference. "I want you to continue to keep your eyes closed and just respond to the movement of my ankle. I pull forward and you move forward. I stop and you stop. Are we good?" Joseph heard something that sounded like yes at which point he began moving slowly through the airway.

"About fifteen more feet to go," Joseph announced to Caesar who still held on to his ankle with his eyes closed as if letting go would let him fall into a deep abyss.

"Ten more feet." He could feel the grip loosening slightly and the circulation returning to his foot.

"Five more feet," and now he could finally hear Caesar breathing again.

"Open your eyes and step down," Joseph instructed him. "There's about a four foot drop to the floor. Everything is going to be alright."

Opening his eyes as instructed, Caesar could see that they had entered the old catacombs, the hall filled with tombs and statues of the dead. "That wasn't so difficult," Caesar said, now that he found himself breathing easily again and his heart beating normally.

"If everything is so good up there," Sarpi commented sarcastically, "Then why don't you step down and let me out of here already?"

"Oh, yes," Caesar quickly apologized as he dropped the four feet to the ground. "Here, let me help you out of there."

"You have helped enough," Paolo knocked his hands away. "I think I can handle it from here on my own."

It took a few seconds for their eyes to adjust to the dimness of the torch light. Then thy realized they were all alone in the catacombs.

"Where is everyone," Joseph inquired.

No sooner had he asked the question when Gyorgy Thurzo appeared at the top of the stairway that led from the catacombs to the level above. "What took you three so long?" he questioned. Not even waiting for the answer, he told them to come up quickly.

"What have you found," Joseph asked.

"Come see for yourself. But be prepared, it is not pretty."

"Is it Reisel? Has something happened to her," Joseph needed to know before he ascended the stone staircase.

"No," Thurzo replied sharply. "We didn't find her. So perhaps that can be interpreted as a good sign. But everything else is a scene straight out of Hell."

The stairway entered onto a landing which opened onto a vestibule on the right and another flight of stairs that continued upward to the next floor by going straight ahead. Turning to the right, Count Thurzo had them follow him into the vestibule, which was nothing but an empty room measuring perhaps fifteen feet square.

"Where is Captain Kartal," Joseph asked."Has has found Reisel?"

"I don't think so," Gyorgy replied. "He was here with his men when we first arrived. They had already been into the next room. I sent them up the next flight of stairs to dispatch any soldiers they came across in the castle."

"But Reisel could be up there," Joseph was concerned. "I have to go up there and find his men before something happens to her."

"I doubt very much she is up there," Thurzo was still cryptic as to his reluctance to go search for her. "Come with me into the next room. You will understand why."

There was an open doorway set into the right half of the far wall which opened into a brightly lit room. The room looked almost exactly as it did when Reisel stumbled upon it almost two months earlier. Just like before, there were several naked bodies of young girls laying dead on the stone floor, their flesh hideously marked by cuts and bruises. Some had large gaping wounds from which it was obvious certain organs had been extracted.

"I'm thinking my father was being literal," Caesar commented when he saw the bodies looking as if they had been eaten.

The metal cage still hung from the ceiling but this time it contained an older, bearded, naked man sprawled flat against its wire flooring.

"Is he dead?" Joseph asked, recognizing that the man trapped in the cage was his future father-in-law.

"No, he's been faking being unconscious from the moment he saw Rashid's men enter the room.

"Joseph, Joseph, is that you," Rabbi Lipmann began stirring from his pretense of unconsciousness, responding to the sound of a familiar voice. His face was bruised and battered, tufts of hair forcefully ripped from his beard, while his arms and legs showed evidence of repeated piercings with a sharp object.

"Where is she," Joseph demanded to know.

"Joseph, thank God it is you," Yom Tov Lipmann appeared grateful to see the young Kahana. "When I saw those Turks enter, I thought that was the end of my life. I didn't know that they were with you."

"Where is Reisel?" Joseph ignored everything else he had to say, only wanting to know one thing, the whereabouts of his fiance'.

"Help me Joseph, take me down from here." Lipmann still didn't answer his question.

"I will leave you rot in there for an eternity if you don't start telling me where she is," Joseph could no longer tolerate his whining.

"She's gone Joseph, That witch took her. I don't know where they were going.

"What do you mean you don't know where," Joseph was furious. "They obviously left you alive for a reason. Tell me what she said."

Reaching his arm out of the cage, Lipmann begged to be released.

"Take him down from there already and get him some clothes," Joseph instructed the men. "Now tell me, what did the Countess say? I know she said something to you!"

"Water," Lipmann's voice croaked. "Please give me some water."

Joseph took the canteen from his belt and held it to Lipmann's lips once they had lowered the cage to the ground. As he attempted to pull the canteen away, Lipmann grabbed his hand, refusing to stop drinking. This time Joseph forcefully yanked his hand away, separating the Rabbi from the canteen. "Now tell me the message, or I swear the next time I hold this canteen to your lips I will see to it that you drown."

"A trade. She says she will make a trade. If you come alone to her home she will return my daughter unharmed."

"A trade? That's all she said to you? It seems strange that she would kidnap Reisel just for the purpose of having me, and then flee from here rather than stay and make the trade? What aren't you telling me?" Joseph demanded to know.

"It's not you she wants, its your blood," the Rabbi provided the missing clue to the Countess's demand."

"A strange request, don't you think Rabbi? But we know of that already. There must be something more." Joseph was not satisfied yet by the answers being delivered by her messenger. "What else did she tell you?"

"She thinks the blood of the Kahana can render her immortal," Lipmann began revealing the truth but it was already known to Joseph.

"And she thinks this because..." Joseph wanted to know how she became aware of his supposed gift of immortality.

"Save my daughter," the Rabbi requested, avoiding to answer the prior question.

"How does she know this?" Joseph shook the bars of the cage with such anger that he managed to toss Rabbi Lipmann from one side to the other.

"Because I told her, Joseph," Lipmann finally confessed. "I thought she would help free my daughter from the marriage proposal you forced her to accept. But I did not know she was the killer you were seeking."

"How did you find out," Joseph demanded to know.

"Find out what?" Lipmann did not comprehend the question.

"That she was the killer? Were you in league with her," Joseph demanded to know. "Did you always know and you hoped I would somehow die on this mission? Did it all start falling apart because I survived everything she tried to do and now she's punishing you for your failure?" Tell me," Joseph screamed at him.

"It is all my fault," Lipmann buried his face into his hands as he began to cry. "Reisel discovered what she was doing to these young girls one night and I refused to believe her. I exposed her accusations to Countess Bathory. I thought they were only the imaginations of a young girl. I didn't know they were true. How could I possibly have known?"

Joseph was disgusted by the excuses. "You stupid old man," he held himself back from saying anything worse. "You couldn't even believe your own daughter. Because the great Rabbi Lipmann knows everything. He is so smart, smarter than the rest of the world. Perhaps if you had learned to listen to someone other than the sound of your own voice, you actually would be a man of God."

Still weeping into his hands, Yom Tov Lipmann pleaded with Joseph. "Save her, Joseph. Save my daughter."

"Oh, I will save her," Joseph had no doubt when he answered. "I will save her, not for you, but for her sake. She does not deserve to pay for your sins."

"Get him out of there, get him dressed, and get him out of my sight," Joseph instructed the men.

"What should we do with him afterwards, Joseph?" Thurzo asked.

"Find him his own transport back to Vienna," Joseph replied. "If comes with us then I don't want to see him until I find Reisel."

"What if we can't save her?" Thurzo asked coldly, knowing that Joseph would not take the question well but it had to be asked.

"I am going to save her," Joseph didn't hesitate to reply. "But if for some reason I can't and she is dead, I will come back and kill her father with my own two hands. This I swear."

Count Thurzo seemed satisfied by that answer.

Chapter Twenty-One

Vienna: December 1610

Captain Kartal's men easily overpowered the small squadron of men that the Countess had left behind to safeguard Castle Bran. Of the few left alive, they were of little use in providing any information regarding the Countess and her nefarious affairs. Even when threatened and knowing that their failure to provide any supportive evidence of Bathory's involvement in the deaths of hundreds of young girls would result in their being tossed to the Turks for execution, they still remained silent. Clearly they were all complicit in this cult that Elizabeth Bathory had resurrected but bound to secrecy by something they feared more than death.

Thurzo had everyone scour the castled from top to bottom looking for anything which may have pointed a finger of blame in the direction of Elizabeth Bathory for all the evils of the past two decades but it was obvious that she had it all physically removed from the castle at the time of her departure, leaving only their word against the highest profile figure of the Hungarian aristocracy. Count Thurzo, feared she still held the upper hand. Nevertheless, they knew their word was all they had to convince Matthias to intercede if there was to be any chance to save Reisel. Trading Joseph was never an option because they knew she would kill them both. Home, as Rabbi Lipmann indicated to Joseph could mean no place other than Cachtice, where Thurzo had no authority unless the Emperor provided it to him.

Before taking the long ride to Vienna, it was time to part ways with Captain Rashid Kartal and his lancers. Whereas they had every right according to the treaty to roam the countryside of Transylvania and Wallachia, they did not have any similar protection under law to enter directly into Austria. There they would been treated as an invading force and Count Thurzo would be unable to protect them. It was difficult for Thurzo to articulate how much he was indebted to the Turkish captain. The two men had gained a healthy respect for one another during their shared travails. Words were not necessary as they embraced forearms and then saluted their farewells.

As they rode off into the distance, Gyorgy Thurzo turned to the three companions and lectured them. "Let that be a lesson to you," he instructed, "The enemy of my enemy truly is my friend."

It was profound but not unheard of, and as Paolo Sarpi was about to mention that it may have already been a common saying, he thought better of it and let Count Thurzo have his moment of sounding profound.

The road to Vienna they knew would be clear, having already dealt with most of the threats that the Countess could turn against them. But to cover the seven hundred and fifty miles, using wagons to haul all the troops would take eighteen days at best. Eighteen days of torment for Joseph Kahana not knowing the condition of his fiance' and not having any plan by which to rescue her. As much as Paolo and Caesar would try to keep his spirits up, they found their friend slipping into a deep melancholy. It certainly didn't help that all this time they held Reisel's father in cuffs, in the last wagon, guarded by the troops. Not so much guarding him from escaping as they were guarding him from Joseph exacting out his threat of revenge. As far as Joseph was concerned, it was unfair that he should be rescued, while his daughter could at that very moment be suffering from indescribable tortures. He wrestled with his restored faith in God, forgetting that Sultan Ahmed had proved it was all merely a test of his worthiness.

Once again he was unable to rationalize how a God that supposedly loved him, would at the same time take everyone he loved away from him. Father, mother, and now Reisel. Deep in his depression he barely ate, he almost never slept and Paolo with all his medical knowledge could do nothing to relieve his anguish.

Ten days into the journey, Joseph was barely able to remain stable in the saddle, weak from the lack of nourishment and his inability to sleep through the nights. Count Thurzo ordered a halt to the convoy, ordering several of his men to lift Joseph out of his saddle and lay him down in the first wagon. "What are we going to do, Paolo?" the Count urgently wanted to know.

"I can make a potion to help him sleep," Paolo thought about some possible solutions. "And we can always force feed him if we have to. But I have nothing that is going to mend his heart and his brain. I'm afraid that if don't find a way to do that we are going to lose him."

"We didn't go through all this to lose him now," the Count was furious but had no idea whom he should address that anger against. "There has to be a solution!"

"Let me help," the voice from the last wagon floated towards the front of the convoy where they were gathered.

"That might push him over the edge," Thurzo commented to Paolo and Caesar.

"Right now," Paolo estimated, "He is at the edge. If there is any chance we can pull him back, then we have to take it."

"I agree," Caesar nodded his affirmation. "Perhaps if he feels his fingers around the Rabbi's throat it will make him feel better." Caesar raised the prospect jokingly but the others thought it was worth consideration.

"Bring him up here," Thurzo commanded the men in the last wagon.

One of the soldiers pulled Rabbi Lipmann from the cart by the collar of his waistcoat, practically dropping him to the ground as the Rabbi scrambled to get his footing after he rolled over the side rail. Pulling him by the ropes that cuffed his hands, he brought the prisoner alongside the first wagon where Joseph lay, staring into the nothingness of the sky above.

"You better not say or do anything that is going to make this worse," Paolo warned the Rabbi or otherwise I'll finish off that first discussion we had.

Rabbi Lipmann ignored the threat, instead resting his tied hands on Joseph's shoulder tenderly. "I have no magic healing prayers, or charms or spells or anything of that order which you all have come to expect over your past few months in dealing with the demons that you've fought," he addressed Joseph's colleagues. "But what I do have is the truth, and I pray to the Almighty that it will be enough." Having addressed the others, Yom Tom Lipmann spoke directly to Joseph. "I hope that if you're listening to me, you can find it in your heart to forgive this old, prejudiced fool. Clearly, you love my daughter more than I ever have. For a father to admit that he wasn't able to love his daughter that much, is a confession that certainly merits divine punishment.

I don't know how it happens that we come to take others for granted. Perhaps we wrap ourselves in scripture thinking God loves us more than anyone else and as a result we lose that capacity to pass that love on to others. But somehow, I came to believe I was special and everyone had to love me more than I needed to love them. I forgot what it was like to love someone with all my heart, to feel like an empty shell when they were gone. Then again, I don't think I've ever known. Seeing you this way only serves to enlighten me as to what love is supposed to be like. I never had any choice in who I was to marry. The council of Rabbis already had that arranged when I was only thirteen. When they said I was to marry Reichel Ashkenazi, I didn't even know who she was. I had never seen her before. It was my duty to obey and I did so willingly. That certainly isn't love!

When the time came, we got married and we performed our duties as instructed and over time we became close. Reichel and I are inseparable, and if you asked me if I love her, I would certainly say 'yes'. But if you were to ask me if I was 'in love' with her, from what I see when you and Reisel are together, and how you are willing to die for her, I would have to answer 'No'. I realize now that I never knew what being 'in love' actually meant.

I have my daughters, boy do I have daughters, six of them, and I thought I loved them, but once again you made me see that if you truly love them, then you believe them, you fight for them and you would die for them. Somewhere I forgot to learn those lessons. I was willing to martyr myself for my beliefs, fight government corruption with my polemics, which continually lands me in prison, but then one must ask, 'How could I truly love my daughters if I was so willing to abandon them, placing a higher value on my mission than on my own children?'

You were right, Joseph Kahana, I failed her. I was a terrible father. I didn't trust her judgment and I didn't believe her when she told me the truth. It only proves that I am everything you think I am and a man not worthy of God's love or protection. How is it that you can be laying here, grieving for her to the point that your heart is breaking and I cannot find it in my own soul to be willing to trade my life for hers. What kind of father is not willing to do that? Yet here I am, and here you are, and God see's which one of us is truly deserving of her love and has made it so.

You accused my teacher of being responsible for the death of your father, and you were right. In our blindness, we wished for the death of all Karaites and if you were to ask me now why we did so, I would have to answer truthfully it is because we fear that God may love you and your kind more. And if you were to ask, how can that be true, then surely I would say that it is because I have seen the embodiment of the spirits of Joshua and Samson and David, and all those that took up the sword on God's behalf in you. As Karaites, you have the willingness to fight for those too weak to fight for themselves, to battle against those that are enemies of the Lord, and somewhere I think we Rabbanites have forgotten that we need you and your kind as much as we need the scriptures to deliver us.

I guess I'm saying that I believe in you now, but Reisel, she never stopped believing in you. From the first day she met you, she believed in you. Even when they had taken her from the cell and were preparing to transport her to the Countess's home, she would say to them that her

Joseph was going to rescue her and that you would make them all pay for their sins. Her faith in you was much stronger than it had ever been in her own father. You cannot let her down now. Perhaps I should be jealous but I'm not. You are the better man. Reisel deserves to be with a man like you. So please, she is waiting for you to come and save her. I know that right now she is praying for you to come. Don't disappoint her. Do what you were meant to do. Be the saviour your family has always been. Save your Reisel, she is calling out to you. I know it. And I believe you can hear her too!"

Lipmann looked up at the Count again, indicating he was finished saying what he had to. "I'm ready to go back now," he began to lift he hands from Joseph's shoulder.

Joseph crossed his arm over his chest in order to hold the Rabbi's hands in place. "Thank you," he responded in a voice that was barely audible. "I can hear her too and I'm going to save her."

"Thank you," Rabbi Lipmann was overwhelmed by the intensity of his gratitude and began to cry. "Save her, please."

Patting her father's hand, Joseph promised that he would.

Lipmann nodded his appreciation to everyone as he was led back to his position in the third cart.

Joseph indicated that he wanted assistance to rise into a sitting position. Repacking several of the feed bags behind his back, they elevated Joseph so that he could now look into the faces of every one gathered about him. He saw the relief in their eyes as he looked from face to face.

"*Temnota nemoze vytlacit Temnotu*" Count Thurzo recited.

"And what exactly does that mean," Paolo was curious.

"Darkness cannot drive out darkness." Gyorgy explained. "An old Slovak saying. The darkness in Joseph's soul needed the light overpowering the darkness in another soul in order to be cured."

"I'd be a little more reticent in using the word cured yet,"Paolo advised. "But obviously an improvement."

"Can I get something to eat," Joseph interrupted their philosophical discussion.

The reception in Vienna was hardly what anyone would consider as being warm and cordial. In fact, their meeting with the Emperor was repeatedly delayed, until Count Thurzo finally decided to play his hand by suggesting that during his exchanges with the Ottoman Sultan, there had been a threat of war breaking out again between the two Empires. Such a threat could not be overlooked and the audience with the Emperor was swiftly arranged.

It was clearly evident from Emperor Matthias' attitude that he was not willing to discuss any of the charges against the Countess Elizabeth Bathory, dismissing the subject almost as soon as it was raised.

"I thought this was to be a meeting regarding the threat from Sultan Ahmed," the Emperor attempted to cut off Count Thurzo from speaking further on the matter.

"It is, your Majesty," Thurzo agreed. "The threat of war is a direct result of concerns regarding the Countess Bathory."

"I doubt the Sultan even knows of the Countess," Matthias objected. "If he doesn't know her, then he certainly isn't going to go to war over her."

"That's right Gyorgy, he doesn't know her," Maximilian confirmed.

"But he does know what she has been doing," Gyorgy intervened, "and he does know who has been supporting Gabriel Bathory with money and munitions. He also knows now who was responsible for tens if not hundreds of young Muslim girls being tortured and disembodied in the Dacian Caves."

"I read your report Gyorgy," Maximilian took over responding for his brother, "and it is clear that it was Count Nadasdy that was responsible for those hideous crimes. He's been dead for six years. You can hardly hold his widow responsible for her dead husband's crimes."

"I can when the widow has continued to perform those same ghastly crimes and therefore was most likely complicit when her husband was responsible."

"An accusation that cannot be proven," Maximilian dismissed the claim.

None of the four could believe what they were hearing. Somehow the Countess had managed to get the Emperor's ear and had pulled it so hard that he was following every thing she said like an unruly child that had just been disciplined.

What about the torture chamber in the Castle Bran?" Gyorgy brought up the recent past. "There were bodies of young girls strewn about the chamber. We were there, we saw them!"

"An unfortunate occurrence when one is not always present in their own castle," Maximilian provided a different account. "Apparently while away, the castle was attacked by a roving squadron of Ottoman soldiers, that killed all of the Countess's men and then raped and killed all of the servant girls she left behind. A terrible tragedy and one which we hold the Sultan accountable for."

Gyorgy could barely restrain himself. "You have Rabbi Lipmann's account of how he was put into a cage in that same chamber, made to witness the torture and murder of these same girls and was in fact tortured himself. How can you deny the existence of his account that it was not the Turks performing these acts?"

"Allow me to answer that," Cardinal Klesl weighed in to the audience, having been sitting all this time in his ministerial chair to the left of the Emperor. "He is a Jew. In fact he is a Jew with a criminal record. A Jew that has expressed his hatred for the Royal family and everyone associated with it. Seriously, do you think his testimony will have any value in a court of law against a highly regarded aristocrat that is well respected in Hungary?"

"I sent you all those documents and letters regarding the establishment of her own private army in Transylvania and Wallachia. What about all the chests of gold and silver they were holding in Bucharest. Surely that money is a reflection of her guilt."

"You've already answered your own question Gyorgy," Maximilian piped in. "Didn't you say Gabriel Bathory is receiving her support? It was this court that made Gabriel the Prince of Transylvania although it was against my better advice. He was only a man of nineteen at the time, barely old enough to wipe his own ass as far as I was concerned. Thankfully his cousin became his benefactor to help guide him properly in good governance."

"You're not serious," Gyorgy was beyond disbelief.

"Very serious," Matthias exerted his imperial oversight. "As Emperor, I can find no wrong doing at all by Elizabeth making herself protector of her younger cousin. Now if we are done, I would like to end this audience. The Crown is grateful for all you have done. You have rid us of this plague of wolf warriors or Omullup as you referred to them, that terrorized the countryside. You have destroyed the coven of witches that was responsible for abducting young girls and sacrificing them in their demonic rituals. We owe you our tremendous gratitude and you all will be well rewarded for what you have done."

Count Gyorgy Thurzo bowed his head and stepped away from the dais. There was nothing further he could say. As a loyal servant of the Crown, he knew if he pressed any further it would only result in a severe reprimand or perhaps even punishment. He was not prepared to push the matter any further.

"Well I am not done!" Joseph Kahana shouted, which shook the guards out of their stupor as they suddenly thought the Emperor was under attack. "What about Reisel? Is she just to die, because you don't have the integrity to stand behind the promises you made to me."

Emperor Matthias was alarmed by the sudden outburst and was not willing to tolerate such an overt act of disrespect. Maximilian knew his brother's demeanour all too well and decided to intervene before the Emperor had a chance to respond. There was something he had always liked in the character of Joseph from the first day they met and he was not willing to see him foolishly throw away his life simply because he was deemed to be disrespectful.

"Joseph, Joseph, we understand your distress at this time completely," he began by trying to soothe the irate Karaite Prince. "We have had every assurance from the Countess that Reisel Lipmann has been a welcome guest at her castle. She is completely unharmed and the Countess guarantees no harm will come to her. In fact she says if you come to visit at her castle, then Reisel can leave at any time afterwards as long as you stay."

"What of your promise that she will be my wife?" Joseph questioned Maximilian's integrity to keep his promises.

"I cannot make a woman love a man, any more than you can," the Archduke responded. "From what I recall, you told her when you first asked for her hand that she could break off the engagement at any time. From what I understand, she no longer wishes to consummate your relationship because of an apparent infidelity that arose between you and the Countess. To me it would appear that the Countess still wants you and you must admit that the advantages of such a relationship far outweigh the gains in marriage to a poor Rabbi's daughter. Think of all you will have achieved. A fine marriage into the aristocracy for your sister. Money beyond your wildest dreams to carry on your legacy. And the chance to be with the wealthiest and most powerful woman in the Empire. The decision is up to you. If you want Reisel Lipmann to go free, then you know what you have to do."

"I know exactly what I have to do," Joseph stated defiantly. "If it should be that only myself and my dog have to lay siege to the castle to free my betrothed, then you can tell the Countess I am coming. But I am coming with my sword in hand."

Seeing that Joseph was seriously contemplating doing as he said in order save Reisel, Caesar felt compelled to speak up to save his friend from committing suicide. "Enough with generating this false story of the beautiful princess that kisses the frog and turns him into the handsome prince." It was a tactful beginning, hardly offensive and managed to raise a few laughs when they drew the comparison to the beautiful countess and the lowly orphan boy. "But we all know how this story ends," Caesar continued. Much in the same way that Century II, Quatrain 90 ends for the both of your Excellencies, according to my father.

"What did your father have to say about us in this regard," Mathias desperately wanted to know."

'Though life and death the realm of Hungary changed:
The law will be more harsh than service:
Their great city cries out with howls and laments,
Castor and Pollux enemies in the arena.'

"Shall I explain it to you, Excellencies?" Caesar offered his services of interpretation.

"Please go ahead," Mathias instructed him to do so.

"It should be obvious who is referred to as Castor and Pollux. The Dioscuri were two brothers, one a prince, the other a demigod. Not that different from an Archduke and an Emperor when you strip away the metaphor. Except in their case they both happen to spend half of their time in Hades."

"And in our case…"

"In your case your Majesty, you and the Archduke are made to fight in the arena, like the Senators of ancient Rome. Forced to fight as gladiators to the death by the new Emperor."

"Need I ask who this new Emperor might be," Mathias already knew the answer to that question.

"Hungary is responsible for life and deaths that result in the Empire. There is only one ruler in Hungary and she will change the laws so that justice becomes meaningless. The cities of the Empire will all cry out because of their suffering and it is all the result of your refusal to take action."

"Be careful what you say son of Nostradamus," the Emperor warned Caesar not to push any further.

"Not me, you Majesty, it is my dead father. As you said, a widow cannot be held accountable to her dead husband, how then can a son then be responsible for his long past father. It was not I but he that wrote Century VIII, Quatrain 14:

'The great credit of gold and abundance of silver
will cause honor to be blinded by lust;
the offense of the adulterer will become known,
which will occur to his great dishonor.'

"How shameful of my father to accuse you have having sold your honour for gold and silver. Yes, she is an adulterer, and true she does blind practically all men by lust, but why would he ever think that it is actually her money that would corrupt your sense of justice and integrity."

"You are mocking me, Caesar de Nostradame, and it matters not to me whose son you are, I will not permit myself to be criticized by someone who has no knowledge of governance and the intrigue of finances to maintain the Empire." Mathias had reached the end of his tolerance. "Leave me now or I will see that all of you spend the rest of your days in a cell."

Maximilian stepped over to his brother and whispered sharply into his ear. He knew that the Emperor had overstepped his authority with his last comment and now sought a way that they could mollify the situation before it grew out of hand. But it was too late as Paolo stepped forward to speak.

"You threaten the Chief Magistrate of Venice!" It was Fra Paolo Sarpi's time to be heard. He had been waiting to seize an opportunity where he could apply his diplomatic pressure and the Emperor's foolish statement had just provided him with that opportunity.

"Fra Sarpi," Maximilian rolled Paolo' name of his tongue as if it was dripping with syrup. "Of course the Emperor had no intention to threaten you. Obviously he knows that both you and Caesar de Nostradame are protected by your citizenship of other states and he would not wish to create any antagonism with either the Venetian or French governments. He became emotional upon hearing about his predicted death by the famed seer Nostradamus and experienced a moment of irrational thought. We ask that you please forgive this momentary lapse."

"No!" Paolo's response was curt.

"No? What do you mean by no?" Maximilian did not understand.

"I believe it is the same word in all our languages," Paolo Sarpi reminded the Archduke. "No can only mean no. I will not forgive this momentary lapse by the Emperor. May I give you a historical lesson that you should take to heart. Never has an empire that is landlocked survived for very long. Without the sea, there is no commercialism, there is no trade, because the only trade routes that remain are overland and that means transporting through hostile territories. You have no sea ports others than those I provide to you on the Italian coast. The Dutch our looking to secure those seaports because of all their increased trade with the Ottoman Empire. Right now I'm giving consideration to provide them with those ports that I previously leased to you."

"You can't do that," Maximilian protested.

"I can do as I please," Paolo Sarpi made himself perfectly clear. "I am the Chief Magistrate of Venice and I alone determine who will have access to those ports."

"But you will cripple us," the Archduke pleaded his case.

"Why not seek more gold and silver from Hungary if you are so concerned about losing your trade and commerce?" Sarpi taunted them.

Turning back to Mathias, his brother explained all the

ramifications of what Paolo Sarpi was threatening. The discussion between them went back and forth for several minutes as Mathias failed to understand why the Chief Magistrate would contemplate undertaking such a drastic measure.

"You would do this because of one simple slip of my tongue where I threatened to place you into a cell. I misspoke and I apologize profusely," the Emperor tried to withdraw his words.

"No, I will do this because of your betrayal of my friend," Paolo puffed up his chest, proud that he finally got to argue a case where the substantive matter was not one of money or profits but having to do with a far more valuable commodity; the integrity of a man's soul.

"You mean Joseph?" Mathias wanted to be certain they were discussing the same motive.

"When I say Joseph, I speak of far more than just a friend. I speak of a man's true value; of a pledge and commitment to do what is right in the Lord's eyes. I speak of a sense of honour and righteous indignation. I speak of chivalry and virtuosity. These are all the characteristics of nobility, that I will defend with the greatest fervour against those that have apparently abandoned the right to be called noble. So once again I will explain to you, I do this for my friend."

"As do I," Count Thurzo was moved by Sarpi's speech, recognizing that there were more important characteristics that defined a noble than a misguided sense of loyalty. "If he goes to Cachtice, he will not be going alone," Gyorgy swore his support.

"And neither do I rescind anything that my father has said," Caesar threw his lot in with the others. "You may be willing to dance with the devil, but I would rather be dancing with those that want to plunge a blade into her dark heart."

Maximilian was moved by their loyalty to one another. It reminded him of a time when he and his two brothers made a pact to support one another no matter what may come. Somewhere, they forgot what it meant to be true brothers. He understood now how these four were able to defeat every obstacle that had been laid in their path. "Gentlemen, if you could please wait outside and give us time to discuss this matter further. I think it will be possible to resolve this matter to everyone's mutual satisfaction. Please be patient I beg you."

"What are you doing Maxi?" they could overhear the Emperor saying as they were leaving the room.

"It is time we talk brother," the Archduke responded, just as the door shut behind them.

Sitting in the outer salon, the four waited patiently for the time when they would be summoned back into the throne room to hear the

Emperor's final decision.

"You have all placed yourselves in precarious positions on my account," Joseph appraised them of their situations. "I can't ask you to help me. This is my concern, my personal battle to fight and I don't want to be responsible for risking your lives as well."

"First of all, you didn't ask, and secondly, it is my life to do with as I choose," Count Thurzo replied.

"And I made a promise to your father," Caesar reminded Joseph. "I told him I would take care of you and that's all I'm doing. It has nothing to do with whether you asked or not."

"And I suppose this had nothing to do with my asking either, Paolo?" Joseph wanted to hear the Venetian's perspective.

"This has everything to do with you asking," Paolo laughed as he gave his answer. "You may not have thought you asked, but the moment you said you were going with Wolf, I assumed if you're too dumb to know the difference between a dog and a wolf, then you're also to dumb to know when to ask your friends for help. So I decided to ask and answer for you. We've been in this from the beginning, and we will see it through to the end. How did that mantra of yours go again, Caesar? The one you did with Joseph's father and Giordano."

"Let me show you," Caesar held out a closed fist to the others, inviting them to press fist to fist against his. "Now repeat after me; One Heart, One Soul, One Mind, We Three...um..., make that Four of a Kind."

"One Heart, One Soul, One Mind, We Four of a Kind," they repeated.

Moments later the two palace guards reopened the doors to the throne room and ushered the four of them back before the Emperor.

"After careful deliberation," the Archduke began, "It was the decision of this council that there may be a way in which this matter concerning the Bathorys can be resolved to everyone's mutual satisfaction. Of course, no matter the outcome, the Crown will require the reassurance that it will not lose its Mediterranean shipping ports or the number of berths at each." Maximilian awaited Sarpi's response.

"In principle, I will agree, assuming that what you have to say is acceptable."

"I will take that as a 'yes'," Maximilian directed the scribe to formalize the response into his notes. "We, being the council of myself, the Emperor and Cardinal Klesl, accept that certain improprieties have been allegedly conducted by the Countess Erzsibet Bathory of Hungary. In order to press formal charges we will require indisputable proof of her committing these crimes. Obtain us that proof and a tribunal will be set up to prosecute her. In the meantime, the allegations of murder, possible treason, as well as subterfuge to undermine the Zsitvatorak Treaty with the Ottoman Empire will be levied against members of her staff, who may have been acting unilaterally without her consent.

In regards to the alleged abduction of Reisel Lipmann, it is the will of the Emperor that he and the Palatine of Hungary will pay a personal visit to the Countess Bathory in Cachtice and will personally escort the girl back to Vienna. Refusal to release the girl into our custody will be considered a crime of kidnapping. The invitation of our presence for dinner on Christmas Day will be immediately dispatched to the Countess Bathory, stipulating that in three days hence we will arrive, discuss any implications of her involvement in these alleged crimes, record her responses, have our Christmas meal and then leave immediately afterwards for Vienna with the girl, Reisel Lipmann in our custody."

No sooner had Maximilian described their intentions, when Caesar felt one of his excruciating migraines pounding the inside of his skull. As he bent over in pain, holding the sides of his head, Paolo Sarpi steadied him in his arms. "I thought these headaches had ended, my friend?" Sarpi was confused.

"Only if I deliver them as a forewarning...in order to prevent what might happen...in this case...because of their decision...it is like they came before...when I was simply confirming what will happen," Caesar struggled to get the words out, breathing deeply with each pause, praying that the pain would subside quickly.

"Another message Caesar?" Maximilian recognized the signs.

"Different this time," Caesar responded. "From my father's Almanac of Apr1562."

"An almanac?" the Archduke sounded intrigued. "Unusual for your father, is it not?"

"He used the almanacs to tell his readers of events that will take place immediately. I'm presuming that means he is telling us what will definitely happen when you go to the Castle in Cachtice."

"As usual, coming from your father I take it that it will not be a pleasant outcome," the Emperor commented.

Caesar began reciting:

'From afar has come a spark of movement
Vain discovery against an infinite people
Of not recognizing the evil of the duties,
In the food one finds death and the End.'

"You are seriously suggesting that she will try to poison us," the Emperor refused to accept the content of the prophecy. "My men will be standing right there. She wouldn't dare to attempt such an act. We would arrest her immediately upon witnessing any foul play."

"And you'll be dead, as well as the Palatine, which leaves her as the only one remaining noble in the room with any authority. Who are your men going to take any orders from? A dead man?" Caesar challenged the Emperor to think about that.

"I cannot imagine that she would dare to undertake such an act against her Emperor," Matthias still refused to accept the prophecy.

"As it says your Majesty, you refuse to recognize the evil of all her doings. The poisoning will take place, because of your inability to move against her now. It is no different than when Moses refused to do as God instructed and he had to be punished for his inactions." Caesar drew the biblical comparison to demonstrate the futility of trying to prevent what was destined to occur."

"Then I simply do not eat the food," the Emperor responded.

"Or drink the drink, or breath the air, or kiss her hand, or a thousand other ways she can find to kill you both. We know she is a master of poisons. At least with food and drink I can actually do something about it," Paolo instructed.

"You will have no idea which poison she might use Fra Sarpi," Klesl interrupted at that moment. Church knowledge of such matters meant he knew that there was no universal antidote for all poisons.

"I see your clerical training as a herbalist was not a complete waste of time," Sarpi ridiculed the Cardinal, knowing that the only true training the church offered was on how to use such toxins for assassination purposes. "But you are correct, Cardinal. There is no universal antidote. So within the hour prior to eating, I will administer a drink of bismuth of charcoal to both of you. That will give you time before the effects of the poison can take effect. Afterwards, I will administer an emetic of tartaric acid that will cause you to vomit, thereby removing the toxin and any remaining poison will be neutralized by the acidic nature of the potion."

"You seriously want me to ingest a poison, in the hope that your potions will render them ineffective, Senor Sarpi. Have you gone mad?" the Emperor was clearly not pleased with that idea.

"As I mentioned previously, your Majesty, the Countess will have a thousand different ways to induce death. At least this one I can deal with. As Nostradamus indicated, this will happen."

"I have full trust in Senor Sapri," Gyorgy Thurzo provided his approval of the plan. If the Emperor is certain that the Countess is not involved in any plot to seize his throne, then there should be no fear of poisoning and Nostradamus will be proven to be both a fraud and a charlatan. But should you now be thinking that she was complicit in all these acts, here is your opportunity to seize all her wealth and all her properties. Suffering a minor case of indigestion in order to make your throne the richest in Europe."

Thurzo's last point definitely caught the interest of the Emperor and his brother. "You say you can do this with confidence, Senor Sarpi," Maximilian needed to be reassured. "The Emperor will not die?"

"Yes," Paolo replied succinctly.

"But we still have a problem of denial," Maximilian thought about it a little further. "She could always claim her cooks took the action upon themselves. That she had no knowledge of their plot to assassinate the Emperor. We need something that is indisputable and directly ties her to the crimes."

"Then we are back to where we started," Thurzo commiserated.

"Perhaps not," Maximilian held his finger in the air. "There was another disappearance this week. Another daughter of an aristocrat. She was supposed to be home from the finishing school two days ago but never showed."

"Who was she," Thurzo asked, surprised that the case had not been handed to him as yet.

"Elana Tsepesh," the Archduke replied. "Fifteen. A little older than the previous cases. Only surviving daughter of Mircea Tsepesh of Transylvania.

Gyorgy Thurzo knew immediately why the case had not crossed his desk as yet. Mircea Tsepesh, son of Petru the Lame, the great-grandson of Vlad Dracul, the one they called the Impaler and still believed to have been the one true Prince of Transylvania. "You're afraid of a civil war," he understood Maximilian's hesitance to reveal any of this previously.

"Not if you can find her alive and she can testify against Erzsibet Bathory," the Archduke provided the details on how civil war could be avoided. "If she's alive and we can strip all power from the Countess, then the Tsepesh family will likely be content with the outcome."

"And if she's dead?"

"Then she was never found and not another word about this."

Chapter Twenty-Two

Cachtice Castle: December 25, 1610

The Emperor and the Palatine arrived at Cachtice Castle in the foothills of Slovakia shortly before noon on Christmas day accompanied by Mathias' personal guard and a full contingent of the Palatine's law enforcement officer's. The view from the carriage window framed an impressive fortress built on three levels that gradually rose skyward from the base of the hill, to the top level from which there were clear views of the Myjava Upland and the town of Cachtice below. The original structure was now over two hundred years old, but the Countess had renovated much of the upper castle, where she kept her residence, in a Renaissance style. The lower castle was built directly into the hillside, with no gates other than those that led into the stables. It wasn't until the middle castle, halfway up the hill, that anyone visiting actually encountered a guardhouse responsible for controlling passage along the road and either permitting or restricting access through the impressive wrought iron gates. The middle castle housed the general servants in one half and served as the barracks for the Countess's well equipped personal forces of approximately one hundred men in the other half. Guests would be escorted by a contingent of Bathory's soldiers at the point they entered through the middle gates to the front gates of the upper castle. Exactly how this would be handled, considering that the Emperor and Palatine were already being escorted by close to one hundred of their own men combined, would need to be seen.

While still at the base of the hill, well below the level of the lower castle, the carriage driver was instructed to bring the horses to a halt. The Emperor's forces stood at attention, no one moving, but well aware that their approach had already been seen from the upper castle. It was time to start unveiling the plan and putting it into action. Paolo Sarpi wanted a last minute briefing with Matthias and Gyorgy to go over the details as they sat across from each other in the Royal carriage.

"We are going to separate at this point before they can actually see us," he informed them. "Caesar and I will move through the castle looking for any evidence that we can use to incriminate the Countess. Meanwhile, Joseph is going to find a way into the castle's dungeons to see if his fiance' is being held captive there. She may be just locked in a bedroom in the upper castle but there are likely other girls down there that will need to be rescued."

"And if she is not down there?" Gyorgy wanted to know how they would deal with that situation should it arise.

"Then it will be up to Caesar and myself to find her if she's being held in the upstairs rooms of the castle. You don't have to worry about any of those details. That is up to us."

"So exactly what do we do," the Emperor wanted specifics.

"As we discussed, you make polite conversation, you eat everything they serve you and you make certain that you can provide us with at least three hours without interruptions. I suspect that she'll have her men closely quartered to wherever you stand your men down. Most of her servants should be busy entertaining you both. That should leave most of the castle empty for us to move around undetected."

"And if it isn't empty?" Gyorgy was not confident that everyone would be positioned exactly as Paolo had presumed.

"Then we use these," Sarpi tapped the rapier attached to his belt.

"Don't get cocky," Thurzo joked but it was more of a warning. "You three aren't the best swordsmen I have ever seen."

"But we're not the worst either," Caesar could not resist adding his comment.

"What if we have our suspicion a certain food is tainted," Matthias wanted to know what he should do in that situation.

"What you do with all the other food that you don't suspect, you eat it," Paolo Sarpi advised. "You cannot leave her with any suspicion that you are on to her, otherwise we may not be able to prove she is conspiring against you."

"It won't be easy to deliberately poison myself," the Emperor confessed.

"That is why you both have your hip flasks filled with the Bismuth of Charcoal. You drink all of it immediately before you sit down for the meal and I swear, you won't be poisoned. I promise." Paolo felt it necessary to repeat the instructions for the charcoal as it certainly wasn't going to be easy to swallow the thick, chalky liquid. "If we are all set, then the three of us will disembark at this point and look for another way in. And just remember, as soon as you know you have been poisoned, you need to seek your way out of there and meet me in this location in a few hours so I can administer the second half of the treatment."

"How will we know we've been poisoned," the Emperor was curious.

"Trust me, you'll know," is all that Sarpi had to say about it.

The carriage rolled upwards towards the middle gates of the guardhouse accompanied by close to fifty mounted soldiers and the other fifty on foot.

"There no room for the whole lot of you," the sentry at the guardhouse informed the Emperor's Master at Arms. "Horses and riders down to the livery. The rest of you can remain here and the carriage can continue on up."

The Master at Arms thought about it and agreed that he could probably send the horses back down to the stables, but then he would order the riders to rejoin them at the upper castle on foot.

The guard still did not agree with that suggestion, insisting that no soldiers would be permitted beyond the middle castle.

"Sergeant, it is Sergeant, isn't it."

"Yes Sir," the guard responded.

"Let me ask you something Sergeant," the Master at Arms continued. "I bet the Countess holds a lot of lavish parties in her castle up there, doesn't she?"

"Yes she does, Sir," the guard agreed.

"I bet you are the man that has to ensure that everyone that attends leaves their personal guards in the barracks here and doesn't take them up to the top."

"That's right Sir." The Sergeant was proud of his responsibilities.

"Those parties are pretty large I guess if you have to keep their men all confined at this level. What would you guess? One hundred guests, perhaps even more."

"Much more at times," the Sergeant estimated.

"Good," replied the Master at Arms. "I want you to imagine that the men behind me are all guests. We'll leave the horses behind but all hundred or so of us guests are going through this gate whether you agree or disagree. Have I made myself clear, Sergeant?"

"It's contrary to my orders, Sir," the Sergeant replied nervously, his hands visibly beginning to shake.

Withdrawing his rapier a third of the way out of the scabbard, the Master at Arms made himself crystal clear. "Are you going to open this gate for the Emperor and his men or do I have to demonstrate what happens to someone that defies imperial orders?"

Still trembling, the Sergeant signaled his men to open the gate, at which point the Emperor's carriage and men advanced along the road continuing on to the Upper Castle, while those on horseback took their animals below, only to return on foot.

Upon reaching the courtyard of the upper castle, the Master at Arms assembled his men into formation and stood awaiting the next set of orders. Similarly, Thurzo's men also took up a position in the courtyard but no sooner had the Count descended from the carriage, he waved his hand in a circular motion, signaling his men to search for any signs of hostility in the immediate area and to stay on alert.

Before the Emperor and Palatine even reached the front door of the castle it swung open wide and they were greeted by the Steward."

"Your Majesty," she bowed in the manner of a man rather than curtsying as one might have expected. "We are honored by your presence. And it is good to see you once again Count Thurzo, please come in."

"If you don't mind," Matthias had a request before stepping through the threshold. "I would be more comfortable if my elite guard could come in as well." Matthias referred to the six man protection unit that was always with him whenever outside his own palace. All six were highly trained combatants that would willingly sacrifice their own lives to protect the Emperor.

"Of course, your Majesty. We want you to be a comfortable as possible. My mistress awaits you in the Salon. Please follow me."

"No sooner had he stepped into the room, the Countess dashed forward to embrace him but was immediately intercepted by one of the elite guardsmen. "Matti, am I no longer permitted to hug my favourite cousin?" the Countess pouted.

Extending his right hand past his guard, Matthias offered his ring, "What can I do Erzsibet, times have changed. Now that I am Emperor the best I can offer is my ring to kiss."

"Oh pooh, Matti, you are becoming just as stuffy as your brother Rudolph. What happened to 'Beth'? Is that no longer permitted? Anyway, please, have a seat. Can I get either of you refreshments?"

Both declined, suggesting that they would wait until dinner for drinks.

"My chefs have prepared a fabulous meal for you, your Majesty," Elizabeth explained as she waited for them to be seated. "It should be ready in the hour. But that gives us plenty of time to discuss urgent matters. It is so good to have this time to talk directly with one another. I understand there have been many accusations leveled against me and I only ask for the opportunity to defend myself."

"Of course Erzsibet," the Emperor Matthias agreed. "I would have it no other way. Someone of your position and stature has the right to refute this dangerous hearsay and of course set the record straight.

"I am so happy that you agree with me, Matthias. There may be others here," an obvious indication suggesting Gyorgy Thurzo, "That may not see this exactly in the same way that we do. But people in our position will always have our detractors and we must learn to expect these annoying and false accusations."

"This is true Erzsibet but some of these accusations do have some factual support that must be dealt with immediately," the Emperor advised.

"Dear cousin, whatever are you referring to?" the Countess asked innocently.

"Perhaps Count Thurzo can explain some of these accusations best," the Emperor deferred to Gyorgy.

"We have testimony that your dead husband was the one responsible for the abductions of the young girls in the Eastern regions from the period of 1592 until 1604."

"Oh my," the Countess feigned surprise. I had no idea that Ferencz was capable of such a horrible crime. He never told me about any of this. I swear to you, that I did not know."

Gyorgy had expected her answer and it was not about to deter him. "In our exploration of the Dacian Caves, we found a device that was used to withdraw the blood from those girls that had been abducted and we believe it to be identical to the device that was used on Maria Zapolya, one of your students that was found dead last Christmas."

"What are you suggesting cousin, that someone that did those terrible crimes in the caves survived and is now terrorizing my students in the same manner as some element of revenge for my not supporting my husband's madness. We will obviously need your protection!"

"Not at all cousin. I'm accusing someone in your household of carrying on your husband's madness either with or without your approval but I suspect the former because of your close association with Annise Darvolya."

"I'm sorry, I don't know anyone by that name."

"Of course you do Cousin," Gyorgy refuted her statement. "She was in your employ from the time your husband died until jut over a year ago when she died. I believe you registered her as Anna Darvula and implied she was your household doctor. Except she never finished medical school and was being charged with several crimes, the worst of which was practicing witchcraft. And while she was with your husband in the Eastern territories not only continued to practice witchcraft but used body parts of these poor girls that were slaughtered by your husband to make her potions. She was in league with the devil and suddenly she is in your employ and the killing continues. What do you call that."

"Coincidence," she replied calmly.

"Perhaps you call the fact that when we entered your castle in Brasov, we found the bodies of multiple young females that had been tortured and killed in the same manner as those we had discovered in the caves as performed by your dead husband's cohorts, a coincidence as well."

"Oh my," the Countess placed a hand over her mouth. "I heard that my castle was invaded by Turks shortly after I left. Perhaps my husband was innocent of these crimes and it were the Turks all along performing these horrible crimes."

"See, that is where the threads of this tapestry you are trying to weave starts to come apart at the seams, Cousin. Those invading Turks as you call them were actually under my command. We took the castle from your men that you had left behind. Those bodies were there from when you and your men were inhabiting your castle. Now that is an undeniable fact." Gyorgy smiled charmingly as he made his statement.

"Oh, look, the sweet meats are ready. I do love them, don't you?" The Countess managed to fluidly change the topic. "Gentlemen, if you don't mind moving into the dining room. Please follow me."

She never even bothered to even attempt to respond to Count Thurzo's last accusation."

As they passed through the hallway, the Countess noted that the Emperor's elite guard still followed. "I'm afraid this time your Majesty there won't be any room in the dining room for your men. But they can wait in the glass sunroom just outside of the dining area. They will be able to see you through the windows at all times."

"That will be fine Erzsibet," the Emperor agreed. "But before we eat, I would like to visit the commode, if you could show me where it is."

"Of course, your Majesty. I will have my Steward show you where it is. Erzsi, please show the Emperor to the Commode."

"I will go as well," Gyorgy Thurzo mentioned. "Need to wash my hands before we eat."

The steward practically appeared out of no where, having never been more than an ear shot away from her mistress all the time they had been in discussion.

Several minutes later the Countess was joined at the dining table by her two guests. The servants ushered in a trays of sweet meats known as collops, made with ground almonds covered in a milk, sugar and rosewater syrup. Both Matthias and Gyorgy appeared hesitant to spoon any into their mouths, until they saw that the Countess was already eating her second spoonful.

"Anything wrong Matthias," she asked.

"No, nothing," the Emperor lied, "I was just admiring how good these looked. I have never tried collops before. It looks delicious."

"I hope you don't mind eating in my small private dining room but I find it so much more intimate when there are only a few people."

"It is fine," the Emperor was satisfied. "But regarding the last issue that was raised by Count Thurzo, perhaps you can provide an explanation for me how these dead mutilated girls appeared in your castle at the time you were residing at Castle Bran."

"Certainly I have an explanation," the Countess responded. "But let's not spoil our meal talking about mutilated bodies, shall we? I prefer that we enjoy our meal and then there will be plenty of time to engage in such discussions afterwards. The entree is ready to be served. I had it prepared especially for you, your Majesty because I know it is one of your favorites. Roasted goose and woodcock, smothered in butter and saffron and then braised in a thick mushroom sauce."

"How did you ever know that?" Matthias asked surprised.

"One of my chefs personally knows one of yours and they delight in trading recipes. I hope it is every bit as delectable as when you have it served in the palace."

"This is delicious, Erzsibet. I think it is even better than my cooks make it. I might have to steal your chef if the rest of the meal tastes as good."

"But regarding the dead girls that we found in Castle Bran," Thurzo made an effort to revive the previous topic of discussion.

"Eat, Gyorgy," Matthias urged his Palatine. "I have already agreed we will withhold such morbid details until after the meal. There is plenty of time."

"Yes, your Majesty," Thurzo had no choice but to agree. He looked up to see that the Countess returned the same charming smile he had offered her earlier.

Finishing the entrees, the servants wheeled out the main course. It was venison, cooked in a berry marinade, and served with creamed white radish.

There was no way of knowing which of the dishes may have been poisoned and failing to suffer any ill effects by that point, the Emperor was beginning to believe that none of it had been poisoned. Perhaps the revered Nostradamus was a fraud after all. By the time they were finished with the main course, out came the Christmas pudding with currants, dried fruit and spices in a thick egg-yolk porridge.

Throughout the meal, a drink known as lambswool, made from hot apple cider and spices, was being continually poured into their mugs by the waiting staff.

Countess Elizabeth kept watching her guests suspiciously, knowing that at any time now, the questioning would begin again. It didn't take long before Thurzo felt they had wasted enough time eating and now it was time to return to serious matters.

"At the same time we found the dead girls in your castle, we also discovered Rabbi Lipmann, a man that you had invited to stay as your guest, imprisoned, naked in a cage with evidence of being tortured. All of which he claims was done on your orders."

"Was he not a criminal?" the Countess asked.

"Yes, he was," Matthias answered the question, feeling somewhat light headed.

"That is not the point," Gyorgy countered as he wiped the sweat from his brow. "Is it hot in here?" his mind was unable to stay focused as he felt the sweat pouring from his body. "And what about his daughter. He says you kidnapped Reisel Lipmann and you are holding her hostage in this castle. Is that true?"

"Yes, very hot," the Emperor replied, as tears welled up in his eyes. "Why am I crying," he could not understand what was happening as he appeared to be losing control his body. "My stomach doesn't feel very good at all."

"Show us Reisel Lipmann," Thurzo demanded.

"She is in her room now. We don't wish to disturb her. Her decision to leave her father was very traumatic for her," the Countess explained.

"Then we will go up to her room and speak to her there," Gyorgy suggested as he rose from the chair. "Take us to her now.

"Erzsi, why isn't this working?" the Countess shouted at her steward.

"Gyorgy," the Emperor reached out with his hand to grab Count Thurzo's sleeve. "Something is wrong. I'm not feeling well."

"I'm experiencing cramps too," the Count reached for his stomach, trying to massage away the pain. "Take us to the girl now!"

"I told you she is not available," the Countess had risen from her chair and was looking frantic. "This isn't right, you both should be dead by now," Elizabeth was suddenly panicking. "Erzsi, what did you do? It's not working!"

From the foyer on the other side of the doors to the small dining room there was a thunderous crash, sounding very much as if there had been an explosion.

"Your Emperor is under attack," Count Thurzo screamed at the elite guard that looked in through the windows of the sun room and were not yet reacting to the commotion. As soon as they heard Thurzo shouting they came charging back through the hallway and burst through the doors. "Get the Emperor out of here. Now! Quickly!" Thurzo continued to scream his orders, saliva flying from his lips. As he followed them out from the room, he saw what looked like at least ten dark robed men crushed beneath a huge iron chandelier. The massive lamp consisted of several concentric rows of candles, which were now tossed and broken everywhere he looked. Perhaps a hundred candles in total. The chandelier had mysteriously fallen from the three story high ceiling of the foyer and caught the men that had obviously assembled in the foyer outside the dining room for nefarious reasons. They wore no particular uniform but Thurzo could see that they were all armed with both swords and knives. There was no time to go after the Countess and her steward. When he looked back, they were already gone. All that was important now was to get back to the meeting place where Paolo Sarpi would have the second treatment waiting. Thurzo could feel that the poison was already rendering him lightheaded and the last thing he recalled was feeling himself lifted on to the shoulders of several men and floating gently down the castle road.

Remaining in the shadows, Joseph with Wolf, Caesar and Paolo skirted the rim of the hill looking for an entrance into the lower castle. They saw where they had taken the horses to be stabled but that presented too much of a risk. Any pathway through the stables would have encountered too many people from stable boys, to grooms to possibly even some of the Countess's mounted soldiers. Everything they needed to do depended on stealth and speed, so they continued to look for another opening.

"Do you hear that," Joseph turned to the others.

They shook their heads.

"Someone is crying," Joseph was convinced he could hear another person.

"Wait a minute," Caesar stopped to listen. "I can hear it now too. It sounds like a woman."

Moving slowly around the base of the hill, the three of them crept silently through the tall grass, searching for the source of the weeping. There was a faint light shining through the shrubbery up ahead. Joseph signaled to the others to follow him. The area was overgrown with vegetation but they continued to push through until they could see the small clearing that lay ahead. Probably no more than ten feet in diameter, had they not followed the sounds of the crying girl, they would have never found it, thinking that the growth of trees, shrubs and long grass extended directly from the foot of the hill without any break.

There in the clearing, at the mouth of a barely visible doorway built into the side of the hill, the woman knelt, tenderly washing the body of a young girl that was barely moving. Every now and then she would sob and cry as the life force ebbed from the near lifeless body. Joseph whispered to the others. "We have to make certain we don't frighten her. If she runs behind that door and locks it, then we'll lose the one chance we have of getting inside. Any suggestions on how we should proceed."

Attracted by the odors that wafted from the concealed doorway, Wolf had already entered the clearing and was standing directly in the doorway waiting for his master to follow. While they were still trying to decide on a suitable action, they failed to notice the woman quivering in terror at the sight of the wolf barring her way back inside. She wanted to scream but the fear of being discovered outweighed her fear of the terrifying beast. It was only when Joseph realized that Wolf was no longer at his side did he look around and saw that the doorway was now secured. It remained now up to him to approach the woman and gain her confidence.

"Don't be afraid," Joseph spoke softly to the young woman. "Everything is going to be fine. You won't be hurt."

Pointing towards Wolf, the woman obviously thought Joseph was actually coming to rescue her from the wild animal. Joseph moved slowly, trying not to make her any more nervous than she already was. He edged himself beside her, until he was screening her view of Wolf with his own body.

"Is he ,still watching us," she asked nervously.

"Probably," Joseph answered calmly. "What is your name?"

"Katalin," she answered but confused as to why he wasn't showing any concern about the wolf standing behind him.

"Katalin, my name is Joseph. No one here is going to hurt you. I promise." Joseph looked down at the young girl that Katalin had been bathing in warm water, her naked body pale, almost white in the sunlight. Her breasts no longer rose or fell with every breath. Her eyes stared blankly towards the trees as the light of life had gone from them. "I am afraid she's dead Katalin." At that moment she burst into tears, a heavy mix of grief and fear. "Did you know her, Katalin? Joseph kept his voice low and monotone, as he tried to soothe the frightened woman.

"Not really," she replied. "So many young girls," she sobbed. "I thought I could save at least one."

"We are here to help you save far more than one, Katalin." Joseph waved for Caesar and Paolo to surface from the bushes. Both men came walking towards her, stopping well short so that they did not appear threatening.

Katalin was still trying to peer around Joseph to see what the wolf was doing, still not convinced that he wasn't a wild animal.

"Don't worry about him either," Joseph flashed a warm smile to ease the woman's concern. "He belongs to me. He won't hurt you."

"All wolves kill," she answered, thinking Joseph ignorant to believe that he could domesticate a wolf's true nature.

"Wolves are like people," Joseph tried to explain. "Some people kill, others don't. That's just the way it is among all the species."

"The wolves here all kill," Katalin advised them.

"Do you see a lot of wolves here," Joseph wanted to know.

"I used to," she answered. "But almost all went away several months ago. They never came back."

"And they won't come back Katalin. We killed them all. Now we are here to rescue any girls in this castle and you can help us."

"I don't know," she was still worried about those inside. "If they catch me they will kill me."

"But you are very brave, Katalin," Joseph praised her. "You know what they will do to you but still you tried to save this girl, and I suspect you tried to save many more. That means that God has been watching over you and keeping you safe thus far. Now He has sent us to end this nightmare but we need your help."

"There is no God in this cursed castle," she groaned. "What God would make me a slave to these monsters all these years? God has abandoned this place."

"How many years have you been here?" Joseph asked.

"Almost five years," she broke into tears again.

Joseph rested his hand on her shoulder. "That's a long time Katalin. I'm sorry we didn't come earlier to rescue you. But obviously God had a purpose for you. That's why you were kept alive all these years."

"Five years ago they abducted me from the streets," she barely got the words out between sobs. "They stripped me naked and the witch, she probed inside me, doing terrible things inside me, It hurt so much" she broke down into tears once again. Catching her breath after about a minute, she attempted to continue her story. "Too old she said." and so she decided to make me her slave. It was my job to feed the girls, assist the witch with the terrible things she did to the others. I didn't want to do it but I didn't want to die. God forgive the things I have done." Once more she broke into a flood of tears, burying her face into Joseph's shoulder.

"I don't know if she's going to be of much help," Paolo had his doubts. "If she can't stop crying, she's only going to attract their attention.

"She knows her way around this castle. We don't," Joseph

appraised their situation quite succinctly. "I think she's exactly what God thinks we need at this moment."

"You have to admit Paolo," Caesar gave his opinion, "There can be only so many coincidences when they're no longer a coincidence."

"If that is supposed to be profound, Caesar, I think you should probably not try so hard," Paolo ridiculed his friend.

"You know what I'm saying," Caesar retorted.

"Strangely enough, I do," Paolo shook his head.

"Katalin," Joseph grabbed her shoulders tenderly. "I need your help. If we are to do God's work, then I need you to tell me how to find where all the girls are being kept. So I need you to dry your tears and tell me very clearly how I can find them."

Holding back the tears, the young woman tried to explain. "It is a labyrinth. If you don't know the way you will get lost."

"I need to know if a girl named Reisel is kept with the others," Joseph tried to make her understand.

"Yes, she is kept with the others but you will get lost," she repeated.

"I understand that Katalin, but you know the way from this doorway as the starting point. There's a pattern for selecting the right path. There always is. Tell me the pattern Katalin. The lives of all those girls still alive in there depends on you."

Closing her yes, the woman imagined herself moving through the different corridors and back to the dungeons where the girls were held prisoner and tortured. "Right, left, left, right, right, left."

"Are you certain?" Joseph wanted her to go through it again in her mind.

"Yes, that is the way," Katilan confirmed her original description.

"I am grateful to you Katalin. Now I need you to help my friends. They are searching for anything that can help prove the Countess has committed these horrendous crimes. You may be able to help them find those things."

"I can try."

"That's all I can ask from you," Joseph wiped the tears from her cheeks. "Now let's go inside and begin putting an end to this nightmare."

Walking into the doorway, the first reaction they had was one of shock and disgust. They had hardly walked a few steps before they found themselves stepping over the bodies of several girls. Joseph knew immediately how they came to be there. These were all the ones that Katalin had been desperately trying to save. Dragging them through the passages in an effort to bring them outside the castle, where she hoped to revive them so they could escape. But alas, all of them had been bled well beyond the point of survival but that did not stop Katalin from trying. Trying and failing, over and over again, but never giving up. Joseph wrapped his arm around Katalin and made her a promise. "They will be avenged. I promise you."

Reaching the first splitting of the corridors, Joseph knew it was time for him to leave the presence of his friends and go rescue Reisel. He cocked his head to the right indicating which way he had to go.

"Any last words of advice from your father," Joseph asked as he prepared to enter the chasm that led into the hollows of the hillside.

"Only this from Century VIII, Quatrain 95 but I think you know all the details already. This is the one your father told me to recall for you. Remember? Must have some special significance but I don't see it:

'The seducer will be placed in a ditch
and will be tied up for some time.
The scholar joins the chief with his cross.
The sharp right will draw the contented ones.'

"Like I said, "Caesar continued, "Nothing we already haven't taken into account. You'll go underground to find Reisel, Thurzo and the Emperor will keep the Countess busy for a few hours, giving us all the time we need to do what we planned. By the time Paolo and I complete our mission, it will be time for him to administer the antidote to both the Emperor and Gyorgy. It either works or we end up burying both of them. But I don't believe the cross refers to a gravestone but to salvation."

"But what about the sharp right and the contented ones?" Joseph could not make any sense of the last line.

"Not exactly certain," Caesar admitted. "But it sounds like a good thing."

"Best guess then. Obviously my father thought this quatrain was important as proof of your ability. That's why he asked me to raise it with you."

"Well then, if right was being used to suggest those that are morally correct, that stand for truth, and wish to correct the sins of the past, then I believe the 'sharp right' must be us four, who else, other than us has dared to fight the evil and corruption that has impregnated this kingdom? Which leads to the next point, that the kingdom represents the contented ones. Those that are satisfied by the status quo, to leave things as they are and not to prosecute anyone. But when we succeed in this mission, then they have no choice but to side with us. So we draw them to our side."

"That is your uncertain, I'm not sure what it exactly means explanation?" Joseph was surprised because it looked as if Caesar had actually given it a lot of thought.

"Stay safe, Joseph," was all Caesar had to say further as he embraced his companion.

"Wolf, I don't know if you can understand me, but bring you master back from there alive, do you hear me," Paolo talked directly to the animal, whose ears perked up as he was being spoken to and the intelligent look on his face almost suggested that he did understand every word. "Bring Reisel back safely," he hugged Joseph as well. "God protect you both."

Joseph had few words to offer before he turned and entered the chasm that led into the dark underbelly of the hill. "God watch over you both as well, my friends." It only took a few steps before he disappeared into the darkness, relying on the weak flickers of light from the torches ahead, Katalin's instructions and Wolf's keen sense of smell to guide him through the labyrinth.

No sooner had Joseph disappeared from view, when Paolo Sarpi readied for their own mission. "We are relying on you Katalin," Sarpi made her aware of the rapier he carried in its scabbard on his belt by fingering the hilt. "I know that Joseph said we can trust you, and he believes in you completely, but how about I remind you that if you betray that trust it will not end well for you. Do you understand?"

The young woman nodded her head vigorously, the white bonnet slipping across her forehead and almost falling off. She readjusted it and Sarpi noticed the tears in her eyes beginning to well up once again.

"Stop terrifying the girl," Caesar was critical of his colleague's tactics. "Don't mind him, he's just a grumpy old man. I am sure you will do your best to help us Katalin," he attempted to calm her nerves.

"I hate it here," she burst into tears again. "I hate all of them. They are monsters and each day they threaten me if I don't do as they say they will do to me what they do to all the others. I never had a choice," she cried.

"I'm sorry Katalin, when all this is over I promise to return you to your family" Sarpi attempted to soften his rhetoric for the girl's sake.

"I don't have any," she answered, still cowering from Sarpi's earlier threat.

"I'm sorry to hear that," he said sincerely. "Truly I am." Turning to Caesar he made another comment. "The perfect victim. No one to turn to. No one to help. No hope of rescue. Unless you're compliant you won't survive. You don't know how much I want to see these animals with their necks stretched on the block."

"It will happen," Caesar confirmed he had the very same wish.

"How can you be so certain?"

"Because there's a book inside that we must find," Caesar

responded. "My father says so. Century III, Quatrain 48 We find it and it is all over for them."

> *'Seven hundred captives bound roughly.*
> *Lots drawn for the half to be murdered:*
> *The hope at hand will come very promptly*
> *But not as soon as the fifteenth death.'*

"I don't hear any mention of a book," Sarpi could not fathom how Caesar managed to arrive at that conclusion.

"My father liked to play with words," Caesar evoked memories of how his father left behind letters of how he selected words that would conceal cryptic messages in his prophecies and then turned them into games that Caesar had to solve. "You read the words 'bound roughly' and immediately you think of rope ties. "But in truth, he wanted to say that there were approximately seven hundred captives so he uses the word 'roughly'. Now what is rough about being bound? Nothing because of course they would be bound since they are prisoners. But other things are bound, such as a book. So he is telling me there is a book that would provide the precise number of girls that have been taken captive and tortured."

"That's it?" Sarpi was still not convinced.

"Of course not," Caesar admonished him. "You should know that by now. So we know about these captives, and we also know there is no hope for them. Over the past two decades they've all been tortured and killed. So why would my father say that their hope is at hand?"

"I don't know," Paolo admitted. "You tell me."

"Because it's not their hope but their chance for justice that is possible because each one of their names is written by hand into this book. That's why he mentioned 'at hand'. And we will find this book fairy quickly, but only after fifteen people die today."

"As long as we're not one of those fifteen," Sarpi prayed. "So my dear," Paolo decided to use a tender reference to put her at ease. "Do you know anything about a book that the Countess might keep a hand written record in."

The young woman thought about if for a second and then recalled that the Countess kept a book in her bedroom that she would write in every day before she went to bed."

"It's a diary," Sarpi was excited by the prospect of finding real evidence. "Have you seen what's in the book," Sarpi asked her.

"I cannot read Sir," she replied.

"Of course not," Paolo commented, realizing that it was a stupid question. Who would bother to teach an abused servant to read.

"Can you show us where this book is? Can you take us there," Caesar asked in a much softer tone than his companion.

"We can take the back stairs to the sleeping rooms," she revealed there was an alternative path they could take.

"Does anyone else use this stairwell," Caesar wanted to know the likelihood of encountering someone else along the way.

"Only the other servants," she reassured him.

Caesar nodded and winked to each other as they pulled their rapiers form the sheaths. "No harm in being prepared," Sarpi expressed his agreement.

Following Katalin, up endless flights of stairs, that extended all the way from the lower castle to the upper castle, they finally found themselves standing behind the false wall that opened on to the oval hallway that separated all the bedroom chambers that ringed the top floor. The central space of the oval, edged by a polished mahogany balustrade and rail, overlooked the three storeys of the residential part of the castle. Katalin peered through little peep hole in the wall, which ensured that when opening the servant's door, they did not accidentally upturn anything or anyone on the other side.

Katalin then pushed on the lever that rotated the wall on its axis, and together they stepped out onto the floral designed carpet that covered the hardwood floors of the hallway. Both Paolo and Caesar needed to take a moment to absorb the breathtaking view of the Renaissance reconstruction of the upper floor. It was magnificent to behold with its domed plaster ceilings, each section of a dome painted with exotic scenes derived from mythological legends. Other than the non-religious nature of the paintings, one could easily mistake it for the beautiful portraits done by Michelangelo in Rome. They were busy admiring these paintings when Katalin returned their attention to their mission of finding the Countess's bedroom.

Caesar could not help but to admire the central railing that ringed the floor, so that when one was to peer over the side they could stare directly into the main foyers and the marble tiled central hallway far below on the first floor. Two massive chandeliers hung from a system of pulleys, one attached to each end of the domed ceiling. Their design seemed at first incongruous with the renovated style of the castle, appearing more medieval in nature, but the iron filigree that ran between the rings of flaming lights managed to render them into beautiful pieces of artwork. Shame though, Caesar thought to himself, no Frenchman would be caught alive attempting to mix these two very different decorative styles.

Katalin led them to the Countess's suite at the far end of the oval balcony. She tried the handle but the door was locked. Clearly the

Countess had been concerned about the Emperor's visit and wished to impede any search that may have been conducted if matters had soured.

"Step aside," Sarpi instructed her as he reached in to the pockets of his robes and pulled out a metal ring with at least twenty-five keys attached.

"I didn't know you had that," Caesar was surprised by his friend's ingenuity as he looked over his shoulder, while Sarpi fiddled with key after key in the lock.

"I'm the Chief Magistrate of Venice," he reminded Caesar. "As such I'm the holder of all the master skeleton keys in the city. Did you know that almost every key is based on five simple master designs. With these you can open almost anything." By the seventh attempt, Paolo Sarpi found the key that clicked as he turned it in the mechanism of the door to the bedroom suite.

"Most impressive," Caesar commented. "Perhaps one day you can lend me those to make a set of copies."

"For what purpose?" Paolo was intrigued as to Caesar's motives.

"The Church has so many secrets it has locked away," Caesar smiled devilishly. "Imagine what I could find with a set of keys like those."

"I might even consider it," Paolo answered. "But for now, we have a job to do." He opened the door, permitting everyone to slip through before he closed it behind himself. Once inside the suite of rooms, the hard part of the task began. Every drawer on every dresser, commode, armoire, night table, vanity table, cupboard had to be searched until they found this diary. For a woman as rich as Elizabeth Bathory, that meant it was going to take a considerable amount of time. The more obvious places close to the bed turned up empty in the search. The drawers where she stored all her clothes offered no sign of the diary either. The three were becoming discouraged after the first hour past and they had nothing to show for their efforts.

"We need to think about this more carefully," Paolo commented to the others. "We need to think like a woman," he stared at Katalin for answers but it was obvious that she could not help in this regard, having never been more than a servant girl in the household. "What would I record in this diary that would make it useful?" he proposed the question to Caesar.

"Obviously the names and details of each of the girls she murdered," Caesar arrived at the obvious.

"But why would she care? That has to be critical to her thinking."

"Because each girl might represent a different attribute," the son of Nostradamus determined. "What does every women want?" the question was rhetorical. "Soft skin, youthful appearance, ample breasts, silky hair, rosy lips, the list is endless my friend."

"Exactly," Sarpi stabbed his finger into the air. "Each girl represents different aspects of beauty. Different organs selected for different purposes. Annise Darvolya may have determined what secretions, from which organs, would deliver the desired response that a vain, aging woman would want. She would need to find a delivery system and what better than using blood, if it was already the way the body normally carried these secretions . She could make pastes, potions, creams from everything she gathered, but she would still have needed to maintain a record of which girl provided a specific bottle and what that bottle was intended to do. And after she died, it automatically became Elizabeth Bathory's responsibility to keep that record up to date. And like any woman, the Countess would sit in front of a mirror, determine what feature she might wish to touch up on a particular day and then she would need to refer to her diary in order to make the right choice. So there's only one place she would keep that book…"

"The vanity," they answered in unison.

"But I checked the vanity," Katalin informed them.

"You checked the drawers," Paolo knew right away that would have been the limit of her search. "But something so important, not to mention so incriminating, would not be left sitting in a drawer where it could easily be discovered."

"A false compartment," Caesar knew where Paolo was leading.

"Precisely,"

Marching into the Countess's dressing room, they began removing every drawer, searching for false backs and false bottoms. Pulling and prodding every leg and corner of the vanity they forced the joints of the exquisite Louis XII dresser to separate but still they found nothing. It wasn't until they pulled the elaborate scroll-work from the base of the mirror that they finally exposed the vertical eight inch wide slot where the diary was hidden. Once removed, Paolo saw that the key to exposing the book was to simply slide the scroll-word to the left as it slid on a thin wooden track, but that didn't matter any more.

Flipping through the pages of the book, Paolo confirmed that it was the diary containing all the details from the girls that had been sacrificed over the years, extending even back to the years her husband was raging his war in the Eastern territories. Feeling victorious, their mission a success, the three of them had paid little attention to the amount of noise they had made taking apart the mirrored vanity. Suddenly they heard what sounded like a door into the bedroom open and then close. It was a surprise, because other than the main doorway from the lounge suite into the bedroom, they had not noticed any other doors leading into the bed chamber.

Whomever it was made no point of trying to remain quiet as they heard him calling out, "Who's in here."

"It is Fizcko," Katalin sounded panicked, her voice trembling as she mentioned his name.

"Fizcko? I've heard that name before," Caesar recollected only to be reminded by Paolo that it was the hunchback in the Countess's employ.

"Please, don't let him find me," the young woman begged, clutching on to Caesar as if her life depended on him. "He's a hideous monster. They let him do terrible things to me. They watch as he violates me over and over again," she burst into tears.

"I hear someone crying," they heard Fizcko say as he began to approach the boudoir. "Is that you little serving girl?" he questioned in what he obviously mistook as a game of hide and seek. "I come to find you little serving girl," he chortled.

"Get ready to charge him when he comes through the doorway," Paolo suggested to Caesar, figuring if they bowl him over then they will be able to subdue him.

What they saw enter into view managed to shock the both of them. Far more than a hunchback, the twisted body sat upon legs far too short for a full grown man. His head was large, too large for the narrow shoulders that supported it, with protuberances of bone jutting from his forehead and chin. One eye drooped well below the other. But his arms and fists were enormous, as if taken them from an ape and then stitched on to his diminutive frame. His startling appearance made them hesitate but once they regained their wits they charged towards their adversary together.

With a backhanded swat of his left arm, Fizcko knocked Paolo across the room, flying at least five feet through the air before he landed hard against the floor. With his right hand he caught Caesar around the throat and held him inches off the ground while he choked the breath from him. Regaining his wits, Paolo drew his rapier and swung it hard against the bony outcropping that twisted along the creature's back. His sword only managed to break skin but could not even make a nick into the osseous ridge that served as Fizcko's spine. But it was enough to gain his full attention and Fizcko flung Caesar to the side as if he was a rag doll. Paolo raised his sword again to strike, but the hunchback moved surprisingly fast, ramming Sarpi into the wall and pinning him against it while he raised his own meaty fist to strike.

Paolo closed his eyes, preparing for the worst but the blow failed to materialize as he heard the sound of a clamorous metallic ring instead.

The arm pinning him against the wall relaxed but didn't release him from his predicament. Then he heard the sound again, but this time he opened his eyes to see Katalin, standing with the bed-warmer in her hands, the cast iron pot at the end of the pole, used to hold the hot coals, already dented from the couple of strikes against Fizcko's skull. The hunchback was dazed but he still fought to retain his consciousness. He let Paolo fall from his grasp and turned to face the little servant girl.

Caesar called to Katalin to toss him the bed warmer. He caught it in full flight and with a mighty swing brought it fully against the left side of Fizcko's head. It hit with such force that the pole of the bed-warmer snapped in two.

Caesar was out of breath, as he stared down at the monstrosity laying on the ground. The blow would have killed any other man, but Fizcko was still breathing, albeit shallowly. Katalin took advantage of this one time she could inflict any pain on her tormentor, kicking him repeatedly in the head until Caesar pulled her away.

"Well that was certainly a sharp right," Paolo commented, "I am definitely content now that I'm not having the life squeezed out of me."

"I am content too," Katalin said excitedly as she managed to throw another two kicks at Fizcko's head, despite Caesar restraining her.

"Promise me that you won't tell Joseph about this 'sharp right' thing," Caesar sought their approval. "I don't think this is the time we want him to start doubting some of my interpretations or to know that his father was having a little joke at my expense."

"My lips are sealed," Paolo promised. Pulling up beside the prone body, Sarpi studied Fizcko carefully. "Amazing," was his first word to the others. "She really did it!" he sounded excited.

"What are you talking about?" Caesar was confused. "What did Katalin do?"

"Not her," Paolo corrected him. "Annise, she did it. She used the humors she obtained from the girls to actually change his physical structure. You see," he pointed to the ridge of protruding and curved vertebra that ran along Fizcko's back, "This developed after treatment. I'm guessing that initially he was a dwarf but Annise managed to induce further growth in the bone. She just couldn't control it properly. It became too dense in some places, and too long in others, causing it to twist out of shape, but essentially she did it. She had found a cure for dwarfism."

"If you think this is a cure, then I think I prefer the disease," Caesar repudiated Paolo's optimism.

Suddenly Fizcko started to grunt more heavily.

"I think he's starting to wake up. We better get out of here," Paolo suggested.

Exiting the boudoir, they still had to be concerned that all the noise they had generated may have alarmed any of the guards that might be patrolling the halls. Paolo slowly opened the outer door to the en-suite and scanned up and down the hall. "All clear," he turned to the others. Leaving the Countess's bedroom, all they had to do now was return to the servant's stairway and make their way to the outside.

Caesar heard what sounded like shoes scuffing against the tile surface far below, as if someone was trying very hard not to make a sound but because of the nature of their foot-ware couldn't succeed. He hung over the rail, looking down at perhaps a dozen dark robed men gathering in the foyer located immediately outside the Countess's private dining room. He peered through the glass ceiling at the Emperor and Gyorgy dining with Elizabeth Bathory, oblivious to the gathering outside their room. In the adjacent sunroom, beneath the same glass ceiling were his elite guard, separated from His Majesty by two sets of doors. "Assassins!" he whispered in a low rumble, loud enough to catch Paolo's attention. They knew they had to do something quickly.

Caesar focused his attention on the massive chandelier that he had critiqued earlier. There it was, consisting of five concentric rings of heavy wrought iron hung from a pulley, the rope attached to a winch and ratchet crank affixed to the wall. The largest outer ring held fifty candles around its circumference, then the next internal ring held, twenty-six, the next fourteen, the next six and finally four on the innermost ring. It hung directly over the foyer far below. Caesar pointed to it and Paolo nodded, understanding exactly what he meant.

"Give me a second and I'll figure out how to release the winch," Paolo studied the mechanism.

"We don't have a second," Caesar told him as he unsheathed his sword and in one swift motion sliced through the heavy cord sending the chandelier hurtling downward like a cannonball to the surface below.

They didn't even bother to see if the massive missile had hit its target. The noise alone they figured would be enough to bring the elite guard running to the defense of their Emperor. Katalin had the servant's door open before they even reached the end of the hallway, With a click of its lock it swung closed and the three of them raced down one flight of stairs after the other until they found themselves outside the lower castle, in the clearing where they had first met the young woman.

They raced to the designated meeting point, waiting impatiently for the Emperor and Gyorgy to arrive. From above, they heard the clang of metal, and knew that the Emperor's men were forcing their way past the sentries that obviously tried to block them. It was surprising that any of the Countess's men would have even attempted to stop the combined force of the Emperor's guard and Thurzo's police officers but then as they suspected, all of the Countess's men were complicit in the murders she had committed. As condemned men they had nothing to loose by resisting. Their failure was hardly noteworthy as they were easily overcome and the elite guard arrived with both Matthias and Gyorgy carried in their arms within minutes of hearing the first sounds of steel against steel.

They laid both leaders on the ground in front of the Chief Magistrate of Venice.

"What in Seven Hells, Sarpi, my gut feels like its being torn apart from the inside," the Palatine complained bitterly.

"I didn't say that you wouldn't suffer any pain," Sarpi corrected him. "All I said was I can slow it down until I had time to give you the tartaric acid to remove most of it from your stomach. Now drink this and we will see what we are dealing with." Paolo gave the Emperor and the Palatine each a cup of the brown foul smelling liquid to drink.

"This is terrible," the Emperor whined, fighting hard to get it past his lips.

"All of it," Paolo Sarpi insisted.

Both did as he said and within seconds they began heaving into the small burlap bags that the magistrate had provided. The retching continued long after there was nothing left to empty from their stomachs.

"Is it supposed to hurt this much," the Emperor continued to complain as he rubbed his belly, trying to ease the pain.

"Yes," Paolo snapped at him, "And be grateful your stomach does hurt. It means that in all likelihood we contained all of it before it managed to go elsewhere in your digestive system. The both of you will recover fully in a few hours. Now let's see what we have."

Peering into the bag, Paolo Sarpi used a long pair of metal tongs to sift through the ingesta. "There it is," his expression was jubilant as he pulled out a cinnamon red coloured mushroom cap. "What a beauty." Looking closely he could see the dull white specks flecked across its rounded surface. "Panther mushrooms," he identified the fungus gleefully. "Death within three hours if not dealt with properly. You now have your proof of treason and attempted murder your Majesty. These weren't picked accidentally, considering they grow in fairy rings in the forest. Every child in Europe knows to fear the fairy rings."

"I only have proof that her cooking staff tried to kill me," Matthias countered the statement.

"What about the assassins," Caesar forced himself into the conversation.

"You two were somehow responsible for all those dead men outside the dining room?" the Emperor was in awe.

"In a way," Caesar replied modestly.

"You should have at least waited until they shouted a threat," the Emperor was still not satisfied. "She'll will probably say they were her kitchen staff and we can't prove otherwise."

Paolo Sarpi could still see that the Emperor was still reluctant to lay any charges directly against the Countess. "All that you say is true," he agreed, throwing Mathias off guard, But we didn't yet have a chance to mention that while you both were busy dining and and keeping the Countess occupied, Caesar and I were going through the Countess's belongings. We found this," Sarpi held up the diary, showing some of the internal pages to both Matthias and Gyorgy. "In her own handwriting," he pointed out. "Descriptions of over six hundred girls and how she committed their murders and what organs and tissues she took from their bodies. I think it will now be simple enough for even the most junior of prosecutors to connect the attempt on your lives with the woman that perpetrated these murders."

"You should hand that diary over to Melchior," Matthias suggested.

"I was going to discuss that with you later your Majesty when you were feeling better, but perhaps we can do it now. I want to be one of the three judges for the tribunal. Since I am the most knowledgeable party of the events and crimes committed by the accused, and recognized as one of the better legal minds in all of Europe, I think that it is a reasonable request. Don't you?" Paolo Sarpi didn't wait for a reply from the Emperor. "So being that it is the likely situation that I will be on the tribunal bench, I will just hold on to this diary for safe keeping." There was no way in the world that Paolo Sarpi was ever going to release custody of that book.

"Well then," the Emperor acquiesced to Sarpi's demand to be one of the judges, "We might as well begin our journey back to Vienna. Gyorgy, I'll leave it to you and your men to wrap everything up here. See to it that you try to take some of the prisoners alive, so that we have at least a few people that can appear in court and be sentenced." The comment was clearly a reference and criticism of the annihilation of everyone that the Countess had left behind at Castle Bran.

"And where is Joseph Kahana? The Emperor sounded concerned. "Shouldn't he be back by now? Someone find out where he is," the Emperor commanded.

Having just left his two companions at the entrance-way, Joseph moved through the shadows, edging himself along the rough stone walls, while avoiding any of the well illuminated areas within the chasm. Wolf plodded along closely at his heels, as if knowing that he too had to avoid being detected.

In his mind he ran over the instructions given to him by Katalin. "Right, left, left, right, right, left." It sounded simple but in the dark one's mind begins to play tricks and you can't help bout wonder if you missed an exit or didn't go far enough. While Joseph tried to ensure that he stayed on the right path, Wolf was already striding ahead as if he knew exactly where to go.

Coming to the last left turn, Joseph was relieved to see the burst of light that lay ahead. He knew it had to be the dungeon, never doubting that Katalin's instruction were correct. He considered himself lucky thus far, no one else had been using the tunnels and other than the sounds of what sounded like water dripping there were no sounds of any activity up ahead.

He looked into the huge chamber and felt his heart race as he saw Reisel sitting naked on her own in one of the cells. There were several other cells, each containing several girls, all of them stripped naked as well. Seeing his beloved shamed in this manor fueled the rage that had been steadily building up inside from the moment he started this mission. Now it had reached the point where he wanted someone to pay for all the cruelty, all the harm, all the suffering they had caused. And for one of the few times in his life, Joseph felt as if he could kill someone without any remorse and certainly without guilt.

"Reisel," he called out, trying not to shout yet overcome by the sheer elation that she was alive and appeared to be unharmed.

Hearing his voice she snapped out of the daydreams she would use to shield herself from the horrors she had seen and raced to the front of he cell, pressing her face to the bars, overcome with excitement that Joseph had come to her rescue. In her jubilation, she didn't even pay attention to her own nakedness, tears of joy streaming down her face as she watched him look around for anything he could use to pry open the cell door.

Leaning against the wall was a heavy metal bar topped by a sculpted bronze rosebud. He didn't know what it was for but it certainly looked like it would be strong enough to wedge between the cell door and the bars. He hefted it in his hands, feeling the weight and nodded his approval. 'This will do nicely,' he thought. He turned and began moving towards her cell, but as he approached he watched the features of her face change from extreme exaltation to abject horror. He new immediately something was wrong.

"Behind you!" Reisel screamed but the warning came too late as Joseph and Wolf were already rushing towards the cell holding Reisel when they became aware of the terrifying growl coming from behind.

As they turned their heads, out of the corner of their eyes they could see rushing upon them the great gray wolf, larger and heavier than any wolf they could imagine. Broad of shoulder, atop which sat its massive head, this truly was the alpha male, that had been absent from all their prior skirmishes with the wolf warriors. This was the last wolf in possession of their mortal enemy and the one whose soul purpose appeared to be the prevention of anyone releasing the imprisoned girls. Before they could even move to one side, the old gray had hurled himself towards Joseph, intent on the kill. The blotches of white fur around the eyes, the mouth and on its chest all indicated the advancing age of the beast, but still it moved as quick as the wind, embodying all the intensity and fury of a major storm.

In desperation, Joseph was able to raise the iron rod at the last second to a position in front of his face, holding it with both hands and then forcibly wedging it between the jaws of the monstrous creature so that its teeth chomped deep into the metal, barely scraping the flesh of Joseph's neck. The hundred pounds of muscular fury was enough to knock Joseph backwards, his head ringing against the bars of the cell and momentarily rendering him semi-conscious in a pain filled daze. Barely an inch from his face, he squirmed at the touch of the hot saliva dripping freely onto his lips. The fetid odour of the drool was enough to overpower his senses, as he felt the strength in his arms quickly dwindling and the fear rising that he could no longer hold back the snarling beast from freeing itself from the iron wedge.

His muscles were strained to their limit, to their point of exhaustion when suddenly the opposing pressure dissipated instantly, and at the same time he heard the crunch of bone, followed by the indescribable howl of pain emerging from the beast. Focused completely on Joseph, the gray wolf had paid no attention at all to the smaller red wolf, which in defense of its master had torn into the hind tibia and calf muscles of its nemesis. Shaking his head back and forth with its prize bone squarely between its jaws, Wolf dragged the much heavier animal off of Joseph to a safe distance at the centre of the chamber.

Overcoming the shock of both the attack and the pain, the gray wolf was able to roll itself sideways, unbalancing Wolf, who immediately lost his footing and fell to the ground, but still continued to grasp the torn leg in his mouth. Stretching his neck and shoulders to look behind, the gray had Wolf's haunches in easy reach, instinctively sinking its own razor sharp teeth close to Wolf's spine as it tore the flesh away. Pools of port coloured blood immediately gathered in the gaping wound as Wolf screamed in pain, releasing the hold on the leg and allowing the old gray to hobble free, slowly rising on to its three good appendages.

Joseph stared haplessly, comparing the shorter stature of Wolf to this beast from Hell, and he knew immediately that the gray completely outmatched his animal in every category. In height, Wolf's head barely reached the shoulders of his opponent. Wolf's forehead may have been broader, but the gray's snout was much longer and when it bared its yellow fangs, each tooth looked the size of dagger blades. Thinking the best chance they had to defeat this beast was to draw him back to where Joseph now stood, having drawn his rapier from the scabbard on his belt, Joseph commanded his wolf-dog to come to his side but Wolf ignored him. "Come here now!" Joseph ordered but now it was clear that Wolf was no longer listening, consumed by animal bloodlust.

The stones where Wolf had been laying were now slick with his blood and as the gray moved counterclockwise, trying to circle around its enemy, it lost the footing of the one good hind leg it was still using, sliding down heavily on its chest as it collapsed. Joseph saw an opportunity to move Wolf to safety. "Come here boy, " he commanded but again Wolf did not respond to the command. The gray was able to pull himself back onto his feet, yelping in pain as it made the mistake of trying to use its damaged back leg. Wolf remained motionless, his wound still dripping profusely but without showing any indication of pain. The big gray lumbered towards its adversary, attempting to not put any pressure on the leg that Wolf had spiked down to the bone.

Oblivious to the size and weight differentials, Wolf was not backing down, not scrambling to run away, and that in itself was drove the gray into an unfathomable rage, evidenced by the snarling, hissing and rumbling growl that managed to terrify even the girls that were well protected behind their iron bars. Wolf still refused to run, focused entirely on his nemesis. No longer feeling any fear or pain, Wolf was still completely oblivious to his master's voice as Joseph continued to beg him to return to his side. That part of him that was still wild knew that in this world of his ancestors, there was only one choice to make. A fight for supremacy; a fight for dominance; a fight until death. Watching carefully, the gray continued moving forward, still limping and staggering as it tried methodically to circle behind Wolf, treating the smaller red wolf like any other prey it had ever hunted.

Wolf made no effort to attack, carefully watching his adversary as if learning each step for the very first time, and once known he began circling as well. Waiting, circling, each would do their spiraling dance of death, darting in quickly with mouths wide open, snapping repeatedly in an effort to try and snare the other, then retreating backwards as quickly as they attacked when their jaws came up empty.

The gray was a well practiced killer, a beast that preyed on anything weaker than itself, and over the years it had made quite a name for itself. This was the werewolf that haunted the forests at night, terrorizing the local farmer's stock and devouring children foolish enough to venture through the woods in the dark. This was the monster that when standing on its hind legs was as tall as any man but three to four times as strong. For years, tales of the monster in the forest had surfaced but none realized that he could never be found because the beast was always safe and secure in this, his master's sanctuary.

Every movement the animal made rippled the heavily developed musculature that bulged as a constant display of strength and prowess. Its long muzzle, now trimmed with the white of age created the illusion of the teeth being twice their normal length. This was a creature of pure savagery, a programmed machine with no other purpose but to kill. Its expectations were simple, thinking of nothing other than inflicting death or dying in the effort. But strength often proves to be a weakness and whether the creature knew it or not, its own limitation of purpose was also its fatal flaw.

Wolf had something the old gray didn't; a combination of wolf cunning but having been raised by Joseph, the imprinting of human intelligence. Unlike his adversary, he could think beyond the blood lust, able to string several thoughts together as if forming a strategy rather than simply attacking blindly. It was that human exposure that rendered him the most formidable opponent the old gray had ever faced. Already he was recovering from the wound inflicted on his flank, as the blood clotted, and he regained his speed and agility. The gray would take a step and in response Wolf would take two or three in the same space of time. It was as if Wolf recognized his ability to move swifter than his clumsier three legged opponent and he began to circle faster, forcing the old gray to spin around on his one good hind leg. Unbalanced from time to time, the gray would attempt to use the damaged leg for support causing it to grunt heavily in obvious pain.

Tiring of this game, the old gray responded with a ferocious roar, fueled by an intensifying rage the more it had to put weight on the damaged leg. A mixture of hate and savagery, the creature was letting that rage overwhelm its other senses, abandoning the normal cunning of the species as it tried to dart into the centre more frequently to snare Wolf in its jaws and put an end to this prolonged stalemate. In response, Wolf nimbly pranced away from each attack, increasing the speed of his circling until the old gray was no longer even trying to pace the outer circumference but merely revolved on a single spot at the centre of Wolf's dance.

Waiting for that one opportunity, Wolf sprang at the old gray, ripping its throat wide open and in the process tearing the jugular which spouted blood in a showering rain. Already in its death throes, Wolf continued to attack, this time disemboweling the beast as he tore into the belly with both teeth and claws. The gray monster lay motionless on the stone floor. Wolf pawed at his nemesis, reaching out repeatedly to prod the muzzle to see if there was any reaction but the spark of life was long gone. Excited by his victory, Wolf stood over the body of his kill and for the first time that Joseph recalled ever hearing, released a feral howl that veritably shook the foundation stones of the castle.

Moving gingerly towards his animal, Joseph carefully held out a welcoming hand to Wolf, unsure of how his pet would react. At first Wolf appeared hesitant, even growling as Joseph approached. Still unsure, Joseph was within a hand's distance of the animal's head when Wolf's demeanour suddenly changed and he whined softly, nuzzling the extended hand and then seeking a pat from his master. Joseph reached out and brought Wolf fully into his embrace, cushioning the animal's head against his chest, as he cried tears of both relief and happiness. With a blood stained tongue, Wolf licked his master's face, but Joseph didn't care. "That's my good boy," Joseph whispered softly into Wolf's ears.

Taking the opportunity to examine the wound on Wolf's flank, Joseph could see it was deep but other than some damage to the muscle and far more extensive damage to the skin, it did not appear to be life threatening. He'd have Sarpi take a look and clean it up once they had completed their tasks in the castle. But now it was time to free everyone from the locked dungeons and get them as far away from the torture site as possible. Picking up the metal rod again, he wedged it between the bars of the cage and the door to Reisel's cell. The centuries old lock easily gave away and the cell door swung open at which point Reisel rushed into his arms and hung around his neck.

"I knew you would come for me," she said, as she shed her own tears of joy and relief.

Letting the rod fall from his hands, it rang loudly as it hit the stone floor but by that time Joseph already had his arms wrapped tightly around the body of his betrothed, lifting her off the ground so that they could share the kiss that each had been wanting for so long.

"I am only sorry it has taken so long my Love," Joseph apologized. "I was worried that you would think I had abandoned you all these months."

"Never!" she exclaimed. "Never would I have thought that. I always knew you'd be coming."

"I tried so hard to be here so long ago," he tried to explain.

Placing a finger to his lips, she answered for him, "I know. They would taunt me, trying to break down my spirit, to crush my feeling for you but in so doing they only reinforced my knowledge that you were coming."

Joseph did not understand, "They taunted you? How?"

"Months ago they told me you had been lost in the Ottoman Empire. That the Turks had probably done them the favour and killed all of you. But then weeks later they told me that their army in Bucharest would manage to slice the heads from the shoulders of all that still remained in your unit. So right then I knew you had survived the Turks. And then about a week after that they told me that their wolves would tear you apart and devour your flesh, so once again I knew you had survived Bucharest. Weeks later they swore that you would fall at Brasov when you attacked the castle, and I knew that you had escaped death by the wolves. And finally they said they would give me the privilege of watching you die in this chamber and then I knew you would be coming to free me. How could I lose hope when it was obvious that God had given you the strength to overcome all of your enemies. They did not even realize that with every event they tried to crush my spirit with, they only raised it higher and gave me the hope that you would be here soon."

Through their own arrogance, Bathory and her servants had provided Reisel the strength and fortitude to survive her captivity.

"But now I need you to take Wolf and leave this castle," Joseph urged her to leave as he searched around to find any discarded clothing in the chamber that he could cover her nakedness with. There was a pile of clothes standing in one corner of the chamber that they must have been accumulating for years, it was piled so high. Tossing whatever looked suitable, he pleaded with her to get dressed quickly. "Wolf will show you the way to the outside. Now go!"

"I don't want to leave you," Reisel at first refused to listen.

"I still have to free everyone else. There may be some of the Countess's men arriving here at any moment. I'm certain they heard all the noise. I can't do what needs to be done if I have to worry about you. So please go. I will be out as soon as I can."

Reisel understood his concern. "I love you," she said as she turned to go.

"And I love you, now please go. Wolf," he commanded. "Go out boy! Go with Reisel! Leave Boy," The animal looked at him whimsically but did not move.

Pointing to the exit, Joseph shouted his order firmly, "Wolf, GO!"

Understanding clearly the tone of the command, Wolf directed Reisel towards the labyrinth that they had used to enter the chamber and soon both of them disappeared from view, giving Joseph the opportunity to get back to the mission of freeing the others.

Wedging the metal rod between the bars, he was able to snap the doors open on the other cells just as he had done with Reisel's cell, Pointing to the same exit where Wolf had gone, he told everyone that had emerged from the open cells to go that way. Most did not understand the words he said but they knew the intent of his finger as it pointed to freedom. Some took the time to grab clothing from the pile in the chamber, others didn't bother, not wishing to spend another second in the dungeons longer than they had to.

While working on the last cell door, Joseph heard the door from the floor above open and knew immediately that someone was coming. He tried to withdraw the rod from between the bars in which it was wedged but it would not give. Pulling as hard as he could, it finally slid out but at the same time he realized he must have activated some mechanism within the rod because the rose bud at the tip suddenly sprang open exposing row upon row of razor like petals.

"What's going on down there?" the voice echoed from the descending stairway into the chambers and reverberated off the walls of the granite stone cells. "Do I have to give you girls a beating again?"

Upon hearing it, Joseph recognized the voice immediately and steadied himself for the inevitable encounter. Laying down the rod, he stood upright and withdrew his rapier once again from its scabbard.

"Ah, so it is you," Captain Rodescu announced his presence when he descended the last stair and stood at the opposite side of the chamber. Once his eyes adjusted to the dim light he noticed the old gray wolf laying dead at the centre of the room. He released a visceral cry of anguish that was more animal than human.

"What have you done?" he shouted in shock and dismay. "My beautiful pet," he bemoaned his loss, "Your are going to pay for this! I swear I'm going to kill you. I don't give a shit what she might say about it any more!"

"Perhaps you should think about this," Joseph attempted to talk his way out of the situation. "Count Thurzo is already here with his men, everyone knows what you all have done, perhaps if you surrender now, I can persuade them to give you a lighter sentence if you cooperate."

"Why don't you just shut the fuck up!" the captain unsheathed his rapier and prepared to attack.

Joseph held up his blade, assuming a defensive stance, readying himself to repel the attack. "Killing me will not change anything."

"Probably not," Captain Rodescu agreed, "But it certainly will feel good and provide me with the satisfaction of revenge for my wolf."

Swiftly moving towards Joseph, he made a lunge, only to have it parried to the side by Joseph's own blade. He rushed forward, faking a thrust and then quickly converting his blow into a side stroke, but once again, Joseph was able to block steel with steel.

"Ah," the Captain took notice, "I see you know a little something about swordsmanship."

"One does not grow up as an orphan on the streets of Brody without learning the means by which to stay alive," Joseph informed him.

Rodescu lunged again, but Joseph parried then drove him back with a couple of swift slashes, the second making a small cut into the fabric over the shoulder of the Captain's doublet.

"Not bad for an amateur," Rodescu commended his opponent. "Let us see how you do against this move." The Captain performed a well rehearsed dance of a lunge, feint, retreat and then backwards slice to the thigh. Joseph managed to avoid all the moves, except for the slice which managed to nick him on the right thigh. A trickle of blood beaded from the cut in his pants but it was so minor Joseph did not even feel it.

"You obviously bleed like any other man," Rodescu commented upon noticing the wound he had inflicted. "Nothing special from what I see, The Countess I believe is mistaken about you."

"She has been mistaken about a lot of things," Joseph informed his opponent. "And because of her mistakes, you are all going to pay for your sins."

"So says the Jew who thinks he can freely walk in the daylight of Austrian society. No matter what titles by which you disguise yourself, you will always be a dirty Jew."

"So be it," Joseph saluted by raising the blade to his brow, followed by a jab and a thrust.

Valerie Rodescu was not prepared for Joseph to suddenly transform into being the aggressor and in so doing, he was forced to take several backwards steps. The Captain parried and then locked his blade beneath the quillon of Joseph's hilt guard. With a quick upward flick, he managed to pry the rapier free of Joseph's hand and send it skirting across the stone floor to the opposite end of the chamber.

Joseph stood weaponless in front of his adversary, his rapier too far away to retrieve and Rodescu just two steps and a plunge from taking his life. A rapacious smile crept across the Captain's face as he prepared to put an end to the duel. He took his first step but surprisingly didn't make any progress, actually sliding backwards on the blood soaked floor. In dismay, he looked down at his feet only to find that he had become entangled in the rope like intestines of his disemboweled wolf. He had not realized when he retreated from Joseph's attack, he had placed his feet into such a precarious position.

As Rodescu tried to free himself from intestinal loops of the old gray wolf, Joseph quickly looked for anything close at hand that he could use to defend himself. The metal rod was just a couple of feet away. Picking it up quickly, Joseph charged directly at the Captain with the rod's open rose petals slicing through the chest of his doublet and burrowing into the flesh underneath. The Captain screamed and cursed in pain as he felt the cut of the first blades pressing against his ribs. It only took a moment for Joseph to understand how the contraption actually worked. He began twisting the rod, watching the rose petals bore deeper and deeper into Rodescu's chest cavity, hearing the snap of ribs and cartilage, all the while the Captain, howling in agony as he was being impaled. Driving forward, twisting, pushing, feeling the spray of blood ejected on to his face, Joseph did not release the rod until the Captain's knees crumpled and his body fell lifeless on top of the beast that he had trained to kill.

Momentarily hanging his head, Joseph reflected on what he had done, on what he had become. There was no remorse, no pangs of guilt but the feeling of satisfaction actually terrified him. It wasn't until he heard the whimpering of the girls remaining in the last unopened cell that he was able to come to grips with what he had done. Not with the fact that he had killed someone, but the fact that there are time where death is the only answer. The fact that he had saved these young girls, innocents not deserving of the torture and horrific deaths that were in store for them, reminded him that sometimes there are just and honourable causes that can only be weighed in the balance of death.

Using the rod as a lever once more, he sprung open the last cell door to free the last two girls. Seeing that the older one was barely moving, huddled naked on the cold stone floor, he urged the younger girl to go find some clothing from the pile to cover her with. The girl responded immediately, grabbing a dress for herself as well as one for the other girl. As Joseph wrapped the girl in the woolen dress, he could not help but notice the wounds covering her body. There were lacerations, some shallow, others deep, from neck to toes. Evidence of needle pricks covered her back and buttocks. But worst of all was the evidence left behind from the mechanical rose bud between her legs. The poor girl was on the threshold of death, having lost an unknown quantity of blood during her torture, but she was hanging on through sheer determination and strength of will and that provided Joseph with hope of her survival. He picked her up in his arms, cradling her like a baby as he began the slow march to the exterior of the castle, praying to God to keep her alive. As if hearing his prayer, the girl in his arms reached up and touched Joseph's face as if to say thank you.

"What's her name?" Joseph asked the other girl that was walking closely beside him, practically hugging his waist, afraid to even move an inch away from her blessed saviour.

"Elana," the girl answered.

"Elana what?" Joseph was eager to know.

"Elana Tsepesh," she replied.

Chapter Twenty-Three

Cachtice: New Year's Eve 1610

As instructed, Gyorgy Thurzo remained behind with his men to put an end to the unholy reign of Countess Bathory once and for all. For his own personal well-being, he had to see it through to the end. If he didn't, he knew his soul would never find any peace. It wasn't because of the number of times that his cousin had attempted to kill him, it wasn't even a result of the over six hundred names of girls she had murdered and listed in her diary. No, this was something that went far deeper than any of those reasons. Reasons that Gyorgy Thurzo had kept buried internally for over ten years and now for the first time he felt the heavy burden on his heart was about to be lifted.

Positioning his men around the base of the hill, some laying prone, others kneeling in the tall grass, they waited for that one fatal mistake when someone from inside the castle would come down from their mountain, seeking out food or water. It had been six days already since he started the siege and he expected any time soon, that opportunity would arise. The cat merely had to wait for the mouse to pop its head out of the hole.

He knew what everyone else was thinking about him. What would drive a man to surrender well over ten years of his life chasing after a phantom that constantly eluded his grasp? Why would a man give up his home life, his family, all the things that mattered to everyone else? The Archduke would say it was his sense of duty, the Emperor, his sense of loyalty, and even the three adventurers that he had spent a year of his life with would attribute it to an idealistic sense of honour and integrity. But they were all wrong. No one ever asked, no one ever thought to ask. He reflected on his time with his three companions and how in the year they spent together, none of them ever inquired into his life. Perhaps they just assumed that what they saw was his life and there was no other existence to talk about.

Yes, Senor Paolo Sarpi could be a pain in the ass, but Thurzo had to admit, he was a damn good investigator. He was confident that as one of the Tribunal judges, justice would be served, otherwise Senor Sarpi would make the Archduke's life a living hell. And as for Caesar de Nostradame, what could he possibly say about Caesar other than one of the strangest human beings that he had ever met. Someone living in this world but at the same time having his foot in some far off place that others could never imagine. How strange it must be to feel like your entire life is merely an extension of the man that came before you and the decisions you made were never really your own. Now Joseph, there was a hard nut to crack, Thurzo thought to himself. As hard as nails, fearless in every respect, able to stare evil directly in its face and not even blink, and yet, the love of a woman, or in this case a girl, could reduce him to hover at the brink of despair, blinded like Samson by his own Delilah . Perhaps that's why he liked him so much, having seen a common thread that ran between their lives.

A strange combination those three, he thought, and yet, together they became something much stronger than their individual parts. Together they would march into Hell and back and do it all again if they needed to without hesitation. Yes, there was an invisible force that bound those three together, a power beyond this world that gave them the ability, if even for the briefest of moments to see through each others eyes and walk in one others shoes

He knew all along that he could be with them, but he could never actually be one of them. Yes, he had his own reason for doing what he did but they never thought to ask. No one ever asks; he accepted that fact. As Palatine of Hungary, bringing the lawless to justice was what it said in the job description. But there were other villains, other murderers that required far less investment in time and sacrifice. No, they never bothered to ask. Most people don't care to know.

"Commander," one of his men called his attention. "Commander look over there. Over by the trees."

Looking out to the distance, Gyorgy could make out the figures of two women standing close to the heavily treed area where Joseph had said they found the clearing and entrance way into the lower castle. He stared harder into the darkness and could now see that it was his cousin Erzsibet and her Steward, Erzsi Majorova. Majorova was reciting some kind of incantation in a mixture of Latin and Hungarian. From the few words he could pick out, he understood it was some sort of protection spell to ward off anyone trying to enter the castle grounds. Looking about he could see that whatever she was doing was unnerving some of his men. He then heard his name mentioned in the spell, cursing it forever and calling down a lifetime of demonic punishments until he begged for death.

He reached under his collar and pulled out the only piece of jewellery he ever wore, a locket that hung from a silver linked necklace. Opening the locket case, Gyorgy Thurzo sighed as he stared at the picture of the beautiful young girl who's life like painting was with him every hour of every day. He blew a kiss to her and wiped away a silent tear. "Tonight Zsari, tonight you get your justice." He closed the locket and placed it back underneath his waistcoat.

While his men stared on in bewilderment, Gyorgy Thurzo loaded his musket with a wad and powder, rammed it down and then loaded his shot with another wad. He raised himself to one knee, resting his right elbow on his thigh to steady his weapon. "This is for you Zsari," as he pulled the trigger. The shot rang out and the incantations stopped as Erzi Majorova slumped to the ground, but still managed to brace herself on one arm that she planted firmly into the earth. The Countess made an effort to lift her Steward back on to her feet, dragging the fallen Erzsi back towards the safety of the clearing.

Count Thurzo ordered his men to attack and the race was on to reach the doorway before the Countess had an opportunity to lock it from the inside. Elizabeth and Erzi managed to escape inside with seconds to spare but not enough time to seal the door behind. The Palatine's officers poured through the opening, only to be momentarily held back by the putrid smell of death and decay. With their torches held high, they viewed the mutilated bodies of young girls just at the inside of the doorway. A short distance, further inside they found another two, in similar condition. Not too far off in the distance they could hear the sound of screaming. The screams took them right, then left and left again. They listened again, and now they veered to the right. More sound coming from the right, and then one more turn to the left brought them face to face with the Countess's servants still performing their diabolical work as if they never knew they were under attack.

"I want them all taken alive," Thurzo shouted to his men. "You five, see to it if there are any of the young girls that can be saved." he pointed to a few of his men that were bent over along the wall, retching as a result of what they had just seen.

"Someone find me some bandages." The Count was furiously shouting orders, in an effort to save any of the victims but his gut told him that none would be saved that day.

It took another couple of hours to clear the castle of the Countess's guards. Most surrendered without any resistance, the scant few that engaged in battle, were either wounded or killed in the one-sided encounters. Gyorgy Thurzo waited patiently for his men to clear the castle and bring out the one person that would definitely put an end to the nightmare. Finding her hiding in the armoire of her bed chambers, two of his guards dragged Elizabeth Bathory screaming and kicking all the way from the third level of the upper castle, down to the plain where the Count was waiting.

Forcing her down upon her knees, Gyorgy Thurzo took the leg irons from his second and tightly secured them around both of Elizabeth's ankles, locking them in place. Leaning over, he whispered into her ear so that none would hear, "My Zsari wishes you a Happy New Year, Cousin."

Epilogue

"And once again we close another chapter of the Kahana Chronicles, John. Everything you ever wanted to know about vampires and werewolves but were afraid to ask."

"I didn't think it possible but once again I'm at a loss for words Doc"

"You at a loss for words, now that is impossible and never going to happen," I disagreed with his claim.

"I'm truly surprised. Usually none of your family heroes ever remain alive by the end of your books. Why suddenly break your string of consistency," he asked.

"Considering, Joseph wasn't married to Reisel yet, I don't think his dying in the book would help to explain my existence very well," I reminded him. "Simply put John, no Joseph, no me!"

"I guess I see your point," John understood now.

"I think I need to remind you John, this is one of those stories that if they ever made it into a movie, the opening screen would say, 'The story you are about to see is true. But the names have not been changed because there were absolutely no innocents to protect. The people, events, places and times are all true. Anyone named was not by coincidence, it was on purpose.' Although I will admit that I can't verify all the interactions I wrote about unfolded exactly as I described them on the pages, I at least can attest to the outcomes of each event as actually happening."

"So what you are trying to say is that justice prevailed in the end," John was obviously curious as to the fate of everyone. "Right?"

"Perhaps not exactly how you would define justice. I can tell you one thing they didn't do, and that was they didn't waste any time before they held the tribunal. In this case justice was swift. Of course, having the diary meant that it was already self incriminating   Elizabeth Bathory's own words spoke for themselves. With over six hundred entries, the only question was possibly how many did she forget to record.

Everything was wrapped up by January 7th, 1611. Fizcko, whose real name was Janos Ujavary received what some thought was a light sentence because they simply beheaded him and then burned his body. Recognizing that he wasn't in full possession of his faculties, the judges felt it would be improper to take any great pleasure in torturing him first much to the disappointment of the public that had gathered for the show."

"Oh, I can definitely see their point," Pearce commented in his usual sarcastic manner. "Ruined a perfectly good afternoon matinee."

"It could have been worse. At least it was for Ilona Jo and Dorottya Szentes. Those two definitely possessed serious sadistic streaks. Even when they knew there was no escaping Gyorgy's forces, which had surrounded the castle, they still couldn't resist torturing those last few girls with which they were caught in the act. They were especially fond of removing appendages as part of their routine, so that is exactly what happened to them. One by one they had their fingers removed. Then they tied them to a stake, set on fire, and burnt alive. After all, we must remember that these were convicted witches and burning at the stake is the only way you can deal with a witch. It was, after all, the traditional punishment.

Katarina Benicka was an interesting case. She was rounded up that last night but wasn't caught engaging in any of the acts of torture with the others. Most likely because she was tending to her mistress at the time as most handmaidens do. But the judges still concluded that she could not have been that close to the Countess without being complicit, so to be on the safe side, they merely beheaded her. No use burning her as a witch if you're not certain.

Now let us not forget Erzsi Majorova, by every account she really was a witch. And according to those that were experts in witchcraft, she was considered a very powerful one. They were initially going to burn her alive at the stake but then they became afraid because she already started reciting incantations during her trial. So the legal question became, how many spells could she still cast while she was being burnt. Too many was the final answer, so they decided they better remove her head immediately, so she couldn't cast any spells and then they burnt her corpse so she couldn't come back."

"Justice was pretty harsh back then," Pearce wasn't impressed by the judges decisions. "Not saying they didn't deserve it but still seems very harsh."

"Those were the times, John. That's how things were done and you may not agree with capital punishment but at least the public never had do worry about any of those five ever getting loose and repeating their crimes."

"But they also make mistakes," Pearce insisted. "History shows many prisoners were executed that never committed a crime. Just look at the Salem witch trials."

"But not in this case," I pointed out. "These people were guilty and there were no mistakes, except..."

"Aha," Pearce jumped on my pause. "So there was a mistake."

"You could call it that. The young woman Katalin ended up being sentenced as well but she wasn't executed because of the help she provided in the rescue of those last few girls. But oddly, the case against her was not for being complicit or participating in any of these heinous murders committed by the others, but instead for the fact that she had multiple opportunities to stop them and she didn't do so."

"That certainly doesn't sound right," Pearce argued. "How could she have possibly stopped them?"

"Today we have all these psychologists to explain to us why people being held captive don't resist their captors. How they can be terrorized into submission so that even when there's an open door to freedom, they are too afraid to step through it. Katalin was one of those victims but we're talking four hundred years ago and there wasn't any psycho-babble to come to her defense. Even as one judge went out of his way to defend her, the other two simply overruled. But at least they reached a compromise. A long term in prison for the failure to run away and report the crimes that were being committed inside the castle. It was too difficult for the others to conceive that she had access to the outside, she wasn't being watched, and yet she didn't take the opportunity to run to the authorities. They couldn't see that the chains she bore mentally meant she was no less a prisoner than anyone of those girls they held in a cell."

"Alright, Doc, what about the big one?" Pearce was eager for me to bring the story to a climactic ending.

"She came from a powerful family with a lot of money," I cautioned him. "Her family pleaded for clemency. After all, it didn't look good for the most powerful reigning family in Hungary to have a serial murderer as their family matron. That dragon on the heraldic shield was beginning to look a lot more like a demon in the public eye the more anyone looked at it."

"So you're telling me she got away with everything she did," Pearce sounded irritated.

"Not exactly," I teased, trying not to tell him everything at once, because it was always so enjoyable watching him become flustered.

"She wasn't executed, if that's what you're asking."

"What then?" he asked abruptly.

"She was sentenced to home detention," I mentioned as if it was no big deal.

"Home detention! Like the home detention they do now-a-days. A serial killer with over a six hundred body count and they just send her home and tell her not to go outside."

"Yes and no," I continued to bait him.

"Okay Doc, what's the real story?" Pearce had reached his limit, so I knew it was time to disclose all.

"Yes, she was sentenced to home incarceration, but it was limited to her bed chambers, which from the description in my book sounds pretty luxurious but they made some renovations. First, they bricked up all the windows, leaving only tiny little slits for sunlight. That prevented anyone from climbing in and certainly stopped her from climbing out. Then, once she was inside her chambers, they bricked up the doorway leaving only a small passage through which they could pass the food trays inward and take the waste out during the day. Other than the sentry that brought the food and removed the waste, she had no contact with any other person. On August 21st, 1614 the guard noticed that the food trays were still laying where he left them in the morning. He called out to her but there was no answer. After reporting his findings, they sent a crew to tear down the brick wall. Elizabeth Bathory was dead."

"Well it wasn't soon enough as far as I'm concerned," Pearce commented. "Still too good for her."

"Some still try to argue that she was innocent of the crimes because there was no official trial record of any charges laid directly against the Countess. But that wasn't entirely accurate, since the over three hundred statements they had from witnesses, some who happened to be victims that survived, and of course from our illustrious heroes of this story, provided enough evidence to convict her without bringing her into the courthouse. Once again, it was simply a political manoeuvre to avoid bringing any further shame and embarrassment on the Bathory family name."

"So her family still continued to remain all powerful and rule over half the Empire, from Hungary eastward." Pearce still struggled with the fact that it did not appear as if justice had been faithfully served.

"Their fall from power was pretty rapid," I informed him. "You know how part of the arrangement between Paolo Sarpi and Emperor Matthias included the restoration of the Sultan's suzerainty over the provinces under his own choice for prince, Gabor Bethlen. But you recall they had Gabriel Bathory in the way of making that arrangement. So conveniently Gabriel was dead at the tender age of twenty-three under suspicious circumstances. So now Sultan Ahmed was once again in control of Wallachia and Transylvania."

"Suspicious circumstances," John laughed at my terminology. "That's certainly an understatement with this lot."

"Then initially all the castles, lands and accumulated wealth of Elizabeth Bathory were distributed to her children. But Matthias found some excuse to seize the inheritance, so that it was all stripped from the Bathorys. But I forgot to mention, the price for not sentencing Elizabeth to death was the writing off of all debts that the Crown owed the Bathory family. So the Habsburgs went from being practically poverty stricken to now being one of the wealthiest families in Europe."

"Not to mention all the money he confiscated from the Maisel family that you reported in *Shadows of Trinity*," Pearce recollected that large sum of money and property that Matthias also had seized in Prague.

"He did give some back to Maisel's nephews," I reminded him. "But certainly kept the mother-load. This time he gave nothing back to the Bathorys."

"So everything worked out for all those involved and they all lived happily ever after." There was that wonderful John Pearce sarcasm surfacing once again.

"I think you could say that," I couldn't really argue otherwise. "Those that committed the crimes got what they deserved. Justice in a morbid sense prevailed. The Bathorys fell from grace and this time the heroes of the story all managed to live out the rest of their normal lives," I informed him.

"But what you call normal isn't exactly what the rest of us would call normal," Pearce took exception to my terminology.

"Well let's see," I thumbed my upper lip. "Paolo Sarpi died twelve years later on January 15th, 1623 from old age. But the Church never stopped trying to assassinate him, even after their promise to stop, but as the storyline said, he couldn't be killed. Now that he was enlightened as to the circular nature of God's universe he became a major proponent of Copernicus, a close friend of Galileo Galilei, Francis Bacon and William Harvey. One might even guess that he may have been one of the Illuminati because of the friends he kept."

"The Illuminati?" Pearce was unfamiliar with that organization.

"I suggest you go read Dan Brown if you want to know more about them," I laughed. "No one in my family belonged, so I won't be writing about it."

"Anything else I should know about his life, Doc?"

"You already know that he was a major critic of the Church but he became one of the first advocates for free speech in the world. In fact I would even go as far as saying he was the father of that notion. Fra Paolo Sarpi as Chief Magistrate of Venice began taking the unprecedented legal action of ensuring that every citizen had the right to express themselves without repercussion."

"So he really did have an impact on future generations," Pearce surmised. "A true American before there even was an America."

"Well, we will talk about America and free speech perhaps in a future book I'll write," I told him. "The two weren't always synonymous."

"So what else did he do," Pearce asked eagerly

"And bombs," I added.

"Huh?"

"You didn't think that part of my story in which he turned the canteens into hand grenades to defeat the witches was fabricated, did you?"

"I may have thought you were taking a bit of literary licence there Doc," John Pearce responded sheepishly

"Hell no," I answered. "Paolo Sarpi spent the rest of his days designing and experimenting with ballistics at the University of Padua. As I said in the story John, these three weren't brought together accidentally, they had special gifts that Nostradamus knew in advance, that once united they would save the world, according to the perspective of the Church and the Crown at that time. So ultimately, their union awakened Paolo's enjoyment of manufacturing and playing with bombs."

"And Caesar," John inquired.

"Well I talked about Caesar's life quite a lot in **Shadows of Trinity,**" I reminded him. Not much more I can say about Caesar that you don't already know. As I told you last time John, take a look at Century III Quatrain 14. Caesar got his reward by ensuring that he honored Yakov's wishes. That meant taking care of his children which honour bound he most certainly did."

'By the bough of the valiant person, The weaker Frenchman, the one who's father was unusual, Honors, riches, workers will be his in his old age, All because he believed in the wise counsel of that gentle man.'

"He lived out the rest of his life in modest luxury tended to by Mademoiselle Claire, he remained a poisoned barb in the side of the Church by using his father's quatrains to expose all the sins of the Vatican, of which he took great pleasure in doing, and then he died at the ripe old age of seventy-six years. I think by most people's standards, that was a pretty good life."

"What about Joseph, Doc?"

"What can I possibly say about my ancestor," I pondered. "He gets the girl."

"Well that was pretty obvious, Doc," John scowled.

"The Emperor did actually have a small temporary bridge built at the Old Jewish Cemetery in Prague so that Joseph could visit his father's grave site. He was probably the last one to visit it before I did in 2017."

"And?"

"And he was my ancestor that actually brought us back into the fold of Rabbinic Judaism, even though we still had our differences that we continually preserved generation to generation. But without his father or any other close family to guide him in Karaite studies and practices, he only had his father-in-law's colleagues to argue the law with on a regular basis. I don't know if the two of them actually developed a a strong liking for one another, but they did achieve a healthy respect for each other once life returned to normal. So, for the next two hundred and twenty years, Joseph's descendants were some of the leading scholars in Jewish law and the family never had to worry about money because the Emperor Matthias rewarded Joseph handsomely. And then came my third great-grandfather, Jacob, who found that letter from Emperor Rudolph and suddenly our world changed dramatically."

"How so, Doc?"

"That story you're going to have to wait for John," I told him.

"I've been waiting for that one for years," Pearce complained. "You never get around to writing it."

"Well, I'm thinking about it now," I informed him. "I even think I might have a title for the book when I get around to writing it."

"Want to share it with the readers?"

"Might call it *The Last Vienna Waltz* or something like that," I speculated.

"So before I forget, what about this Otto guy and Joseph's sister?" Pearce asked next.

"Interestingly, the Oettingen-Wallerstein nobility did manage to become well established and earn its place in German history. Quite a few generals produced in that house. But they always had one thing going against them and that was Tanit did raise her children to be Jewish by religion and that continued to be the household religion for succeeding generations. But in the nineteenth century, Germany was not prepared to have a Jewish aristocratic family any longer, especially one so highly placed in the nobility. So the family was stripped of their entitlements and their nobility and now they are no different from anyone else. Just an interesting footnote in history."

"Anything else you would like to tell the readers about?" Pearce kept jotting down everything I said in his notebook

"Strangely enough my family did end up residing in Transylvania. Piatra Neamt to be exact. Up in the Eastern Carpathian Mountain range. But that wasn't until long after Joseph died, and only once the family began spreading out from Galicia. Perhaps they remembered the Sultan's invitation because it is certainly hard to explain why we moved south-east rather than west, which was the usual migration pattern in Europe. Not to suggest the Carpathian mountains aren't beautiful but they would have seemed a little remote compared to the bustling commercial center of Brody. Perhaps if I start doing more research I will find there was a specific reason why my ancestors returned to the land of vampires and werewolves. Maybe there's still even a bit of Transylvania left in my immortal blood. I guess you'll just have to wait until my next story, John, to find out."

www.ingramcontent.com/pod-product-compliance
Lightning Source LLC
Chambersburg PA
CBHW031824090426
42741CB00005B/126